Explorations in the Learning Sciences, Instructional Systems and Performance Technologies

Volume 3

Series Editors
J. Michael Spector, Athens, GA, USA
Susanne LaJoie, Montreal, Quebec, Canada

For further volumes:
http://www.springer.com/series/8640

Rafael A. Calvo • Sidney K. D'Mello
Editors

New Perspectives on Affect and Learning Technologies

 Springer

Editors
Rafael A. Calvo
School of Electrical and
Information Engineering
The University of Sydney
Sydney, NSW, Australia
Rafael.Calvo@sydney.edu.au

Sidney K. D'Mello
Department of Psychology
Institute for Intelligent Systems
University of Memphis
Memphis, TN, USA
sdmello@memphis.edu

ISBN 978-1-4614-2993-7   ISBN 978-1-4419-9625-1 (eBook)
DOI 10.1007/978-1-4419-9625-1
Springer New York Dordrecht Heidelberg London

Printed on acid-free paper

Springer is part of Springer Science+Business Media (www.springer.com)

About the Authors

Shazia Afzal has recently completed a PhD in Computer Science and Technology from the University of Cambridge in 2010. She also holds a Bachelors in Information Technology from JMI in India and worked as software engineer for a while before taking up the Gates Cambridge Scholarship for a PhD degree at Cambridge. She received the Best Paper Award at the tenth IEEE International Conference on Advanced Learning Technologies (ICALT) held in July 2010 in Tunisia. Her research interests include human–computer interaction (HCI), affective computing, educational technology, and social signal processing.

Ivon Arroyo is a Research Scientist in the Department of Computer Science at UMASS Amherst. She has carried out research on how students learn and perceive mathematics with intelligent tutoring systems at the K-12 level in public school settings. She is PI or Co-PI of several NSF and DoEd grants that predicted student emotions in real time and designed mathematics tutors for students with learning disabilities. She holds a Doctorate in Mathematics and Science Education and Bachelor's and Master's degree in Computer Science. She is the author of more than 50 research articles, is a Fulbright Fellow, an elected member of the executive committee of AIED (2004–2007), and was finalist for the Best Paper Awards at AIED 2009, ITS 2010, and EDM 2010, one of them for an article entitled "Emotion Sensors Go to School."

Roger Azevedo is a Professor at McGill University. He is the Director of the Laboratory for the Study of Metacognition and Advanced Learning Technologies. His research includes examining the role of cognitive, metacognitive, affective, and motivational processes during self-regulated learning with advanced learning technologies. He is also interested in using various interdisciplinary methods in the detecting, tracking, and modeling of self-regulatory processes with intelligent multiagent learning environments. He has authored over 200 peer-reviewed publications in several interdisciplinary fields. Dr. Azevedo received his PhD in Applied Cognitive Science from McGill University and did his postdoctoral training in Cognitive Psychology at Carnegie Mellon University.

Ryan S.J.d. Baker is presently Assistant Professor of Psychology and the Learning Sciences in the Department of Social Science and Policy Studies at Worcester Polytechnic Institute. His primary research interests are in educational data mining, disengagement, metacognition, motivation, affect, human–computer interaction, artificial intelligence in education, and quantitative field observation methods. His publications have received two awards and have been in the final lists of five others. Baker received his PhD in Human–Computer Interaction from Carnegie Mellon University in 2005. He also holds an MS in Human–Computer Interaction from Carnegie Mellon University and a BSc in Computer Science from Brown University.

Benedict du Boulay is Professor of Artificial Intelligence in the School of Informatics at the University of Sussex. Following a Bachelor's degree in Physics, he spent time in industry and in school as a secondary school teacher before returning to university to complete his PhD working on Logo. He is interested in modeling and developing students' metacognition and motivation. He is a former Editor of the International Journal of Artificial Intelligence in Education, is on the Editorial Board of the International Journal of Technology, Instruction, Cognition, and Learning, and has edited/written 8 books and written some 160 papers.

Winslow Burleson, Assistant Professor of Human–Computer Interaction at ASU, directs the Motivational Environments research group (http://hci.asu.edu). Author of over 60 scientific publications, including "best paper" at AIED 2009, and ten patents, he received a PhD in Affective Computing from the MIT Media Lab, a BA from Rice, and an MSE from Stanford. He worked with the Life Long Kindergarten research groups and the Entrepreneurial Management Unit at Harvard Business School, IBM Research, NASA-SETI Institute, the Space Telescope Science Institute, and UNICEF. NSF, NASA-JPL, Deutsche Telekom, iRobot, LEGO, and Microsoft and Motorola support his research. He frequently serves on NAE, NAS, and NSF committees.

Rafael A. Calvo, PhD (2000), is an Associate Professor at the University of Sydney – School of Electrical and Information Engineering and Director of the Learning and Affect Technologies Engineering (Latte) research group. He has a PhD in Artificial Intelligence applied to automatic document classification and has worked at Carnegie Mellon University and Universidad Nacional de Rosario, and as a consultant for projects worldwide. Rafael is author of numerous publications in the areas of affective computing, learning systems and web engineering, recipient of four teaching awards, and a Senior Member of IEEE. Rafael is Associate Editor of IEEE Transactions on Affective Computing.

Amber Chauncey Strain is a PhD student in the Department of Psychology and the Institute for Intelligent Systems at the University of Memphis. She has a BS in Psychology from Middle Tennessee State University, and an MS in Cognitive Psychology from the University of Memphis. Her research interests include the broad areas of cognitive and educational psychology, cognitive science, emotions, and emotion regulation during learning. Specifically, her interests include self-regulated learning, causal influence of emotions on self-regulation, and the role of emotion regulation strategies on affective, metacognitive, and cognitive processes during complex learning.

Cristina Conati is an Associate Professor of Computer Science at the University of British Columbia. Dr Conati's research is at the intersection of Artificial Intelligent, Human–Computer Interaction and Cognitive Science, with focus on User-Adaptive Interfaces, Intelligent Tutoring Systems, and Affective Computing. She published over 60 strictly refereed articles, and her work received the Best Paper Awards from the international conferences on User Modeling, AI in Education, Intelligent User Interfaces, and the Journal of User Modeling and User-Adapted Interaction.

David G. Cooper is a PhD candidate in Computer Science at the University of Massachusetts Amherst focusing on computational models of emotion. He holds an MS in Computer Science from the University of Massachusetts Amherst and a BS in Cognitive Science from Carnegie Mellon University. He has published work on affective computer tutors, cognitive agent architectures, emotional robotics, evolutionary agent learning, and sensor data fusion. His research interests include biologically inspired computation, emotional and cognitive models of human interaction, and sensor integration for computer awareness.

Sidney K. D'Mello is a Research Assistant Professor in the Institute for Intelligent Systems at the University of Memphis. His primary research interests are in the affective, cognitive, and learning sciences. More specific interests include affective computing, artificial intelligence in education, human–computer interactions, speech recognition and natural language understanding, and computational models of human cognition. He has authored over 100 papers and presentations in these areas. D'Mello received his PhD in Computer Science from the University of Memphis in 2009. He also holds an MS in Mathematical Sciences from the University of Memphis and a BS in Electrical Engineering from Christian Brothers University.

Andy Dong is an Associate Professor of Design and Computation at the University of Sydney. His primary research area is language use in design: How does language enact design, what are the linguistic properties of language use in design, and what are the sociolinguistic codes of the language of design? He has published extensively on language use in design, including a monograph, The Language of Design: Theory and Computation (Springer, London). More broadly, his research programs address design competence, the "first principles" of knowledge about designing, including how linguistic and design competence intersect and how societies organize to support design.

Kate Forbes-Riley is a Senior Research Associate with the Learning Research and Development Center, at the University of Pittsburgh. She obtained a PhD in Computational Linguistics in 2003, and an MSE in Computer and Information Science in 2001 at the University of Pennsylvania. She also holds a BA in Linguistics from Dartmouth College. Her current research concerns affect/attitude prediction and adaptation in spoken dialogue tutorial systems, and her research interests center on (para-)linguistic aspects of discourse and dialogue.

Heather Friedberg is an Undergraduate Research Assistant and Current Senior at the University of Pittsburgh. Her research interests are artificial intelligence and natural language processing. She graduated with a BS in Computer Science and a BA in Linguistics in April 2011, and is continuing her Masters in Computer Science at the University of Pittsburgh.

Peter Goodyear is Professor of Education and Codirector of the CoCo Research Centre at the University of Sydney. He is also a Senior Fellow of the Australian Learning and Teaching Council and an Australian Research Council Laureate Fellow. He has been carrying out research on technology-enhanced learning since the early 1980s and teaches educational design methodology. His latest books are students' experiences of e-learning in higher education: the ecology of sustainable innovation, (Routledge, with Rob Ellis) and technology-enhanced learning; design patterns and pattern languages (Sense Publishers, with Simeon Retalis). He edits the journal Instructional Science.

Art Graesser is Professor of Psychology, Adjunct Professor of Computer Science, and Codirector of the Institute for Intelligent Systems at the University of Memphis. His primary research interests are in cognitive science, discourse processing, and the learning sciences. Some of his more specific interests include knowledge representation, question asking and answering, tutoring, text comprehension, inference generation, conversation, reading, education, memory, expert systems, artificial intelligence, and human–computer interaction. He served as Editor of the journal *Discourse Processes* (1996–2005) and is the Current Editor of *Journal of Educational Psychology*. In addition to publishing over 400 articles in journals, books, and conference proceedings, he has written two books and edited nine books. He has designed, developed, and tested cutting-edge software in learning, language, and discourse technologies, including AutoTutor, Coh-Metrix, HURA Advisor, SEEK Web Tutor, MetaTutor, ARIES, Question Understanding Aid (QUAID), QUEST, and Point&Query.

Mary Helen Immordino-Yang, ED.D. is an affective neuroscientist and human development psychologist who studies the neural, psychophysiological and psychological bases of social emotion and culture and their implications for development and schools. She is Assistant Professor of Education and of Psychology at the University of Southern California. A former junior high school teacher, she earned her doctorate at Harvard University (2005). She is Associate Editor for North America of the journal Mind, Brain and Education, the inaugural recipient of the Award for Transforming Education through Neuroscience, and a recipient of the Cozzarelli Prize from the US National Academy of Sciences.

Slava Kalyuga is Associate Professor at the School of Education, UNSW, where he received a PhD and has worked since 1995. His research interests are in cognitive processes in learning, cognitive load theory, and evidence-based instructional design principles. His specific contributions include detailed experimental studies of the role of learner prior knowledge in learning (expertise reversal effect); the redundancy effect in multimedia learning; the development of rapid online diagnostic assessment methods; and studies of the effectiveness of different adaptive procedures for tailoring instruction to levels of learner expertise. He has authored three books and over 50 refereed papers and book chapters.

Blair Lehman is a PhD student in the Department of Psychology and Institute for Intelligent Systems at the University of Memphis. She has her BA in Psychology and Spanish from Rhodes College. Her research interests include the general areas of cognitive psychology, emotion, education, cognitive science, and intelligent tutoring systems. More specific interests include tutoring (human and computer), emotions during learning, affective computing, and state standards and assessments.

James C. Lester is Professor of Computer Science at North Carolina State University. His research in intelligent tutoring systems, computational linguistics, and intelligent user interfaces focuses on intelligent game-based learning environments, affective computing, and tutorial dialogue. He received the BA, MSCS, and PhD degrees in Computer Science from the University of Texas at Austin, and the BA degree in History from Baylor University. He has served as Program Chair for the ACM International Conference on Intelligent User Interfaces and the International Conference on Intelligent Tutoring Systems. He is Editor-in-Chief of the International Journal of Artificial Intelligence in Education.

Diane Litman is presently Professor of Computer Science, Senior Scientist with the Learning Research and Development Center, and faculty in Intelligent Systems, all at the University of Pittsburgh. Litman's current research focuses on enhancing the effectiveness of intelligent tutoring systems through spoken language processing, affective computing, and machine learning. Dr Litman has been Chair of the North American Chapter of the Association for Computational Linguistics, and a member of the editorial boards of Computational Linguistics and User Modeling and User-Adapted Interaction. Dr Litman is the author of over 150 peer-reviewed articles, and the winner of several Best Paper Awards.

Rosemary Luckin is Professor of Learner Centred Design at the London Knowledge Lab and an EPSRC Advanced Research Fellow. Her research explores how to most effectively scaffold learning across multiple technologies, locations, subjects, and times. This work is interdisciplinary and encompasses education, psychology, artificial intelligence, and HCI. It investigates the relationship between people, the concepts they are trying to learn and teach, the contexts within which they operate, and the resources at their disposal. Professor Luckin is also a Nonexecutive Director of Becta (the UK government agency leading the national drive to ensure the effective and innovative use of technology throughout learning).

Scott W. McQuiggan is presently with the Education Practice at SAS Institute Inc. Scott has focused on an interdisciplinary research agenda combining artificial intelligence, education, educational psychology, human factors and human-computer interaction, and psychology. His primary interests center on investigating student interactions with new learning technologies, such as intelligent tutoring systems, game-based learning environments, and narrative-centered learning environments. Scott received his PhD in Computer Science from North Carolina State University in 2009. He also holds an MS in Computer Science from North Carolina State University and a BS in Computer Science from Susquehanna University.

Beverly Park Woolf is a Research Professor in the Computer Science Department at the University of Massachusetts Amherst. Her research focuses on building tutoring systems using artificial intelligence mechanisms and cognitive models to improve a computer's ability to adapt to students needs. Dr Woolf has authored more than 200 papers, wrote the book "Building Intelligent Interactive Tutors," and was lead author for "Roadmap for Educational Technology." Woolf received a PhD in Computer Science, an EdD in Education, an MS in Computer Science from the University of Massachusetts, and a BA from Smith College.

Reinhard Pekrun holds the chair for Personality and Educational Psychology at the University of Munich. His research focuses on achievement emotions, educational assessment, and the implementation of effective learning environments. Pekrun has authored more than 200 publications in these areas, including the state-of-the art volume Emotion in Education (San Diego 2007) and numerous articles in leading journals, such as Journal of Educational Psychology. Pekrun is a Fellow of the International Academy of Education and Past-President of the Stress and Anxiety Research Society. He is active in policy implementation and development and serves on a number of committees on school reform.

Genaro Rebolledo-Mendez is a full-time researcher at the Faculty of Informatics of the Universidad Veracruzana, México. He is also visiting Research Fellow at the IDEAS Lab, Sussex University, UK and the Serious Games Institute, Coventry University, UK. Genaro's interest is the design and evaluation of educational technology that adapts sensitively to affective, motivational, and cognitive differences among students. To do so, he studies how cognitive and affective differences impact students' behavior while interacting with educational technology and how, in turn, technology impacts students' learning. To that end, he uses techniques from artificial intelligence, computer science, education, and psychology.

Peter Robinson is Professor of Computer Technology at the University of Cambridge, where he leads work on computer graphics and interaction. His research concerns new technologies to enhance communication between computers and their users, and new applications to exploit these technologies. He pioneered the use of video and paper as part of the user interface, with recent work, including desk-size projected displays and tangible interfaces. He has also investigated the inference of people's mental states from facial expressions, vocal nuances, body posture and gesture, and other physiological signals, and also considered the expression of emotions by robots and cartoon avatars.

Ma. Mercedes T. Rodrigo is an Associate Professor of the Department of Information Systems and Computer Science and Director of the Office of International Programs of the Ateneo de Manila University in the Philippines. Her research interests are in the areas of affect and learning, modeling student cognition, and computer science education. In 2008–2009, she was a Fulbright Senior Research Fellow at the Pittsburgh Science of Learning Center in Carnegie Mellon University. She received a PhD in Computer Technology in Education from Nova Southeastern University, an MS in Applied Computer Science from the University of Maryland Eastern Shore, and a BS in Computer Science from the Ateneo de Manila.

Jennifer L. Sabourin is a PhD student in the Department of Computer Science at North Carolina State University working in the Intellimedia Group. Her research focuses on artificial intelligence applications in education with specific interest in affect, self-regulated learning, and collaboration. Jennifer graduated from NC State in 2008 with a BS. in Computer Science and minors in both Psychology and Cognitive Science. She holds a National Science Foundation Graduate Research Fellowship.

Vanessa Singh is a graduate student in the Department of Psychology at the University of Southern California. She received her BA in Psychology from the University of Delhi, India and an MSc in Neuroscience from the Max Planck Research Institute, Tuebingen, Germany. Her MSc dissertation work was completed under the guidance of Prof. Nikos Logothetis. Her current work with Prof. Antonio Damasio at USC is in the field of Social and Affective Neuroscience. Specifically, she applies neuroimaging techniques of functional MRI and EEG to study the neural networks underlying social emotion and moral reasoning.

Contents

Contributors

Shazia Afzal Computer Laboratory, University of Cambridge, William Gates Building, Cambridge, CB3 OFD, England, UK
e-mail: Shazia.Afzal@cl.cam.ac.uk

Ivon Arroyo Department of Computer Science, University of Massachusetts, Amherst, MA, USA
e-mail: ivon@cs.umass.edu

Roger Azevedo Laboratory for the Study of Metacognition and Advanced Learning Technologies and Department of Educational and Counselling Psychology, McGill University, Montreal, Canada
e-mail: roger.azevedo@mcgill.ca

Ryan S.J.d. Baker Department of Social Sciences and Policy Studies, Worcester Polytechnic Institute, Worcester, MA, USA
e-mail: rsbaker@wpi.edu

Benedict du Boulay Interactive Systems Research Group, School of Informatics, University of Sussex, Brighton, BN1 9QH, UK
e-mail: B.du-Boulay@sussex.ac.uk

Winslow Burleson School of Computing, Informatics, and Decision System Engineering, Arizona State University, Tempe, AZ, USA
e-mail: winslow.burleson@asu.edu

Rafael A. Calvo School of Electrical and Information Engineering, The University of Sydney, Building J 03, Sydney, New South Wales, Australia
e-mail: Rafael.Calvo@sydney.edu.au

Amber Chauncey Strain Department of Psychology, Institute for Intelligent Systems, University of Memphis, Memphis, TN, USA
e-mail: astrain@memphis

Cristina Conati Department of Computer Science, University of British Columbia, Vancouver, BC V6T 1Z4, Canada
e-mail: conati@cs.ubc.ca

David G. Cooper Department of Computer Science, University of Massachusetts, Amherst, MA, USA
e-mail: dcooper@cs.umass.edu

Sidney K. D'Mello Department of Psychology, Institute for Intelligent Systems, University of Memphis, Memphis, TN, USA
e-mail: sdmello@memphis.edu

Andy Dong Faculty of Architecture, Design and Planning, University of Sydney, Sydney, North South Wales, Australia
e-mail: andy.dong@sydney.edu.au

Kate Forbes-Riley Learning Research and Development Center, University of Pittsburgh, Pittsburgh, PA, USA
e-mail: forbesk@cs.pitt.edu

Heather Friedberg Computer Science and Linguistics, University of Pittsburgh, Pittsburgh, PA, USA
e-mail: haf13@pitt.edu

Peter Goodyear CoCo Research Centre, University of Sydney, Sydney, North South Wales, Australia
e-mail: Peter.Goodyear@sydney.edu.au

Art Graesser Department of Psychology, Institute for Intelligent Systems, University of Memphis, Memphis, TN, USA
e-mail: a-graesser@memphis.edu

Mary Helen Immordino-Yang Brain and Creativity Institute; Rossier School of Education, University of Southern California, Los Angeles, CA, USA
e-mail: immordin@usc.edu

Slava Kalyuga School of Education, University of New South Wales, Sydney, North South Wales, Australia
e-mail: s.kalyuga@unsw.edu.au

Blair Lehman Department of Psychology, Institute for Intelligent Systems, University of Memphis, Memphis, TN, USA
e-mail: balehman@memphis.edu

James C. Lester Department of Computer Science, North Carolina State University, Engineering Building II, Raleigh, NC 27695-8206, USA
e-mail: lester@ncsu.edu

Diane Litman The Learning Research and Development Center and Department of Intelligent Systems, University of Pittsburgh, Pittsburgh, PA, USA
e-mail: litman@cs.pitt.edu

Rosemary Luckin The London Knowledge Lab, University of London, London, UK
e-mail: r.luckin@ioe.ac.uk

Scott W. McQuiggan SAS Institute, Inc., Cary, NC, USA
e-mail: scott. mcquiggan@sas.co

Beverly Park Woolf Department of Computer Science, University of Massachusetts, Amherst, MA, USA
e-mail: bev@cs.umass.edu

Reinhard Pekrun Department of Psychology, University of Munich, Munich, Germany
e-mail: pekrun@lmu.de

Genaro Rebolledo-Mendez Faculty of Informatics, Av. Jalapa esq. Av. Avila Camacho, Col. Centro, 91020, Jalapa, Veracruz, Mexico
e-mail: grebolledo@uv.mx

Peter Robinson Computer Laboratory, University of Cambridge, William Gates Building, Cambridge, England, UK
e-mail: Peter.Robinson@cl.cam.ac.uk

Ma. Mercedes T. Rodrigo Department of Information Systems and Computer Science, Ateneo de Manila University, Metro Manila 1108, Philippines
e-mail: mrodrigo@ateneo.edu

Jennifer L. Sabourin Department of Computer Science, North Carolina State University, Raleigh, NC, USA
e-mail: jlbobiso@ncsu.edu

Vanessa Singh Department of Psychology, University of Southern California, Los Angeles, CA, USA
e-mail: vanessa1@usc.edu

Part I
Theoretical Perspectives

Introduction

Rafael A. Calvo and Sidney K. D'Mello

Introduction

When we step into a meeting, or attend a lecture, can we genuinely leave our emotions at the door? Can we magically dissociate our decision-making processes from the effects of boredom, interest, anxiety, delight, anger, or pleasure? Do we not experience utter joy and elation when a much anticipated grant gets funded? Do we not clench our fists and cry out in anger when we feel that a reviewer has treated us unfairly? It is clear that as complex human beings, emotions intersect every aspect of our lives. They bias every decision, influence every action, impact every memory, and govern every social interaction.

Neuroscientists have shown that a person with full cognitive abilities intact, but lacking normal emotional responses, is incapable of making decisions that are essential for life. While popular wisdom and folklore has often argued for the separation of emotion from reason, we now understand that this is neither realistic nor desirable. Affect and cognition weave together to form our experience and behavior as we engage in everyday activities. Simply put, we are affected by affect.

Learning at deeper levels of comprehension, problem solving, and high stakes testing are similarly affected by affect. We experience negative emotions (such as irritation, frustration, anger, and sometimes rage) when we experience failure, make mistakes, and struggle with troublesome impasses. We also experience positive emotions (such as delight, excitement, and eureka) when tasks are completed, challenges are conquered, insights are unveiled, and major discoveries are made. These trajectories of positive and negative affective states presumably lead to different learning outcomes. Affective states (emotions, feelings, moods)

R.A. Calvo (✉)
School of Electrical and Information Engineering, The University of Sydney,
Building J 03, Sydney, New South Wales, Australia
e-mail: Rafael.Calvo@sydney.edu.au

R.A. Calvo and S.K. D'Mello (eds.), *New Perspectives on Affect and Learning Technologies*,   3
Explorations in the Learning Sciences, Instructional Systems and Performance Technologies 3,
DOI 10.1007/978-1-4419-9625-1_1, © Springer Science+Business Media, LLC 2011

such as engagement, flow, and curiosity presumably promote learning while frustration, boredom, and lack of self-confidence inhibit learning.

Given the pervasiveness of affect in learning activities, our ability to make significant advancements in developing effective educational interventions will rely on understanding the intricate dance between affect, cognition, and motivation. Once we have a better grasp on the impact of emotions, either as facilitators or inhibitors of learning, we will have made significant progress toward improving the efficacy of our interventions. This book is particularly focused on technological interventions, where computer programs deliver individualized instruction in a manner that is sensitive to learners' affective and cognitive states. The book does not attempt to cover the full breadth of affective phenomena described, for example, in the Handbook of Affective Sciences (Davidson, Scherer, & Goldsmith, 2003), but rather focuses on affective phenomena that are directly influenced by, or are influential to learning, and generally, within the time span of a specific learning activity. It is also important to note that the term *affect* is used quite generally in this book and encompasses feelings, prototypical emotions, moods, affective traits, and affect-cognitive amalgamations such as confusion, interest, and engagement.

Understanding the complex interplay between cognition and emotion and developing effective interventions to regulate student emotions is a highly interdisciplinary endeavor that spans psychology, education, computer science, engineering, neuroscience, and artifact design. Highlighting cutting-edge research from these fields to understand student affect coupled with the practical goal of developing learning environments that coordinate affect and cognition to promote learning is the major goal of this book.

Learning, Affect, and Technology in Close Relationships

Figure 1 presents a triangle with three entities and three interactions that are relevant to this book. Different lines of research have contributed to understanding different parts of this triangle. The top-left circle in the triangle represents research on human

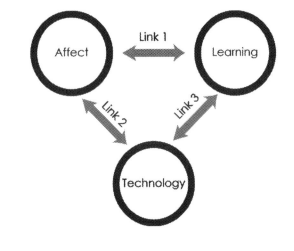

Fig. 1 Relationships between affect, learning activities, and technology

affective phenomena (Dalgleish & Power, 1999; Lewis, Haviland-Jones, & Barrett, 2008). Deciphering human emotions is one of the great unanswered questions about human nature and has been at the core of theoretical and empirical research for over a century (Darwin, 2002; Ekman, 1992; Lazarus, 1991; Russell, 2003; Scherer, Schorr, & Johnstone, 2001; Tomkins, 1962). Contemporary theories view emotions as expressions (Darwin, 1872; Ekman, 1992), embodiments (Barrett, Mesquita, Ochsner, & Gross, 2007), outcomes of cognitive appraisals (Ortony, Clore, & Collins, 1988; Scherer et al., 2001), social constructs (Keltner & Haidt, 2001), and products of neural circuitry (Damasio, 2003; Davidson, 1998; Panksepp, 2000), and some recent attempts have been made to integrate these views (Russell, 2003).

Research linking emotions and human activities has provided evidence on how emotions influence cognitive processes (e.g., Lane & Nadel, 2002), including memory, attention, deliberation, and action selection (Bower, 1981; Isen, 2001; Mandler, 1976). Our impetus here is on learning activities (the top-right of the triangle) including problem solving, text comprehension, test taking, etc. (Schutz & Pekrun, 2007), and we focus on the many ways these activities are affected by emotion (Link 1).

The development of technologies that compute affect, the third entity in Fig. 1, is primarily in the purview of computer science, engineering, artificial intelligence (AI), and human–computer interaction (HCI) research. Emotions were not a substantial topic of research in these fields until the last decade, until Rosalind Picard coined the term "affective computing (AC)" (Picard, 1997) in her influential 1997 book. Inspired by the inextricable link between emotions and cognition, the field of AC aspires to narrow the communicative gap between the highly emotional human and the emotionally challenged computer by developing computational systems that recognize and respond to the affective states (e.g., moods, emotions) of the user.

Link 2 encompasses affect-sensitive or affect-aware technologies. These systems are being developed in a number of domains including gaming, mental health, and learning. In addition to developing systems to help users regulate their emotions, technology has also been used to learn about emotions. Similar to how a physician uses technology to diagnose disease (e.g., a stethoscope to monitor the heart), neuroscientists, for example, have used fMRI and other techniques to understand the neural circuitry that underlies emotion (Dalgleish, Dunn, & Mobbs, 2009; Davidson, 1998; Immordino-Yang & Damasio, 2007; Panksepp, 1998). Finally, learning activities can be paired with technology, independent of affect, as is usually the case. This is illustrated by Link 3 in Fig. 1. This link includes research in the areas of computer-supported learning, e-learning, intelligent tutoring systems (ITS), and AI in education (Biswas, Leelawong, Schwartz, & Vye, 2005; Graesser, Jeon, & Dufty, 2008; Koedinger & Corbett, 2006; VanLehn et al., 2007; Woolf, 2009). The focus of much of this research is on designing technological interventions to promote more effective learning outcomes. ITS take this goal a step further by developing interventions that are sensitive to the cognitive states, knowledge levels, and learning styles of individual students.

This book, and the series of which it is part, focuses on exploring links between affect and learning with technology. In particular, this edited volume brings leading researchers whose work combines the three entities described above: student affect, learning activities, and technology. Each of these three entities is important in providing an accurate and detailed account on affect and learning. If the learners' affect is not taken into account, and the research assumes learning as a "cold" cognitive process, the understanding of the learning phenomena is limited; this is aptly demonstrated by extensive multidisciplinary evidence presented throughout this book. If basic research on affect and learning is not considered in the development of technologies, researchers might end up developing affect-aware tools that have little impact, or worse, a negative effect, on learning. Finally, technology can also be used to advance basic research on affect and learning by providing tools to monitor the dynamic rollercoaster of student emotions that arise, morph, and decay during learning. In summary, an interdisciplinary position that integrates research from all three entities is the most promising way forward.

Aims and Scope

The last decade has seen an explosion of basic research on affect and learning, as well as technological advances in monitoring and responding to emotions, in order to heighten motivation and engagement, boost self-efficacy, and optimize learning. While much of the traditional research in AC is focused on building technologies that recognize and adapt to affective states, it is important that this focus is expanded. In addition to innovative technologies having the potential to adapt to user emotions, they can also be used to inform our understanding of the emotional processes and affective dynamics that underlie learning activities.

Existing methods for studying the impact of affect within real-world activities are fundamentally difficult, since they depend on the subjective judgment of the subjects themselves, or third party experts and novices. They require the laborious manual collection of data, often by experts that are costly and a limited resource. Much of the research described in this book is aimed toward the development of objective methods to model the enormous variety of affective features in human behavior, language, and physiology. Rather than relying only on data collected before and after an activity, these models would use the micro behavioral information that can be collected with different type of sensors and video cameras.

This book is designed to act as a catalyst to advance research in affective learning technologies by highlighting recent advances, discussing open problems, and setting the stage for future research in this area. This book focuses on technological interventions that aspire to promote learning gains by responding to emotions, while simultaneously helping uncover some critical learning-centered affective phenomena. This edited volume brings together recent research in the area of AC with an emphasis on affect and learning. The "new perspectives" come from the intersection of several research themes including

- Theories of affect, cognition, and learning
- Basic research on emotion, cognition, and motivation applied to learning environments

- Pedagogical and motivational strategies that are sensitive to affective and cognitive processes
- Multimodal human computer interfaces with a focus on affect recognition and synthesis
- Recent advances in affect-sensitive computer learning environments
- Design issues in the development of affect-sensitive learning environments
- Novel methodologies to investigate affect and learning
- Neuroscience research on emotions and learning

Overview of Contributions

The book is divided into three parts. In the first part, *Theoretical Perspectives,* the authors discuss the conceptual changes that are driving the renewed interest in affect and learning, and present theoretical perspectives of relevance to education and learning environments. The second part, *Case Studies,* features exemplary studies that span from basic research on affect and learning to state-of-the-art affect-sensitive learning technologies. The third part of the book, *Interdisciplinary Perspectives,* features diverse views related to affect and learning from cognitive load, creativity and design, and neuroscience, followed by a summative conclusion of current research in the field and possible avenues for future research.

The first three chapters present unique theoretical perspectives on affect and learning. Art Graesser and Sidney D'Mello (Chap. 2) begin by introducing theories that integrate cognition and emotion during learning. They emphasize the role cognitive disequilibrium, confusion, and impasses in driving inquiry and promoting deep comprehension. In Chap. 3, Reinhard Pekrun provides a categorization of the emotions that arise in learning activities (called academic emotions) and describes a theory that relates these academic emotions with their antecedents and consequents. In Chap. 4, Benedict du Boulay tackles the very pertinent question of how to engage students who lack motivation by providing theoretically grounded pedagogical strategies that can be implemented in computer tutors.

The case studies feature research projects, mostly from the ITS community, that address important questions on affect, learning, and describe novel technologies that monitor emotions while helping learners regulate their emotions. In particular, researchers have found it challenging to develop protocols and techniques to collect ecologically valid data, an essential component for the design of affect-sensitive learning systems. Addressing this issue in Chap. 5, Shazia Afzal and Peter Robinson discuss approaches to collecting and annotating naturalistic affective data. Cristina Conati, in Chap. 6, discusses how causes and effects can be combined to model user affect in educational games. The goal here is to build affective user models with an explicit representation of the possible *causes* of an affective reaction, as well as its *behavioral effects.* In Chap. 7, James Lester, Scott McQuiggan and Jennifer Sabourin, examine a wide-range of issues emerging from systematic investigations of learner affect during interactions with narrative-centered learning environments.

There are a number of practical and challenging issues that arise when one attempts to engineer affect-sensitive learning environments. These systems must address the problem of integrating sensors that monitor multiple signals, such as physiology, facial expressions, and contextual cues. Some systems also need to automate the process synthesizing emotions via avatars or animated pedagogical agents. Importantly, all systems need to adapt their pedagogical and motivational strategies in a manner that is sensitive to each learner's emotions, knowledge states, needs, and learning styles. In Chap. 8, Win Burleson presents his work on building an agent platform with classifiers that can recognize affect and drive the real-time behavior of a learning companion. Often emotional-intelligence capabilities need to be retrofitted on top of existing systems, introducing an entirely unique set of challenges. Sidney D'Mello, Blair Lehman, and Art Graesser describe, in Chap. 9, their work on the Affective AutoTutor, which is an affect-sensitive version of the influential dialog-based AutoTutor system (Graesser et al., 2004). They also provide early evidence of the efficacy of affect-sensitivity in promoting learning gains, particularly at deeper levels of comprehension.

It is important to acknowledge that we are only beginning to understand how best to adapt an affect-sensitive tutor's behavior to be responsive to learner affect. In Chap. 10, David Cooper, Ivon Arroyo, and Beverly Woolf address this issue by describing actionable affective processing techniques and illustrating their use in affective learning companions. Their chapter also describes the deployment of affect-detection systems in classroom environments.

Most would agree that metacognitive processes are as important as affective and cognitive processes, and there is a paucity of research exploring complex interactions between affect, cognition, and metacognition. Although this is a challenging research area, it offers several opportunities for innovative discoveries to be made. Roger Azevedo and Amber Strain discuss these challenges and their own approach with the MetaTutor system in Chap. 11.

In addition to affect, motivation and engagement are equally important constructs that warrant serious consideration. Chapter 12, by Genaro Rebolledo, Rosemary Luckin, and Benedict du Boulay, provide guidance on implementing a form of motivational scaffolding that adapts to learner affect. They focus on personalization (user modeling plus scaffolding) within a narrative supported learning environment. They also discuss their iterative development methodology that should inform the development of similar systems. Detecting engagement/disengagement, and adapting to it, is a formidable challenge addressed by Kate Forbes-Riley, Diane Litman, and Heather Friedberg in Chap. 13. They present an approach for annotating student disengagement and its source during spoken dialogs with a computer tutor as an initial, yet critical step, toward this goal.

Generalizing the outcomes of so many different projects and platforms is quite challenging. To what extent do insights gleaned from one system generalize to another? This is a difficult issue to address since each research group tends to focus on a single system. In Chap. 14, Ma. Mercedes Rodrigo and Ryan Baker address this very issue by comparing the incidence and persistence of learners' affective states during interactions with an impressive array of learning environments.

The third part of the book features interdisciplinary perspectives from researchers outside the ITS community, which constitute the majority of authors in this book. This section begins with a chapter by Slava Kalyuga (Chap. 15), who presents the cognitive aspects that underlie the expertise reversal effect. He presents an impressive synthesis of cognitive-load research within multimedia learning environments and discusses how insights gleaned from this avenue of research can be applied to affect-sensitive learning environments.

Chapter 16, by Andy Dong, examines the representation of affect through language, with a particular focus on its three meta-functions in creative thinking and design: to help break stimulus–response bonds; to control the pacing and sequencing of actions; and to evaluate situations according to beliefs and values. The chapter then discusses links between affect and creativity and their implications for building learning technologies.

Armed by emerging evidence from neuroscience, Mary Helen Immordino-Yang and Vanessa Singh (Chap. 17), construct an argument which claims that: (a) emotion and cognition are inextricably bound and involve both the body and the mind, and (b) learning is often accompanied by learners' internalization of subjective interpretations of other people's beliefs, and feelings, and actions.

Peter Goodyear's chapter (Chap. 18) encourages us to revisit the underlying motivation and framing of our research field, where technology, learning and affect meet in interesting ways. It is known that affective phenomena are contextually bound and situated in a social and physical world. Goodyear's argument transcends the body of evidence pertaining to this interrelatedness and opens a discussion into the type of activities that AC *should* support. One important point is that a deeper understanding of learning cannot be achieved by reducing the rich social nature of human behavior (including learning) to the actions of isolated individuals, as is the case with most ITSs. Hence, it might be necessary to reconceptualize the role of learning technologies in order to meet twenty-first century outcomes, an activity that, in our view, should take place in an interdisciplinary forum such as the one advocated in this book.

We conclude the book (Chap. 19) by taking stock of the various threads of research on affect, learning, and technology. We emphasize significant accomplishments and suggest possible avenues that are particularly promising for future research.

References

Barrett, L., Mesquita, B., Ochsner, K., & Gross, J. (2007). The experience of emotion. *Annual Review of Psychology, 58*, 373–403.

Biswas, G., Leelawong, K., Schwartz, D., & Vye, N. (2005). Learning by teaching: A new agent paradigm for educational software. *Applied Artificial Intelligence, 19*(3–4), 363–392.

Bower, G. (1981). Mood and memory. *American Psychologist, 36*, 129–148.

Dalgleish, T., Dunn, B., & Mobbs, D. (2009). Affective neuroscience: Past, present, and future. *Emotion Review, 1*(4), 355–368.

Dalgleish, T., & Power, M. (Eds.). (1999). *Handbook of cognition and emotion*. Sussex: Wiley.

Damasio, A. (2003). *Looking for Spinoza: Joy, sorrow, and the feeling brain*. Orlando: Harcourt.

Darwin, C. (1872). *The expression of the emotions in man and animals*. London: John Murray.

Darwin, C. (2009). *The expression of the emotions in man and animals,* Anniversary Edition. Oxford University Press.

Davidson, R. J. (1998). Affective style and affective disorders: Perspectives from affective neuroscience. *Cognition & Emotion, 12*, 307–330.

Davidson, R. J., Scherer, K. R., & Goldsmith, H. H. (2003). *Handbook of affective sciences*. New York: Oxford University Press.

Ekman, P. (1992). An argument for basic emotions. *Cognition & Emotion, 6*(3–4), 169–200.

Graesser, A., Jeon, M., & Dufty, D. (2008). Agent technologies designed to facilitate interactive knowledge construction. *Discourse Processes, 45*(4–5), 298–322.

Graesser, A., Lu, S. L., Jackson, G., Mitchell, H., Ventura, M., Olney, A., et al. (2004). AutoTutor: A tutor with dialogue in natural language. *Behavioral Research Methods, Instruments, and Computers, 36*, 180–193.

Immordino-Yang, M. H., & Damasio, A. R. (2007). We feel, therefore we learn: The relevance of affective and social neuroscience to education. *Mind, Brain and Education, 1*(1), 3–10.

Isen, A. (2001). An influence of positive affect on decision making in complex situations: Theoretical issues with practical implications. *Journal of Consumer Psychology, 11*, 75–85.

Keltner, D., & Haidt, J. (2001). Social functions of emotions. In T. J. Mayne & G. A. Bonanno (Eds.), *Emotions: Current issues and future directions* (pp. 192–213). New York: Guilford Press.

Koedinger, K., & Corbett, A. (2006). Cognitive tutors: Technology bringing learning sciences to the classroom. In R. K. Sawyer (Ed.), *The Cambridge handbook of the learning sciences* (pp. 61–78). New York: Cambridge University Press.

Lane, R., & Nadel, L. (2002). *Cognitive neuroscience of emotion series in affective science*. USA: Oxford University Press.

Lazarus, R. (1991). *Emotion and adaptation*. New York: Oxford University Press.

Lewis, M., Haviland-Jones, J., & Barrett, L. (Eds.). (2008). *Handbook of emotions* (3rd ed.). New York: Guilford Press.

Mandler, G. (1976). *Mind and emotion*. New York: Wiley.

Ortony, A., Clore, G., & Collins, A. (1988). *The cognitive structure of emotions*. New York: Cambridge University Press.

Panksepp, J. (1998). *Affective neuroscience: The foundations of human and animal emotions*. New York: Oxford University Press.

Panksepp, J. (2000). Emotions as natural kinds within the mammalian brain. In M. Lewis & J. M. Haviland-Jones (Eds.), *Handbook of emotions* (2nd ed., pp. 137–156). New York: Guilford.

Picard, R. (1997). *Affective computing*. Boston: MIT Press.

Russell, J. (2003). Core affect and the psychological construction of emotion. *Psychological Review, 110*, 145–172.

Scherer, K., Schorr, A., & Johnstone, T. (Eds.). (2001). *Appraisal processes in emotion: Theory, methods, research*. London: London University Press.

Schutz, P. A., & Pekrun, R. (2007). *Emotion in education*. San Diego: Academic.

Tomkins, S. S. (1962). *Affect imagery consciousness: Volume I, the positive affects*. London: Tavistock.

VanLehn, K., Graesser, A., Jackson, G., Jordan, P., Olney, A., & Rose, C. P. (2007). When are tutorial dialogues more effective than reading? *Cognitive Science, 31*(1), 3–62.

Woolf, B. (2009). *Building intelligent interactive tutors*. Burlington: Morgan Kaufmann Publishers.

Theoretical Perspectives on Affect and Deep Learning

Art Graesser and Sidney K. D'Mello

The first author's study of emotions began in 1974 when he was a teaching assistant in George Mandler's course on emotions at University of California at San Diego. That was a special moment in history when the cognitive revolution was in full swing and the interdisciplinary field of cognitive science was emerging. George Mandler's mission at that time was to make sure that emotions and consciousness were seriously embraced in the cognitive research communities in addition to the standard components of cold cognition: perception, attention, memory, judgment, decision making, problem solving, language, and so on. Mandler was busy writing *Mind and Emotion* (1976), a book that was the precursor of another book he published in 1984, called *Mind and Body: Psychology of Emotions and Stress.* The 1984 book was selected as the first interdisciplinary William James Book Award by the American Psychological Association. And here we are, approximately four decades later, following some of Mandler's footsteps.

The textbook in Mandler's 1974 course described two dozen theories of emotions, a clear sign that the scientific study of emotions was floundering at a pretheoretical stage. The science of emotions has seemed to progress somewhat after 40 years of research. There are now fewer major theories (perhaps 5–10) according to Pekrun's review in this edited volume, the recent *Handbook of Emotions* edited by Lewis, Haviland-Jones, and Barrett (2008), and Calvo and D'Mello's (2010) review of affect detection in the computer and social sciences. Theoretical convergence is one signal of progress in science.

One of Mandler's fundamental lessons was to resist the temptation of confusing words and psychological mechanisms. The fact that we have a word, label, or phrase to describe an emotion (e.g., shame, hope, catharsis, ecstasy) does not mean that we should reify it to the status of a scientific construct. The words we use to describe

S.K. D'Mello(✉)
Department of Psychology, Institute for Intelligent Systems,
University of Memphis, Memphis, TN, USA
e-mail: sdmello@memphis.edu

R.A. Calvo and S.K. D'Mello (eds.), *New Perspectives on Affect and Learning Technologies,*
Explorations in the Learning Sciences, Instructional Systems and Performance Technologies 3,
DOI 10.1007/978-1-4419-9625-1_2, © Springer Science+Business Media, LLC 2011

emotions are products of folklore, the historical evolution of the language, the social context of interpretation, and other cultural fluctuations that are guided by principles very different from scientific theories of psychological mechanisms. This lesson has been accepted by contemporary theories of emotions that differentiate the fundamental psychological dimensions of valence and intensity from the folklore, labels, and contextual interpretations of emotions (Barrett, 2006; Russell, 2003). It is therefore pointless to debate over whether confusion or guilt is an emotion, mood, affective state, or purely cognitive state. Researchers who debate over the precise meaning and theoretical status of particular emotion terms are better suited for a career in lexicography or ordinary language philosophy – not the science of emotions. We know that there are deep connections between cognition, affect, motivation, and social interaction so it is a waste of time to argue whether particular psychological states come under the umbrella of affect. In fact, the inextricable link between affect and cognition is sufficiently compelling that some claim the scientific distinction between emotion and cognition to be artificial, arbitrary, and of limited value (Lazarus, 1991, 2000).

This chapter focuses on connections between affect and cognition that are prevalent during complex learning. Complex learning occurs when a person attempts to comprehend difficult material, to solve a difficult problem, and to make a difficult decision. This requires learners to generate inferences, answer causal questions, diagnose and solve problems, make conceptual comparisons, generate coherent explanations, and demonstrate application and transfer of acquired knowledge. This form of learning can be contrasted with shallow learning activities such as memorizing key phrases, definitions, and facts (Graesser, Ozuru, & Sullins, 2009). Deep learning is inevitably accompanied by failure and the learner experiences a host of affective states, while they are more affectively neutral in shallow learning sessions that resonate with blasé comprehension.

For example, complex learning occurs when a person attempts to comprehend a legal document, to fix a broken piece of equipment, or to decide whether to take a new job in another city. Comprehension, reasoning, and problem solving normally require conscious reflection and inquiry because there is a discrepancy between (a) the immediate situation and (b) the person's knowledge, skills, and strategies. The person is in the state of *cognitive disequilibrium* which launches a trajectory of cognitive and affective processes until equilibrium is restored or disequilibrium is dampened. It is assumed that cognitive disequilibrium is ubiquitous in complex learning so we need a theoretical framework to understand its dynamics.

Cognitive Disequilibrium

Deep learning occurs when there is a discrepancy between the task at hand and the person's prior knowledge and the discrepancy is identified and corrected. Otherwise, the person already has mastered the task and by definition there is no learning. The discrepancy creates cognitive disequilibrium. Cognitive disequilibrium occurs when there are obstacles to goals, interruptions of organized action sequences, impasses, system breakdowns, contradictions, anomalous events, dissonance, incongruities, negative feedback, uncertainty, deviations from norms, and novelty. One question is how the person handles the disequilibrium over time. Another question is what gets learned. Answers to these questions depend on characteristics of the learner and the task, as will be discussed in this chapter.

Cognitive disequilibrium may occur at many cognitive levels, starting with sensation and extending to the person's self-concept and social interaction. Consider some concrete examples of cognitive disequilibrium.

Sensation: A crowd at a rock concert receives loud sounds and bright lights that are outside of the scope of typical stimuli. The sensory neurophysiological system responds while the person experiences shock, surprise, and eventually stress.

Perception: Modern art museums display works that deviate from our normal perception of reality. The deviations from perceptual and cognitive schemas draw attention and encourage explanation. Patrons notice many of the deviations from expectations and norms: An elephant in a lecture hall, a naked person in a church, a dog sitting at a bar. They experience surprise or curiosity at the novelty (see Silvia, 2009 for a discussion on emotions and psychological aesthetics)

Comprehension: Readers of a novel spend time trying to comprehend atypical or anomalous events in a text they read. Why did Patty Hearst become attracted to her kidnappers? Why does the author or narrator bother mentioning that the main character has a scar? Readers get surprised or confused while reading these ideas that do not coherently fit in.

Action: The piano player is repeatedly interrupted by audience members while singing her favorite songs. She becomes irritated or frustrated.

Memory: A grandfather tries to remember his account number while trying to draw out some money for vacation. He slaps his head in frustration.

Problem solving: A student tries to solve a math problem on an exam for admission to college. He has an anxiety attack when he gets stuck.

Writing: A doctoral student has a writing block before a proposal deadline. Frustration advances to rage, and occasionally aggression.

Decision making: A mother's child gets a sprained ankle so she searches the Web to find out what to do. One Web site recommends ice, another heat, whereas others have a more complex story. The mother experiences confusion and anxiety at the contradictions until she reads a Web site with the complete answer or simply gives-up and sees a doctor.

Argumentation: The teenager argues with her parents on why she wants a tattoo. The parents explain that it will take 2 years to get rid of it so she changes her mind. The parents are hoping that the teenager's resentment will shift to epiphany and enlightenment.

One could go on with this exercise of mapping affective states onto cognitive processes. Cognitive equilibrium launches cognitive and affective processes at multiple levels of cognition and these are the foundations of deep learning. The role of cognitive disequilibrium on learning and emotions has been known for decades (Festinger, 1957; Graesser, Lu, Olde, Cooper-Pye, & Whitten, 2005; Lazarus, 1991; Mandler, 1976; Piaget, 1952; Stein, Hernandez, & Trabasso, 2008). What we do not know very much about is the trajectory of cognitive-affective processes over time and also the impact of these trajectories on learning.

Some generalization can be made about the impact of cognitive disequilibrium on the body and brain. We know that activities of the sympathetic nervous system increase when there is cognitive disequilibrium compared to a neutral state. We know that anomalies trigger EEG activities of the N400 (Kutas & Hillyard, 1980). We know that the amygdala and other components of the limbic system are involved when there are emotions aligned with learning. The body and brain participate in complex learning. These activities are part of the emotions that people experience (see Chap. 17 by Immordino-Yang and Michael Connell).

Our recent research has also unveiled some generalizations about the types of emotions that accompany cognitive disequilibrium during complex learning. The affective states are not particularly pleasant during the disequilibrium phase, but the more positive emotions do emerge as equilibrium is restored. We have documented in a number of studies (Baker, D'Mello, Rodrigo, & Graesser, 2010; Craig, Graesser, Sullins, & Gholson, 2004; D'Mello & Graesser, in press-a; Lehman, Matthews, D'Mello, & Person, 2008) that the prominent emotions that occur during problem solving, reasoning, and comprehension of technical material are the negative affect states of confusion, frustration, boredom, curiosity, and anxiety; the positive affective states of delight and a genuine flow experience (i.e., when time flies and fatigue is invisible, Csikszentmihalyi, 1990) are comparatively rare, although most students do often experience sustained engagement with the task. Surprise and delight occasionally occur but they are comparatively infrequent. It is important to acknowledge that these affective states are very different from Ekman's (1992) six basic universal emotions: anger, disgust, fear, joy, sadness, and surprise. Our landscape of learning-centered emotions in a typical academic learning environment is very different from Ekman's big six.

We have discovered that the affective state of confusion is the best predictor of learning among these affect states (Craig et al., 2004; D'Mello & Graesser, in press-b; Graesser, Jackson, & McDaniel, 2007; Graesser, D'Mello, Chipman, King, & McDaniel, 2007). Confusion is a signature of thoughtful reflection, reasoning, and problem solving so this affect state is expected to be diagnostic of deep learning. Jackson and Graesser (2007) also reported that students had the lowest ratings of enjoyment during learning in those conditions where they learned the most. Thus, liking is not positively correlated with deep learning. As one student succinctly put it, "Thinking hurts!"

Positive emotions hopefully emerge after cognitive disequilibrium shifts to equilibrium. Our analysis of sequences of affect states support the claim that there are *virtuous* cycles of cognition and affect (D'Mello & Graesser, in press-a; D'Mello, Taylor, & Graesser, 2007). Delight occurs when goals are met and problems are solved. We expect the delight to be more extreme when the task is more difficult, when there has been a time-consuming commitment, and when the goal has high utility. Our best interpretation of Csikszentmihalyi's flow state is that it is an emergent affect state from a set of smaller-scale cycles that involve modest challenges, high engagement, timely achievement, and delight. This is experienced while playing games so an important pedagogical mission is to design games that smuggle in serious learning (Conati, 2002; Gee, 2003; Shaffer & Graesser, 2010). When learners get a sudden insight that solves a difficult problem, they have a very positive eureka (aha!) experience. However, our research has revealed that eureka experiences are extremely rare during complex learning (Craig et al., 2004).

Cognitive disequilibrium can also spawn unfortunate trajectories of negative affective states, or what we have sometimes called *vicious* cycles (D'Mello & Graesser, in press-a; D'Mello et al., 2007). When the learners experience repeated failures, confusion transitions into frustration, which in turn may result in disengagement and boredom. The learner attributes the failure to one or more potential causes (Dweck, 2002; Weiner, 1986), such as their own limited abilities, the subject matter being boring, or the learning environment being inadequate. These attributions are of course unfortunate. It would be better for the learners to take on the obstacle as a challenge and to work harder, but unfortunately many students do not have a strong enough self-concept to take that leap. The ideal learner is an academic risk taker (Meyer & Turner, 2006) who wants to master the material rather than being prisoners of extrinsic rewards and positive feedback.

Timing and Regulation of Affective States

The time-course of the different affect states during complex learning has only recently been initiated (D'Mello & Graesser, in press-b). One would hope that frustration and boredom do not last too long and that the learning environment would stretch the window of delight and flow. Exactly where confusion lies is an excellent question. Perhaps some confusion is good, but not too much because the student runs the risk of transitioning to frustration, disengagement, and boredom, as discussed above. D'Mello and Graesser (in press-b) have tracked the affect states while students work on difficult questions with the AutoTutor system (see Chap. 9) on computer literacy. We found that the half-life duration of surprise and delight were significantly shorter than that of confusion, boredom, and engagement/flow, with frustration in between. The fact that surprise had a short duration is intuitively plausible. A person would appear insane if they exhibited a lengthy stretch of surprise. One might like delight to last longer, but perhaps happiness is fleeting, particularly when the learning environment is sufficiently dynamic so there is no time for a student to revel in their achievements.

Basic research on the temporal chronometry of emotions offers minimal guidance on understanding the time-course of affective states during complex learning. The claim is sometimes made that true emotions are short-lived, lasting 2–4.5 s or less whereas moods can last hours and emotional traits can last years (Ekman, 1984; Rosenberg, 1998). This chapter addresses affective states during complex learning so we are most concerned about states that last seconds to minutes. Given the lack of research on this important topic, we can only offer speculations on the basis of general theories in the cognitive, learning, and social sciences.

We assume that the cognitive and task constraints play a central role in dictating the time-course of cognitive disequilibrium and affiliated affective states mentioned above. However, these states and processes are mediated by self-concepts, goals, meta-knowledge, social interaction, and the learning environment (Calvo & D'Mello, 2010; Pekrun, 2006, Chap. 3; Schutz & Pekrun, 2007). Below we discuss these factors in a bit more detail.

Cognitive Processes of the Learning Task

Some cognitive processes are executed automatically and unconsciously, such as those aligned with sensation, perception, and recognition memory. Familiarity, novelty, and positive vs. negative valence of a word are examples of these fast automatic processes that are executed in less than a second (Mandler, 1976; Zajonc, 1984). Surprise is elicited quickly and unconsciously, with a short duration, when the source of cognitive disequilibrium involves sensory, perceptual, and pattern recognition processes. This includes surprise that follows quick flashes of insight when the appropriate content accrues in working memory. Novelty can elicit curiosity under conditions that are mediated by the person's prior knowledge and interests. In contrast, there is the risk of boredom or low engagement when the stimuli and tasks have low novelty for a sustained period of time (Berlyne, 1960).

The automatic cognitive processes and associated affective states are ubiquitous in everyday life, particularly when we are living on auto-pilot throughout the day. However, central to deep learning are the more conscious and deliberate cognitive processes that occur in difficult learning activities that involve comprehension, reasoning, and problem solving. As the learners struggle with challenges, there is cognitive disequilibrium at multiple levels. When the degree of cognitive disequilibrium meets or exceeds some threshold T_a, the person experiences confusion. When this threshold is exceeded for a long enough duration (D_b) or cycles of interaction with the world, then there is the risk of frustration; and with a longer duration (D_c) or cycles of interaction with the world, the risk of disengagement and boredom. At the other extreme, the degree of cognitive disequilibrium may be lower than a different threshold T_d when there is not enough novelty, challenge, or source of disequilibrium for the person to be engaged; when this occurs for a lengthy duration that exceeds some value (D_e), there is the risk of boredom. Thus, boredom can result from a sustained period of too much disequilibrium as well as too little, a curvilinear prediction analogous to the Yerkes-Dodson law and a recent assertion by Reinhard Pekrun (see Chap. 3).

The durations and thresholds obviously depend on the complexity of the stimuli and tasks, as well as the person's cognitive appraisal of the situation, cognitive demands, and their emotions (Ortony, Clore, & Collins, 1988; Scherer, 2009). As illustrated below, the parameters are systematically affected by the person's self-concept, goals, meta-knowledge, and social interaction.

Self-Concept

Academic risk takers have a high priority in mastering the material so they push the envelope in taking on challenging tasks, even to the point of tolerating failure and negative feedback (Meyer & Turner, 2006). In contrast, the cautious learner prefers safe tasks that ensure success and positive feedback. The duration parameters would therefore be longer before the academic risk takers would encounter frustration (D_b) and disengagement (D_c). It is also conceivable that their parameter values for D_c would be longer, T_a would be higher, and T_d would be lower to the extent that they master the material and have interest. Interest in the topic is an important dimension of self-concept. People presumably persist longer and are more patient on subject matter and tasks that they view as interesting and that are within the realm of what they consider important for them to know about.

Goals

The learners' goals presumably influence the parameter values in a systematic manner. If there is a high value on the task goal and a high expectation they can complete the goal, then the values of all three duration parameters would increase and T_d would decrease, but the status of T_a is uncertain. Learners of course persist on content that is relevant to their goals even when their prior knowledge about the material is modest (McCrudden & Schraw, 2007). The parameter values are likely to vary as a function of intrinsic vs. extrinsic rewards and as a function of mastery vs. performance goals (Deci & Ryan, 2002; Dweck, 2002; Pekrun, 2006).

Metaknowledge

Metaknowledge is knowledge that a person has about cognition, pedagogy, emotions, and communication (Graesser, D'Mello, & Person, 2009). Psychological research has supported the conclusion that the accuracy and sophistication of most people's metaknowledge is unspectacular. For example, Maki's (1998) extensive review of the research on comprehension calibration has indicated that there is only a 0.27 correlation between college students' ratings on how well they understand technical texts and their scores on an objective test of comprehension. During tutoring, it is the students with higher domain knowledge who are more prone to express to the tutor that they do not understand something (Graesser & Person, 1994; Miyake & Norman, 1979). This suggests that high domain knowledge would lower the threshold of T_a: It is the knowledgeable student who would be more sensitive to various sources of cognitive disequilibrium. Regarding emotions, our research has led us to conclude that students' knowledge of their emotions during learning is not sufficiently trustworthy for us to automatically believe what they report (D'Mello, Craig, & Graesser, 2009). We need to compare the students' self judgments with those of peers, judges trained on emotions, master teachers, automated sensing devices (D'Mello & Graesser, 2010), and physiological measures. The gold standard of truth remains a mystery.

Social Interaction

Contemporary theories of emotion assume that emotions are constrained and sometimes defined by social interactions with others. Students typically do not want to appear inadequate to their teachers and too brainy to their peers. They become anxious when they take instructors' exams and the high-stakes tests administered by the government. These pressures presumably influence the threshold and duration parameters, but there is no systematic research as to how. A tutor who is supportive, empathetic, and polite is likely to influence the parameters in a way that minimizes the occurrence of frustration, boredom, and disengagement (Johnson & Valente, 2008; Lepper & Woolverton, 2002).

Learning Environments

Features of the learning environment have perhaps the most robust influence on the trajectories of cognition and affect during complex learning. We know that a system's feedback on the students' performance has a large impact, particularly when it signals cognitive disequilibrium (D'Mello & Graesser, in press-a; Graesser et al., 2008). Students sometimes are confused or frustrated when the system is unresponsive to the student or not coherently connected to what the student is saying or doing. Students are more motivated when they have some options and choices (Lepper & Woolverton, 2002), but not when they are saturated with requests for trivial decisions.

Many learning environments are entirely under student control. Students can move at their own pace when they read books and interact with hypermedia, for example. Unfortunately, students learn surprisingly little deep knowledge when left to read a textbook on their own (VanLehn et al., 2007). Their metacomprehension skills are inadequate so they cannot reliably detect whether they are understanding the material. Similarly, the strategies of self-regulated learning and question asking are underdeveloped for most students (Azevedo & Cromley, 2004; Graesser & McNamara, 2010) so they tend to be guided by shallow rather than deep learning. Students need substantial training and scaffolding of metaknowledge, self-regulated learning, and question asking before they can productively use some of the more complex learning environments.

Conclusions

There has been some progress on advancing theoretical perspectives on affect and learning during the last 40 years. This chapter has focused on the affective states that occur during deep learning, when students struggle to comprehend difficult subject matter and when they solve challenging problems that require reasoning and conscious reflection. We have argued that cognitive disequilibrium is a fundamental driver of deep learning. Cognitive disequilibrium occurs when there are obstacles to goals, interruptions of organized action sequences, impasses, system breakdowns, contradictions, anomalous events, dissonance, incongruities, negative feedback, uncertainty, deviations from norms, and novelty. A number of emotions are affiliated with cognitive disequilibrium, but notably confusion, frustration, boredom, anxiety, engagement/flow, surprise, and delight. The transitions and timing of these affective states depend on the cognitive tasks, self-concept, goals, meta-knowledge, social interaction, and features of the learning environment.

We believe that an important next phase of research is to build learning environments that are sensitive to student emotions during the course of facilitating deep learning. The systems need to detect and track the learners' emotions automatically, with sufficient reliability and accuracy. The systems need to respond to the learners in ways that are sensitive to the learners' emotions in addition to their cognitive states. We also welcome systems that will train the students how to productively self-regulate their learning in ways that reflect a mature understanding of their own meta-cognition, meta-emotions, and other forms of meta-knowledge (see Chap. 11 by Azevedo & Chauncey). We imagine a day when the students understand the meaning of confusion, its pedagogical value, how to manage it, how to use it to guide learning, and maybe even how to enjoy it.

Acknowledgments   The research on was supported by the National Science Foundation (ITR 0325428, ALT-0834847, DRK-12-0918409), and the Institute of Education Sciences (R305H050169, R305B070349, R305A080589, R305A080594). Any opinions, findings, and conclusions or recommendations expressed in this material are those of the authors and do not necessarily reflect the views of NSF or IES.

References

Azevedo, R., & Cromley, J. G. (2004). Does training on self-regulated learning facilitate students' learning with hypermedia. *Journal of Educational Psychology, 96*, 523–535.

Baker, R. S., D'Mello, S. K., Rodrigo, M. T., & Graesser, A. C. (2010). Better to be frustrated than bored: The incidence, persistence, and impact of learners' cognitive-affective states during interactions with three different computer-based learning environments. *International Journal of Human-Computer Studies, 68*, 223–241.

Barrett, L. (2006). Are emotions natural kinds? *Perspectives on Psychological Science, 1*, 28–58.

Berlyne, D. E. (1960). *Conflict, arousal, and curiosity*. New York: McGraw Hill.

Calvo, R. A., & D'Mello, S. K. (2010). Affect detection: An interdisciplinary review of models, methods, and their applications. *IEEE Transactions on Affective Computing, 1*, 1–20.

Conati, C. (2002). Probabilistic assessment of user's emotions in educational games. *Applied Artificial Intelligence, 16*(7–8), 555–575.

Craig, S., Graesser, A., Sullins, J., & Gholson, J. (2004). Affect and learning: An exploratory look into the role of affect in learning. *Journal of Educational Media, 29*, 241–250.

Csikszentmihalyi, M. (1990). *Flow: The psychology of optimal experience*. New York: Harper and Row.

D'Mello, S. K., Craig, S. D., & Graesser, A. C. (2009). Multi-method assessment of affective experience and expression during deep learning. International Journal of Learning Technology, 4, 165–187.

D'Mello, S., & Graesser, A. C. (2010). Multimodal semi-automated affect detection from conversational cues, gross body language, and facial features. *User Modeling and User-adapted Interaction, 20*, 187.

D'Mello, S. K., & Graesser, A. C. (in press-a). Emotions during learning with AutoTutor. In P. Durlach and A. Lesgold (Eds.), *Adaptive technologies for training and education*. Cambridge: Cambridge University Press.

D'Mello, S., & Graesser, A. (in press-b). The half-life of cognitive-affective states during complex learning. Cognition and Emotion.

D'Mello, S., Taylor, R., & Graesser, A. (2007). Monitoring affective trajectories during complex learning. In D. McNamara & G. Trafton (Eds.), *Proceedings of the 29th Annual Cognitive Science Society* (pp. 203–208). Austin: Cognitive Science Society.

Deci, E., & Ryan, R. (2002). The paradox of achievement: The harder you push, the worse it gets. In J. Aronson (Ed.), *Improving academic achievement: Impact of psychological factors on education* (pp. 61–87). Orlando: Academic.

Dweck, C. (2002). Messages that motivate: How praise molds students' beliefs, motivation, and performance (in surprising ways). In J. Aronson (Ed.), *Improving academic achievement: Impact of psychological factors on education* (pp. 61–87). Orlando: Academic.

Ekman, P. (1984). Expression and the nature of emotion. In K. Scherer & P. Ekman (Eds.), *Approaches to emotion* (pp. 319–344). Hillsdale: Erlbaum.

Ekman, P. (1992). An argument for basic emotions. *Cognition & Emotion, 6*(3–4), 169–200.

Festinger, L. (1957). *A theory of cognitive dissonance*. Stanford: Stanford University Press.

Gee, J. P. (2003). *What video games have to teach us about language and literacy*. New York: Macmillan.

Graesser, A. C., & McNamara, D. S. (2010). Self-regulated learning in learning environments with pedagogical agents that interact in natural language. *Educational Psychologist, 45*, 234–244.

Graesser, A. C., D'Mello, S. K., Chipman, P., King, B., & McDaniel, B. (2007). Exploring relationships between affect and learning with AutoTutor. In R. Luckin, K. Koedinger, & J. Greer (Eds.), *Artificial intelligence in education: Building technology rich learning contexts that work* (pp. 16–23). Amsterdam: IOS Press.

Graesser, A. C., D'Mello, S. K., Craig, S. D., Witherspoon, A., Sullins, J., McDaniel, B., et al. (2008). The relationship between affect states and dialogue patterns during interactions with AutoTutor. *Journal of Interactive Learning Research, 19*, 293–312.

Graesser, A. C., D'Mello, S., & Person, N. K. (2009). Metaknowledge in tutoring. In D. Hacker, J. Donlosky, & A. C. Graesser (Eds.), *Handbook of metacognition in education* (pp. 361–382). New York: Taylor & Francis.

Graesser, A. C., Jackson, G. T., & McDaniel, B. (2007). AutoTutor holds conversations with learners that are responsive to their cognitive and emotional states. *Educational Technology, 47*, 19–22.

Graesser, A., Lu, S., Olde, B., Cooper-Pye, E., & Whitten, S. (2005). Question asking and eye tracking during cognitive disequilibrium: Comprehending illustrated texts on devices when the devices break down. *Memory and Cognition, 33*, 1235–1247.

Graesser, A. C., Ozuru, Y., & Sullins, J. (2009). What is a good question? In M. McKeown (Ed.), *Festscrift for Isabel Beck*. Mahwah: Erlbaum.

Graesser, A. C., & Person, N. K. (1994). Question asking during tutoring. *American Educational Research Journal, 31*, 104–137.

Jackson, G. T., & Graesser, A. C. (2007). Content matters: An investigation of feedback categories within an ITS. In R. Luckin, K. Koedinger, & J. Greer (Eds.), *Artificial intelligence in education: Building technology rich learning contexts that work* (pp. 127–134). Amsterdam: IOS Press.

Johnson, W. L., & Valente, A. (2008). Tactical language and culture training systems: Using artificial intelligence to teach foreign languages and cultures. In *Proceedings of the 20th Innovative Applications of Artificial Intelligence (IAAI) Conference.* Los Angeles: Alelo.

Kutas, M., & Hillyard, S. A. (1980). Reading senseless sentences: Brain potentials reflect semantic incongruity. *Science, 207,* 203–208.

Lazarus, R. (1991). *Emotion and adaptation.* New York: Oxford University Press.

Lazarus, R. (2000). The cognition-emotion debate: A bit of history. In M. Lewis & J. Haviland-Jones (Eds.), *Handbook of emotions* (pp. 1–20). New York: Guilford Press.

Lehman, B., Matthews, M., D'Mello, S., & Person, N. (2008). What are you feeling? Investigating student affective states during expert human tutoring sessions. In B. Woolf, E. Aimeur, R. Nkambou, & S. Lajoie (Eds.), *Proceedings of the 9th international conference on Intelligent Tutoring Systems* (pp. 50–59). Berlin: Springer.

Lepper, M., & Woolverton, M. (2002). The wisdom of practice: Lessons learned from the study of highly effective tutors. In J. Aronson (Ed.), *Improving academic achievement: Impact of psychological factors on education* (pp. 135–158). Orlando: Academic.

Lewis, M., Haviland-Jones, J., & Barrett, L. (Eds.). (2008). *Handbook of emotions* (3rd ed.). New York: Guilford Press.

Maki, R. H. (1998). Text predictions over text material: Metacognition in educational theory and practice. In D. J. Hacker, J. Dunlosky, & A. C. Graesser (Eds.), *Metacognition in educational theory and practice* (pp. 117–144). Mahwah: Lawrence Erlbaum Associates Publisher.

Mandler, G. (1976). *Mind and emotion.* New York: Wiley.

McCrudden, M. T., & Schraw, G. (2007). Relevance and goal-focusing in text processing. *Educational Psychology Review, 19,* 113–139.

Meyer, D., & Turner, J. (2006). Re-conceptualizing emotion and motivation to learn in classroom contexts. *Educational Psychology Review, 18*(4), 377–390.

Miyake, N., & Norman, D. A. (1979). To ask a question, one must know enough to know what is not known. *Journal of Verbal Learning and Verbal Behavior, 18*(3), 357–364.

Ortony, A., Clore, G., & Collins, A. (1988). *The cognitive structure of emotions.* New York: Cambridge University Press.

Pekrun, R. (2006). The control-value theory of achievement emotions: Assumptions, corollaries, and implications for educational research and practice. *Educational Psychology Review, 18,* 315–341.

Piaget, J. (1952). *The origins of intelligence.* New York: International University Press.

Rosenberg, E. (1998). Levels of analysis and the organization of affect. *Review of General Psychology, 2*(3), 247–270.

Russell, J. (2003). Core affect and the psychological construction of emotion. *Psychological Review, 110,* 145–172.

Scherer, K. R. (2009). The dynamic architecture of emotion: Evidence for the component process model. *Cognition and Emotion, 23,* 1307–1351.

Schutz, P. A., & Pekrun, R. (Eds.). (2007). *Emotion in education.* San Diego: Academic.

Shaffer, D. W., & Graesser, A. (2010). *Using a quantitative model of participation in a community of practice to direct automated mentoring in an ill-defined domain.* Workshop at Intelligent Tutoring Systems (ITS), Pittsburgh, PA.

Silvia, P. J. (2009). Looking past pleasure: Anger, confusion, disgust, pride, surprise, and other unusual aesthetic emotions. *Psychology of Aesthetics Creativity and the Arts, 3*(1), 48–51.

Stein, N., Hernandez, M., & Trabasso, T. (2008). Advances in modeling emotions and thought: The importance of developmental, online, and multilevel analysis. In M. Lewis, J. M. Haviland-Jones, & L. F. Barrett (Eds.), *Handbook of emotions* (3rd ed., pp. 574–586). New York: Guilford Press.

VanLehn, K., Graesser, A. C., Jackson, G. T., Jordan, P., Olney, A., & Rose, C. P. (2007). When are tutorial dialogues more effective than reading? *Cognitive Science, 31,* 3–62.

Weiner, B. (1986). *An attributional theory of motivation and emotion.* New York: Springer.

Zajonc, R. (1984). On the primacy of affect. *American Psychologist, 39,* 117–123.

Emotions as Drivers of Learning and Cognitive Development

Reinhard Pekrun

Settings of learning abound with emotions. Remember the last time you studied some educational material? Depending on your goals and the contents of the material, you may have enjoyed learning or been bored, experienced flow forgetting time or been frustrated about too many obstacles, felt proud of your progress or confused and ashamed of lack of accomplishment. Furthermore, these diverse emotions affected your effort, motivation to persist, strategies for learning, and cognitive concepts – even if you were unaware of these effects. Empirical findings corroborate that learners experience a wide variety of emotions (Pekrun, Goetz, Titz, & Perry, 2002). Until recently, these emotions did not receive much attention by researchers, two exceptions being studies on test anxiety (Zeidner, 1998, 2007) and on the links between causal attributions and achievement emotions (Weiner, 1985). During the past 10 years, however, there has been growing recognition that emotions are of critical importance for human learning and cognitive development (Linnenbrink-Garcia & Pekrun, 2011; Schutz & Pekrun, 2007).

In this chapter, I consider emotions and their functions for learning. In the first section, I will outline different concepts describing relevant emotions. Next, the effects of emotions on learning and development are addressed. In the third section, I summarize research on the individual and social origins of emotions related to learning. The chapter is concluded by considering principles of reciprocal causation and their implications for emotion regulation.

R. Pekrun (✉)
Department of Psychology, University of Munich, Munich, Germany
e-mail: pekrun@lmu.de

R.A. Calvo and S.K. D'Mello (eds.), *New Perspectives on Affect and Learning Technologies*,   23
Explorations in the Learning Sciences, Instructional Systems and Performance Technologies 3,
DOI 10.1007/978-1-4419-9625-1_3, © Springer Science+Business Media, LLC 2011

Concepts of Emotion

Emotion, Mood, and Affect

Emotions are multifaceted phenomena involving coordinated psychological processes, including affective, cognitive, physiological, motivational, and expressive components (Scherer, 2009). For example, a student's anxiety before an exam can be comprised of nervous, uneasy feelings (affective); worries about failing the exam (cognitive); increased heart rate or sweating (physiological); impulses to escape the situation (motivation); and an anxious facial expression (expressive). As compared to intense emotions, *moods* are of lower intensity and lack a specific referent. Different emotions and moods are often compiled in more general constructs of *affect*. Two variants of this term are used in the research literature. In the educational literature, affect is often used to denote a broad variety of motivational constructs including self-concept, beliefs, emotions, etc. (e.g., McLeod & Adams, 1989). In contrast, in emotion research, affect refers to emotions and moods more specifically. In this research, the term is often used to refer to omnibus variables of positive vs. negative emotions and moods, with positive affect being compiled of various positive states (e.g., enjoyment, pride, satisfaction) and negative affect consisting of various negative states (e.g., anger, anxiety, frustration).

Valence and Activation

Two important dimensions describing emotions and affect are *valence* and *activation*. In terms of valence, positive (i.e., pleasant) states, such as enjoyment and happiness, can be differentiated from negative (i.e., unpleasant) states, such as anger, anxiety, or boredom. In terms of activation, physiologically activating states can be distinguished from deactivating states, such as activating excitement vs. deactivating relaxation. These two dimensions are orthogonal, making it possible to organize affective states in a two-dimensional space including four broad categories of emotions: *positive activating* (e.g., enjoyment, hope, pride); *positive deactivating* (e.g., relief, relaxation); *negative activating* (e.g., anger, confusion, anxiety, shame); *negative deactivating* (e.g., hopelessness, boredom; Pekrun, 2006; Table 1).

Object Focus

Emotions can also be grouped according to their object focus. For explaining the functions of emotions for learning, object focus is critical because it determines if emotions pertain to the task at hand or not. In terms of object focus, the following broad groups of emotions and moods may be most important for learning and cognitive development.

Table 1 A three-dimensional taxonomy of achievement emotions

Object focus	Positive[a]		Negative[b]	
	Activating	Deactivating	Activating	Deactivating
Activity	Enjoyment	Relaxation	Anger Frustration	Boredom
Outcome	Hope Pride Gratitude	Contentment Relief	Anxiety Anger Shame	Hopelessness Disappointment

[a] Positive = pleasant emotion
[b] Negative = unpleasant emotion

General and specific moods: Learners may experience moods that lack a referent, but may nevertheless influence their performance. Moods can be generalized in terms of good vs. bad mood, being experienced as a low-intensity feeling in the background of one's conscious mind that is just positive (pleasant) or negative (unpleasant), does not capture much attention, and lacks any clear differentiation of specific affective qualities. Alternatively, moods can be qualitatively distinct, as in joyful, angry, or fearful mood.

Achievement emotions: These are emotions that are linked to activities (e.g., learning) or outcomes (e.g., success and failure) that are judged according to achievement-related standards of quality. Accordingly, two groups of achievement emotions are activity emotions, such as enjoyment or boredom during learning, and outcome emotions, such as hope and pride related to success, or anxiety and shame related to failure. Combining the valence, activation, and object focus (activity vs. outcome) dimensions renders a three-dimensional taxonomy of achievement emotions (Pekrun, 2006; see Table 1).

Epistemic emotions: Emotions can be caused by cognitive qualities of task information and of the processing of such information. A prototypical case is cognitive incongruity triggering surprise, curiosity, and confusion, as well as anxiety and frustration if the incongruity cannot be dissolved (Craig, Graesser, Sullins, & Gholson, 2004; D'Mello & Graesser, 2010). As these emotions pertain to the epistemic aspects of learning and cognitive activities, they can be called epistemic emotions (Pekrun & Stephens, in press). During learning, many emotions can be experienced either as achievement emotions or as epistemic emotions, depending on the focus of attention. For example, the frustration experienced by a student not finding the solution to a science problem can be regarded as an epistemic emotion if it is focused on the cognitive incongruity implied by a nonsolved problem, and as an achievement emotion if the focus is on personal failure and inability to solve the problem.

Topic emotions: Emotions can be triggered by the contents covered by learning material. Examples are the empathetic emotions pertaining to a protagonist's fate when reading a novel, the emotions triggered by political events dealt with in political lessons, or the emotions related to topics in science class. Topic emotions do not directly pertain to learning and problem solving, but can strongly influence learners' interest in learning material (Ainley, 2007).

Social emotions: Learning and development are situated in social contexts. Even when learning alone, students do not act in a social vacuum; rather, the goals, contents, and outcomes of learning are socially constructed. By implication, settings of learning induce a multitude of social emotions related to other persons, such as admiration, envy, or contempt related to the success and failure of others, or love or hate in the relationships with classmates and teachers (Weiner, 2007).

Functions for Learning and Cognitive Development

Cognitive and neuroscientific research suggest that emotions are fundamentally important for human learning and development. Specifically, experimental mood studies have found that emotions influence a broad variety of cognitive processes that contribute to learning, such as perception, attention, memory, decision making, and cognitive problem solving (e.g., Clore & Huntsinger, 2007; Loewenstein & Lerner, 2003). However, one fundamental problem with much of this research is that it used global constructs of positive vs. negative affect or mood, but did not attend to the specific qualities of different kinds of emotions. This implies that it may be difficult to use the findings for explaining learning in real-world contexts. Specifically, it is not sufficient to differentiate positive from negative affective states, but imperative to also attend to the degree of activation and to the affective qualities implied.

As such, the minimum necessary is to distinguish between the four groups of emotions outlined earlier (positive activating, positive deactivating, negative activating, negative deactivating). For example, both anxiety and hopelessness are negative (unpleasant) emotions; however, their effects on students' engagement can differ dramatically, as anxiety can motivate a student to invest effort in order to avoid failure, whereas hopelessness likely undermines any kind of engagement. Moreover, even within each of the four categories, it may be necessary to further distinguish between distinct emotions. For example, both anxiety and anger are activating negative emotions; however, paradoxically, whereas anxiety is associated with avoidance, anger is related to approach motivation (Carver & Harmon-Jones, 2009).

As proposed by Pekrun's (1992a, 2006) cognitive/motivational model of emotion effects, the emotions grouped in the four valence x activation categories can influence various processes underlying human learning, including (1) attention and memory processes; (2) motivation to learn; (3) use of learning strategies; and (4) self-regulation of learning. In the following sections, I summarize research on the effects of emotions on these processes and on resulting learning outcomes.

Attention and Memory

Emotions consume resources of the working memory by focusing attention on the object of emotion. This effect was first addressed in interference models of test anxiety, which posited that anxiety involves worries and task-irrelevant thoughts that interfere with performance on complex and difficult tasks (see Zeidner, 1998). Interference models of anxiety were expanded by resource allocation models postulating that any emotion can consume cognitive resources (Ellis & Ashbrook, 1988). However, the resource consumption effect is likely bound to emotions that have task-extraneous objects and produce task-irrelevant thinking, such as worries about impending failure on an exam in test anxiety. In contrast, in task-based surprise and positive task-related emotions such as epistemic curiosity and enjoyment of learning, the task is the object of emotion. In these affective states, emotional arousal serves to focus attention on the task, and working memory resources can be used for task completion.

Corroborating these expectations, empirical studies with K-12 and university students have found that negative emotions such as anger, anxiety, shame, boredom, and hopelessness are associated with task-irrelevant thinking and reduced flow, whereas enjoyment is related negatively to irrelevant thinking and positively to flow (Linnenbrink, 2007; Pekrun, Goetz, Daniels, Stupnisky, & Perry, 2010; Pekrun et al., 2002; Zeidner, 1998).

Beyond working memory, emotions also influence long-term storage and retrieval of information, including mood-congruent memory recall and retrieval-induced forgetting and facilitation. Mood-congruent retrieval (Parrott & Spackman, 2000) implies that mood facilitates the retrieval of like-valenced material, with positive mood facilitating the retrieval of positive self-related information, and negative mood facilitating the retrieval of negative information. By implication, positive mood can foster positive self-appraisals and thus benefit motivation to learn and performance; in contrast, negative mood can promote negative self-appraisals and thus hamper motivation and performance.

Retrieval-induced forgetting implies that practicing some learning material impedes later retrieval of related material that was not practiced, presumably because of inhibitory processes in memory networks. In contrast, retrieval-induced facilitation implies that practicing enhances memory for related, unpracticed material (Chan, McDermott, & Roediger, 2006). With learning material consisting of disconnected elements, such as single words, retrieval-induced forgetting has been found to occur. For example, after learning a list of words, practicing half of the list can impede memory for the other half due to interference effects. In contrast, facilitation has been shown to occur for connected materials consisting of elements that show strong interrelations. For example, after learning coherent text material, practicing half of the material can lead to better memory for the non-practiced half.

Emotions can influence retrieval-induced forgetting. Specifically, negative mood can undo forgetting, likely because it inhibits spreading activation in memory networks which underlies retrieval-induced forgetting (Bäuml & Kuhbandner, 2007). Conversely, positive emotions should facilitate retrieval-induced facilitation since they promote the relational processing of information underlying such facilitation. This would imply that negative emotions can be helpful for learning lists of unrelated material (such as lists of foreign language vocabulary), whereas positive emotions should promote learning of coherent material.

Motivation to Learn

Emotions can profoundly influence learners' motivational engagement. The little empirical evidence available to date suggests that emotions influence students' adoption of achievement goals. Specifically, pleasant emotions were found to have positive effects, and unpleasant emotions negative effects, on college students' adoption of mastery goals (Daniels et al., 2009; Linnenbrink & Pintrich, 2002). In line with this evidence, positive achievement emotions such as enjoyment of learning, hope, and pride have been shown to relate positively to K-12 and college students' interest and intrinsic motivation, whereas negative emotions such as anger, anxiety, shame, hopelessness, and boredom related negatively to these motivational variables (Pekrun et al., 2002, 2010; Pekrun, Goetz, Perry, Kramer, & Hochstadt, 2004; Zeidner, 1998).

However, as addressed in Pekrun's (1992a, 2006) cognitive/motivational model, motivational effects may be different for activating vs. deactivating emotions. This model posits that activating positive emotions (e.g., joy, hope, pride) promote motivational engagement, whereas deactivating emotions (e.g., hopelessness, boredom) simply undermine engagement. In contrast, effects are posited to be more complex for deactivating positive emotions (e.g., relief, relaxation) and activating negative emotions (e.g., anger, frustration, confusion, anxiety, and shame). For example, relaxed contentment following success can be expected to reduce immediate motivation to reengage with learning contents, but strengthen long-term motivation to do so. Regarding activating negative emotions, anger, anxiety, and shame have been found to reduce intrinsic motivation, but to strengthen extrinsic motivation to invest effort in order to avoid failure, especially so when expectations to prevent failure and attain success are favorable (Turner & Schallert, 2001). Due to these variable effects on different kinds of motivation, the effects of these emotions on students' overall motivation to learn can be variable as well.

Use of Learning Strategies

Experimental mood research has shown that positive and negative moods impact problem solving. Specifically, positive mood can promote flexible, creative, and holistic ways of solving problems and a reliance on generalized, heuristic knowledge structures (Fredrickson, 2001; also see Dong, 2011). Conversely, negative mood has been found to promote focused, detail-oriented, and analytical ways of thinking (Clore & Huntsinger, 2007). A number of theoretical explanations have been proffered for these findings. For example, in mood-as-information approaches, it is assumed that positive affective states signal that all is well (e.g., sufficient goal progress), whereas negative states signal that something is wrong (e.g., insufficient goal progress; Clore & Huntsinger, 2009). "All is well" conditions imply safety and the discretion to creatively explore the environment, broaden one's cognitive horizon, and build new actions, as addressed by Fredrickson's (2001) broaden-and-build theory of positive emotions. In contrast, "all is *not* well" conditions may imply a threat to well-being and agency, thus making it necessary to focus on these problems in analytical, cognitively cautious ways. Furthermore, positive emotions may facilitate flexible problem solving via increasing brain dopamine levels (Ashby, Isen, & Turken, 1999), and negative moods may promote effort investment and performance on analytical tasks by inducing a need for "mood repair" (e.g., Schaller & Cialdini, 1990).

Judging from the experimental evidence on problem solving, positive activating emotions such as enjoyment of learning should facilitate use of flexible, holistic learning strategies like elaboration and organization of learning material or critical thinking. Negative emotions, on the other hand, should sustain more rigid, detail-oriented learning, like simple rehearsal of learning material. Correlational evidence from studies with college students generally supports this view (Linnenbrink, 2007; Pekrun et al., 2002, 2004; Pekrun, Goetz, Frenzel, Barchfeld, & Perry, 2011). However, for deactivating positive and negative emotions, these effects may be less pronounced. Deactivating emotions, like relaxation or boredom, may produce shallow information processing rather than any more intensive use of learning strategies.

Self-Regulation of Learning

Self-regulation of learning includes the use of meta-cognitive, meta-motivational, and meta-emotional strategies (Wolters, 2003) making it possible to adopt goals, monitor and regulate learning activities, and evaluate their results in flexible ways, such that learning activities can be adapted to the demands of academic tasks. An application of these strategies presupposes cognitive flexibility. Therefore, positive emotions should foster self-regulation and the implied use of meta-strategies, whereas negative emotions can motivate the individual to rely on external guidance. Correlational evidence from studies with college students is generally in line with these propositions (Pekrun & Stephens, in press). However, the reverse causal direction may also play a role in producing such correlations – self-regulated learning may instigate enjoyment, and external directions for learning may trigger anxiety.

Overall Effects on Learning Outcomes

Since different mechanisms can contribute to the functional effects of emotions, the overall effects on learning and cognitive development are inevitably complex and may depend on the interplay between different mechanisms, as well as between these mechanisms and task demands. Nevertheless, it seems possible to derive inferences from the existing evidence and the above considerations.

Positive emotions: Traditionally, it was assumed that positive emotions, notwithstanding their potential to foster creativity, are often maladaptive for cognitive performance as a result of inducing unrealistically positive appraisals, fostering nonanalytical information processing, and making effort expenditure seem unnecessary by signaling that everything is going well. From this perspective, "our primary goal is to feel good, and feeling good makes us lazy thinkers who are oblivious to potentially useful negative information and unresponsive to meaningful variations in information and situation" (Aspinwall, 1998, p. 7).

However, as noted, positive mood has typically been regarded as a unitary construct in experimental mood research. As argued earlier, such a view is inadequate because it fails to distinguish between activating vs. deactivating moods and emotions. As detailed in Pekrun's (1992a, 2006) cognitive/motivational model, *deactivating* positive emotions, like relief or relaxation, may well have the negative performance effects described for positive mood. These emotions can reduce task attention and can lead to superficial information processing, thus making effects on overall achievement variable. In contrast, *activating* positive emotions, such as task-related enjoyment, curiosity, or pride, focus attention on the task, promote relational processing of information, promote intrinsic motivation, and facilitate use of flexible learning strategies and self-regulation, thus probably exerting positive effects under most task conditions.

Related empirical evidence is scarce, but supports the view that activating positive emotions can enhance learning. Specifically, K-12 and college students' enjoyment of learning, hope, and pride was found to correlate positively with their interest, effort invested in studying, elaboration of learning material, self-regulation of learning, and academic performance (Buff, Reusser, Rakoczy, & Pauli, 2011; Pekrun et al., 2002, 2011). General positive affect has also been found to correlate positively with students' engagement (Linnenbrink, 2007). However, some studies have found null relations (Linnenbrink, 2007; Pekrun, Elliot, & Maier, 2009). Also, caution should be exercised in interpreting the reported correlations. Linkages between emotions and achievement are likely due not only to performance effects of emotions, but also to effects of performance attainment on emotions, implying reciprocal rather than unidirectional causation.

Negative activating emotions: As noted, emotions such as anger, anxiety, and shame reduce cognitive resources available for task purposes and undermine intrinsic motivation. On the other hand, these emotions can induce motivation to avoid failure and facilitate the use of more rigid learning strategies. By implication, the effects on learning outcomes depend on task conditions and may well be variable, similar to the effects of positive deactivating emotions.

The available evidence supports this position. Specifically, it has been shown that *anxiety* impairs performance on complex or difficult tasks that demand cognitive resources, whereas performance on easy and less complex tasks may not suffer or is even enhanced. In line with experimental findings, field studies have shown that test anxiety correlates moderately negatively with students' academic performance (Hembree, 1988; Zeidner, 1998, 2007). Again, in explaining the correlational evidence, reciprocal causation of emotion and performance has to be considered. Linkages between test anxiety and achievement may be caused by effects of success and failure on the development of test anxiety, in addition to effects of anxiety on achievement. Furthermore, zero or positive correlations with performance variables have sometimes been found, in line with the view that anxiety can exert variable effects. Anxiety likely has deleterious effects in many students, but it may facilitate overall performance in those who can productively use the motivational energy provided by anxiety (also see Lang & Lang, 2010).

Few studies have addressed the effects of negative activating emotions other than anxiety. As with anxiety, *shame* and *anger* showed moderately negative correlations with students' academic achievement (Pekrun et al., 2004, 2011) and negatively predicted their exam performance, even when controlling ability and trait affect (Pekrun et al., 2004, 2009). However, as with anxiety, the underlying mechanisms may be complex and imply more than just negative effects (e.g., Turner & Schallert, 2001), especially so when students are able to maintain positive expectancies making it possible to use these emotions for strengthening motivation and effort. Similarly, negative activating epistemic emotions can also well promote students' learning and cognitive development. Specifically, *confusion* during learning has been found to correlate positively with learning gains, presumably because it instigates motivation to think and reflect on existing cognitive schemas (Craig et al., 2004; D'Mello & Graesser, in press), thus promoting conceptual change.

Negative deactivating emotions: In contrast to negative activating emotions, negative deactivating emotions, such as boredom and hopelessness, may uniformly impair performance by reducing cognitive resources, undermining both intrinsic and extrinsic motivation, and promoting superficial information processing. The little evidence available corroborates that boredom and hopelessness relate uniformly negatively to students' learning (Craig et al., 2004; Pekrun et al., 2010).

In sum, theoretical expectations, experimental evidence, and findings from field studies suggest that emotions have profound effects on learning and cognitive development. As such, administrators, educators, and designers of learning environments should pay attention to the emotions experienced by learners. Most likely, the effects of enjoyment of learning are beneficial, whereas hopelessness and boredom are detrimental. The effects of emotions like anger, anxiety, shame, or confusion are more variable. Likely, the effects of anxiety and shame on complex learning are negative in the average student, whereas epistemic emotions like confusion can contribute to promoting cognitive development.

Origins of Emotions

Given the relevance of emotions for learning, it pays to analyze their origins as well. In this section, I provide a short overview of current perspectives on the individual and social antecedents of emotions related to learning (for more comprehensive treatments, see Schutz & Pekrun, 2007; Zeidner, 1998).

Individual Antecedents: Appraisals and Achievement Goals

Emotions can be caused and modulated by numerous individual factors, including situational perceptions, cognitive appraisals, neurohormonal processes, and sensory feedback from facial, gestural, and postural expression (Davidson, Scherer, &

Goldsmith, 2003). However, the emotions experienced in situations of learning pertain to culturally defined demands in settings that are a recent product of civilization. In these settings, the individual has to learn how to adapt to situational demands while preserving individual autonomy – inevitably a process guided by individual goals and appraisals.

Appraisals: In test anxiety studies, appraisals concerning threat of failure have been addressed as causing anxiety, including appraisals of the likelihood and subjective importance of failure, and of possibilities to cope with this threat. For example, a student may experience anxiety when she thinks failure on an important exam is likely, and that this threat is not sufficiently controllable. Empirical research confirms that test anxiety is closely related to perceived lack of control over performance in terms of low self-concept of ability, low self-efficacy expectations, and unfavorable academic control beliefs (Zeidner, 1998).

In attributional theories explaining emotions following success and failure, perceived control plays a central role as well. In B. Weiner's (1985, 2007) approach, attributions of success and failure to various causes are held to be primary determinants of these emotions. For example, pride is assumed to be aroused by attributions of success to internal causes such as ability and effort. Shame is seen to be instigated by failure attributed to internal causes that are uncontrollable (like lack of ability), and gratitude and anger by attributions of success and failure, respectively, to external causes that are under control by others. Empirical findings from scenario studies and field research were largely in line with Weiner's propositions (Weiner, 1985).

While test anxiety theories and attributional theories have addressed outcome emotions pertaining to success and failure, they have neglected activity-related emotions. In Pekrun's (2006; Pekrun, Frenzel, Goetz, & Perry, 2007) control-value theory of achievement emotions, core propositions of the transactional stress model and attributional theories are revised and expanded to explain a broader variety of emotions. The theory posits that achievement emotions are induced when the individual feels in control of, or out of control of, achievement activities and outcomes that are subjectively important – implying that appraisals of control and value are the proximal determinants of these emotions (e.g., Goetz, Frenzel, Stoeger, & Hall, 2010).

The theory proposes that enjoyment of achievement activities is instigated when these activities are experienced as both controllable and valuable. For example, a student is expected to enjoy studying when she feels competent to master the learning material and perceives the material as interesting. Conversely, boredom is induced when the activity lacks any incentive value. The anticipatory outcome emotions hope and anxiety, related to potential success and failure, respectively, are thought to arise when there is some lack of control, implying uncertainty about these achievement outcomes, paired with subjective importance of these outcomes. For example, a student would feel anxious before an exam if he expects that he could fail and perceives the exam as important. If he is sure to succeed or does not care, there is no need to be anxious. Hopelessness is thought to be triggered when achievement seems not controllable at all, implying subjective certainty about failure.

Finally, retrospective outcome emotions such as pride and shame are induced when success and failure, respectively, are perceived to be caused by internal factors implying control, or lack of control, about these outcomes (for further details, see Pekrun, 2006).

Achievement goals: To the extent that cognitive appraisals are proximal determinants of achievement emotions, more distal individual antecedents such as achievement goals should affect these emotions by first influencing appraisals (Fig. 1; Pekrun, 2006). Specifically, Pekrun's (2006; Pekrun, Elliot, & Maier, 2006, 2009) control-value theory implies that mastery goals should focus attention on the controllability and positive values of task activities, thus promoting positive activity emotions such as enjoyment of learning, and reducing negative activity emotions such as boredom. Performance-approach goals should focus attention on the controllability and positive values of success, thus facilitating positive outcome emotions such as hope and pride, and performance-avoidance goals should focus attention on the uncontrollability and negative value of failure, thus inducing negative outcome emotions such as anxiety, shame, and hopelessness.

The available evidence corroborates that learners' goals affect their emotions. The relation between performance-avoidance goals and test anxiety is best documented, but recent research also shows clear relations for mastery goals and activity emotions (positive for enjoyment, negative for boredom), and for performance goals and outcome emotions other than anxiety, such as pride, shame, and hopelessness

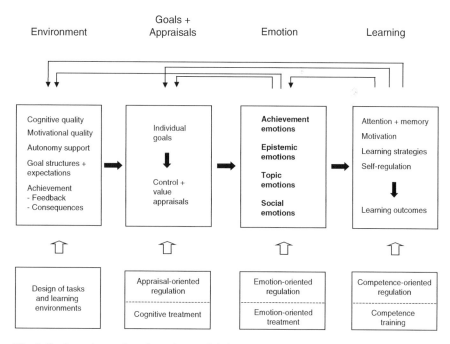

Fig. 1 Reciprocal causation of emotions and their antecedents and outcomes

(Daniels et al., 2009; Linnenbrink, 2007; Linnenbrink & Pintrich, 2002; Pekrun et al., 2006, 2009). The close relation between achievement-related goals and subsequent emotions also implies that emotions can function as mediators of the effects of achievement goals on learning (Pekrun et al., 2009).

The Influence of Tasks and Environments

The impact of task design and learning environments on learners' emotions is largely unexplored, with the exception of research on the antecedents of test anxiety (Wigfield & Eccles, 1990; Zeidner, 1998, 2007). Lack of structure and clarity in classroom instruction and exams, as well as excessively high task demands, high achievement expectancies from important others, competition in classrooms, negative feedback after performance, and negative consequences of poor performance (e.g., public humiliation) correlate positively with students' test anxiety, likely because these factors reduce perceived control and increase the importance of avoiding failure. Furthermore, the format of tasks has been found to be relevant. Open-ended formats (e.g., essay questions) seem to induce more anxiety than multiple-choice formats, likely due to higher working memory demands which are difficult to meet when working memory capacity is used for worrying about failure. In contrast, giving individuals the choice between tasks and relaxing time constraints has been found to reduce test anxiety, presumably so because perceived control is enhanced under these conditions (Zeidner, 1998).

The quality of tasks, expectations from significant others such as parents and teachers, and functional importance of achievement likely influence academic emotions other than anxiety as well. The following factors may be relevant for a broad variety of emotions (Fig. 1; Pekrun, 2006; Pekrun & Stephens, in press).

Cognitive quality: The cognitive quality of tasks and instruction as defined by their structure, clarity, and potential for cognitive stimulation likely has a positive influence on perceived competence and the perceived value of tasks (e.g., Cordova & Lepper, 1996), thus positively influencing learners' emotions. The cognitive quality of tasks in terms of inducing appropriate levels of cognitive incongruity may be of primary importance for the arousal of epistemic emotions such as surprise and curiosity. In addition, the relative difficulty of tasks can influence perceived control, and the match between task demands and competences can influence subjective task value, thus also influencing emotions. If demands are too high or too low, the incentive value of tasks may be reduced to the extent that boredom is experienced (Csikszentmihalyi, 1975; Pekrun et al., 2010).

Motivational quality: Teachers and peers deliver both direct and indirect messages conveying academic values. Two approaches of inducing emotionally relevant values in indirect ways may be most important. First, if tasks and environments are shaped such that they meet students' needs, positive activity-related emotions should be fostered. For example, learning environments that support cooperation should help students fulfill their needs for social relatedness, thus making working on academic tasks more enjoyable and promoting social engagement as discussed earlier. Second, teachers' own enthusiasm in dealing with tasks can facilitate the adoption of achievement values and related emotions (Frenzel, Goetz, Lüdtke, Pekrun, & Sutton, 2009; Turner, Meyer, Midgley, & Patrick, 2003). Observational learning and emotional contagion may be prime mechanisms mediating these effects (Hatfield, Cacioppo, & Rapson, 1994).

Autonomy support: Tasks and environments supporting autonomy can increase perceived control and, by meeting needs for autonomy, the value of related achievement activities (Tsai, Kunter, Lüdtke, & Trautwein, 2008). However, these beneficial effects likely depend on the match between individual competences and needs for academic autonomy, on the one hand, and the affordances of these environments, on the other. In case of a mismatch, loss of control and negative emotions could result.

Goal structures and social expectations: The goal structures provided in academic settings conceivably influence emotions in two ways. First, to the extent that these structures are adopted, they influence individual achievement goals and any emotions mediated by these goals (e.g., Roeser, Midgley, & Urdan, 1996). Second, goal structures determine relative opportunities for experiencing success and perceiving control, thus influencing control-dependent emotions. Specifically, competitive goal structures imply, by definition, that some individuals have to experience failure, thus inducing negative outcome emotions such as anxiety and hopelessness in these individuals. Similarly, the demands implied by an important other's unrealistic expectancies for achievement can lead to negative emotions resulting from reduced subjective control.

Feedback and consequences of achievement: Cumulative success can strengthen perceived control, and cumulative failure can undermine control. In environments involving frequent assessments, performance feedback is likely of primary importance for the arousal of emotions. In addition, the perceived consequences of success and failure are important, since these consequences affect the instrumental value of achievement outcomes. Positive outcome emotions (e.g., hope for success) can be increased if success produces beneficial long-term outcomes (e.g., future career opportunities), provided sufficient contingency between one's own efforts, success, and these outcomes. Negative consequences of failure (e.g., unemployment), on the other hand, may increase achievement-related anxiety and hopelessness (Pekrun, 1992b).

In sum, individual antecedents as well as social environments and academic tasks shape students' academic emotions and, consequently, any emotion-dependent engagement with learning. Environments, goals, and appraisals can induce, prevent, and modulate students' emotions, and they can shape their objects and contents. Depending on individual goals and the learning environment provided, students' academic life can be infused with positive affect and joyful task engagement, or with anxiety, shame, frustration, hopelessness, and boredom.

Reciprocal Causation and Emotion Regulation

Emotions influence learning and development, but learning outcomes are expected to reciprocally influence appraisals, emotions, and the environment (Linnenbrink & Pintrich, 2002; Pekrun, 2006; see Fig. 1). As such, emotions, their antecedents, and their effects are thought to be linked by reciprocal causation over time. For example, emotions influence students' adoption of achievement goals, but these goals reciprocally influence students' emotions. Such reciprocal causation can take different forms and can extend over fractions of seconds (e.g., in linkages between appraisals and emotions), days, weeks, months, or years. Positive feedback loops likely are commonplace (e.g., teachers' and students' enjoyment reciprocally reinforcing each other by mutual emotional contagion; Frenzel et al., 2009), but negative feedback loops can also be important (e.g., when failure in solving a cognitive problem instigates frustration in a student, and frustration motivates the student to solve the problem).

Reciprocal causation has implications for the regulation of emotions, for the treatment of excessively negative emotions, and for the design of "emotionally sound" (Astleitner, 2000) learning environments. Emotions can be regulated and changed by addressing any of the elements involved in the cyclic feedback processes between emotions, their effects, and their antecedents. Regulation and treatment can target (a) the emotion itself (*emotion-oriented* regulation and treatment, such as using drugs to cope with anxiety or employing interest-enhancing strategies to reduce boredom; Sansone, Weir, Harpster, & Morgan, 1992); (b) the control and value appraisals underlying emotions (*appraisal-oriented* regulation and treatment; e.g., attributional retraining, Ruthig, Perry, Hall, & Hladkyj, 2004); (c) the competences determining individual agency (*competence-oriented* regulation and treatment; e.g., training of learning skills); and (d) tasks and learning environments (*design of tasks and environments*). Empirical evidence on ways to regulate and modify emotions related to learning is still largely lacking to date, with the single exception of research on the modification of test anxiety (Zeidner, 1998; see also Nett, Goetz, & Hall, 2010).

Conclusion

As argued in this chapter, emotions are critically important for human learning and cognitive development. However, much of the research supporting this conclusion has been conducted by cognitive psychologists and neuroscientists in laboratory studies, thus being removed from the reality of learning situations in academic and work contexts. Except for studies examining test anxiety, which has been a popular construct in educational research since the 1950s (Zeidner, 1998), research on emotions in real-world learning settings is clearly in a nascent stage. Educational research is just beginning to acknowledge the importance of affect and emotions.

Of specific importance, little is known to date about emotion regulation and the design of learning tasks and learning environments targeting emotions other than anxiety. As yet, the few attempts to design learning environments that foster learners' positive emotions have met with partial success at best (e.g., Glaeser-Zikuda, Fuss, Laukenmann, Metz, & Randler, 2005). The success story of test anxiety research suggests, however, that future research can be successful in developing ways to shape learning settings so that adaptive emotions fostering learners' engagement are promoted and maladaptive emotions prevented.

References

Ainley, M. (2007). Being and feeling interested: Transient state, mood, and disposition. In P. A. Schutz & R. Pekrun (Eds.), *Emotion in education* (pp. 147–163). San Diego: Academic.

Ashby, F. G., Isen, A. M., & Turken, A. U. (1999). A neuropsychological theory of positive affect and its influence on cognition. *Psychological Review, 106*, 529–550.

Aspinwall, L. (1998). Rethinking the role of positive affect in self-regulation. *Motivation and Emotion, 22*, 1–32.

Astleitner, H. (2000). Designing emotionally sound instruction: The FEASP-approach. *Instructional Science, 28*, 169–198.

Bäuml, K.-H., & Kuhbandner, C. (2007). Remembering can cause forgetting – but not in negative moods. *Psychological Science, 18*, 111–115.

Buff, A., Reusser, K., Rakoczy, K., & Pauli, C. (2011). Activating positive affective experiences in the classroom: "Nice to have" or something more? Learning and Instruction, *21*, 452–466.

Carver, C. S., & Harmon-Jones, E. (2009). Anger is an approach-related affect: Evidence and implications. *Psychological Bulletin, 135*, 183–204.

Chan, C. K., McDermott, K. B., & Roediger, H. L. (2006). Retrieval-induced facilitation: Initially nontested material can benefit from prior testing. *Journal of Experimental Psychology: General, 135*, 533–571.

Clore, G. L., & Huntsinger, J. R. (2007). How emotions inform judgment and regulate thought. *Trends in Cognitive Sciences, 11*, 393–399.

Clore, G. L., & Huntsinger, J. R. (2009). How the object of affect guides its impact. *Emotion Review, 1*, 39–54.

Cordova, D. I., & Lepper, M. R. (1996). Intrinsic motivation and the process of learning: Beneficial effects of contextualization, personalization, and choice. *Journal of Educational Psychology, 88*, 715–730.

Craig, S. D., Graesser, A. C., Sullins, J., & Gholson, B. (2004). Affect and learning: an exploratory look into the role of affect on learning with AutoTutor. *Journal of Educational Media, 29*, 241–250.

Csikszentmihalyi, M. (1975). *Beyond boredom and anxiety*. San Francisco: Jossey-Bass.

D'Mello, S., & Graesser, A. C. (2010). Modelling cognitive-affective dynamics with hidden Markov models. In R. Catrambone & S. Ohlsson (Eds.), *Proceedings of the 32nd annual Cognitive Science Society conference* (pp. 2721–2726). Austin: Cognitive Science Society.

D'Mello, S., & Graesser, A. C. (in press). The half-life of cognitive-affective states during complex learning. *Cognition and Emotion*.

Daniels, L. M., Stupnisky, R. H., Pekrun, R., Haynes, T. L., Perry, R. P., & Newall, N. E. (2009). A longitudinal analysis of achievement goals: From affective antecedents to emotional effects and achievement outcomes. *Journal of Educational Psychology, 101*, 948–963.

Davidson, R. J., Scherer, K. R., & Goldsmith, H. H. (Eds.). (2003). *Handbook of affective sciences*. Oxford: Oxford University Press.

Dong, A. (2011). The role of affect in creative minds. In R. Calvo & S. D'Mello (Eds.), *New Perspectives on Affect and Learning Technologies* (Explorations in the learning sciences, instructional systems and performance technologies, Vol. 3) New York: Springer.

Ellis, H. C., & Ashbrook, P. W. (1988). Resource allocation model of the effect of depressed mood states on memory. In K. Fiedler & J. Forgas (Eds.), *Affect, cognition, and social behavior*. Toronto: Hogrefe International.

Fredrickson, B. L. (2001). The role of positive emotions in positive psychology: The broaden-and-build theory of positive emotions. *American Psychologist, 56*, 218–226.

Frenzel, A. C., Goetz, T., Lüdtke, O., Pekrun, R., & Sutton, R. E. (2009). Emotional transmission in the classroom: Exploring the relationship between teacher and student enjoyment. *Journal of Educational Psychology, 101*, 705–716.

Glaeser-Zikuda, M., Fuss, S., Laukenmann, M., Metz, K., & Randler, C. (2005). Promoting students' emotions and achievement – instructional design and evaluation of the ECOLE-approach. *Learning and Instruction, 15*, 481–495.

Goetz, T., Frenzel, A. C., Stoeger, H., & Hall, N. C. (2010). Antecedents of everyday positive emotions: An experience sampling analysis. *Motivation and Emotion, 34*, 49–62.

Hatfield, E., Cacioppo, J. T., & Rapson, R. L. (1994). *Emotional contagion*. New York: Cambridge University Press.

Hembree, R. (1988). Correlates, causes, effects, and treatment of test anxiety. *Review of Educational Research, 58*, 47–77.

Lang, J. W. B., & Lang, J. (2010). Priming competence diminishes the link between cognitive test anxiety and test performance: Implications for the interpretion of test scores. *Psychological Science, 21*, 811–819.

Linnenbrink, E. A. (2007). The role of affect in student learning: A multi-dimensional approach to considering the interaction of affect, motivation, and engagement. In P. A. Schutz & R. Pekrun (Eds.), *Emotion in education* (pp. 107–124). San Diego: Academic Press.

Linnenbrink, E. A., & Pintrich, P. R. (2002). Achievement goal theory and affect: An asymmetrical bidirectional model. *Educational Psychologist, 37*, 69–78.

Linnenbrink-Garcia, L., & Pekrun, R. (2011). *Students' emotions and academic engagement* [special issue]. *Contemporary Educational Psychology, 36*(1).

Loewenstein, G., & Lerner, J. S. (2003). The role of affect in decision making. In R. J. Davidson, K. R. Scherer, & H. Hill Goldsmith (Eds.), *Handbook of affective sciences* (pp. 619–642). Oxford: Oxford University Press.

McLeod, D. B., & Adams, V. M. (Eds.). (1989). *Affect and mathematical problem solving: A new perspective*. New York: Springer.

Nett, U. E., Goetz, T., & Hall, N. C. (2011). Coping with boredom in school: *An experience sampling perspective*. Contemporary Educational Psychology, 36, 49–59.

Parrott, W. G., & Spackman, M. P. (2000). Emotion and memory. In M. Lewis & J. M. Haviland-Jones (Eds.), *Handbook of emotions* (2nd ed., pp. 476–490). New York: Guilford Press.

Pekrun, R. (1992a). The impact of emotions on learning and achievement: Towards a theory of cognitive/motivational mediators. *Applied Psychology, 41*, 359–376.

Pekrun, R. (1992b). The expectancy-value theory of anxiety: Overview and implications. In D. G. Forgays, T. Sosnowski, & K. Wrzesniewski (Eds.), *Anxiety: Recent developments in self-appraisal, psychophysiological and health research* (pp. 23–41). Washington: Hemisphere.

Pekrun, R. (2006). The control-value theory of achievement emotions: Assumptions, corollaries, and implications for educational research and practice. *Educational Psychology Review, 18*, 315–341.

Pekrun, R., Elliot, A. J., & Maier, M. A. (2006). Achievement goals and discrete achievement emotions: A theoretical model and prospective test. *Journal of Educational Psychology, 98*, 583–597.

Pekrun, R., Elliot, A. J., & Maier, M. A. (2009). Achievement goals and achievement emotions: Testing a model of their joint relations with academic performance. *Journal of Educational Psychology, 101*, 115–135.

Pekrun, R., Frenzel, A., Goetz, T., & Perry, R. P. (2007). The control-value theory of achievement emotions: An integrative approach to emotions in education. In P. A. Schutz & R. Pekrun (Eds.), *Emotion in education* (pp. 13–36). San Diego: Academic Press.

Pekrun, R., Goetz, T., Daniels, L. M., Stupnisky, R. H., & Perry, R. P. (2010). Boredom in achievement settings: Control-value antecedents and performance outcomes of a neglected emotion. *Journal of Educational Psychology, 102*, 531–549.

Pekrun, R., Goetz, T., Perry, R. P., Kramer, K., & Hochstadt, M. (2004). Beyond test anxiety: Development and validation of the Test Emotions Questionnaire (TEQ). *Anxiety, Stress and Coping, 17*, 287–316.

Pekrun, R., Goetz, T., Titz, W., & Perry, R. P. (2002). Academic emotions in students' self-regulated learning and achievement: A program of quantitative and qualitative research. *Educational Psychologist, 37*, 91–106.

Pekrun, R., Goetz, T., Frenzel, A. C., Barchfeld, P., & Perry, R. P. (in press). Measuring emotions in students' learning and performance: The Achievement Emotions Questionnaire (AEQ). *Contemporary Educational Psychology, 36*, 36–48.

Pekrun, R., & Stephens, E. J. (in press). Academic emotions. In K. R. Harris, S. Graham & T. Urdan (Eds.), *APA educational psychology handbook* (Vol. 2). Washington, DC: American Psychological Association.

Roeser, R. W., Midgley, C., & Urdan, T. C. (1996). Perceptions of the school psychological environment and early adolescents' psychological and behavioral functioning in school: The mediating role of goals and belonging. *Journal of Educational Psychology, 88*, 408–422.

Ruthig, J. C., Perry, R. P., Hall, N. C., & Hladkyj, S. (2004). Optimism and attributional retraining: Longitudinal effects on academic achievement, test anxiety, and voluntary course withdrawal in college students. *Journal of Applied Social Psychology, 34*, 709–730.

Sansone, C., Weir, C., Harpster, L., & Morgan, C. (1992). Once a boring task always a boring task? Interest as a self-regulatory mechanism. *Journal of Personality and Social Psychology, 63*, 379–390.

Schaller, M., & Cialdini, R. B. (1990). Happiness, sadness, and helping: A motivational integration. In R. Sorrentino & E. T. Higgins (Eds.), *Handbook of motivation and cognition: Foundations of social behavior* (Vol. 2, pp. 265–296). New York: Guilford Press.

Scherer, K. R. (2009). The dynamic architecture of emotion: Evidence for the component process model. *Cognition and Emotion, 23*, 1307–1351.

Schutz, P. A., & Pekrun, R. (Eds.). (2007). *Emotion in education*. San Diego: Academic Press.

Tsai, Y.-M., Kunter, M., Lüdtke, O., & Trautwein, U. (2008). What makes lessons interesting? The role of situational and individual factors in three school subjects. *Journal of Educational Psychology, 100*, 460–472.

Turner, J. C., Meyer, D. K., Midgley, C., & Patrick, H. (2003). Teacher discourse and sixth graders' reported affect and achievement behaviors in two high-mastery/high-performance mathematics classrooms. *Elementary School Journal, 103*, 357.

Turner, J. E., & Schallert, D. L. (2001). Expectancy-value relationships of shame reactions and shame resiliency. *Journal of Educational Psychology, 93*, 320–329.

Weiner, B. (1985). An attributional theory of achievement motivation and emotion. *Psychological Review, 92*, 548–573.

Weiner, B. (2007). Examining emotional diversity on the classroom: An attribution theorist considers the moral emotions. In P. A. Schutz & R. Pekrun (Eds.), *Emotion in education* (pp. 73–88). San Diego: Academic Press.

Wigfield, A., & Eccles, J. S. (1990). Test anxiety in the school setting. In M. Lewis & S. M. Miller (Eds.), *Handbook of developmental psychopathology: Perspectives in developmental psychology* (pp. 237–250). New York: Plenum Press.

Wolters, C. A. (2003). Regulation of motivation: Evaluating an underemphasized aspect of self-regulated learning. *Educational Psychologist, 38*, 189–205.

Zeidner, M. (1998). *Test anxiety: The state of the art*. New York: Plenum.

Zeidner, M. (2007). Test anxiety in educational contexts: What I have learned so far. In P. A. Schutz & R. Pekrun (Eds.), *Emotion in education* (pp. 165–184). San Diego: Academic Press.

Towards a Motivationally Intelligent Pedagogy: How Should an Intelligent Tutor Respond to the Unmotivated or the Demotivated?

Benedict du Boulay

Introduction

This paper delineates some of the pedagogy needed by a motivationally intelligent tutoring system. Such a system combines the expertise and knowledge of systems able to reason and react effectively at the cognitive and metacognitive levels with those able to reason and react at the affective and meta-affective levels. Three big problems face the designer of such systems. First is determining the internal motivational states of learners given their behaviours, their demeanours and what they say. Second is figuring out what might have caused that state. Third is choosing how to act or react in a way that is likely to make the situation better (Avramides & du Boulay, 2009; du Boulay, Rebolledo-Mendez, Luckin, & Martinez-Miron, 2007). The main argument of this paper is around the second and third steps: identifying the causation of negative motivational states and remediating those states.

Motivational States

Pintrich (2003) categorised research on motivation as falling into the three overlapping areas of "Values," "Expectancies" and "Feelings." Here, Values refer to the personal, social and cultural rationale that underpins the learner's participation in the educational activity in question. Expectancies refer to the learners' expectations of their lived experience of doing the learning, for example in terms of success or failure. Feelings refer to the emotions engendered by the learning experience: frustration (say)

B. du Boulay (✉)
Interactive Systems Research Group, School of Informatics, University of Sussex,
Brighton, BN1 9QH, UK
e-mail: B.du-Boulay@sussex.ac.uk

R.A. Calvo and S.K. D'Mello (eds.), *New Perspectives on Affect and Learning Technologies,*   41
Explorations in the Learning Sciences, Instructional Systems and Performance Technologies 3,
DOI 10.1007/978-1-4419-9625-1_4, © Springer Science+Business Media, LLC 2011

when a problem is hard, elation when the solution seems to appear from nowhere, or boredom when the material or the interaction is dull. Generalising from this analysis of the literature we characterise the motivational state of a learner as a triple of "Feelings, Expectancies, Values." As time unfolds, the things that happen to learners, the things that they do and their own reflections on these change their appraisal of the degree of fit of the Values and Expectancies components of the triple. In its turn, the motivational state helps determine the extent to which, and the method by which, the learner engages (or not) in ongoing activity that may be "constructive" or "unconstructive" (Rosiek, 2003) with respect to normal educational goals. Negative motivational states are regarded as those where the causal chain of events has resulted in mismatches or violations of Values or confirmation or disconfirmation of Expectancies, so giving rise to the feeling associated with the negative motivational state and possibly also to unconstructive behaviour such as passivity or gaming the system.

A convenient way to refer to a motivational state is via the main feeling associated with it. So we can talk about the feeling of elation (say), but also of the motivational state within which elation is the main feeling. Two learners may feel equally elated, but be in different motivational states when their Expectancies and Values are different. So for example, an elated learner who rather expected to do well will be in a different motivational state from one who expected to do badly.

Various researchers have developed ways to detect particular feelings associated with the motivational states that occur in learning. For example, these include frustration (Kapoor, Burleson, & Picard, 2007) as well as more positive feelings such as interest, excitement and confidence (Arroyo et al., 2009). In broader terms, attempts have been made to detect learners' overall motivation (see, e.g. Johns & Woolf, 2006). In narrower terms others have detected particular symptoms of negative motivational states such as when learners engage in potentially mal-adaptive learning behaviours, e.g. "gaming the system" (for a review see, e.g. Baker et al., 2008).

Adopting an effective pedagogic response to negative feelings or unconstructive behaviours will depend on the reason why the learner is in that motivational state or exhibiting that behaviour. For example, Baker et al. (2008) examined 13 hypotheses as to why learners might game the system and found supporting evidence for several of them including dislike of the subject matter, lack of self-drive, and frustration with the level of the material or with the difficulty of reading it. We could add further hypotheses. For example, the learner may never have wanted to be in this class in the first place and was persuaded into it by ambitious parents. By contrast they may find the issue of seeking out the weak points in the system's tutorial strategy just inherently more interesting than the material they are supposed to learn from the tutor. More mundanely, they might find the material just dull, or indeed too easy. By contrast the learner might have imported feelings from some event prior to logging-on to the system (a row at breakfast with mum, for instance), or may lack confidence in their ability to solve the problems posed by the system. Each of these needs to be dealt with in a different way, and that is what this paper is about.

Motivational Intelligence for Computer Tutors

Several researchers argue that cognition and emotion are interwoven in learning and hard to disentangle, both for the learners themselves and for their tutor's understanding of their learning (see, e.g. Bickhard, 2003). A consequence of this is that the tutor needs to reason about both the likely emotional and the likely cognitive consequences of a tutorial intervention if it is to succeed in acting in a motivationally intelligent way. For example, just preventing the learner from engaging in gaming behaviour by adjusting the way the help mechanism works may only succeed in encouraging the learner's (possible) frustration to emerge in other ways (Baker et al., 2008).

The multifaceted aspects of motivation and the interwoven nature of cognition and emotion make the design and development of motivationally intelligent tutors especially complex. The aim of this chapter is to try to tease apart some of the factors that might assist in the design of the diagnostic and remedial components of motivationally intelligent tutors. The work described is at an early stage, without empirical support as yet. So the diagnostic part corresponds in part to the hypothesis generation stage of the work of Baker et al. (2008). The remedial part corresponds in part to the to strategy generation proposals on managing mood, attitudes, and interpersonal stances of Blanchard, Volfson, Hong, and Lajoie (2009). For example, they suggest that a tutor might improve learners' attitudes to learning by considering their self-efficacy and their personal goals.

This chapter concentrates on negative motivational states as these need to be dealt with if the learner is to make good progress. Positive motivational states are also important to the tutor, not just as a goal to achieve in their right, but also as states to be recorded as potential sources of encouragement and reflective advice to the learner should things not go so well later. For example, as we see later in this chapter, one way to counter certain kinds of anxiety (say) is to remind the learner about past learning episodes where the anxiety turned out to be unfounded. Detecting positive states poses similar difficulties to detecting negative states, but ongoing good performance and effort on the learning task at hand are a good guide. Recording both positive and indeed negative motivational states opens up the possibility for the tutor to be more proactive, possibly heading off a shift towards an unwanted negative motivational state before the feelings or behaviour that would accompany it manifest themselves.

The chapter is organised into five sections. The next section looks briefly at the kinds of data available about motivational states and at the kinds of learner state that are normally distinguished in such systems. The main section of the paper takes three motivational states whose associated feelings are frustration, anxiety and boredom. For each of these motivational states it suggests a set of pedagogic tactics to remediate that state. These tactics respond differently to the different causal chains arising from Values and Expectancies issues. Finally, there is a conclusions section with some indications of future directions.

Diagnosing Motivational States

This section looks briefly at the kinds of data potentially available to the tutor, and the temporal or pedagogical granularity with which that data is observed and considered. It also considers the kinds of motivational state into which learners are typically categorised.

Kinds of Data

Much of the contemporary work is focused on broadening the bandwidth of data available to the tutor beyond what can be gleaned from the learners' responses, either in terms of dealing with the domain itself or in terms of self-reports about their cognitive, metacognitive and affective reactions to what is going on. As technology becomes more sophisticated and cheaper we find cameras being used to record focus of attention and facial expression, sensors to record skin conductance, heart rate and brain waves, pressure sensors to record posture and wriggling in the chair, linguistic analysis to infer affect (see, e.g. Dong, 2011) as well as the force exerted on the mouse (see, e.g. D'Mello et al., 2008). Each of these channels provides clues of differing quality with respect to the emotional state of the learner, with some being good for confirming some states and others being good for disconfirming other states (Arroyo et al., 2009).

In addition to looking at the emotional state there are also clues to be found in the learner's unconstructive behaviour. In diagnosing negative motivational states, we may classify this crudely into (1) the presence of unconstructive activities that are mal-adaptive, or into (2) the absence of constructive activity that should occur. So in terms of mal-adaptive activity we list gaming the system and other misuses of the help facility, engaging in off-topic activities such as surfing the web or using email instead of studying, or making poor choices as to the difficulty of the problems tackled (whether too easy or too hard). In terms of mal-adaptive inactivity we might list a general lack of activity at all, listlessness, passivity and failure to engage.

It is completely understandable as to why researchers are keen to find ways to ascertain learner's motivational states with as little intrusion as possible. However, there are limits as to how accurately even a human teacher can gauge the learner's state, not least when the learner may wish to mask it (Balaam, Luckin, & Good, 2009).

The chapter assumes that it is going to be difficult to distinguish between some motivational states just from the sensor data and the external behaviour on their own, and just as difficult to distinguish Values issues from Expectancies issues. This suggests that the motivationally intelligent tutoring system needs to engage in some kind of dialogue with the learner, just as a human teacher would need to do in similar circumstances. In order to sidestep the obvious problems of NLP-based interactions, we currently favour some kind of menu-based interaction, similar to those employed elsewhere to gauge motivational states (Arroyo et al., 2009; del Soldato & du Boulay, 1995). This might be triggered in two stages. The first stage might simply ascertain the learner's perceived motivational valence (positive or negative). Should this be negative and should the demeanour of the learner give other causes for concern, the system might then ask the learner to choose as many items from a set of menu items that might apply, somewhat along the lines of:

- I don't see why are we learning this   O
- This is too hard   O
- This is dull   O
- This is too easy   O
- Something happened outside the lesson which upset me   O
- I would rather be doing something else   O
- There is no problem, I am feeling fine   O
- There is a problem but it's private   O
- Other . . .

In addition there could be a text box for the learner to type in whatever they want. While this would not be reacted to directly by the system, it could be used by the system-designer to improve the menu items over the longer term.

Temporal and Pedagogical Granularity

Many tutors focus most of their attention on the problem at hand or at least on the current session. A few (e.g. Weber & Brusilovsky, 2001) look back to the detail of interactions in previous sessions, and none (as far as we know) anticipate the sessions yet to come and reason about how best to plan for the future *from a motivational point of view*. As tutors cover greater amounts of material and the interaction data logged by the tutor becomes more extensive, issues around the how best to exploit what may be many hours of motivational experience with a particular learner come to the fore.

Distinctions Made Amongst Learner States

There are differing views as to how best to categorise the possible types of motivational state that a learner may be in. Given the tri-faceted view of motivation espoused, some of the categories are based around Expectancies, some around Values and some around Feelings. While the occurrence of pure strong emotions in a learning situation is rare (disgust, anger, surprise), more nuanced emotional states (feelings) are common. Some researchers focus on emotions per se (e.g. Conati & Maclaren 2005) and some on motivational states that are designated in terms of their emotional component (see, e.g. Graesser et al., 2008).

A simple but effective method to distinguish affective states is simply between the positive and the negative (the valence) and react both to absolute values of valence and to changes of valence (Zakharov, Mitrovic, & Johnston, 2008). In their work on understanding the phenomenon of gaming the system, Baker et al. (2008) distinguish between learner characteristics (such as goals, attitudes, beliefs, general approaches and emotions) rather than motivational states as such, though there is overlap with Expectancies, Values and Feelings. In trying to calibrate the utility of different sensors, Arroyo et al. (2009) distinguish between learners who are Confident, Frustrated, Excited and Interested. Graesser and his colleagues distinguish the states of Confusion, Frustration, Boredom, Flow/Engagement, Eureka and Neutral (Graesser et al., 2008).

Others adopt a subset of the emotion states developed by OCC theory (Ortony, Clore, & Collins, 1988), or variations on this, to reason about the causality in learning situations. So, for example, Conati and Maclaren (2005) distinguish the emotions of Joy, Distress, Admiration and Reproach as part of their approach to modelling the causes of emotion in the classroom. Following classroom-based empirical work with adolescents, Balaam, Fitzpatrick, Good, and Luckin (2010) asked her participants to distinguish between Happy, Tired, Proud, Bored, Nervous, Angry and Frustrated.

The purpose of the chapter is to show how a system might react effectively to a range of negative motivational states, where the reactions would attempt to deal with the underlying causes. So we examine Frustration, Boredom and Anxiety.

Motivational Pedagogy

This section looks at the three different negative motivational states whose main feeling is experienced by the learner as: frustration, anxiety or boredom. In each case we examine that state from the point of view of Values and Expectancies and for each of these we sketch possible causes of that state together with possible remedial actions that might be taken by the tutor.

It is worth stressing that learning difficult material can be hard work and that solving tricky problems can be frustrating. Being frustrated or anxious about outcomes (say) is a natural aspect of learning. Indeed as Pekrun points out (see Pekrun, 2011) the same emotion can have either an "activating" or a "deactivating" effect, depending on how the learner appraises the situation. The motivationally intelligent tutor will recognise this by putting more effort into helping the learners become more aware of these issues themselves and assist them to manage these feelings, than into changing the flow of activity so as to avoid situations that lead to these feelings (Avramides & du Boulay, 2009).

We distinguish two kinds of causes of a transition towards a negative (or more negative) motivational state:

1. *Values-based*: underpinning most formal educational situations there will be a set of values around desirable learner behaviours and learner outcomes. To the extent that the learner "goes along" with these all may be fine, but there may be times where the learner cannot understand the value of a particular activity or outcome, or if it can be understood, its personal value cannot be appreciated. For example, a learner

who really cannot see the point of learning about Pythagoras' Theorem will feel at odds with a situation where that is the goal. So we concentrate on mismatched or violated Values between those of the learner and those of the educational situation.

2. *Expectancies-based*: learners have expectations about how well or badly they are going to succeed in an educational activity and whether it will conclude with a successful or unsuccessful outcome. They will also have views about how much agency and control they are in a position to exert and also about the nature of learning and skill acquisition. For example, they may limit their effort and misinterpret errors as evidence not only that they cannot exercise some skill, *but cannot imagine ever coming to be able to acquire it*. So we concentrate on confirmed and disconfirmed Expectancies.

It is important to note that feelings may also be imported from external or past events. First are feelings not directly linked to the learning situation per se. For example, a learner may be angry about events that happened outside the classroom, or may be anxious about some future event unconnected with the learning in hand: for example, an ongoing feud with another learner in a different class. Rather than seeking causes in terms of Values and Expectancies within the learning, the tutor would need to help the learners distance themselves from such external causes of the negative state, if an optimal state for learning is to be maintained. This might even involve abandoning the learning activity for the moment to give time and space for this distancing.

By contrast, feelings may be imported from the recollection of previously experienced similar learning situations. A learner who has experienced anger, anxiety or frustration about mathematics (say) in the past may well re-experience these feelings in a new, but apparently similar, learning situation. In this case, the tutor should reason about the Values and Expectancies of the learner to anticipate this kind of possibility and attempt to forestall the development of the feelings afresh, for example by reassurance, or by reference to positive motivational states previously experienced.

The system should be able to gain some diagnostic leverage by examining the time signature of the onset of a motivational state. In the tables below we look back simply at the motivational valence (positive/negative) of the learner at the beginning of the session, and on average in the previous session. This helps to distinguish those motivational states that can become negative quite quickly (frustration) from those where the build-up is likely to be slower (anxiety, boredom). Knowing something of the personality of the learner will also help identify the state in terms of the nature of the behavioural consequences (symptoms) of that state. In the tables that follow, motivational valence is designated as "−ve" for negative, "neutral" for neutral, and "+ve" for positive. "Any" means that the motivational valence can take any value.

Anxiety

Pekrun (see Pekrun, 2011) provides a detailed account of the different antecedents and different consequences of anxiety. He also emphasises, as we do, that the antecedents of any particular emotion can vary from one individual to another, and the consequences

Table 1 Anxiety

Valence start of session	Valence previous session	Motivational facet	Possible cause	Remedial possibility
Neutral or −ve	Neutral or −ve	Values	Ongoing mismatch of values	Try to re-orientate values
Neutral or −ve	Any	Expectancies	Work has started to look too difficult and there is fear of failure	Reassure by finding evidence to the contrary *or* make the task easier *or* offer more domain level support

for the learner's behaviour also vary. Here we distinguish anxiety arising from issues around Values from that arising from issues around Expectancies (see Table 1).

Where there is anxiety arising from a mismatch of values, this may focus on the alternative activities that the learner might have been engaged in rather than the ones that she does not value. A way to try to deal with this is to help the learner either to value the current activity or the overall goals of the learning within which the current activity is situated. By contrast, anxiety arising from lack of confidence or fear of failure requires a different approach in terms of reassurance and support.

Frustration

Frustration (see Table 2) is often associated with a greater degree of arousal than anxiety considered earlier and so may pose different kinds of remedial pressure (Russell, 1980). In considering the Values aspect, the learner may have something else in mind to do, rather than simply not seeing the point of the current activity. Frustration is also likely to have few precursors from earlier in the session or from the previous session, but arise out of a specific activity. At the Expectancies level the learner can get frustrated if the work is too hard or indeed too easy, so these need to be distinguished in order to take sensible steps.

Frustration about the work being too easy is perhaps more properly regarded as a Values issue, arising from the sense that the learner's time is not being well used.

Boredom

Like frustration, boredom in educational settings has a higher degree of arousal than anxiety (Sidney D'Mello & Graesser, 2010), though not all agree (Russell, 1980). So one may observe various mal-adaptive activities like gaming the system, chatting to other learners, or being a nuisance. In terms of behavioural cues these may be just the opposite of listlessness and lack of effort – though the effort may well be misdirected (see Table 3).

Table 2 Frustration

Valence start of session	Valence previous session	Motivational facet	Possible cause	Remedial possibility
Any	Any	Values	Would rather be doing something else	Discuss comparative value of two activities. Discuss rescheduling two activities
Any	Any	Expectancies	Work has started to look too difficult or too easy	*Too hard*: reassure by finding evidence to the contrary *or* make the task easier *or* offer more domain-level support
				Too easy: make the work more challenging
			Unable to exercise personal choice in the current activity	Offer more control

Table 3 Boredom

State start of session	State previous session	Motivational facet	Possible cause	Remedial possibility
Neutral or – ve	Any	Values	Would rather be doing something else	Discuss comparative value of two activities. Discuss rescheduling two activities
			Cannot see the point of the current activity	Try to re-orientate values
Any	Any	Expectancies	Work has started to look too easy	Make the work more challenging or add interest and excitement
			Unable to exercise personal choice in the current activity	Offer more control

Discussion

In terms of Values the main remedial method is to attempt to align (or realign) the learner's values with those inherent in the course being taken. In terms of Expectancies, it is important to distinguish the learner's realistic expectancies from unrealistic ones. Unrealistically negative expectancies may be countered by evidence of success in similar circumstances in the past. Unrealistically positive expectancies can either be ignored for the moment or a note of caution suggested, depending on the likely impact of failure on that learner. Realistically negative expectancies may be dealt with by negotiating over whether the task difficulty should be adjusted. Realistic positive expectancies can be affirmed.

In terms of feelings, it is important to distinguish feelings that have been imported into the learning situation from outside from those emanating directly from the learning situation itself. In the former case it may be possible to acknowledge the feelings arising from outside while trying to minimise their effects within the lesson. For feelings arising directly from the learning situation it will be important to decide whether the feelings are well-founded (similar to the realistic/unrealistic distinction for Expectancies). Of course, the feelings need to be acknowledged whether or not they are well-founded as we assume that the learner is not misrepresenting how she feels. For example, a learner who feels (well-foundedly) ashamed over a poor performance may be consoled and a strategy put in place to improve performance. However, in dealing with learners who feels (ill-foundedly) ashamed over a perfectly adequate performance effort may be devoted to helping them to take a more realistic view of their own and others' performances.

Conclusion

This chapter has argued that dealing with poorly motivated learners requires knowledge of the causes of the negative feelings and mal-adaptive behaviour associated with their motivational state. So, noting that the learner is gaming the system, and determining that they are frustrated (say) is just the first step. One needs to work back to the causes of that frustration in terms of Expectancies or Values in order to have some hope of deploying a remedial action that may make the situation better. In working back to the causes one is very likely to have to go beyond simply observing learners' behaviours and demeanours to find out directly from them why they believe that they feel and act as they do.

Making the causation behind learner demotivation explicit is potentially beneficial to the learner as well as to the motivationally intelligent tutor. From the learner's point of view, attempting to be explicit about the causation of the poor motivation and then experiencing the remedial tactic suggested by the tutor should build up the learner's own understanding of motivation, in other words, improve his or her meta-motivational insight. For the tutor, each of these episodes of diagnosis and remediation can itself become an example that can be used with the learner later: "remember when you said that you were feeling .... and you tried doing .... well I think you may be in a similar situation again". Referring to a past incident like this should further increase the learner's meta-motivation.

The pedagogic tactics in the tables above have not yet been implemented in a working system. Once deployed, they could be evaluated in terms of process measures such as decreased frequency or severity of negative motivational states, improved persistence in problem-solving or following set-backs, decreased off-topic or mal-adaptive learning behaviour, more sensible choice of problem difficulty, and so on. In terms of outcome measures one might expect benefits such as increased learning gain, improved willingness to engage with future learning and increased meta-motivational insight.

Acknowledgments I thank Katerina Avramides, Madeline Balaam, Martin van Zijl and the Intelligent Computer Tutor Group at University of Canterbury, New Zealand for many helpful comments on a draft of this paper.

References

Arroyo, I., Cooper, D. G., Burleson, W., Woolf, B. P., Muldner, K., & Christopherson, R. (2009). Emotion sensors go to school. In V. Dimitrova, R. Mizoguchi, B. du Boulay & A. Grasser (Eds.), *Artificial intelligence in education. Building learning systems that care: From knowledge representation to affective modelling* (Vol. Frontiers in Artificial Intelligence and Applications 200, pp. 17–24). Amsterdam: IOS Press.

Avramides, K., & du Boulay, B. (2009). Motivational Diagnosis in ITSs: Collaborative, reflective self-report. In V. Dimitrova, R. Nizoguchi, B. du Boulay & A. Graesser (Eds.), *Artificial intelligence in education. Building learning systems that care: From knowledge representation to affective modelling* (Vol. Frontiers in Artificial Intelligence and Applications 200, pp. 587–589). Amsterdam: IOS Press.

Baker, R., Walonoski, J., Heffernan, N., Roll, I., Corbett, A., & Koedinger, K. (2008). Why students engage in "gaming the system" behaviours in interactive learning environments. *Journal of Interactive Learning Research, 19*(2), 185–224.

Balaam, M., Fitzpatrick, G., Good, J., & Luckin, R. (2010). *Exploring affective technologies for the classroom with the subtle stone.* Paper presented at the Proceedings of the 28th international conference on Human factors in computing systems (CHI 2010). Atlanta, Georgia.

Balaam, M., Luckin, R., & Good, J. (2009). Supporting affective communication in the classroom with the Subtle Stone. *International Journal of Learning Technology, 4*(3–4), 188–215.

Bickhard, M. H. (2003). *An integration of motivation and cognition BJEP Monograph Series II, Number 2 – Development and Motivation* (Vol. 1, pp. 41–56). British Psychological Society. Leicester, UK.

Blanchard, E. G., Volfson, B., Hong, Y. -J., & Lajoie, S. P. (2009). Affective artificial intelliegnce in education: From detection to adaptation. In V. Dimitrova, R. Mizoguchi, B. du Boulay & A. Grasser (Eds.), *Artificial intelligence in education. Building learning systes that care: From knowledge representation to affective modelling* (Vol. Frontiers in Artificial Intelligence and Applications 200, pp. 81–88). Amsterdam: IOS Press.

Conati, C., & Maclaren, H. (2005). Data-driven refinement of a probabilistic model of user affect. In L. Ardissono, P. Brna & A. Mitrovic (Eds.), *User Modeling 2005, 10th International Conference, UM 2005, Edinburgh, Scotland, UK, Proceedings* (Vol. Lecture Notes in Artificial Intelligence 3538, pp. 40–49). Berlin: Springer.

D'Mello, S., & Graesser, A. (2010). Mining Bodily Patterns of affective experience during learning. In R. S. J. d. Baker, A. Merceron & P. I. J. Pavlik (Eds.), *Proceedings of the 3rd International Conference on Educational Data Mining* (pp. 31–40). Pittsburgh.

D'Mello, S., Jackson, T., Craig, S., Morgan, B., Chipman, P., White, H., et al. (2008). *AutoTutor Detects and Responds to Learners Affective and Cognitive States.* Paper presented at the Workshop on Emotional and Cognitive Issues at the International Conference on Intelligent Tutoring Systems. Montreal, Canada.

del Soldato, T., & du Boulay, B. (1995). Implementation of motivational tactics in tutoring systems. *International Journal of Artificial Intelligence in Education, 6*(4), 337–378.

Dong, A. (2011). The role of affect in creative minds. In R. Calvo & S. D'Mello (Eds.), *Explorations in the learning sciences, instructional systems and performance technologies.* New York: Springer.

du Boulay, B., Rebolledo-Mendez, G. R., Luckin, R., & Martinez-Miron, E. (2007). Motivationally intelligent systems: Diagnosis and feedback. In R. Luckin, K. R. Koedinger & J. Greer (Eds.), *Artificial intelligence in education: Building technology rich learning contexts that work*

(Vol. Frontiers in Artificial Intelligence and Applications 158, pp. 563–565). Amsterdam: IOS Press.

Graesser, A. C., D'Mello, S. K., Craig, S. D., Witherspoon, A., Sullins, J., McDaniel, B., et al. (2008). The relationship between affective states and dialog patterns during interactions with auto tutor. *Journal of Interactive Learning Research, 19*(2), 293–312.

Johns, J., & Woolf, B. P. (2006). *A dynamic mixture model to detect student motivation and proficiency.* Paper presented at the Proceedings of the 21st national Conference on Articifial Intelligence (AAAI-06). Boston, MA.

Kapoor, A., Burleson, W., & Picard, R. W. (2007). Automatic prediction of frustration. *International Journal of Human-Computer Studies, 65*(8), 724–736.

Ortony, A., Clore, G. L., & Collins, A. (1988). *The cognitive structure of emotions.* Cambridge: Cambridge University Press.

Pekrun, R. (2011). Emotions as drivers of learning and cognitive development. In R. Calvo & S. D'Mello (Eds.), *Explorations in the learning sciences, instructional systems and performance technologies.* New York: Springer.

Pintrich, P. (2003). Motivation and classroom learning. *Handbook of Psychology: Educational Psychology, 7,* 103–122.

Rosiek, J. (2003). Emotional scaffolding: An exploration of the teacher knowledge at the intersection of student emotion and the subject matter. *Journal of Teacher Education, 54*(4), 399–412.

Russell, J. A. (1980). A circumplex model of affect. *Journal of Personality and Social Psychology, 39*(6), 1161–1178.

Weber, G., & Brusilovsky, P. (2001). ELM-ART: An adaptive versatile system for web-based instruction. *International Journal of Artificial Intelligence in Education, 12*(4), 351–384.

Zakharov, K., Mitrovic, A., & Johnston, L. (2008). Towards emotionally-intelligent pedagogical agents. In B. P. Woolf, E. Aïmeur, R. Nkambou & S. L. Lajoie (Eds.), *Intelligent Tutoring Systems, 9th International Conference, ITS 2008, Montreal, Canada, Proceedings* (Vol. Lecture Notes in Computer Science 5091, pp. 19–28). Berlin: Springer.

Part II
Case Studies

Natural Affect Data: Collection and Annotation

Shazia Afzal and Peter Robinson

Introduction

Learning has a strong affective quality that impacts overall performance, memory, attention, decision making and attitude (Kort, Reilly, & Picard, 2001; Lisetti & Schiano, 2000). We know from a multitude of studies in different educational contexts that learners experience a wide range of positive and negative emotions and that these influence their cognitive functioning and behaviour (Pekrun, Goetz, Titz, & Perry, 2002). Not surprisingly then, affective diagnoses constitute a significant aspect of expert human mentoring (Lepper, Woolverton, Mumme, & Gurtner, 1993). Computer-based learning environments aim to emulate the social dynamics of human teacher–learner interactions to make learning with computers more immersive, engaging and hence more effective.

Effective tutoring by humans is an interactive and guided process where learner engagement is constantly monitored to provide remedial feedback and to maximise the motivation to learn (Merrill, Reiser, Ranney, & Trafton, 1992). Indeed, formative assessment and feedback is an important aspect of effectively designed learning environments and should occur continuously and unobtrusively, as part of the instruction (Bransford, Brown, & Cocking, 1999). In naturalistic settings the availability of several channels of communication facilitates the constant monitoring necessary for such an interactive and flexible learning experience (Picard et al., 2004). One of the biggest challenges for computer tutors then is to achieve the mentoring capability of expert human teachers. To give such a capability to a machine tutor entails giving it the ability to infer affect. This idea of incorporating emotional intelligence in computers has motivated efforts towards automatic perception of

S. Afzal (✉)
Computer Laboratory, University of Cambridge, William Gates Building,
15 JJ Thomson Avenue, Cambridge CB3 0FD, England, UK
e-mail: Shazia.Afzal@cl.cam.ac.uk

R.A. Calvo and S.K. D'Mello (eds.), *New Perspectives on Affect and Learning Technologies*, 55
Explorations in the Learning Sciences, Instructional Systems and Performance Technologies 3,
DOI 10.1007/978-1-4419-9625-1_5, © Springer Science+Business Media, LLC 2011

affect. It reflects the growing understanding of the centrality of emotion in the teaching–learning process and the fact that as yet this crucial link has not been addressed in machine–learner interactions (O'Regan, 2003).

Current methods for measuring emotions can be broadly categorised as Subjective/Objective and Qualitative/Quantitative. In the context of learning, an additional categorisation as Snapshot/Continuous can be defined based on the timing of the emotion measurement (Wosnitza & Volet, 2005). Snapshot type measurements are done immediately before/after the learning process while continuous measurements are process oriented and give access to the ongoing emotional experience. Consequently, snapshot measures provide only a limited window into the anticipated or reflected emotions at the end of the learning experience as against the continuous measures that provide direct access to emotions as they unfold during learning. Table 1 categorises some common methods for measuring emotional experience during learning.

For intervention to be effective, remedial action has to be appropriately timed – particularly in the case of strong emotions. Given the complex and transient nature of emotions, any retrospective accounts are problematic because of issues related to the potential for multiple levels of awareness making it difficult to dissociate an emotional experience from previous or related memories; reappraisals and reconstruction of meanings during recall (Schutz, Hong, Cross, & Obson, 2006). This necessitates dynamic evaluation of learners' emotions but without disrupting the learning task itself. Ideally then, an unobtrusive, quantitative, and continuous account of emotional experience is a suitable method of enquiry. Amongst the methods listed in Table 1, nonverbal behaviour analysis, in the lower right quadrant, offers a reasonable fit to this requirement (Pekrun, 2005; Picard et al., 2004). Analyses of expert tutoring sessions have indeed revealed that affective diagnoses depend heavily on inferences drawn from facial expressions, body language, intonation, and paralinguistic cues (Lepper et al., 1993). Advances in the field of affective computing (Picard, 1997) have opened the possibility of emotion recognition from its nonverbal manifestations like facial expressions, head pose, body gestures, voice and physiology. The field is promising, yet in a formative stage as current technologies need to be validated for reliability outside controlled experimental conditions.

Machine perception of affect is a challenging problem given the inherent difficulty in conceptualising affect and the technical constraints in access, measurement and fusion of emotional signals from the verbal and nonverbal channels. Comparing previous work in affect sensing in learning environments, Afzal and Robinson (2010) emphasise the range in the affect constructs measured, the information

Table 1 Methods for measuring emotional experience

	Snapshot (before/after learning)		Continuous (during learning)	
	Qualitative	Quantitative	Qualitative	Quantitative
Subjective	Open interviews Emotional probes Stimulated recall	Questionnaires Surveys	Emotional diaries Think-aloud	Experience/time-sampling
Objective	Structured interviews	Transcripts analysis Video analysis	Observational analyses	Interactional content Nonverbal behaviour analysis

sources used, the varied learning contexts and the specific computational approach adopted. It highlights the variety in modelling techniques that range from rule-based systems to complex probabilistic models; the different ways in which affect is conceptualised in these systems based on whether a dimensional, discrete or appraisal-based stance is adopted; the array of interactional as well as behavioural measures used to infer affect; and importantly, the nature and focus of the learning setup used. However, this diversity in the measured affect constructs, the specific learning environments and the channels used as information sources; makes it difficult to comment on the overall performance of a system and determine its efficiency in a broad sense. This inability to make generalisable claims is an acknowledged limitation of affect-sensing technologies (Pantic & Rothkrantz, 2003) and makes it challenging to establish the merit and success of a particular system satisfactorily and with confidence. Nevertheless, what is apparent is a growing understanding of the importance of affect modelling in learning and this substantiates further research in the area.

Automatic inference using machine learning relies on extensive training data which serves as the ground-truth for development and evaluation of appropriate algorithms. For viable applications of affect-sensitive technology the use of naturalistic over posed data is being increasingly emphasised. Dealing with the complexity associated with naturalistic data is, however, a significant problem. Nonverbal behaviour is rich, ambiguous and hard to validate, making naturalistic data collection and labelling a tedious, expensive and time-consuming exercise (Abrilian, Devillers, & Martin, 2006; Cowie, Douglas-Cowie, & Cox, 2005; Ekman & Rosenberg, 1997; El Kaliouby & Teeters, 2007; Picard, 1997). This chapter documents the collection and subsequent annotation of data obtained in a learning scenario. The conceptual and methodological issues encountered during data collection are discussed, and problems with labelling and annotation are identified.

Data Collection

Our research involves modelling the affective aspects of learner experience in computer-based learning scenarios. As such we are interested in studying how non-verbal behaviour from multiple-cues like facial expressions, eye-gaze and head posture can be used to infer a learner's affective state during interaction and learning with a computer tutor. The final objective is to abstract this behaviour in terms of features that can enable automatic prediction and reliable computational modelling of affect states. The need for representative data is therefore essential in order to carry out realistic analyses, to develop appropriate techniques and eventually to perform validation of the inferences.

Ideally, a database should depict naturalism, limited or no experimental control, and be contextually relevant. Although a number of databases exist, these are often oriented to prototypical representations of a few basic emotional expressions being mostly recorded using scripted scenarios under constrained settings. Such extreme expressions of affect rarely occur, if at all, in HCI contexts. The applicability of such data therefore becomes severely limited because of observed deviation from real-life (Cowie et al., 2005; Ekman & Rosenberg, 1997) and for our purpose their lack of relevance to a naturalistic situation like learning with a computer. For developing applications that are generalisable to real-life situations there is now an increasing shift from easier to obtain posed data to more realistic naturally occurring data in the target scenarios. This is based on evidence that naturalistic head and facial expressions of affect differ in configuration and dynamics from posed/acted ones and are in fact, mediated by separate neural pathways (Cohn & Schmidt, 2004; Ekman & Rosenberg, 1997; Pantic & Patras, 2006). The dominant role of situational context in the nature and meaning of emotion (Russell & Fernandez-Dols, 1997) further emphasises the use of context-relevant corpora. Therefore, to ensure ecological validity of our research and a more meaningful interpretation, it was necessary to study the affect patterns in situ, as they occur. This motivated our data collection exercise details of which are presented in the following sections.

Encoders. Eight participants, three males and five females in the age group of 21–32, were recruited to serve as encoders of emotional behaviour. The term encoder is used to denote these participants as being the source or examples for affective data obtained (Ekman & Rosenberg, 1997). All were regular and proficient computer users ($M=20$ h of computer usage/week) so there was no effect of comfort level or exposure to the task requirements. Two of the participants wore glasses while one sported a beard. All participants reported as being happy, relaxed or in anticipation at the onset of experiment. They were informed that they would be video recorded during the interaction but remained naïve to the actual purpose of the experiment until after the experiment was completed.

Setup. All interaction was computer based and the recording setup was based on guidelines in Frank, Juslin, and Harrigan (2005). The experiment was conducted in a usability lab with a mock living room or personal office environment effect. It was chosen to facilitate video recording without compromising the naturalism of the desired behaviour. Standard computing equipment, that is, a desktop computer with a mouse and keyboard was used for the experiment. A video camera was mounted on top of the computer screen to allow video recording of the participants' upper body focusing mainly on the face. Additionally, a screen-capture utility, Camtasia™ Studio (2006), was used to obtain a complete interaction record for reference.

Procedure. Participants were run individually in the usability lab and were observed via a one-way mirror from the adjoining room. This ensured that they were alone during the tasks and were not disturbed by an additional presence. Formal consent for recording was obtained in writing from all participants prior to the experiment. Participants were video recorded while doing two tasks: an interactive map-based geography tutorial and a card matching activity. The session finished by completion of some expressivity test questionnaires, the self-annotation of videos, and subsequently, a semi-structured interview.

The tutorial enabled participants to study the countries and landscapes of different continents followed by a test of their learning. It served as a platform to observe facial affect signs when the learner is in complete control of the pace and strategy of the learning task. There was no time limit on this task but participants took on average about 20 min to complete this activity.

The second task was an adaptation of a card sorting activity meant to demonstrate the effect of situational anxiety on higher mental activities (Skemp, 1971). Cards having one, two, three or four of either squares, circles, crosses or triangles in red, green, blue or yellow were used – all figures on a card being alike and of the same colour. Participants had to sort the cards against four category cards based on a changing criterion. The four category cards – one red triangle, two green squares, three yellow crosses and four blue circles, were laid out and the participants were asked to sort the remaining cards first by colour, then by shape, then by number and finally in consecutive changing order of first by colour, second by shape, third by number and so on. This task is supposed to inhibit reflective intelligence leading to lowered performance and thus, decreased motivation (Skemp, 1971). We were interested to see if this was accompanied by observable changes in facial expressions.

The two tasks were chosen to encourage a variety of emotion expressions and their sequence order was varied across participants. The card activity contained three triggers/events presented only once per participant during the game interaction (order-varied): the screen blanking out for 5 s, a match not being possible and variation in feedback/scoring. These are not dramatic deviations from the task and were used to induce raction to some common interaction events. In the first case, the screen went to sleep for 5 s without warning but recovered immediately after. In the second event, the participants were asked to match a dummy card against the category cards. The dummy card had five diamond shapes in black and white and thus could not be matched according to any of the game rules. The change in feedback event was implemented by replacing the correct/incorrect answer text with a happy/sad smiley, respectively.

Results. Approximately 4 h of video data were collected from the eight participants. Observation of the videos revealed a significant variability in the emotional behaviour of participants. Individual differences in expressivity were in fact quite striking. Some participants were animated and displayed a wide range of expressions while others were notably inexpressive. There was difference even in the way participants reacted to the triggered events. Consistently across the encoders, more emotional expressions occurred during the card game than during the tutorial highlighting the impact of task difference on nonverbal behaviour. While the puzzle evoked quick jerky movements, the tutorial elicited more engaging and sustained gestures. As individual and task differences seem to influence perceived emotional behaviour, it is reasonable to suggest that emotion inference technology will need to address these in design and function.

Annotation and Labelling

Automatic prediction using machine learning relies on extensive training data which in this case implies preparation of labelled representative data. This requires observational assessments on data to be represented in a quantifiable manner via annotation. It involves developing a protocol to catalogue observations and to represent the behaviour of interest using an appropriate coding scheme in terms of desired labelling constructs. Our annotation method evolved from various domain-relevant decisions related to the choice of labelling constructs and modality, anticipated technical constraints in the target scenario, relation to context and ease of interpretation. Before elaborating on the annotation process itself, we outline the choices and practices from nonverbal behaviour research that provides the framework for the annotation procedure.

Coding Scheme. Coding schemes are theoretical stances that embody the behaviours or distinctions that are important for exploring the data. It is possible to locate these along a continuum, with one end anchored by physically based schemes – schemes that classify behaviour with clear and well-understood roots in physiology, and the other end by socially based schemes – schemes that deal with behaviour whose very classification depends far more on the mind of the investigator (and others) than on the mechanisms of the body (Bakeman & Gothman, 1997). Relevant examples of physiologically based coding schemes are FACS, MAX and MPEG-4 which, although more standardised and comprehensive, are complex, require extensive training and involve specialised procedures. Socially based coding schemes on the other hand, are observational systems that are rooted in social processes and follow from cultural tradition or negotiation amongst observers as to a meaningful way to view and categorise behaviour. As a result, they require considerably more inference and potentially sensitive observers. To contrast with physically based schemes, these examine behaviour or messages that have more to do with social categories of interaction like smiling or happiness rather than with physiological elements of behaviour like amplitude or a specific facial configuration (Manusov, 2005). Since our goal was to quantify behaviour into the different affect categories, a socially based coding scheme was deemed more appropriate.

Level of Measurement. Determining the level of measurement is an important choice when examining nonverbal behaviour using a socially based coding scheme. It concerns the amount of behaviour examined and the extent to which the assessment involves more concrete indicators of behaviour's occurrence or more abstract assessments of the social meaning of behaviour (White & Sargent, 2005). The distinction can be referred to as macro- vs. micro-level of measurement and is in general related to the level of abstraction adopted. We reconcile the two abstraction levels by following a hierarchical labelling process where an inferential level coding of extracting emotionally salient segments is followed by two levels of more focused coding along the pre-selected affect states.

Coding Unit. The coding unit refers to the decisions about when to code within an interaction and the length of time the observation should last. It has two broad variants – event based and interval based. Event-based coding involves decision making triggered by a behavioural event of interest while interval-based coding assesses pre-determined intervals of time within an interaction. Event-based coding provides a realistic way of segmenting behaviours but it may result in loss of time information unless precise onset and offsets are noted. Interval-based coding on the other hand is easy to use but requires selecting an optimal time interval and may truncate behaviour unnaturally. Choosing one over the other depends upon the research view and the level of accuracy required, complexity of the coding scheme and the frequency of behaviour occurrence (Bakeman & Gothman, 1997). It is also possible, as in Graesser et al. (2006), to combine both approaches and record what they term as voluntary judgements along with regularly polled timestamps. We, however, used interval-based coding to allow an easy and systematic observation in the first annotation round, but as discussed further on, had to replace it with an event-based coding.

Labelling Construct. Annotation schemes for affect commonly employ either categorical, dimensional or appraisal-based labelling approaches (Cowie et al., 2005). In addition, free-response labelling may also be used for richer descriptions. We use a variant of categorical labelling in which raters are asked to choose from preselected domain-relevant emotional descriptors namely: confused, interested, surprised, happy, bored, and neutral. These were derived using Baron-Cohen's (2004) lexical taxonomy of complex mental states that groups together 412 emotion concepts into 24 exclusive groups. Confusion, for example, includes states like unsure, puzzled, baffled and clueless while Happy includes pleased, cheerful, relaxed, calm, enjoying, etc. These descriptors thus refer to non-basic affective-cognitive emotions of broader semantic scope and are pertinent in learning situations.

To familiarise the raters with their meaning and scope, a list of these emotion groups along with the emotion concepts they encompass (Baron-Cohen, Golan, Wheelwright, & Hill, 2004) was provided at the beginning of the coding session. To reduce the bias of forced choice on selected affect labels – an often listed drawback in categorical methods (Russell & Fernandez-Dols, 1997), coders are allowed to define their own category or label under a residual "Other" option if the perceived state is not represented by the provided categories. This ensures a degree of flexibility in coding and allows raters to express their responses in their preferred vocabulary or response mode.

Raters. Selecting raters or coders is an important aspect of designing annotation studies as they should be able to discern meaning from behaviour and make judgements effectively. We attempted three modes of annotation with respect to raters: self-annotation by encoders themselves, experts and non-experts. The term expert is used to denote raters who have some degree of formal experience as opposed to non-experts whose skills of emotion perception come from experience in day to day social interaction.

Reliability Measures. Inter-rater reliability measures for nominal data include raw agreement, Scott's pi, Cohen's kappa, Fleiss' kappa, and Krippendorff's alpha (Hayes & Krippendorff, 2007). Since our approach involves multiple raters rating multiple categories – often uneven across coders, we use Fleiss' kappa to report inter-rater reliability (Fleiss, Levin, & Paik, 2003). Kappa is a statistical measure that calculates the degree of agreement in classification over that expected by chance and is scored as a number between 0 and 1, where 1 indicates perfect agreement.

Having set the scope of the annotation framework in terms of general methodological decisions, we will now describe the three iterations of annotation that were applied to the data.

First Annotation

Design. The very first annotation was performed by participants themselves immediately after the experiment. The objective was to use this self-annotation as a triangulation method when comparing felt emotions and observed behaviour. Given the specific research setup and the type of labelled data sought, none of the standard self-report instruments were found suitable (Isomursu, Tahti, Vainamo, & Kuutti, 2007). As such, self-annotation was implemented using an interval-based coding system through fixed-time slots. Participants were prompted to rate their agreement on each of the pre-selected categories based on a Likert scale ranging from Strongly Agree to Strongly Disagree after every 20 s of elapsed video. A free-response option to allow subjective descriptions as well as an "Other" option was also provided. Annotation was implemented to allow a split-screen viewing of recorded behaviour with the time-synchronised interaction record obtained via screen capture to encourage context-sensitive judgment in a sequential manner. The idea was to retain the natural evolution of the behaviour and preserve the temporal dynamics of interaction.

Results. The purpose of obtaining self-report was to get a subjective account of emotional behaviour. Observation of the labelling process however, indicated otherwise. Although participants responded differently to watching their own expressions – some surprised, mimicking and laughing at themselves, and others embarrassed, rushing through the video; the reactions did not suggest that they associated a subjective feeling with these but rather interpreted the expression as if it belonged to another person in a social setting. This level of cognitive mediation was perceived as confounding the self-labelling purpose. It seemed that participants were more interested in "watching" themselves and rushed through the coding part. They also complained that 20 s was a very tiny interval and that "nothing major" was happening. Three participants left the coding mid-way complaining of boredom. None of the participants had a problem with the annotation interface or the procedure itself but found watching themselves and "creating" a meaning from their videos hard and uneventful. For these reasons, the self-annotation was considered unreliable and was discarded. Although the self-annotation was not successful in itself it helped re-assess certain choices in light of the data and shaped the next level of annotation:

- Emotional behaviour in the videos was subtle and gradual making interval-based coding extremely tedious. Deciding on an optimal time interval relative to the observed behaviour in such a case was difficult. Thus, switching to event-based coding was deemed appropriate for maximising the annotation value and effort.
- Although easy to use, interval-based coding artificially truncates behaviour resulting in information loss and arbitrary segments. As such, it would fail to

account for emotional transitions occurring at the periphery of time intervals and depending on the frequency of such occurrences could severely affect the quality of training data required for machine learning. This further endorsed switching to event-based coding.

- Finally, a more objective labelling using multiple external raters was adopted to improve reliability of annotation. In the application context, this would correspond to taking a tutor-centric view.

The shift to event-based coding meant, however, that we could no longer use the recorded screen data to interpret the visual behavioural records as the segmented video clips corresponding to emotional events were of a granularity (a few seconds; see next section) that made the screen capture fragments of no meaningful value. Without an acceptable level of temporal history, the screen records therefore had no perceived value for further annotation. A more qualitative analysis of the participants' general emotional behaviour, specifically to study their reaction to the events/triggers in the game, was conducted preliminary discussion of which appears elsewhere (Afzal, Morrison, & Robinson, 2009).

Second Annotation

Design. Using event-based coding, the original videos were segmented into 105 non-neutral segments using ELAN.[1] ELAN is a free, multimodal annotation tool providing multi-layer annotation features. A single application window gives powerful playback options along with flexible annotation modes to give an overall view of the annotation density over a video. However, as with other video annotation tools, it is accompanied with a strong learning curve and requires considerable practice to achieve proficiency in use. It is therefore suitable only for an expert annotator, unless an appropriate level of training is provided.

As the eventual purpose was to compile a database of training clips, extraction of video segments corresponding to the transcribed annotations was required. The process of video extraction is time consuming and computationally expensive when dealing with large amounts of data. The annotations or labels assigned in ELAN were exported to and processed using VirtualDub.[2] VirtualDub is a free video processing utility which is streamlined for fast linear operations over video and also allows batch processing. It provides a powerful and versatile scripting framework called Sylia which can be used to program the entire video extraction process efficiently using scripts. The annotation files generated in ELAN were parsed to produce Sylia scripts which were then batch processed in VirtualDub to produce the annotation-based video clips.

---

[1] http://www.lat-mpi.eu/tools/tools/elan
[2] http://www.virtualdub.org

The mean duration of extracted clips was 3.4 s (SD = 2.5), ranging from a minimum of 0.6 s to a maximum of 16 s. The segmentation was based on changes in the blanket expression where behaviour seemed consistent over a period of time. This essentially meant extracting portions of video that contained perceived emotional behaviour as against portions with no observable changes in the facial expressions or head gestures (Abrilian, Devillers, Buisine, & Martin, 2005; El Kaliouby & Teeters, 2007). During the annotation, care was taken to preserve the temporal boundaries while demarcating the emotional segments. The manual annotation process followed by the corresponding automatic video extraction reduced the original video corpus of approximately 4 h to less than 6 min at 30 fps. While this was a substantial gain in required annotation effort it highlighted how scantily the interaction was accompanied by changes in the observed visual modality.

Results. Three expert raters labelled the 105 pre-segmented clips independently. Raters could replay a video as many times as they wished. A primary and optional secondary emotion label was allowed for each video clip. Enforcing a simple majority rule resulted in 75% of videos getting classified into one of the pre-selected emotion categories. Table 2 (column A) summarises the distribution of emotion categories obtained this way when at least two out of the three raters agreed.

Taking primary labels into account, Fleiss' overall kappa was 0.35 indicating fair agreement. Agreement by chance was ruled out, but weakly. Given the low inter-rater reliability, the labelling results remained questionable. Moreover, the expert raters indicated that the video segments often displayed multiple emotions and that a second level of more intensive segmentation would improve judgement accuracy. A finer level of further segmentation was therefore done where segments corresponding to holistic expression changes were extracted. Unlike the first segmentation which was based on distinguishing emotional from non-emotional content, the focus now was to identify occurrences of sufficiently distinct emotional episodes. This meant demarcating the onset and offset of expression changes that provided enough context to be meaningful on their own. This increased the total number of video clips from 105 to 247. A third level annotation on these was designed, as described in the next section.

Table 2 Distribution of video clips across emotion categories

| Annotations | A | | B | |
| | 3 Experts, 105 clips | | 108 Coders, 247 clips | |
	Number	Proportion (%)	Number	Proportion (%)
Confused	26	24.8	73	29.6
Interested	18	17.1	35	14.2
Surprised	12	11.4	40	16.2
Bored	5	4.8	19	7.7
Happy	16	15.2	35	14.2
Annoyed	0	0	13	5.3
Neutral	3	2.9	29	11.7
Other	25	23.9	3	1.2

Third Annotation

Design. The corpus now consisted of 247 video clips with a mean duration of 2.8 s (SD = 1.86), ranging from a minimum of 0.4 s to a maximum of 16 s. An online labelling interface was set up to facilitate access to a large number of raters. The coding scheme was modified so that for each video clip raters were required to mark the following: the emotion they attributed to the video clip, their confidence level (from 1 to 10) and whether they could perceive more than one emotion in the clip (yes/no). The decision time for emotion judgement was also recorded. A video clip was played only once in order to get the initial reaction and to control the effects of replaying across raters. The focus at this level of annotation was to analyse emotion judgements from a large number of raters and improve annotation results. All raters underwent a training session before the actual labelling during which they were familiarised with the emotions taxonomy as well as the annotation interface.

Results. 108 Raters, 39 male and 69 female, signed up for the online study and coded an average of 20 videos each. They were aged between 18 and 56 years (*M* = 28.28, SD = 6.20) and were of diverse ethnicities and background. A total of 2,221 annotations were obtained so that each video was coded on average 8.99 times (SD = 0.13). Emotion labels present under "Other" category were parsed using emotion taxonomies, GALC (Scherer, 2005) and Mind Reading (Baron-Cohen et al., 2004) in order to group semantically similar terms into macro-classes. For example, pleased, amused, and enjoying, were grouped together under happy.

Inter-rater reliability estimated using Fleiss' weighted kappa for multiple ratings per video with multiple raters (Fleiss et al., 2003) was 0.20 overall, indicating slight agreement. Individual kappa agreements for the emotion categories were: confused 0.2, interested 0.1, surprised 0.2, bored 0.1, happy 0.5 annoyed 0.1, neutral 0.2 and other 0.1. Only happy showed a good agreement while others got marginal kappa values.

The inter-coder reliability results were not convincing enough to accept the emotion annotations as the true class based simply on raw agreement. In order to enhance the reliability of final annotations, we adopted a weighted system of classification by using the coders' confidence level ratings obtained during the annotation procedure. This way emotion labels were assigned a weight equivalent to the coders' confidence level and the maximum weighted emotion label was taken as the true label for a video clip. For example, a video clip coded as happy with confidence 9 by Coder 1, confused with confidence 1 by Coder 2, happy with confidence 7 by Coder 3, and surprised with confidence 9 by Coder 4; would be classified as happy since the total confidence weight for emotion happy is the highest (9 + 7). Table 2 (column B) shows the final assignment of video clips to the emotion classes by applying the weighting rule. Approximately 30% of the videos were classified as confused as against the least proportion for *Other* at 1%. This highlights the occurrence of confusion as a dominant emotion associated with learning followed by surprised, interested and happy. Only 8% of the videos were classified as bored which is not surprising considering the nature and duration of the experimental task used in data collection.

Discussion

Having clearly labelled samples is a pre-requisite for designing automatic classifiers. The annotation process reveals that this is indeed very difficult to obtain from naturalistic data. Even for a human expert, it is difficult to define what constitutes an emotion. Segmenting the original videos into emotionally salient clips was the most challenging and time-consuming process. Demarcating the beginning and end of emotional expressions was incredibly challenging as they often overlap, co-occur or blend subtly into a background expression. In retrospect, pre-segmentation of videos should ideally be validated by a second and if possible, more raters even though some noise is unavoidable because of the difficulty in marking precise boundaries and judging the exact onset, peak and offset of expressions.

To complicate things further, re-visiting the data often changes judgements as familiarity habituates a rater to the range of facial signs of the encoders. The more familiar a face becomes, the more meaning you can discern from it. The whole process is unavoidably subjective and therefore dependent on the affect decoding skills and experience of raters. Gender-wise annotation results, for example, revealed that on average, female raters were more confident in their judgement ($M = 7.54$, $SD = 0.16$) than males ($M = 7.42$, $SD = 0.25$) and took less time to take a decision ($M = 11.71$, $SD = 0.46$) than males ($M = 12.38$, $SD = 0.77$). Although these differences were not statistically significant at $p < 0.05$, there is extensive evidence in nonverbal behaviour research showing that women are better than men in nonverbal decoding ability (Elfenbein, Marsh, & Ambady, 2002; Riggio & Riggio, 2005). Nonverbal decoding ability measures the accuracy of nonverbal cue processing and is a subset of interpersonal sensitivity. As such, quantitative affect decoding measures like PONS, CARAT, Empathic Accuracy or the Empathy Quotient (see Riggio & Riggio, 2005) can be used to pre-screen annotators, indicate when training might be required as well as serve as reliability indicators for labelled data. Given the established individual differences in emotion judgement, inclusion of such measures might help improve and facilitate annotation of behavioural data.

Another factor that comes to fore from the annotation results is the prevalent ambiguity in emotion judgements. 38.7% of the total videos were perceived as containing more than one emotion. Female raters on average made higher use of this option than males (approximately 27% more) again emphasising heightened gender sensitivity to emotion perception. This is consistent with the findings of Abrilian et al. (2006) whose coding results on natural interview data also revealed that female coders perceived ambiguity in emotions 25% more than male coders. In general, the ambiguity in emotion perception shows that the occurrence of one emotion does not rule out the presence of another and an ideal automatic emotion inference system should be able to track co-occurring emotions.

During annotation itself, people find it difficult to articulate what they perceive in words. This is understandable because in everyday life emotion perception is rarely expressed in explicit terms and is subtly intertwined in social interactions. Consequently, raters often used a combination of labels and even phrases to express their judgements. The "Other" category was liberally used during labelling which reveals the dependence of raters' active vocabulary on annotation. A possible alternative would be to balance free-form responses with fixed-choice alternatives in order to maximise accuracy while ensuring a degree of standardisation. Having taxonomies that allow parsing or mapping of free-form lexical emotion labels into different levels or groups of emotions would be of great help to standardise annotation results. Taxonomies like the GALC (Scherer, 2005) and Mind Reading (Baron-Cohen et al., 2004) though not entirely comprehensive as yet, are good examples of this.

Finally, using multiple layers of annotation may help to reduce the subjectivity of annotations and get more convergent results. Abrilian et al.'s (2005) multi-level annotation framework is exemplary in that it combines emotion, context and multi-modal annotations to overcome issues related to temporality and abstraction. However, as in any comprehensive coding technique, the coding-time, expertise and cost remain the main constraints.

To get a flavour of related work in the learning community, consider D'Mello, Picard, and Graesser (2007) and D'Mello, Taylor, Davidson, and Graesser (2008) ensemble of emotion assessment techniques including observations by external observers, emote-aloud procedure, cued-recall, coding of videos by trained experts as well as post hoc self-rating of emotions to analyse and contrast emotion judgements. Their findings provide novel empirical evidence on the nature and relationship of emotional accounts across self, peers and teachers. In another example, Baker, Rodrigo, and Xolocotzin (2007) conduct real-time observations using peripheral vision in classrooms. They use a team of six trained observers, working in pairs, to code categories of behavioural or affective states in 20-s intervals. In contrast, Conati and Maclaren (2009) use a dialogue box permanently alongside their educational game to allow participants to volunteer emotional self-responses but report having to introduce game event-related pop-up dialogue boxes to overcome the lack of volunteered responses. Similarly, Arroyo et al. (2009) use a problem-based mathematics tutor to collect self-report on one of four emotions after every 5 min of interaction. The emotion to be queried is selected randomly and rated on a five-point continuous scale to analyse relationships with learning-related concepts. In general, balancing the quantity and timing of emotion measurement requires careful consideration as ultimately it is the specific research view, user profile and the eventual purpose of data analysis that determines the best strategy to be used. In our case, decisions were mostly driven by the requirements of representative data for training automatic affect classifiers.

Summary and Conclusions

For affect recognition technology to reliably operate in target applications, we need context-specific corpora to serve not only as repositories of sample data, but importantly to shape our understanding of the problem itself. This chapter has described one such attempt to capture naturalistic emotional data in a computer-based learning scenario. We have described the data collection process and the annotation framework in detail and have discussed important observations and results arising from these. A self-regulated learning task was used to collect samples of emotional behaviour in an unconstrained setting. The data obtained went through three levels of annotation each giving a new insight into the nature of the problem. It was found that the main problems in annotation are derived from the dynamic nature of emotions, the ambiguity in categorisation and the high subjectivity of emotion perception. Inter-rater reliability was found to be quite low which rather than being an error of measure, as one could interpret, is in fact an acknowledged observation reported for naturalistic data and highlights the difficulty in ascribing emotions in real-life data (Abrilian et al., 2005; Cowie et al., 2005). What is important, however, is to reflect on how we can decide on an optimal metric of recognition accuracy for evaluating automatic classifiers when we lack a reliable and objective ground-truth in the first place.

References

Abrilian, S., Devillers, L., Buisine, S., & Martin, J.-C. (2005). EmoTV1: Annotation of real-life emotions for the specification of multimodal affective interfaces. *Proceedings of 11th International Conference on Human-Computer Interaction (HCI 2005)*, Las Vegas, USA.

Abrilian, S., Devillers, L., & Martin, J.-C. (2006). Annotation of emotions in real-life video interviews: Variability between coders. *International Conference of Language Resources & Evaluation*. Genoa, Italy.

Afzal, S., Morrison, C., & Robinson, P. (2009). Intentional affect: An alternative notion of affective interaction with a machine. *Proceedings of British HCI*. Cambridge, UK.

Afzal, S., & Robinson, P. (2010). Measuring affect in learning – Motivation and methods. *10th IEEE International Conference on Advanced Learning Technologies (ICALT)*. Tunisia.

Arroyo, I., Cooper, D. G., Burleson, W., Woolf, B. P., Muldner, K., & Christopherson, R. (2009). Emotion Sensors Go to School. In V. Dimitrova, R. Mizoguchi, B. du Boulay & A. Grasser (Eds.), *Artificial Intelligence in Education. Building Learning Systems that Care: from Knowledge Representation to Affective Modelling* (Vol. Frontiers in Artificial Intelligence and Applications 200, pp. 17–24). Brighton, UK: IOS Press.

Bakeman, R., & Gothman, J. M. (1997). *Observing interaction: An introduction to sequential analysis*. Cambridge, UK: Cambridge University Press.

Baker, R., Rodrigo, M., & Xolocotzin, U. (2007). The dynamics of affective transitions in simulation problem-solving environments. In: Paiva, A., Prada, R., Picard, R.W. (Eds.), ACII 2007. LNCS, vol. 4738, pp. 666–677. Springer, Heidelberg.

Baron-Cohen, S., Golan, O., Wheelwright, S., & Hill, J. (2004). *Mind reading: The interactive guide to emotions*. London: Jessica Kingsley.

Bransford, J. D., Brown, A. L., & Cocking, R. R. (1999). *How people learn: Brain, mind, experience and school*. Washington, DC: National Academy Press.

Camtasia Studio. (2006). Version 3.1. TechSmith Software.

Cohn, J. F., & Schmidt, K. L. (2004). The timing of facial motion in posed and spontaneous smiles. *International Journal of Wavelets, Multiresolution and Information Processing, 2*, 1–12.

Conati, C., & Maclaren, H. (2009). Empirically building and evaluating a probabilistic model of user affect. *User Modeling and User-Adapted Interaction, 19*(3), 267–303.

Cowie, R., Douglas-Cowie, E., & Cox, C. (2005). Beyond emotion archetypes: Databases for emotion modelling using neural networks. *Neural Networks, 18*, 371–388.

D'Mello, S., Picard, R. W., & Graesser, A. (2007). Towards an affect-sensitive auto-tutor. *IEEE Intelligent Systems, 22*(4), 53.

D'Mello, S., Taylor, R., Davidson, K., & Graesser, A. (2008). Self versus teacher judgements of learner emotions during a tutoring session with AutoTutor. In B. Woolf et al. (Eds.), ITS 2008, LNCS 5091, (pp 9–18). Springer-Verlag.

Ekman, P., & Rosenberg, E. L. (1997). *What the face reveals: Basic and applied studies of spontaneous expression using facial action coding system (FACS).* New York: Oxford University Press.

El Kaliouby, R., & Teeters, A. (2007). Eliciting, capturing and tagging spontaneous facial affect in autism spectrum disorder. *International Conference on Multimodal Interfaces.* Aichi, Japan.

Elfenbein, H. A., Marsh, A. A., & Ambady, N. (2002). Emotional intelligence and the recognition of emotion from facial expressions. In L. F. Barrett & P. Salovey (Eds.), *The wisdom of feelings: Processes underlying emotional intelligence* (pp. 37–59). New York: Guilford.

Fleiss, J. L., Levin, B., & Paik, M. C. (2003). The measurement of interrater agreement. In J. L. Fleiss, B. Levin, & M. C. Paik (Eds.), *Statistical methods for rates & proportions* (3rd ed., pp. 598–626). Hoboken, NJ: Wiley.

Frank, M. G., Juslin, P. N., & Harrigan, J. A. (2005). Technical issues in recording nonverbal behaviour. In J. A. Harrigan (Ed.), *The new handbook of methods in nonverbal behaviour research.* New York: Oxford University Press.

Graesser, A. C., McDaniel, B., Chipman, P., Witherspoon, A., D'Mello, S., & Gholson, B. (2006). Detection of emotions during learning with AutoTutor. In R. Son (Ed.), Proceedings of the 28th Annual Meetings of the Cognitive Science Society (pp. 285–290). Mahwah, NJ: Erlbaum.

Hayes, A. F., & Krippendorff, K. (2007). Answering the call for a standard reliability measure for coding data. *Communication Methods and Measures, 1*(1), 77–89.

Isomursu, M., Tahti, M., Vainamo, S., & Kuutti, K. (2007). Experimental evaluation of five methods for collecting emotions in field settings with mobile application. *International Journal of Human-Computer Studies, 65*, 404–418.

Kort B., Reilly, R. & Picard R. (2001) An affective model of interplay between emotions and learning: reengineering educational pedagogy—building a learning companion, In T. Okamoto, R. Hartley, Kinshuk & J. P. Klus (Eds.), *IEEE International Conference on Advanced Learning Technology: Issues, Achievements and Challenges* (Madison, WI, IEEE Computer Society), 43–48.

Lepper, M. R., Woolverton, M., Mumme, D. L., & Gurtner, J. (1993). Motivational techniques of expert human tutors: Lessons for the design of computer-based tutors. In S. P. Lajoie & S. J. Derry (Eds.), *Computers as cognitive tools* (pp. 75–105). Hillsdale, IN: Erlbaum.

Lisetti, C., & Schiano, D. (2000). Facial expression recognition: Where human computer interaction, artificial intelligence and cognitive science intersect. *Pragmatics and Cognition, 8*(1), 185–235.

Manusov, V. L. (2005). *Sourcebook of nonverbal measures: Going beyond words.* Mahwah, NJ: Lawrence Erlbaum.

Merrill, D. C., Reiser, B. J., Ranney, M., & Trafton, J. G. (1992). Effective tutoring techniques: A comparison of human tutors and intelligent tutoring systems. *Journal of the Learning Sciences, 2*, 277–305.

O'Regan, K. (2003). Emotion and e-learning. *Journal of Asynchronous Learning Networks, 7*(3), 78–92.

Pantic, M., & Patras, I. (2006). Dynamics of facial expression: Recognition of facial actions and their temporal segments from face profile image sequences. *IEEE Transactions on Systems, Man, and Cybernetics, 36*(2), 433–449.

Pantic, M., & Rothkrantz, L. J. M. (2003). Toward an affect-sensitive multimodal human-computer interaction. *Proceedings of the IEEE, 91*(9), 1370–1390.

Pekrun, R. (2005). Progress and open problems in educational emotion research. *Learning and Instruction, 15*, 497–506.

Pekrun, R., Goetz, T., Titz, W., & Perry, R. P. (2002). Academic emotions in students' self-regulated learning and achievement: A program of qualitative and quantitative research. *Educational Psychologist, 37*, 91–105.

Picard, R. W. (1997). *Affective computing*. Cambridge, MA: MIT.

Picard, R. W., Papert, S., Bender, W., Blumberg, B., Breazeal, C., Cavallo, D., et al. (2004). Affective learning – A manifesto. *BT Technology Journal, 22*, 253–269.

Riggio, R. E., & Riggio, H. R. (2005). Self-report measures of emotional and nonverbal expressiveness. In V. Manusov (Ed.), *The sourcebook of nonverbal measures: Going beyond words* (pp. 105–111). Mahwah, NJ: Erlbaum.

Russell, J. A., & Fernandez-Dols, J. M. (1997). *The psychology of facial expression*. Cambridge, UK: Cambridge University Press.

Scherer, K. (2005). What are emotions? And how can they be measured? Social Science Information, 44(4), 695–729.

Schutz, P. A., Hong, J. Y., Cross, D. I., & Obson, J. N. (2006). Reflections on investigating emotion in educational activity settings. *Educational Psychology Review, 18*, 343–360.

Skemp, R. R. (1971). *The psychology of learning mathematics*. Hillsdale, NJ: Erlbaum.

White, C. H., & Sargent, J. (2005). Researcher choices and practices in the study of nonverbal communication. In V. L. Manusov (Ed.), *Sourcebook of nonverbal measures: Going beyond words*. Mahwah, NJ: Lawrence Erlbaum.

Wosnitza, M., & Volet, S. (2005). Origin, direction and impact of emotions in social online learning. *Learning and Instruction, 15*(5), 440–464.

Combining Cognitive Appraisal and Sensors for Affect Detection in a Framework for Modeling User Affect

Cristina Conati

Introduction

Digital games are one of the most promising media for the development of innovative educational content (e.g., de Castell & Jenson, 2007; Gee, 2003). They integrate game design concepts with instructional design techniques in order to better address the learning needs of this generation, which highly regards interactive, experiential learning. While there is ample evidence that educational games (edu-games from now on) are more appealing than traditional learning environments, there is still limited empirical research that supports evidentiary claims about what is learned through play, what are the pedagogical and new media constructs required to have games that teach, and what is the interplay between entertainment and learning.

In our research, we have addressed this problem by hypothesizing that a key role in edu-game effectiveness is played by learners' individual differences, both long-term (e.g., preexisting knowledge, personality traits) and short-term (e.g., interaction goals, emotional state, learning state). The more the edu-game understands about its current learner, the better it can *adapt* the interaction to fit the learner's needs. In particular, by monitoring both the learner's affective states and his or her learning trajectory, a *user-adaptive* edu-game should be better able to strike the right balance between instruction and entertainment, leveraging the latter when there is need to revive the learner's motivation and engagement.

In the context of this research, we have been investigating how to build user models that can help an educational game understand how to best support a profitable interaction with the learners. We then use these models to experiment on how to provide user-adaptive interventions that address the interplay of affect and learning.

C. Conati (✉)
Department of Computer Science, University of British Columbia,
2366 Main Hall, Vancouver, BC V6T 1Z4, Canada
e-mail: conati@cs.ubc.ca

R.A. Calvo and S.K. D'Mello (eds.), *New Perspectives on Affect and Learning Technologies*,   71
Explorations in the Learning Sciences, Instructional Systems and Performance Technologies 3,
DOI 10.1007/978-1-4419-9625-1_6, © Springer Science+Business Media, LLC 2011

A distinguishing feature of our research is that we are looking at affective user models that rely on an explicit representation of both the *potential causes* of a user affective reaction, as well as the *behavioral effects* of that reaction. The advantage of such a model is twofold. First, by relying on both causes and effects as sources of information, the model is more resilient to limitations of each individual source and thus it can more accurately assess *which* affective state the user is in. Second, by having an explicit representation of *why* the student is in a given emotional state, the model provides the game with valuable additional information to decide how to react to that state, if necessary.

Most existing efforts to recognize user affect have either relied solely on detection of behavioral reactions (e.g., Healey & Picard, 2005; Prendinger, Mori, & Ishizuka, 2005), or have blended context and effect information as features to build classifiers that predict the user emotion but cannot tell why they occur (e.g., Cooper, Muldner, Arroyo, Park Woolf, & Burleson, 2010; D'Mello & Graesser, 2010).

In the rest of this chapter, we first describe the general approach and its theoretical underpinnings. Next, we describe the Prime Climb game, the testbed we have been using to apply the framework in practice. We then introduce the general steps needed to build an affective user model following our approach, and discuss how these steps were implemented to build the affective model for Prime Climb. We conclude by reporting results on the model's performance, followed by a discussion of future work.

The Affect-Modeling Framework

Our approach relies on Dynamic Decision Networks (DDN) to leverage information on both the possible causes and the observable effects of the user's affective reaction. Figure 1 shows a high-level representation of two time-slices in our DDN-based framework for modeling user affect (Conati, 2002). Each time-slice represents the system belief over relevant elements of the world after an interaction event of interest, such as a user's action (left slice) or an action from an interface agent (right slice). As the figure shows, the network can combine evidence on both the causes and effects of emotional reactions to assess the user's emotional state after each event. Links between variables in different time-slices represent relevant temporal dependencies, such as permanence or decay.

The subnetwork above the nodes *Emotional States* is the predictive component of the framework, representing the relations between emotional states and their possible causes as described in the OCC cognitive theory of emotions (Ortony, Clore, & Collins, 1988). According to this theory, emotions derive from one's appraisal of the current situation (consisting of events, agents, and objects) with respect to one's goals, preferences, and attitudes. For instance, depending on whether an event (e.g., the outcome of an interface agent's action) fits or does not fit with one's goals, one will feel either joy or distress in relation to the event. If the current event is caused by a third-party agent, one will feel admiration or reproach

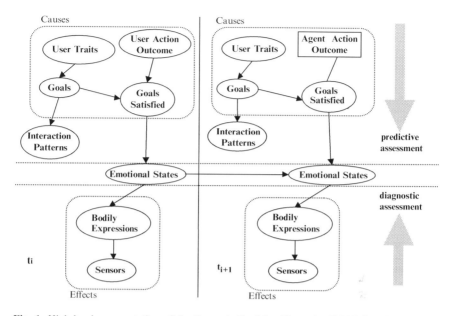

Fig. 1 High-level representation of the Dynamic Decision Networks (DDN) for affective user modeling

toward the agent; if that agent is oneself, one will feel either pride or shame. Based on this structure, the OCC theory defines 22 different emotions, which are inherently linked to context, and modulated both by factors more cognitive in nature (e.g., goals) as well as by affective elements such as attitudes and dispositions (e.g., liking/disliking not necessarily justified by objective reasons).

We based our model on the OCC theory because its intuitive representation of the causal nature of emotions lends itself well to devising computational models that can assess not only which emotions a user feels, but also why. Our OCC-based DDN includes variables for goals that a user may have during the interaction with a system that includes an interface agent (nodes *Goals* in Fig. 1). The events subject to the user's appraisal are the outcomes of the user's or the agent's actions (nodes *User Action Outcome* and *Agent Action Outcome* in Fig. 1). Agent actions are represented as decision variables in the framework, indicating points where the agent decides how to intervene. The fit of events with user's goals is modeled by the nodes class *Goals Satisfied*, which in turn influences the user's *Emotional States* (we call this part of the model the *appraisal-subnetwork*). Assessing user goals is not trivial, especially if asking the user about them during interaction is too intrusive, as is the case during game playing. Thus, our DDN also includes nodes (the *goal-assessment subnetwork*) to infer user goals from their interaction patterns and relevant traits (e.g., personality).

The subnetwork below the nodes *Emotional States* is the model's diagnostic part, representing the interaction between emotional states and their observable effects. *Emotional States* directly influence user *Bodily Expressions*, which in turn affect the output of *Sensors* that can detect them. Our framework is designed to modularly combine data from any available sensor, and gracefully degrade in the presence of partial or noisy information. It should be noted that the only temporal dependencies explicitly represented in Fig. 1 are between emotion variables, to account for the impact of the emotional state at time *t* on the emotional state at time *t* + 1 (representing, for instance, the fact that the negative impact of a mismatched goal on one's emotion also depends on the preexisting emotional state). Other temporal dependencies may be relevant (e.g., between goals, as we discuss in Conati & Maclaren, 2009a), but require extra complexity to be captured reliably. Their absence in Fig. 1 should be seen as simplifying assumptions to be revised if empirical evaluations show a need for it.

Going from the high-level framework described here to concrete user models obviously requires filling in a large amount of often nontrivial details. In the rest of the chapter, we illustrate the process in the context of building an affective user model for an edu-game on number factorization, described next.

The Prime Climb Educational Game

In Prime Climb, students in sixth and seventh grade practice number factorization by pairing up to climb a series of mountains. Each mountain is divided into numbered sectors (see Fig. 2), and players must try to move to numbers that do not

Fig. 2 The Prime Climb interface

share common factors with their partner's number, otherwise they fall. To help students, Prime Climb includes the Magnifying Glass, a tool that allows players to view the factorization for any number on a mountain in the PDA device displayed at the top-right corner on the game interface (see Fig. 2). Each student also has a pedagogical agent (Fig. 2) that provides individualized support, both on demand and unsolicited, when the student does not seem to be learning from the game.

When providing unsolicited hints, the agent currently decides when and how to intervene based solely on a probabilistic model that assesses how the player's factorization knowledge evolves during game playing (*learning model* from now on, described in (Manske & Conati, 2005)). The agent's interventions are structured as hints given at incremental levels, with the goal of triggering student reasoning about number factorization as they play (Conati & Manske, 2009).

- The first (*focus*) level aims to channel the student's attention on the skill that requires help. For instance, the agent says "Think about how to factorize the number you clicked on" if the student model predicts that the student does not know how to factorize that number.
- The second (*tool*) level is a hint that encourages the student to use the magnifying glass to see relevant factorizations.
- The third (*bottom-out*) level gives either the factorization of a number or which factors are in common between two numbers.

Students can choose to progress through the various levels by asking for further help. Otherwise, the agent goes through the progression when it needs to intervene on the same skill more than once. The above hints are provided regardless of the correctness of the student's move, if the learning model assesses that the student needs help with the relevant number factorization skills.

The affective user model described in the next section is designed to capture the affective reactions elicited in the student by his or her interaction with the game and the agent. It will eventually be integrated with the learning model to make agent interventions and game dynamics sensitive to both cognitive and affective states of the user.

Building the Affective Model

In this section, we illustrate the general steps needed to apply the framework described in the previous section to a specific learning environment (LE). For each step, we also discuss how the framework was applied to build the affective model for the Prime Climb game. We divide the description in two subsections, one for the causal and one for the diagnostic part of the model, since these two components are conceptually separate and could be adopted in isolation if desired, as it was done, for instance, in Conati and Maclaren (2009a).

Defining the Causal Component of the Affective Model

Define which emotions should be modeled. The OCC theory defines 22 emotions starting from the appraisal mechanism described in the previous section. These emotions include:

- Reactions related to how an occurring event impacts one's goals (*joy/distress* toward the event, *admiration/reproach* if the event was generated by a third party, *pride/shame* if was generated by oneself)
- Reactions about how an event impacts others that one may *like/dislike* (*happy-for/resentment* if the impact is positive, *pity/gloating* if the impact is negative)
- Emotions related to the prospective effects of an event (e.g., *hope/fear, relief/disappointment*)

Clearly, not all 22 emotions are always relevant for specific LEs. For instance, a one-user LE cannot elicit emotions related to other users. Even when a specific emotion is potentially relevant, inclusion in the model is a tradeoff between its impact on the interaction and the cost of modeling the dynamics that bring that emotion to bear. For instance, in Prime Climb we currently model 6 of the 22 OCC emotions: emotions toward game states (*joy/regret*), and related emotions toward the agent (*admiration/reproach* in the OCC theory) or toward oneself (*pride/shame*). The first four emotions were often informally observed during interaction with Prime Climb, and have been consistently self-reported by students during a variety of studies (Conati & Maclaren, 2009a). The *pride/shame* pair is clearly relevant to any kind of reward-based interaction, however, we have no formal evidence on the extent of its occurrence because of difficulties in obtaining reliable self-reports 'more on this in a later section'. Still, once the model is set up to capture *admiration/reproach*, adding *pride/shame* has little overhead because the only additional factor that needs to be tracked to distinguish between these two emotion pairs is whether the Prime Climb state currently appraised has been generated by the Prime Climb agent or by the student. In contrast, while we have substantial evidence that emotions toward the climbing partner (i.e., another student) arise frequently during game play, they are currently not included in the model because of the added complexity involved in modeling a two-player interaction. Because of this complexity, we decided to first evaluate the feasibility of the approach with the simpler model described here.

Define student goals. This step requires us to define the set of goals that students may have when using the target LE. These goals can either be well-defined objectives set by the game itself (*fixed goals* from now on) or more *subjective goals* still influenced by the type of interaction that the LE supports but not as obviously related to it as fixed goals are. While fixed goals can be easily defined from an analysis of the LE, the relevant set of subjective goals must be derived empirically by observing actual student interactions. For instance, observations and interviews of students playing Prime Climb uncovered six high-level non-mutually exclusive goals (*Have Fun, Avoid Falling, Beat Partner, Learn Math, Succeed By Myself and Wanting Help*). While some of these goals naturally derive from to the structure of

Prime Climb (*Have Fun, Avoid Falling, Learn Math*) others are more arbitrary. For instance, the goal *Beat Partner* is actually in contrast to the nature of Prime Climb, since the two players are supposed to collaborate, when climbing. The goals *Succeed By Myself* and *Wanting Help* intuitively seem mutually exclusive; however, we observed that they can in fact co-exist for students who express a general preference to succeed by themselves but end up wanting help during especially challenging episodes. We have collected the data to instantiate goal-related variables and their prior probabilities in the Prime Climb model via user studies in which students were given a post-game questionnaire to assess which of the above goals they experienced during game playing. The post-questionnaire includes goal-related statements to be ranked on a Likert scale (1–5), and there are multiple statements per goal, to increase the reliability of the students' answers (e.g., "I wanted to learn math by playing the game," "I didn't want to think about math when I was playing the game"). The questionnaire also includes an open-ended question gauging the presence of any additional goal, but none were found.

Define means for goal assessment. The goal set defined in the previous step specifies the range of goals each student *may* have while interacting with the target LE, not which goals the student actually pursues at any given point in time. So, unless goals are specifically set by the LE during interaction, they need to be inferred. One option is to endow the interface with an unobtrusive way for students to specify their goals while playing. Alternatively, the system needs to perform *goal recognition*, i.e., infer the goals dynamically as the student interacts with the system. In Prime Climb, we adopted the second approach, as eliciting student goals explicitly during game playing was deemed too intrusive. In particular, we leverage the fact that user goals are influenced by *user personality* (Costa & McCrae, 1992) and affect user *interaction patterns*, which in turn can be inferred by observing the outcomes of individual user actions. Thus, observations of both the relevant user traits and action outcomes can provide the DDN with indirect evidence for assessing user goals.

We derived the data to build the portion of the DDN that exploits this evidence for goal assessment via a series of Wizard of Oz studies where pairs of students interacted with the game while an experimenter controlled the pedagogical agent (Zhou & Conati, 2003). Students reported their goals via the questionnaire described above. Information on student personality is included in the model based on the Five-Factor Model (Costa & McCrae, 1992), which represents personality as five domains – *neuroticism*, *extraversion*, *openness*, *agreeableness* and *conscientiousness*. Data to instantiate the prior and conditional probabilities for the variables that represent these domains in the model was collected through a standard personality test (Graziano, Jensen-Campbell, & Finch, 1997). Interaction logs were mined to define the relationships between student goals (assessed via the goal post-questionnaire) and interaction behaviors. This process resulted in the goal assessment subnetwork shown in Fig. 3, where all nodes are binary variables. More details on the construction of this part of the model can be found in Zhou and Conati (2003).

Define appraisal relationships. Following the OCC appraisal model, a student's emotional state depends on whether his or her goals are satisfied or not during the interaction with a LE. Modeling this process in a DDN requires identifying how

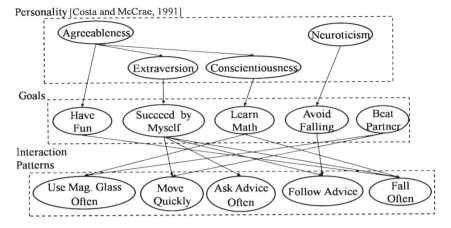

Fig. 3 Goal assessment portion of the model

each relevant game state relates to the set of possible student goals in terms of appraisal. Some of these relations can be defined intuitively. In Prime Climb, for instance, if the student has the goal *Avoid Falling*, a successful move likely satisfies it, while a fall likely does not. If the student has the goal *Beat Partner*, only a move that brings the player ahead of the partner on the mountain is likely to satisfy this goal. Other appraisal relationships must be derived empirically. For instance, we could not define a priori which events satisfy student goals *Have Fun* or *Learn Math*. Similarly, although an unsolicited hint from the Prime Climb agent intuitively violates the goal *Succeed-by-myself* and satisfies *Want-Help*, it is unclear how the various types of hints are appraised with respect to these goals given that they vary substantially in the amount of help that they provide. We defined the appraisal relationships in the Prime Climb affective model through a user study in which students, after game playing, were asked to rate propositions of the type "I <*goal-related action*> when <*game event*>." In each proposition, <*goal-related action*> is a statement related to one of target appraisal goals (e.g., "learnt math," "had fun") and <*game event*> is a relevant event in the Prime Climb interaction (e.g., "I fell," "the agent suggested to use the magnifying glass"). Figure 4 shows the appraisal relations derived from this process with respect to the outcome of student actions. More details about the process and the resulting model can be found in (Conati & Maclaren, 2009a).

Defining the Diagnostic Component of the Affective Model

Define sensors for the diagnostic part of the model. The choice of sensors to be included in the model largely depends upon the type of emotional states that the model must capture. There has been considerable success in linking individual

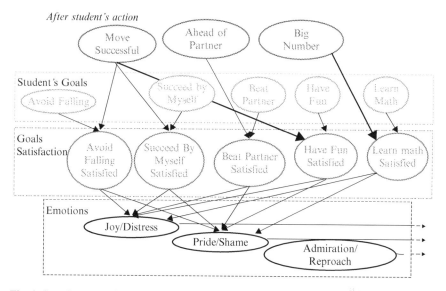

Fig. 4 Sample excerpt from the Prime Climb appraisal network

bodily/physiological expressions to the affective dimensions of valence and arousal, such as heart beat and measures of skin conductance (e.g., Prendinger et al., 2005), various facial expressions (e.g., Lang, Greenwald, Bradley, & Hamm, 1993), acoustic–prosodic and lexical speech features (Litman & Forbes-Riley, 2004). There have also been results on combinations of sensors as detectors of specific emotions. For instance, Healey and Picard (2005) report 89% accuracy in recognizing four levels of driver anxiety by integrating measurements from five physiological sensors, three video-cameras and a microphone. Cooper et al. (2010) linked measurements from a mouse that captures pressure placed on its various points, as well as camera-detected facial expressions with high student interest during interaction with an intelligent LE for math. They also linked facial expressions with high levels of student excitement. D'Mello and Graesser (2010) found that facial expressions as coded by external judges can discriminate among student states of confusion, boredom, frustration, and neutral. Although existing results can help guide the choice of sensors, the final selection should always be empirically validated, as sensors performance highly depends upon a variety of factors such as whether the emotions are spontaneous or artificially elicited, age of participants, and the interaction context.

In our research, empirical evaluations of the causal part of the Prime Climb model (Conati & Maclaren, 2009a) suggested that its performance could be improved by including information on the valence of the student affective states, leading us to experimenting with a sensor that would serve this purpose. More specifically, the causal model proved to be unable to reliably capture *regret* toward the agent because it could not capture the shifts that some students experience between the goals *Succeed-by-myself* and *Wanting Help* at critical times of game playing. This confusion causes the model to misjudge how students react to the agent's interventions (or lack thereof) at those times. Accurate goal recognition can be extremely challenging, but this particular problem could be alleviated if the Prime Climb model can detect when the student moves to a state of negative valence after an agent action. A sensor that has shown to be a good detector of negative affect is the electromyography (EMG) placed on the corrugators muscle on the forehead (Lang, Greenwald, Bradley, & Hamm, 1993). EMG sensors measure muscle activity by detecting surface voltages that occur when a muscle is contracted. When placed on the corrugator muscle on the forehead, the signal gets excited by this muscle's movements, and previous studies linked greater EMG activity in this area with expressions of negative affect.

Adding sensors to the model. The bottom part of Fig. 1 shows the most complete incarnation of this step, where the connection between affective states and sensors predictions is defined through the bodily expression that each sensor captures. Having the connection between affective states and sensors go through bodily expressions is advisable when using multiple sensors to detect a specific bodily expression (e.g., a videocamera and an EMG to detect eyebrow movements). This configuration requires the specification of both the conditional probabilities that express each sensor's reliability in detecting the target bodily expression, as well the conditional probabilities that encode the reliability of that bodily expression as an indicator of the target emotional state. Alternatively, sensor measurements can be directly linked to the target emotional state, as we did in our first exploration of the EMG sensor for the Prime Climb model.

Since we wanted the EMG sensor to provide information on affective valence, two new nodes were added to each time slice of the affective model: *Valence* and *Signal Prediction* (see Fig. 5, left), both binary. The *Valence* node represents the model's overall prediction for the student's affective valence the *Signal Prediction* node encodes whether the EMG signal predicts positive/negative valence at a time of interest. The conditional probability table (CPT) for *Valence* given *Emotional States* is defined so that the probability that valence is positive/negative is proportional to the number of positive/negative emotion nodes. The CPT for *Signal Prediction* given *Valence* represents the probability of observing an EMG prediction of positive or negative valence, given the student's actual affective valence. To instantiate this CPT, we ran a user study to collect both EMG evidence and accompanying affective labels.

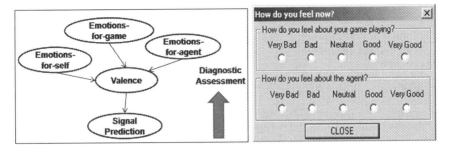

Fig. 5 Adding electromyography (EMG) data to the model (*left*); emotion self-report box (*right*)

The study involved 41 students (sixth and seventh grade) and its design was similar to the studies we used to instantiate other parts of the model. Here, however, each student had an EMG sensor placed on the forehead. During game play, students periodically self-reported their emotions via the dialog box shown in Fig. 5, a self-reporting mechanism that we have extensively validated and used throughout this research (Conati, 2004; Conati & Maclaren, 2009a).[1]

The log files from the study include all relevant game events (e.g., a student's successful climbs and falls, agent interventions), the student's reported emotions and the EMG signals sampled at 32 Hz. These log files were analyzed to generate a set of datapoints of the form *<affective valence, signal prediction>*, where a datapoint is created for each logged event that can be associated with an emotion self-report. The value for *affective valence* (positive or negative) is derived from that self-report; the value for *signal prediction* (also positive or negative) is computed by analyzing the EMG signal in the 4 seconds following the event. The analysis yielded 196 datapoints, which were used to instantiate the CPT for the *Signal Prediction* node in Fig. 5 by calculating the frequencies of the various combinations of *signal prediction/affective valence* value pairs in the data set. More details on this process can be found in (Conati & Maclaren, 2009b).

Model Evaluation

The data from the study described in the previous section was used to evaluate the resulting Prime Climb affective model with respect to two main questions

1. Is the goal assessment mechanism sufficiently accurate to support our appraisal-based modeling approach?
2. How does the model using only causal information compare to the model that includes diagnostic information from the EMG sensor?

The general evaluation methodology is to compare various versions of the model by using a Prime Climb simulator. The simulator is used to feed log files from the study to each model that is to be evaluated. Model predictions of affect are collected at points in which students generated their emotion self-reports, and compared with the reported emotions (in this study, 170 reports of Joy, 14 reports of Distress, 127 reports of Admiration, and 28 reports of Distress).

To answer question 1, we compared the performance of the causal model with the goals assessed via the mechanism described earlier against a model where goals were set based on student post-questionnaire responses from the study. The model's performance when using goal assessment increased significantly for *Distress* and

---

[1] Currently, the dialog box only elicits information on emotions towards the game and the agent because dealing with three pairs of emotions turned out to be too overwhelming for students.

for *Reproach*, mostly because dynamic goal assessment can capture to some extent the changes in student goals during interaction, which the alternative model cannot do since goal values as set up-front. The performance of the model with goal assessment for *Joy* and *Admiration* decreased slightly (from 69.6 to 68.7% for *Joy*, from 67.2 to 66% for *Admiration*) but the decrease is not statistically significant. Thus, from a practical standpoint, the model using the probabilistic goal assessment performs better than the model using explicit evidence on student's goals. The only way to further improve goal information in the model would be to obtain self-reports on students' goals periodically during interaction.

To answer question 2, we compared the performance of the causal model against the performance of the model that includes EMG. We found that, for datapoints corresponding to strong, consistent emotional states (e.g., when students reported emotions with the same valence toward the game and the agent) the complete model performs significantly better than the predictive model. Accuracy for reproach went from 39 to 63%, bringing overall accuracy on emotions toward the agent to 73% (against 61% for the causal mode). Accuracy for emotions toward the game went from 72.6 to 76.9%, also a statistically significant increase. In contrast, the addition of the EMG sensor made no difference for data points corresponding to weaker or conflicting emotional states (e.g., states in which students reported at least one emotion to be neutral, or emotions with opposite valence toward game and agent). In the presence of weak emotions, likely the affective reaction is not strong enough to generate movements of the corrugators muscle that are detectable by the EMG sensor. Thus, adding to the model more sensitive sensors for valence detection may alleviate this problem. In the case of conflicting emotions, the addition of the EMG brings no value because it captures overall valence but does not help discriminate valence at the level of the individual emotion pairs. This problem calls for refinement in the goal assessment process, to better capture shifts between goals or goal priority during interaction.

Conclusions

We have presented an approach to modeling user affect that combines explicit information on both causes and effects of emotional reaction. One advantage of this approach is that using both 'of these' sources increases model accuracy. A second advantage is that, by assessing not only which emotions the student is feeling but also *why* they arise, this model enhances a LE's ability to adequately respond to these emotions. For instance, if the LE can recognize that the user feels a negative emotion because of something wrong the user has done (*shame* in our models) it may provide hints aimed at making the user feel better toward herself. If the LE recognizes that the user is upset because of its own behavior (*reproach* in our models), it may take actions to make amends. These specific interventions are more difficult to identify with approaches that do not have such an explicit representation of the reasons underlying user emotions (e.g., Cooper et al., 2010; D'Mello &

Graesser, 2010). This added value, however, comes with increased model complexity. Implementing the appraisal mechanism that enables causal assessment requires defining relationships between student traits, goals, and events. This process often involves laborious data collection, as we illustrated in this chapter, with our experience in building the affective model for the Prime Climb edu-game. It is our long-term objective to compare the approach presented here with lighter-weight models, to better understand if and when the added cost is worth the effort.

A more immediate goal is to integrate the predictions of the Prime Climb affective model with the existing model of student learning, so that game dynamics and agent interventions can be tailored to both. Toward this end, we are conducting user studies to understand specific limitations of agent hints based solely on the learning model, and how affect-sensitive responses may overcome these limitations. We are also exploring ways to elicit explicit information on student goals at selected times during interaction in order to better cope with situations in which the model cannot reliably assess these goals. The objective here is to maximize the value of this information for the model, without excessive disruption to game play. Similarly, we want to investigate if and when it is appropriate to explicitly ask students about their emotions, to cope with situations in which the model does not have sufficient information to generate a confident assessment.

References

Conati, C. (2002). Probabilistic assessment of user's emotions in educational games. *Journal of Applied Artificial Intelligence, 16*(7–8), 555–575.

Conati, C. (2004). How to evaluate models of user affect? In In Elisabeth André, Laila Dybkjær, Wolfgang Minker, & Paul Heisterkamp (Eds.),*Proceedings of ADS'04, Tutorial and Research Workshop on Affective Dialog Systems*. (pp. 288–300), Kloster Irsee, Germany.

Conati, C., & Maclaren, H. (2009a). Empirically building and evaluating a probabilistic model of user affect. *User Modeling and User-Adapted Interaction, 19*(3), 267–303.

Conati, C., & Maclaren, H. (2009b). Modeling user affect from causes and effects. In *Proceedings of UMAP 2009, First and Seventeenth International Conference on User Modeling, Adaptation and Personalization*. pp 4–15. Springer, LNCS 5535.

Conati, C., & Manske, M. (2009). Evaluating adaptive feedback in an educational computer game. In Hannes Högni Viljálmsson (Eds.), *Proceedings of Intelligent Virtual Agents (IVA) 2009* (pp. 146–158). Amsterdam, The Netherlands: Springer, LNCS 5773.

Cooper, D., Muldner, K., Arroyo, I., Park Woolf, B., & Burleson, W. (2010). Ranking feature sets for emotion models used in classroom based intelligent tutoring systems. In P. De Bra, A. Kobsa, & D. Chin (Eds.), *Proceedings of UMAP 2010* (pp. 135–146). Big Island, HI, USA: Springer, LNCS 6075.

Costa, P. T., & McCrae, R. R. (1992). Four ways five factors are basic. *Personality and Individual Differences, 13*, 653–665.

D'Mello, S., & Graesser, A. C. (2010). Multimodal semi-automated affect detection from conversational cues, gross body language, and facial features. *User Modeling and User-Adapted Interaction, 20*(2), 147–187.

de Castell, S., & Jenson, J. (2007). Digital games for education: When meanings play. *Intermedialities, 9*, 45–54.

Gee, J. P. (2003). *What video games have to teach us about learning and literacy*. New York: Palgrave Macmillan.

Graziano, W. G., Jensen-Campbell, L. A., & Finch, J. F. (1997). The self as a mediator between personality and adjustment. *Journal of Personality and Social Psychology, 73*, 392–404.

Healey, J. A., & Picard, R. W. (2005). Detecting stress during real-world driving tasks using physiological sensors. *IEEE Transactions on Intelligent Transportation Systems, 6*(2), 156–166.

Lang, P., Greenwald, M., Bradley, M., & Hamm, A. (1993). Look at pictures: Affective, facial, visceral, and behavioral reactions. *Psychophysiology, 30*, 261–273.

Litman, D. J., & Forbes-Riley, K. (2004). Predicting student emotions in computer-human tutoring dialogues. In Donia Scott (Ed.), *42nd Annual Meeting of the Association for Computational Linguistics (ACL)* (pp. 352–359). Barcelona, Spain.

Manske, M., & Conati, C. (2005). Modelling learning in educational games. *Proceedings of the 12th International Conference on AI in Education*. Amsterdam, The Netherlands.

Ortony, A., Clore, G. L., & Collins, A. (1988). *The cognitive structure of emotion*. New York: Cambridge University Press.

Prendinger, H., Mori, J., & Ishizuka, M. (2005). Recognizing, modeling, and responding to users' affective states. In Liliana Ardissono, Paul Brna & Antonija Mitrovic (Eds.), *UM'05 10th International Conference on User Modeling*. (pp. 60–69). Edinburgh, UK. Springer, LNCS 3538.

Zhou, X., & Conati, C. (2003). Inferring user goals from personality and behavior in a causal model of user affect. In Johnson, Lewis & Andre, Elisabeth (Eds.), *IUI'03, International Conference on Intelligent User Interfaces* (pp. 211–218). Miami, FL.

Affect Recognition and Expression in Narrative-Centered Learning Environments

James C. Lester, Scott W. McQuiggan, and Jennifer L. Sabourin

Affect has begun to play an increasingly important role in intelligent tutoring systems. The intelligent tutoring system community has seen the emergence of work on affective student modeling (Conati & Mclaren, 2005), detecting frustration and stress (Burleson, 2006; McQuiggan, Lee, & Lester, 2007), modeling agents' emotional states (André & Mueller, 2003; Graesser, Person, & Magliano, 1995), devising affect-informed models of social interaction (Johnson & Rizzo, 2004; Paiva et al., 2005), detecting student motivation (de Vicente & Pain, 2002), and diagnosing and adapting to student self-efficacy (Beal & Lee, 2005). All of this work seeks to increase the fidelity with which affective and motivational processes are understood and utilized in intelligent tutoring systems in an effort to increase the effectiveness of tutorial interactions and, ultimately, learning.

This level of emphasis on affect is not surprising given the impact it has been shown to have on learning outcomes. Student affective states influence problem-solving strategies, the level of engagement exhibited by the student, and the degree to which he or she is motivated to continue with the learning process (Kort, Reilly, & Picard, 2001; Picard et al., 2004). All of these factors have the potential to influence both how students learn in a single session and their learning behaviors in the future. Consequently, developing techniques for keeping students in an affective state that is conducive to learning has been the focus of much recent work (Arroyo, Woolf, Royer, & Tai, 2009; Chaffar & Frasson, 2004; D'Mello et al., 2008; Forbes-Riley, Rotaru, & Litman, 2008).

Unfortunately, there is not yet a clear understanding of how emotions occur during learning and this problem is compounded by evidence that individual learning environments can strongly impact students' emotional experiences (Rodrigo & Baker, 2011). It is also unclear which emotional states are optimal for individual

J.C. Lester (✉)
Department of Computer Science, North Carolina State University,
Engineering Building II, 890 Oval Drive, Raleigh, NC 27695-8206, USA
e-mail: lester@ncsu.edu

R.A. Calvo and S.K. D'Mello (eds.), *New Perspectives on Affect and Learning Technologies*,   85
Explorations in the Learning Sciences, Instructional Systems and Performance Technologies 3,
DOI 10.1007/978-1-4419-9625-1_7, © Springer Science+Business Media, LLC 2011

students. This is likely to vary based on student needs and experience. Affective experiences may also have immediate and long-term effects on how students perceive learning and their levels of confidence and motivation moving forward. Finally, current research on how best to respond to student affect has yielded varying and often conflicting conclusions (Beal & Lee, 2005; Shute, 2008). For these reasons, it is challenging to design affective support systems for learning environments.

The goal of this research is to examine these issues within narrative-centered learning environments. These environments embed the educational process within a story with the objective of leveraging narrative's motivating features such as compelling plots, engaging characters, and fantastical settings (Malone & Lepper, 1987). These environments also offer the potential for creating affective experiences that complement those provided by more typical interactive learning environments (McQuiggan, Robison, & Lester, 2010). The ability to understand and control the emotional experiences of students in narrative-centered learning environments could lead to significant gains for student learning and motivation.

Related Work

There is a strong connection between affect and learning. Teachers and tutors alike motivate students to learn and craft educational experiences to increase student efficacy to support learning (Meyer & Turner, 2007). Affect influences the cognitive, motivational, and behavioral processes of students (Linnenbrink & Pintrich, 2001), and it appears that affect impacts learning and cognition in at least four ways: memory, strategy use, attention, and motivation (Pekrun, 1992). Therefore, a critical requirement of pedagogically successful intelligent tutoring systems is providing them with the ability to recognize, understand, and respond to student affect.

Work on affect recognition (Picard, 1997) has explored a variety of physical cues, which are produced in response to affective changes in the individual. These include visually observable cues such as body and head posture, facial expressions, and posture, and changes in physiological signals such as heart rate, skin conductivity, temperature, and respiration (Ekman & Friesen, 1978; Frijda, 1986). Psychologists have used electroencephalograms (EEG) to monitor users' brain activity for detection of task engagement (Pope, Bogart, & Bartolome, 1995) and user attention (Mekeig & Inlow, 1993). Heart rate measurements have been used to adapt challenge levels in computer games (Gilleade & Allanson, 2003), detect frustration and stress (Prendinger, Mayer, Mori, & Ishizuka, 2003), and monitor anxiety and stress (Healey, 2000). Galvanic skin response (GSR) has been used to sense user affective states, such as stress (Healey), student frustration for learning companion adaptation (Burleson, 2006), frustration for lifelike character adaptation in a mathematical game (Prendinger et al., 2003), and multiple user emotions in an educational game (Conati, 2002).

Recent work seeking to characterize the affective experience of learners interacting with intelligent learning environments has considered student affective trajectories occurring during learning. D'Mello, Taylor, and Graesser (2007) studied the likelihood of affective transitions among six affective states (boredom, flow, confusion, frustration, delight, and surprise) that were found to be relevant to complex learning (Craig, Graesser, Sullins, & Gholson, 2004). In general, learners are likely to persist in the same affective state (e.g., transitioning from a state of boredom to boredom is likely, and in some cases, significantly more likely than transitioning to another affective state). This analysis was conducted in the AutoTutor learning environment (Craig et al.; D'Mello et al., 2007). Baker, Rodrigo, and Xolocotzin (2007) were able to replicate many of the findings of D'Mello et al. (2007) when they calculated the likelihood of affective transitions in the Incredible Machine: Even More Contraptions, a simulation-based learning environment (2007). Baker et al. (2007) extended their analyses to investigate how usage choices affect emotion transitions. This work found that bored and confused learners are particularly likely to game the system. Further, it was found that students who game the system are unlikely to transition into a confused state (Baker et al.). An understanding of learners' affective experiences will inform the next generation of affect response modules that seek to optimize learning experiences.

Empathetic approaches to user affect have been shown to alter the affective state of the user as well as other qualities such as motivation (D'Mello et al., 2008; McQuiggan et al., 2010). Recent work has yielded models of when an empathetic response is appropriate (McQuiggan & Lester, 2007), how it ought to be delivered and when parallel or reactive empathy is preferable (McQuiggan, Robison, et al., 2008). These behaviors have also been shown to have an impact on the affective experiences of students (McQuiggan et al., 2010). Other work with empathetic synthetic agents has explored their affective responsiveness to biofeedback information and the communicative context (Prendinger & Ishizuka, 2005). Additional work has supplemented empathetic virtual agents capable of mimicking the emotional state of students with motivational statements that provide feedback regarding students success and efforts (Arroyo et al., 2009). It has also yielded agents that interact with one another and with the user in a virtual learning environment to elicit empathetic behaviors from its users (Paiva et al., 2005).

Affective Reasoning in CRYSTAL ISLAND

CRYSTAL ISLAND (Fig. 1) is a narrative-centered learning environment that is being created in the domain of microbiology for middle school students. It features a science mystery set on a recently discovered volcanic island where a research station has been established to study the unique flora and fauna.

The user plays the protagonist, Alex, who is attempting to discover the source of an unidentified infectious disease at the research station. The story opens by introducing the student to the island and the members of the research team for which her father serves as the lead scientist. As members of the research team fall ill, it is her task to discover the cause and the specific source of the outbreak. She is free to

Fig. 1 Crystal Island learning environment

explore the world and interact with other characters while forming questions, generating hypotheses, collecting data, and testing her hypotheses. Throughout the mystery, she can walk around the island and visit the infirmary, the lab, the dining hall, and the living quarters of each member of the team. She can pick up and manipulate objects, and she can talk with characters to gather clues about the source of the disease. In the course of her adventure she must gather enough evidence to correctly identify the type and source of the disease that has infected the camp members.

The approaches to affective support used in Crystal Island are based on the widely accepted appraisal theory of human emotions and one that is particularly well suited for computational modeling (Marsella & Gratch, 2009; Smith & Lazarus, 1990). According to this model (Fig. 2), individuals compare events in the environment to their goals and beliefs to develop an understanding of how these events impact their personal situation. This appraisal results in an emotional state as well as associated action tendencies and physiological responses. Upon experiencing this emotion, individuals are then likely to engage in emotion regulation behaviors (*coping*). Since the emotional state was determined by an interaction of the environment and the individuals' beliefs, one of these must be altered in order to attenuate the affective state. This distinction leads to two separate types of coping strategies: emotion focused and problem focused. These strategies attempt to alleviate emotional experiences by attempts to alter either one's own beliefs or the external environment, respectively.

Affective support in Crystal Island attempts to mirror this process of appraisal. The system itself has its own internal goals and beliefs that are often based on empirical data-driven models of user interaction. The system compares its own goals (e.g., student learning, positive affect, etc.) with the variables it is able to observe in the environment to create an assessment of the current situation of the user interaction. Based on this assessment it considers multiple strategies of intervening to aid student development. These strategies also take on a problem-based or

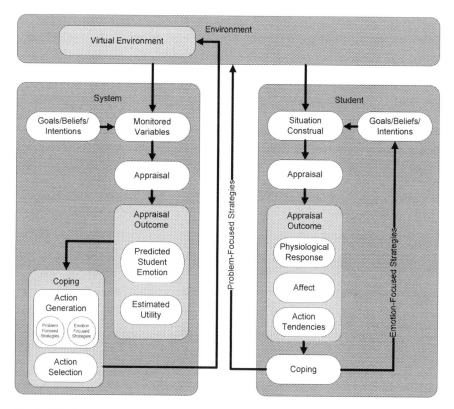

Fig. 2 Affective support in CRYSTAL ISLAND

emotion-based focus, mirroring the coping strategies individuals use during affective appraisal. However, the system cannot directly affect the appraisal process of the individual student. Instead, it must affect the environment in some way, such as through character-driven feedback, in order to encourage coping strategies and consequent reappraisal in students.

Empirical Findings

In order to examine the necessity and direction of affect sensitivity in narrative-centered learning environments, it is important to first focus on categorizing the affective experiences of students as they interacted with the CRYSTAL ISLAND environment. Primarily, it is important to distinguish how these affective experiences differed from those reported in more typical tutoring environments and problem solving non-narrative games. An initial study showed some interesting similarities and differences between the affective experiences in CRYSTAL ISLAND (McQuiggan et al., 2010), The Incredible Machine: Even More Contraptions (Baker et al., 2007), and AutoTutor (D'Mello et al., 2008). The Incredible Machine is a commercially available problem solving game in which students attempt to accomplish goals by building machines out of many everyday items while AutoTutor is a natural language-based intelligent tutoring system that aids students solving computer literacy and physics problems.

While the three environments are very different, several important findings were replicated in all three settings. First, the emotion of *flow* is the most commonly reported emotion in each environment, accounting for between 28 and 61% of all reports in individual studies. Interestingly, in the tutoring environment the reported levels of *flow* were only marginally higher than those of *boredom* and *confusion*, each accounting for nearly a quarter of all reports. In the two game-based environments, however, *confusion* and *boredom* together accounted for less than 20% of reports. The similarities and differences between affective experiences between the environments indicate both that it is important to examine narrative-centered learning environments for their specific impact on student affect and also that the results of these findings may provide insight to other learning environments despite the different approaches to instruction.

This initial study also replicated the finding that students tend to remain in the same emotional state over time. D'Mello et al. (2007) refer to this tendency as a *virtuous* or *vicious cycle*, depending on whether the persisting affective state is positive or negative. The continued support for this finding in very different learning environments suggests that affective intervention strategies should be developed to promote virtuous cycles and to prevent vicious ones.

Affect Recognition

In our laboratory we have investigated inductive approaches to recognizing student affective states, levels of self-efficacy, and several other cognitive and affective constructs. By recognizing student affect we hope to inform pedagogical planning and control modules of learning environments, such as CRYSTAL ISLAND, to improve tutorial and affective interactions. Likewise, by diagnosing self-efficacy we hope to better inform the pedagogical decisions bearing on the selection of problem difficulty by ensuring that the student has not only mastered the concept but believes in his or her abilities to utilize acquired knowledge.

Various models of emotion have been induced from observations of student behavior in CRYSTAL ISLAND to predict student self-reported affective states. We have investigated models that predicted affective state from a set of six emotional states (*excitement, fear, frustration, happiness, relaxation,* and *sadness*) using naïve Bayes and decision trees resulting in the best performing model with 95% accuracy. We then investigated approaches to early prediction of student frustration by collapsing the dataset to two states: *Frustration* and *Not Frustration*. To create models that make accurate predictions of student frustration as early as possible, we again use training data collected from observations of students interacting with CRYSTAL ISLAND. From this data, we then induced n-gram models, naïve Bayes, support vector machines, and decision trees to make early predictions of student frustration. These induced models were able to predict student frustration up to 30 s before confirmation of student frustration (self-reported frustration), with the best performing model achieving 89% accuracy (McQuiggan et al., 2007).

A foundational study to investigate the prospect of using the inductive approach to model self-efficacy in an online tutorial system produced models that were able to classify student self-efficacy as *High Efficacy* or *Low Efficacy* with 87% accuracy (McQuiggan, Mott, & Lester, 2008). Models were constructed from representations of ongoing situations in the online tutorial system. A second empirical study was designed to investigate the potential and the value of creating models of self-efficacy in more complex interactive learning environments (McQuiggan, Mott, & Lester). Models of self-efficacy were induced from observations of student behavior in the CRYSTAL ISLAND environment including representations of subject actions, locations, and other world state information. The highest performing induced naïve Bayes models correctly classified 85.2% of instances in the first empirical study and 82.1% of instances in the second empirical study. The highest performing decision tree models correctly classified 86.9% of instances in the first study and 87.3% of instances in the second study.

Affective Feedback

Recognizing student's affective states in real time provides little benefit without being able to provide intelligent responses aimed at improving the student's emotions during the learning experience. To this end we have examined a variety of methods for determining how best to provide affective feedback to students that is both natural and helpful in maintaining affective states that are conducive to learning. Given the rich interactive and social nature of CRYSTAL ISLAND's virtual characters, endowing these agents with the ability to respond directly to students' emotional states seemed to be a promising mechanism for emulating natural human–human affect sensitivity. While virtual character feedback is currently limited to text-based responses to self-reported affective states, a variety of types of feedback within this paradigm have been explored to gain understanding of the most effective mechanisms for supporting students' affective experience.

The first attempts to model ideal affective feedback examined students reactions to parallel and reactive empathy (McQuiggan, Robison, et al., 2008; McQuiggan et al., 2010), where parallel empathy occurs when the virtual character mimics the student's emotional state in an attempt to demonstrate an understanding of the situation and the student's perception of it. Alternatively, reactive empathy occurs when the character attempts to motivate the student to enter a more positive state. In this case, the character may not directly mimic the student's own emotional state but will still demonstrate an understanding of the situation and use this as a basis for motivating a more positive emotional state (Davis, 1994). An initial model of agent feedback was developed using machine learning techniques and a corpus of data collected from students interacting with empathetic virtual agents (McQuiggan, Robison, et al., 2008). In this study, subjects were given the opportunity to rate whether each empathetic response was helpful and appropriate in real time. This data was then used to determine the instances in which parallel or reactive empathetic statements should be used.

However, it seemed that perhaps students ranking of the quality of responses might not be indicative of whether the responses were actually useful in improving students' affective experiences. Therefore, transition models were created to determine if parallel and reactive empathetic statements would differentially impact the consequent emotional state of the student, and, if so, how they would be different. The results of this analysis revealed very interesting trends. In general, it appeared that parallel empathetic responses in which the character mimics the same emotional state to the student had a strong tendency to encourage virtuous and vicious cycles. Students feeling positive would remain positive and vice-versa for students experiencing negative states. Alternatively, when subjects received motivating, reactive empathetic statements they tended to reverse affective states. This meant that a student feeling negatively would respond to the motivation and had a higher likelihood to report subsequent positive affective states. However, when a student in a positive state received motivating empathetic feedback, they would react negatively and had a high likelihood of transitioning into a negative state. It is hypothesized that the source of this response lies in an adverse response toward being told to "feel better" when one is already feeling relatively well. Based on these findings, a simplified model of empathetic feedback was developed in which agents would respond with parallel empathy to positive emotional states and reactive empathy to negative states.

While empathetic statements seemed useful for supporting student emotion, they seemed to focus too much on the affective state of the student, perhaps neglecting the important cognitive processes of the student. The emotional states of the students in the learning environment are likely strongly impacted by their ability to understand and maneuver the virtual learning environment, and it may be the case that providing additional cognitive support could alleviate some of the same negative emotions perhaps more effectively than affect-focused empathetic statements. Therefore, a follow-up study examined the use of task-based feedback (in addition to empathetic feedback) that guided students through the learning task and reinforced their past successes. Using a methodology similar to the one in the initial, empathy-only study, models were learned based on of students' ratings of the quality of empathetic and task-based feedback.

Risk and Utility of Affect-Sensitive Behavior

The initial findings of the differential responses of affective feedback indicated the power that the virtual characters had in influencing student affective states. It became clear that it was plausible that in trying to support student emotional experiences it could also risk inducing unintended negative emotions. Just as responding to another individual's emotional states in human–human communication is full of uncertainty, the same uncertainty is magnified in human–agent interactions, which lack access to many of the important cues available to human interlocutors. Quantifying this uncertainty became the next important step in informing affective behavior.

In order to take a first step toward quantifying the expected risk or utility associated with affective feedback we first analyzed the emotional transitions students were likely to experience when presented with varying qualities of emotional feedback (Robison, McQuiggan, & Lester, 2009). This analysis yielded interesting results that confirmed the need for measuring uncertainty and risk. The results indicated that providing affective feedback to students in a positive state was highly risky and should be avoided. While an appropriate response could support positive emotions, inappropriate feedback could cause students to transition into very negative emotional states. Because students are likely to stay positive when left on their own, it is best to avoid intervention. When students are in a highly negative emotion, the converse holds: though an inappropriate response may prolong a negative state, the chance to perhaps improve their state offers such a great benefit that it is worth attempting an intervention, even when the system is unsure of the best type of feedback to give. While these findings are simple, the types of responses given to moderately negative emotions (i.e., *boredom*) require further study. For these states, students are likely to transition to positive states with appropriate feedback, but will transition to more negative states when feedback is inappropriate. In this case, the ability to measure uncertainty in the best type of feedback and weigh this with expected utility values becomes important in developing affect-sensitive virtual characters.

Conclusions and Future Work

The capability to recognize, understand, respond to, and express affect offers significant potential for improving the quality of interaction in interactive learning environments. In interactive learning environments, there is potential to create effective learning experiences through adaptations that account for student emotion and efficacy and can respond effectively through complex socio-constructs such as empathy. By endowing these systems with the ability to detect and properly respond to student affect, we may be able to encourage positive states for both immediate and long-term learning gains.

While current results are promising and provide some insight into how to properly support students' affective experiences and the importance of these efforts, there are many areas that are yet to be explored. For instance, initial work has examined *which* affective states students report while engaging in learning activities. Future work will examine *when* and *why* these states occur. If a student is experiencing frustration, it is likely very important to understand the source of that frustration in order to properly respond to it. The student may be experiencing difficulties with the learning material or the controls of the environment, or she may simply be irritated by characters who are attempting to provide feedback. Understanding the sources of affective states will not only help identify the most appropriate interventions but will also contribute to better designs that will enable negative emotions to be effectively managed.

Another important line of work will be understanding how the affective experiences of students influence learning gains and interactions in the environment. For instance, it is hypothesized that when a student experiences a negative emotion he or she may disengage from the learning aspects of the environment, focusing exclusively on the narrative features. This may or may not hinder overall learning as it may indicate successful emotion regulation or metacognitive behaviors. Understanding emotional impacts on learning will also contribute to the development of an empirically based utility measure of emotion that can be used in conjunction with measures of risk and benefit associated with interactive interventions. In this way, agent behavior can be driven by long-term learning goals rather than just short-term affective goals.

In addition to understanding how emotion impacts learning and student game-play, it will be important to examine how individual traits and beliefs may guide these phenomena. Previous work has already indicated the strong impact that personality traits and learning beliefs can have on emotional experiences of students. Examination of factors such as goal orientation, personality, self-efficacy and beliefs about the nature of learning in conjunction with student affect will help to provide systems that can tailor support to individual student needs and experiences.

Finally, combining the aspects of emotion recognition and expression discussed above into a unified system will provide insight into how affect-sensitive virtual environments might contribute to student learning. To date, each of the systems and findings discussed has been examined in isolation, focusing on one small piece of a large and complex puzzle. The ability to utilize each component of knowledge in an affect-sensitive learning environment offers significant promise for promoting effective learning that is accompanied by positive affective experiences.

Acknowledgments The authors wish to thank the members of the IntelliMedia research lab for their assistance in implementing CRYSTAL ISLAND, Omer Sturlovich and Pavel Turzo for use of their 3D model libraries, Valve Software for access to the Source™ engine and SDK. This research was supported by the National Science Foundation under REC-0632450, DRL-0822200, CNS-0540523, IIS-0812291, DRL-1007962. This material is based upon work supported under a National Science Foundation Graduate Research Fellowship. Any opinions, findings, and conclusions or recommendations expressed in this material are those of the authors and do not necessarily reflect the views of the National Science Foundation.

References

André, E., & Mueller, M. (2003). Learning affective behavior. In J. Jacko & C. Stephanidis (Eds.), *Proceedings of the 10th International Conference on Human-Computer Interaction* (pp. 512–516). Mahwah, NJ: Lawrence Erlbaum.

Arroyo, I., Woolf, B., Royer, J., & Tai, M. (2009). Affective gendered learning companions. In *Proceedings of the 14th International Conference on Artificial Intelligence in Education* (pp. 41–48).

Baker, R., Rodrigo, M., & Xolocotzin, U. (2007). The dynamics of affective transitions in simulation problem-solving environments. In *Proceedings of the 2nd International Conference on Affective Computing and Intelligent Interactions* (pp. 666–677). Lisbon, Portugal.

Beal, C., & Lee, H. (2005). Creating a pedagogical model that uses student self reports of motivation and mood to adapt ITS instruction. *Workshop on Motivation and Affect in Educational Software, in Conjunction with the 125th International Conference on Artificial Intelligence in Education*. Amsterdam, Netherlands.

Burleson, W. (2006). *Affective learning companions: Strategies for empathetic agents with real-time multimodal affective sensing to foster meta-cognitive and meta-affective approaches to learning, motivation, and perseverance*. PhD thesis, Massachusetts Institute of Technology, Cambridge, MA.

Chaffar, S., & Frasson, C. (2004). Using an emotional intelligent agent to improve the learner's performance. *Proceedings of the Workshop on Social and Emotional Intelligence in Learning Environments in conjunction with the International Conference on Intelligent Tutoring Systems*. Maceio, Brazil.

Conati, C. (2002). Probabilistic assessment of user's emotions in educational games. *Applied Artificial Intelligence, 16*, 555–575.

Conati, C., & Mclaren, H. (2005). Data-driven refinement of a probabilistic model of user affect. In L. Andrissono, P. Brna & A. Mitrovic (Eds.), *Proceedings of the 10th International Conference on User Modeling* (pp. 40–49). New York: Springer.

Craig, S. D., Graesser, A. C., Sullins, J., & Gholson, B. (2004). Affect and learning: An exploratory look into the role of affect in learning with AutoTutor. *Journal of Educational Media, 29*(3), 241–250.

D'Mello, S., Jackson, T., Craig, S., Morgan, B., Chipman, P., White, H., et al. (2008). AutoTutor detects and responds to learners affective and cognitive states. In *Proceedings of the Workshop on Emotional and Cognitive issues in ITS in conjunction with the 9th International Conference on Intelligent Tutoring Systems* (pp. 31–43).

D'Mello, S., Taylor, R. S., & Graesser, A. (2007). Monitoring affective trajectories during complex learning. In *Proceedings of the 29th Annual Meeting of the Cognitive Science Society* (pp. 203–208). Austin, TX.

Davis, M. (1994). *Empathy: A social psychological approach*. Madison, WI: Brown and Benchmark Publishers.

de Vicente, A., & Pain, H. (2002). Informing the detection of the students' motivational state: An empirical study. In S. Cerri, G. Gouardères & F. Paraguaçu (Eds.), *Proceedings of the 6th International Conference on Intelligent Tutoring Systems* (pp. 933–943). New York: Springer.

Ekman, P., & Friesen, W. (1978). *The facial action coding system: A technique for the measurement of facial movement*. Palo Alto, CA: Consulting Psychologists Press.

Forbes-Riley, K., Rotaru, M., & Litman, D. (2008). The relative impact of student affect on performance models in a spoken dialogue tutoring system. *User Modeling and User-Adapted Interaction, 18*(1–2), 11–43.

Frijda, N. H. (1986). *The emotions*. New York: Cambridge University Press.

Gilleade, K., & Allanson, J. (2003). A toolkit for exploring affective interface adaptation in videogames. In *Proceedings of Human–Computer Interaction International* (pp. 370–374). Crete, Greece.

Graesser, A. C., Person, N., & Magliano, J. (1995). Collaborative dialog patterns in naturalistic one-on-one tutoring. *Applied Cognitive Psychology, 9*, 359–387.

Healey, J. (2000). *Wearable and automotive systems for affect recognition from physiology*. PhD thesis, Massachusetts Institute of Technology, Cambridge, MA.

Johnson, L., & Rizzo, P. (2004). Politeness in tutoring dialogs: "Run the factory, that's what I'd do." In J. Lester, R. M. Vicari & F. Paraguaçu (Eds.), *Proceedings of the 7th International Conference on Intelligent Tutoring Systems* (pp. 67–76). New York: Springer.

Kort, B., Reilly, R., & Picard, R. (2001). An affective model of interplay between emotions and learning: Reengineering educational pedagogy – building a learning companion. In T. Okamoto, R. Hartley & J. P. Kinsuk (Eds.), *Proceedings of IEEE International Conference on Advanced Learning Technology: Issues, Achievements and Challenges* (pp. 43–48). Madison, WI: IEEE Computer Society.

Linnenbrink, E., & Pintrich, P. (2001). Multiple goals, multiple contexts: The dynamic interplay between personal goals and contextual goal stresses. In S. Volet & S. Jarvela (Eds.), *Motivation in learning contexts: Theoretical advances and methodological implications* (pp. 251–269). New York: Elsevier.

Malone, T., & Lepper, M. (1987). Making learning fun: A taxonomy of intrinsic motivations for learning. In R. Snow & M. Farr (Eds.), *Aptitude, learning, and instruction: Cognitive and affective process analyses* (Vol. 3, pp. 223–253). Hillsdale, NJ: Erlbaum.

Marsella, S., & Gratch, J. (2009). EMA: A model of emotional dynamics. *Journal of Cognitive Systems Research, 10*(1), 70–90.

McQuiggan, S., Lee, S., & Lester, J. (2007). Early prediction of student frustration. In A. Paiva, R. Prada & R. W. Picard (Eds.), *Proceedings of the 2nd International Conference on Affective Computing and Intelligent Interaction* (pp. 698–709). Lisbon, Portugal: Springer.

McQuiggan, S., & Lester, J. (2007). Modeling and evaluating empathy in embodied companion agents. *International Journal of Human Computer Studies, 65*(4), 348–360.

McQuiggan, S., Mott, B., & Lester, J. (2008). Modeling self-efficacy in intelligent tutoring systems: An inductive approach. *User Modeling and User-Adapted Interaction, 18*(1–2), 81–123.

McQuiggan, S., Robison, J., & Lester, J. (2010). Affective transitions in narrative-centered learning environments. *Educational Technology & Society, 13*(1), 40–53.

McQuiggan, S., Robison, J., Phillips, R., & Lester, J. (2008). Modeling parallel and reactive empathy in virtual agents: An inductive approach. In L. Padgham, D. Parkes, J. Müller & S. Parsons (Eds.), Proceedings of the 7th International Joint Conference on Autonomous Agents and Multi-Agent Systems (pp. 167–174). Estoril, Portugal: International Foundation for Autonomous Agents and Multiagent Systems.

Mekeig, S., & Inlow, M. (1993). Lapses in alertness: Coherence of fluctuations in performance and EEG spectrum. *Electroencephalography and Clinical Neurophysiology, 86*, 23–25.

Meyer, D., & Turner, J. (2007). Scaffolding emotions in classrooms. In P. Schutz & R. Pekrun (Eds.), *Emotion in education* (pp. 243–258). New York: Elsevier.

Paiva, A., Dias, J., Sobral, D., Aylett, R., Woods, S., Hall, L., et al. (2005). Learning by feeling: Evoking empathy with synthetic characters. *Applied Artificial Intelligence, 19*, 235–266.

Pekrun, R. (1992). The impact of emotions on learning and achievement: Toward a theory of cognitive/motivational mediators. *Applied Psychology: An International Review, 41*(4), 359–376.

Picard, R. (1997). *Affective computing.* Boston: MIT.

Picard, R., Papert, S., Bender, W., Blumberg, B., Breazeal, C., Cavallo, D., et al. (2004). Affective learning – a manifesto. *BT Technology Journal, 22*(4), 153–189.

Pope, A., Bogart, E., & Bartolome, D. (1995). Biocybernetic system evaluates indices of operator engagement in automated yask. *Biological Psychology, 40*, 187–195.

Prendinger, H., & Ishizuka, M. (2005). The empathic companion: A character-based interface that addresses users' affective states. *Applied Artificial Intelligence, 19*, 267–285.

Prendinger, H., Mayer, S., Mori, J., & Ishizuka, M. (2003). Persona effect revisited: Using biosignals to measure and reflect the impact of character-based interfaces. In T. Rist, R. Aylett, D. Ballin & J. Rickel (Eds.), Proceedings of the 4th International Working Conference on Intelligent Virtual Agents (Kloster Irsee, Germany, September 15–17) (pp. 283–291). New York: Springer.

Robison, J., McQuiggan, S., & Lester, J. (2009). Evaluating the consequences of affective feedback in intelligent tutoring systems. In *Proceedings of the International Conference on Affective Computing & Intelligent Interaction* (pp. 37–42). Amsterdam, The Netherlands.

Rodrigo, M. T., & Baker, R. (2011). Comparing the incidence and persistence of learners' affect during interactions with different educational software packages. In R. Calvo & S. D'Mello (Eds.), *Explorations in the learning sciences, instructional systems and performance technologies.* New York: Springer.

Shute, V. J. (2008). Focus on formative feedback. *Review of Educational Research, 78*(1), 153–189.

Smith, C., & Lazarus, R. (1990). Emotion and adaptation. In L. A. Pervin (Ed.), *Handbook of personality: Theory and research* (pp. 609–637). New York: Guildford.

Advancing a Multimodal Real-Time Affective Sensing Research Platform

Winslow Burleson

Introduction

Expert human tutors focus approximately half of their interactions on the affective and motivational engagement of their students (Lepper, Woolverton, Mumme, & Gurtner, 1993). In stark contrast, the vast majority of Intelligent Tutoring Systems (ITS) pay little or no attention to students' emotional experiences. To redress this, the Affective Agent Research Platform has been advanced, demonstrating the ability to sense elements of student frustration and respond in real time with affective support. While the work has been advanced within the context of a challenging educational activity, the architecture and lessons from its implementation are broadly applicable and readily deployable within a wide range of settings, e.g., workplace, automotive, assistive care, etc.

A new platform for affective agent research has been developed. The platform has a modular architecture that is facilitated by a centralized system server. The platform integrates an array of multimodal affective sensors that send information to the Data Logger. A real-time Behavior Engine and Character Engine are used to present a 3-D scriptable expressive humanoid agent within a graphical virtual environment. The platform also uses classifier algorithms to detect elements of user's affective experience. The research platform and architecture focus on the sensing and analysis of signals related to affect, and on the ability to interpret and respond to these, in real time, with an expressive scriptable agent. The Behavior Engine and Character Engine include dynamically scripted character attributes at multiple levels. This approach is particularly suited to affective expression. This platform can be used to explore several affective findings in the social, behavioral, and learning sciences.

W. Burleson (✉)
School of Computing, Informatics, and Decision System Engineering,
Arizona State University, Tempe, AZ, USA
e-mail: winslow.burleson@asu.edu

R.A. Calvo and S.K. D'Mello (eds.), *New Perspectives on Affect and Learning Technologies*, 97
Explorations in the Learning Sciences, Instructional Systems and Performance Technologies 3,
DOI 10.1007/978-1-4419-9625-1_8, © Springer Science+Business Media, LLC 2011

The user sits in front of a wide screen plasma display. On the display appears an agent and 3-D environment. The user can interact with the agent and can attend to and manipulate objects and tasks in the environment. In the studies reported here the Towers of Hanoi puzzle was used with seven disks. The chair that the user sits in is instrumented with a high-density pressure sensor array and the mouse detects applied pressure throughout its usage. The user also wears a wireless skin conductance sensor on a wristband with two adhesive electrode patches on his or her hand and forearm. Three cameras in the system, a video camera for offline coding, and the blue eyes camera, record and sense additional elements of human behavior.

This multimodal approach to recognizing affect uses more than one channel to sense a broad spectrum of information. This approach applies techniques from psychophysiology, emotion communication, signal processing, pattern recognition, and machine learning, to make a classification from this data. Since any given sensor will have various problems with noise and reliability, and will contain only limited information about affect, the use of multiple sensors should also improve robustness and accuracy of classification.

This paper will present the affective agent research platform and findings from investigations employing it by describing the system architecture, sensing system, behavior modules, and research findings.

System Development

System Architecture

The system has several modules: a System Server, Sensors, Data Logger, Behavior Engine, Character Engine, and Classifier (Fig. 1). Each sensor sends its signal via UDP packets through a socket to the Data Logger. The Behavior Engine uses algorithms

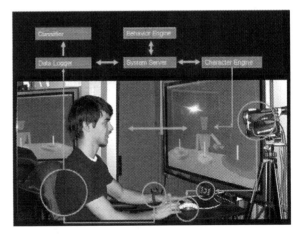

Fig. 1 System architecture and sensors listed *right* to *left*: video camera, blue eyes camera, pressure mouse, skin conductance sensor, and posture chair

and thresholds to decide when and how to direct the character's actions, which are then performed by the Character Engine. The Character Engine controls the character actions, elements in an OpenGL virtual environment (disks and slideshow display). Because the character and its environment are operated as a single component, this virtual environment also enables the Character Engine to monitor the user's mouse clicks and disk movements. All information that is received by the System Server is time stamped and logged in a text file for analysis. The system comprises several machines and languages which exhibit differing data rates, and benefit from many contributors. Each module is connected with UDP or TCP sockets. The system architecture is modular allowing additional modules to be added in a similar manner.

Sensors

The multimodal sensor system consists of a Pressure Mouse, a Wireless BlueTooth skin conductance sensor (Strauss et al., 2005), a Posture Analysis Seat, a Facial Action Unit analysis using the Blue Eyes camera system, and Head Tracking. This system expands upon the earlier work (Kapoor, Mota, & Picard, 2001), that used only facial and postural information. Through the combination of all these modalities, the agent system is provided with a better understanding of the affect and interactions of the user and is also able to determine the contribution of each of the sensors to the modeling of affect (Cooper et al., 2011; Kapoor, Burleson, & Picard, 2007; Kapoor, Picard, & Ivanov, 2004).

Game State

While game state (in this case of the Towers of Hanoi disks) is not a traditional sensor, it is used by the system as a source of data and is treated as a sensor channel in a manner similar to each of the other sensors. The system records the disk state after each move, checks if it is legal or illegal, increments the move count, calculates the optimal number of moves to the end of the game (Rueda, 2004), and evaluates progress in terms of number and significance of regressions. This data can also be used to explore users' engagement and intent: understanding of the game, proceeding in a focused way, or becoming disengaged.

Pressure Mouse

The Pressure Mouse has eight force-sensitive-resisters that capture the amount of pressure that is put on the mouse throughout the activity (Reynolds, 1999). Users who have been administered a frustration-inducing online application form have been shown to produce increasing amounts of pressure related to their level of frustration (Dennerlein, Becker, & Picard, 2003).

Wireless BlueTooth Skin Conductance

In collaboration with Gary McDarby, at Media Lab Europe, Carson Reynolds and Marc Strauss, at the MIT Media Lab, developed a wireless version of an earlier "glove" that senses skin conductance. While the skin conductance signal does not explain anything about valence – how positive or negative the affective state is – it does tend to be correlated with arousal or how activated the person is. High levels of arousal tend to accompany significant and attention-getting events (Boucsein, 1992).

Posture Analysis Seat

The Posture Analysis Seat utilizes the TekScan sensor pad system developed for medical and automotive applications (Tekscan, 1997). The system uses pattern recognition techniques while watching natural behaviors to "learn" what behaviors tend to accompany states such as interest and boredom (Mota & Picard, 2003). The system thus detects the surface-level behaviors (postures) and their mappings during a learning situation in an unobtrusive manner so as not to interfere with the natural learning process. Through the chair, significant detection of nine static postures and four temporal patterns associated with levels of learner interest has been demonstrated.

Blue Eyes Camera System

Kapoor and Picard (Kapoor & Picard, 2003) have been developing automatic tools for computer vision and machine learning that are capable of detecting facial movements and head gestures used as conversational cues and communications of emotion. The system currently detects some upper facial features such as eyes and eyebrows, as well as their motion and action: eyes squinting or widening, eyebrows being raised, and head nods and shakes. These techniques are being extended to include lower facial features like cheeks and the mouth, which express smiles, fidgets, and tension. The data logging includes full frame synchronized capture of the Blue Eyes (Haro, Essa, & Flickner, 2000) camera images at 20 Hz, giving the opportunity to code for additional facial action units as they are identified.

Head Tracking

The Head Tracking System (Morency, Rahimi, & Darrell, 2003; Morency, Sundberg, & Darrell, 2003) is built upon the Small Vision System developed by SRI International and the MEGA-DCS stereo camera (Videre Design, 2010). This system also incorporates a real-time head nod and head shake algorithm (Kapoor et al., 2001) and provides information on the intersection of the user's gaze and the screen plane. This plane can be shifted to various reference depths within the environment to ascertain the virtual object that a user is directing their head toward. This type of sensing helps to facilitate shared attention behaviors.

This simulation used a wide plasma screen that provides greater spatial resolution between objects. This caused users to move their head to a greater extent than they would on a smaller screen and to attend to different objects and points of interest. This facilitates the use of the head tracker.

The head tracker employed proved to be unreliable. After less than 10 min of interaction it would fail to reacquire the position of the users head. Therefore, it was not used in the studies reported here.

Video Capture

The video camera recorded the user and the onscreen activity. It was positioned so as to acquire both an image of the user and an image of the screen that is reflected in a mirror positioned behind the users head. This setup was chosen so as not to miss any of the features of the user/character interaction and provide true (same image) synchronization. When the system is initialized, a datagram signal is sent to start the DirectX video capture and the time is noted in the log.

Behavior Engine and Character Engine

A 3-D virtual environment is presented on a wide screen plasma display. This OpenGL Virtual Environment can display a character, virtual disks, selectable text and buttons, and images for a slide show presentation. The system can also play audio files. While direct user driven interaction with the environment occurs only through the pressure mouse, this information along with each sensor's information is used by the Behavior Engine to determine the behavior of the character and virtual environment (e.g., resetting the disks if the user makes an illegal move). While the Behavior Engine determines the behavior, the animation of the character is managed by the Character Engine through the use of Character Behavior Scripts which contain two types of events, scripted events and serendipitous events. Scripted events are sequences of text that explicitly tell the character what actions to undertake. They are predetermined events which can be called upon by the system to elicit specific interactions. For example, in Table 1 the script on the left instructs the character to move its mouth for several seconds with a broad smile. Longer sequences can be scripted to expand the behavioral repertoire to include the introduction of the character to the user, a slide show presentation, and the delivery of precisely controlled *affect support* or *task interventions* (e.g., supportive comments when classification made from sensor data indicates they might be beneficial to users). Examples of *affective support* and *task support* dialogues appear later in this chapter. In contrast to the predetermined scripted events, serendipitous events are real-time interactions driven by sensors and algorithms. In Table 1, the script on the right instructs

Table 1 Character behavior scripts that present the two types of events that are supported by the character engine, scripted events and serendipitous events, e.g., based on the value of behavior_smile_value

Scripted events	Serendipitous events
Sequence talk	Sequence talk_variable_smile
smile. 8	**smile. 8**
mouth .3	mouth .3
wait .4	wait .4
then	then
mouth .4	mouth .4
wait .2	wait .2
then	then
mouth .5	mouth .5
wait .4	wait .4
then	then
mouth .3	mouth .3
wait .6	wait .6
then	then
mouth .2	**smile behavior_smile_value**
wait .7	mouth .2
	wait .7
then	then
mouth .4	mouth .4
wait .2	wait .2
then	then
mouth .3	mouth .3
wait .1	wait .1
then	then
mouth .5	mouth .5
wait .1	wait .1
then	then

the character to move its mouth for several seconds. Initially, the character displays a broad smile (smile .8).

Midway through this script the smile value is updated. The value in the "behavior_smile_value" enables the character to tailor its smile expression to respond to the user. If the user is not smiling, then the character uses the new "behavior_smile_value" and stops smiling, half way through the script. For example, if the Blue Eyes camera detects a user's smile at 80% confidence this information is transmitted to the Data Logger. The Behavior Engine will then aggregate 2 s of Blue Eyes data from the Data Logger and determine, according to its algorithms, whether it should or should not tell the character to smile at this time. A running average of the previous 2 s of data is calculated for each sensor mapped channel. If the average value crosses either of the preset thresholds for that channel then behavior changes are invoked in the character. These behavioral changes are implemented with a 4-s delay. Such a delay is long enough so that the character's mirroring behavior is not consciously detected by users, yet short enough for the mirroring to have a social effect (Bailenson, 2005). It is also a means of creating a limited form of empathy (mirroring emotional expression). The Behavior Engine sends the appropriate value of the "behavior_smile_value" variable to the Character Engine. This value is then used whenever the variable is encountered in a Character Behavior Script. This enables a real-time serendipitous interaction that responds to the users' detected expressions. This strategy can also be used in a loop to update the "behavior_smile_value," to respond serendipitously to the user, continuously.

The "Serendipitous Events" column of Table 1 demonstrates that the scripting language includes variables that monitor the state of the virtual world, such as the "behavior_smile_value." This is one type of layering between prescripted behaviors and serendipitous events that can occur. Another type of layering occurs when the Character Behavior Scripts run multiple sequences in parallel. The "introduction script" can call "sequence talk" to elicit mouth movements. Calling "sequence talk" will interleave the mouth movements with the actions already called for by the "introduction script." Calling "sequence_talk_variable_smile" instead of "sequence talk" would combine these two layering methods. Since the scripts can call actions and sequences based on traditional control structures, such as "if" conditionals and "while" loops, the scripts are quite flexible. In this way, the system can be developed with a rich combination of prescripted and serendipitous behaviors.

By separating serendipitous events from scripted events this control-architecture allows the character behavior to combine information from the behavior repertoire with real-time affective information and run them in parallel. When the character delivers an intervention it can use the affective information from a serendipitous event to customize the delivery in real time. This ability to layer behavior allows the character to adapt its expressivity to the users and enables it to repeat the same scripted events with differing affects.

Character's Expression of Emotion

The emotional expression of the character is very rich. The Character Engine contains internal scalar variables or "knobs" that can be modified over time by the script. These knobs include posture (stooped vs. erect), knees more bent or unbent, rate of eye blink, face coloration, sidling (side-stepping), energy level (snappy, quick movement vs. slow movement), involvement (body follows gaze direction more or less), and jitteriness (for creating more or less nervous appearance). Face affect knobs constitute an integrated subsystem. (Perlin, 1997). These include head turn, nod and tilt, eyebrows up/down, eye gaze direction, eyes open/closed, eyelid centers, up/down, mouth open/closed, mouth corners up/down, mouth narrow/wide, sneering. Each of these controls can either have the same value for the left and right sides of the face, or can be given left/right asymmetric values. The latter case is used for such gestures as winking and one-sided sneering or smiling (see Fig. 2).

Fig. 2 The agent is capable of a rich continuum of diverse expressions

Rather than providing only a high-level emotional API, this system provides lower-level physical affect knobs, which the scriptwriter can combine to create the appearance of higher-level or more subtle emotional affects. In particular, by providing lower-level controls, such as mouth corners raised, rather than "smile," this enables script writers to create the appearance of a very rich set of emotional states.

Other knobs that control physical appearance are also being used for this project. The system allows the programmer to control, at run-time, physical attributes such as height, girth, knee angle, leaning forward and backward, and swaying speed and magnitude. In order to maximize the empathic effect of mirroring, a subset of these are being used to roughly match the individual user's physical characteristics (such as elements of posture, agitation, arousal, and facial expression) in real time. These capabilities can prove to be useful in other contexts, as well.

Crafting Character Expression

The architecture of scripted events, serendipitous events, and control knobs for affective expression is used for nonverbal communication. The goal for these interactions is to develop an empathetic relationship between the character and the user where the character "mirrors" the frustration and engagement of the user. Features of the user's emotional state are inferred by the Behavior Engine, and the Character Engine is instructed to direct the character to visually mirror aspects of the user's state. In this way, a virtual actor can appear to mirror users' emotional state without the virtual actor itself needing to have an extensive internal emotional model; the emotional state model is the built in the Classifier algorithms. Also, the "mirroring" can be conducted with variation that looks natural, so that it does not appear to be an exact duplication of what the user does.

Table 2 Mapping of sensors to character behavior

Sensor	Character behavior
Pressure mouse	Magnitude of character swaying motion
Skin conductance	Pigmentation of the skin tone (pale to flush)
Posture analysis seat	Leaning forward and leaning back
Blue eyes camera system	Smile, fidget, head movement, and head tilt

The mapping between the sensors and the character behaviors are shown in Table 2. The pressure exerted on the pressure mouse drives the apparent agitation of the character, which "sways" more at times of elevated pressure. The skin conductance sensor is mapped to changes in the color of the character; it becomes redder at times of greater arousal. The posture of the character, in terms of the interpersonal distance with the user, is controlled by the posture chair sensor and the associated Behavior Engine algorithms. The character's facial expressions and head movements are informed by data from the Blue Eyes camera system.

Developing the Nonverbal Mirroring Conditions

The data collected by the Data Logger from pilot study participants was used to develop two experimental conditions for nonverbal mirroring, *sensor-driven nonverbal mirroring* and *prerecorded nonverbal interaction*. Data from pilot studies was processed to decompose each of the prerecorded sensor channels into several features and to calculate from the feature values the averages for short time chunks for the duration of each participant's experience. Statistically typical data files were selected to drive the character's behavior during the *prerecorded nonverbal interaction* condition.

The *prerecorded nonverbal interactions* were used by the System Server to provide prerecorded data to the Behavior Engine. To determine which files to make available to the System Server, the mean values and the standard deviations of each of the behavior-mapped data channels and features (pressure, skin conductance, leaning forward or back, smile, fidget, and head tilt) for each participant were analyzed. Each participant's files were given a rank based on their proximity to the mean values relative to the other files, for each channel and feature. The ranks were summed and the files with the lowest overall ranking (e.g., the ones closet to the mean) were investigated as candidates for driving the *prerecorded nonverbal interaction* condition. There were five files that had lower overall rankings than the others; these files also had no outlier rankings. These five files were then provided to the System Server, Behavior Engine and onward to the Character Engine and the resulting character behaviors were observed to determine the suitability of the interactions that they produced. The interactions were deemed suitable for all five files by two separate observers. Noting that Bailenson used multiple prerecorded files in his experiments (Bailenson, 2005) so as not to bias the interactions in the prerecorded condition by the anomalies of any single prerecorded file, the five suitable files were all made available to the System Server. One file, selected at random, was used per participant in the *prerecorded nonverbal interaction* condition.

The *sensor-driven nonverbal mirroring* employs the sensor mapping described above in Table 2. If data for a channel was not available for a period greater than 3 s (e.g., when a participants pupils are not detected or if the skin conductance electrode as become detached) then in order to continue to display reasonable character behavior the individual channel would receive *prerecorded nonverbal interactions* from the randomly selected prerecorded file that was assigned to each participant at the start of the activity, until real-time data for that channel was available again.

Character Dialogue

In addition to nonverbal interactions the character interacts with the user through an asynchronous voice dialogue (Burleson, Picard, & Perlin, 2004). The character speaks using Microsoft's "Eddie" voice scripted with Text-Aloud, a text-to-speech application. When there are questions the words are presented in a text bubble, as well, for the user to read. Users may respond by clicking on the available text responses. In the experiment and the pilot studies, this asynchronous dialogue is used during the introduction, when the character presents the Towers of Hanoi activity and again during the intervention when the character provides tutorial support to participants. The character engine also supports the ability for the character to present a slide show; this feature is used to enable the character to present a persuasive message based on Dweck's treatments which have been shown to improve learners' self theories of intelligence and goal mastery orientation (Dweck, 1999).

Dialogue Sequence for the Affective Support
and the Task Support Interventions

The following sequences present the tutorial support dialogue that the character provides as an intervention to participants in the experiment. It should be noted that while there are many elements of emotional intelligence, and many interesting methods for providing and studying affective support and task support there are practical limitations such as sample size and the time, effort, and expense, involved in running large numbers of participants that limit the number of conditions that can be studied. The interventions described in this chapter are informed by Klein and Bickmore's work on empathetic interventions (Bickmore & Picard, 2004; Klein, Moon, & Picard, 2002) and by Dweck's work on teaching metacognitive strategies that relate to meta-affective skill (Dweck, 1999; Dweck, 2004). Due to these multiple interests and due to the limitations mentioned above, the *affective support* intervention in the studies reported here has been designed to combine both empathetic interactions (with respect to the learners' levels of frustration) and reinforcement of meta-affective skills. This *affective support* intervention is juxtaposed by a *task support* intervention that is neither empathetic nor supportive of meta-affective skill. These two interventions were developed as stark contrasts (see Table 3).

Table 3 Highlighted cells were used in studies reported here

	Empathetic (with respect to frustration)	Not empathetic (with respect to frustration)
Meta-affective skill support	The *affective support* used in this study includes Empathy and meta-affective skill support	Not empathetic, meta-affective skill
Other interventions (task, traditional metacognition, break taking, play, etc.)	Empathetic, other intervention (task, metacognitive, etc.)	The *task support* used in this study is not Empathetic and does not support meta-affective skills

Affective support includes empathy and meta-affective skill support while *task support excludes* both of these elements of emotional intelligence. Other cells of the table represent other types and combinations of intervention strategies, which are interesting areas for further research

Dialogue for Affective Support

The dialogue in the *affective support* sequence was adaptive to participants' responses, so only excerpts are presented here.

> I'm sorry I don't know more about this activity so I could help you through it. I do know that many people find it frustrating. On a scale from 1 to 7, how frustrated are you feeling right now?'
>
> 1. This is one of the most frustrating times I have ever felt while using a computer; 2., 3…. .7. Absolutely not frustrated at all.

An adaptive response is given. For example, if the participant selects number 1 the following response is provided.

> It sounds like you are extremely frustrated with this activity. Is that about right?" Yes/No

If the answer from the participant is "No" then the following "repair" is stated:

> Sorry about that, to clarify, how frustrated are you?
>
> 1. This is one of the most frustrating times I have ever felt while using a computer; 2. 3… 7. Absolutely not frustrated at all.

The dialogue then continues with:

> Wow, that must be really tough. I am really sorry doing this activity is making you feel that way.
>
> How much effort do you feel you have been putting into this activity?"
>
> 1. Absolutely no effort at all; 2., 3…7. An enormous amount of effort.

Another adaptive response is given, based on frustration and effort responses, for example if seven was selected as the effort response the dialogue then continues with:

> It is probably really aggravating to have to stick with this activity when you are already putting in a lot of effort and finding it so frustrating. Please remember that it is ok to be frustrated. It is great that you are aware of how you feel. Remember, frustration sometimes tells you to try things differently. It is like a navigation sign that says, "slow down as you

might want to change direction." Take a breath and be determined to keep thinking of different ways to solve the problem. You are creative and there are always many things you can try. Maybe one of them will work!

Remember, the mind is like a muscle that when exercised may not feel good, but it is getting stronger through exercise. If you stick with it and keep trying hard, you WILL get better and smarter.

Do you think that you will be able to try these strategies?

1. Yes, I think I can; 2., 3., …, 7 No, I do not think I can

Another adaptive response is provided. For example, if seven is selected the response is as follows:

It can be hard, but remember that's a sign that you are learning, stick with it and you will learn a lot.

I have to go now. Thank you for letting me watch you do this activity.

Watching you has helped me learn too. Sorry that I have to leave now.

How do you feel about continuing the activity?

1. I am very willing to stick with it; 2., 3., …., 7. I am not at all willing to stick with it.

One of the following two responses is provided based on the participant's answer:

Great, good luck! Please try as hard as you can. If you feel like you would like to stop there are a few buttons in the upper right hand corner that you can press.

I'm sorry that I have to ask you to continue anyway. Please just try as hard as you can. If you feel like you would like to stop there are a few buttons in the upper right hand corner that you can press.

Bye bye.

Participants are then presented with a choice of goodbye responses which they can select.

"Ok, bye I was glad to have you here"; "Ok, bye"; or, "Ok glad you are finally going"

Dialogue for Task Support

The dialogue in the *task support* sequence does not adapt to the participant responses, so it is presented in its entirety in this section.

1. I'm sorry I don't know more about this activity so I could help you through it. I do know that many people find it frustrating. On a scale from 1 to 7, how frustrated are you feeling right now?
2. How much effort do you feel you have been putting into this activity? (1–7 scale)
3. Ok, well, here are some tips others have told me they think about while doing the activity. You can think about where you want the big disk to go and then try to move all of the other disks out of the way. These disks can go to another pole so that you can move the big disk to where you want it. Remember that if you get all of the disks that are in the way out of the way then you can move the disk that you want to move. Another way to think about this

is to think about the small disks that are in the way. If you move these out of the way then you can move the disk that you want to move. Some people try to do this in as few moves as possible. Do you think that you will be able to try these strategies (1–7 scale)?

4. Well, just give it your best. I have to go now. Thank you for letting me watch you do this activity. Watching you has helped me learn too. Sorry that I have to leave now.

5. How do you feel about continuing the activity? (scale of 1–7. 1= willing to continue, 7 not willing.

6. Well try as hard as you can. If you feel that you need to stop there will be a few buttons in the upper right hand corner that you can press.

7. Bye, bye

Participants are then presented with a choice of goodbye responses which they can select ("Ok, bye I was glad to have you here", "Ok, bye", "Ok glad you are finally going").

Testing the System

The system was tested in a series of pilot studies. Initial data collection showed that there were gaps in the frequency that data from each channel was collected. Reducing the number of sensors used improved the collection rate so it was determined that the Data Logger was getting overloaded, and it was upgraded.

Once the Data Logger was functioning properly further pilot studies collected additional data from participants. Figure 3 shows the data collected from a single pilot participant in each of the various sensor channels. The data from these participants was then used to inform the design of the character's nonverbal mirroring

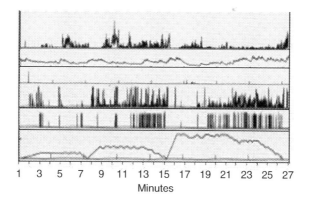

Fig. 3 Normalized graphs of data showing: (1) pressure mouse data proportional to the force applied on the mouse surface; (2) wireless BlueTooth skin conductance in microSiemens; (3) posture analysis seat with nine discrete posture states (this participant did not change their posture very much); (4) blue eyes camera classification in % confidence of a smile; (5) blue eyes camera classification in % confidence of a fidget; and (6) game state representing the least number of moves, for an optimal solution from the current configuration of the disks

behavior, described above, and to train the classifier algorithms, discussed in the next section.

Affective Classifier

The simplest "affective classifier" for an empathetic agent is to recognize user movements and use these to move a character. This simple classifier enables the character to engage in mirroring or mimicking, such as leaning toward the user, smiling, nodding, and so forth. This can be recognized with the current pattern recognition tools that have been developed for each of the sensors (Kapoor & Picard, 2005) and is currently implemented in the decisions and directions of the Behavior Engine.

A more advanced affective classifier has also been developed discerning elements of the user's affective states, such as "Stuck." By coupling data from all of the different sensor channels, this classifier achieves an improvement over any one channel (Kapoor et al., 2007, 2004). The current classifier can detect if an individual is likely to choose to keep engaging in a task, or whether the learner is frustrated or likely to benefit from outside help (quitting) with 79% accuracy (chance = 58%) (Kapoor et al., 2007). While most of the learning conducted by the classifier is done offline, in parallel with algorithm development, this system can also detect some kinds of users' affective states in real-time. This real-time ability was not necessary in the study reported here since it was desirable to keep agent responses constant despite user differences. Therefore, this more advanced classifier has not been used in the experimental methodology. Analysis of the user data was conducted offline, after the experiment, to determine the emotional state of the users at various times throughout their experience with the activity.

The analysis occurs in several steps. Labeling of the data comes from four sources: in situ self-labeling by the user's clicking on the quit button, self-report from the user surveys, the sensor feature data algorithms, and from human coding of the video data. The raw sensor data is processed for features, such as "startle events" in skin conductance, high pressure exerted on the pressure mouse, the ratio of leaning forward to leaning backward, and the confidence of detection of specific features (smiles and mouth fidgets) by the Blue Eyes facial expression camera. This information is chunked into 3 second time periods and averaged for each feature within those periods. A joint analysis, of all of the sensors, for the series of 3 second time sequences is conducted using unsupervised and semi-supervised clustering procedures: training with Hidden Markov Models, State Vector Machines, and Dynamic Bayesian Networks. The process that has been most promising is the use of the five most significant features for 150×3 second timeframes. These five features include the: mean skin conductance, mean seat activity ratio of forward posture to backward posture seat forward/back ratio, mean confidence level of mouth fidget, and mean head tilt. Training on these and classifying with the "leave one out" method, yields 79% accuracy for an SVM with RBF kernel learning the parameters. (Kapoor et al., 2007).

Summary of the Affective Agent Research Platform

The Affective Agent Research Platform has been synthesized and iteratively tested. It is composed of several sensors that are relevant to the detection of affective states. It has a modular architecture with a System Server core that is flexible to facilitate additional modular improvements to the system capabilities. It has a character that exhibits behaviors that are broadly expressive and interactive through scripted behavioral repertoire and serendipitous events that use sensor events mapped to character behavior to provide *sensor-driven nonverbal mirroring*. Through pilot studies the system has been refined and an offline Classifier capability has been developed that can detecting participant's likelihood of quitting with an accuracy of 79%.

References

Bailenson, J. N. (2005). Personal conversation. W. Burleson.

Bickmore, T., & Picard, R. W. (2004). Establishing and maintaining long-term human-computer relationships. *Transactions on Computer-Human Interaction, 12*(2), 293–327.

Boucsein, W. (1992). *Electrodermal activity*. New York: Plenum Press.

Dennerlein, J., Becker, T., Johnson, P., Reynolds, C., & Picard, R. W. (2003). Frustrating computer users increases exposure to physical factors. *Proceedings of the international ergonomics association*, August 24–29, Seoul, Korea Here is the pdf: http://affect.media.mit.edu/pdfs/03. dennerlein-etal.pdf.

Burleson, W., Picard, R. W., & Perlin, K. (2004). A Platform for affective agent research. *International conference on autonomous agents and multiagent systems*. New York: Columbia University.

Cooper, D. G., Arroyo, I., & Woolf, B. P. (2011). Actionable affective processing for automatic tutor interventions. In R. Calvo & S. D'Mello (Eds.), *Explorations in the learning sciences, instructional systems and performance technologies*. New York: Springer.

Dweck, C. S. (1999). *Self-theories: Their role in motivation, personality and development*. Philadelphia: Psychology Press.

Dweck, C. S. (2004). Personal Conversation.

Haro, A., Essa, I., & Flickner, M. (2000). Detecting and tracking eyes by using their physiological properties, Dynamics and Appearance. *In Proceedings of IEEE Computer Vision and Pattern Recognition* 2000 Conference, Hilton Head, SC, June 2000. [PS.Z <http://www.cc.gatech.edu/ cpl/projects/pupil/pupil.ps.Z> | PDF <http://www.cc.gatech.edu/cpl/projects/pupil/pupil.pdf>]. Also available as Georgia Tech, GVU Center Tech Report No. GIT-GVU-TR-99-46.

Kapoor, A., Burleson, W., & Picard, R. (2007). Automatic prediction of frustration. *International Journal of Human Computer Studies, 65*(8), 724–736.

Kapoor, A., Mota, S., & Picard, R. (2001). *Towards a learning companion that recognizes affect. AAAI Fall Symposium*. North Falmouth.

Kapoor, A., Picard, R. W., & Ivanov, Y. (2004). Probabilistic Combination of Multiple Modalities to Detect Interest. *International Conference on Pattern Recognition*. Cambridge.

Kapoor, A., & Picard, R.W. (2005). Multimodal affect recognition in learning environments. ACM MM'05, November 6-11, Singapore. PDF <http://web.media.mit.edu/~ash/papers/ACM2005. pdf>.

Kapoor, A., Qi, Y., & Picard, R. W. (2003). Fully automatic upper facial action recognition. IEEE International workshop on analysis and modeling of faces and gestures (AMFG 2003) held in conjunction with ICCV 2003, October 2003, Nice, France. TR 571 <http://vismod.media.mit. edu/pub/tech-reports/TR-571-ABSTRACT.html>.

Klein, J., Moon, Y., & Picard, W. (2002). This computer responds to user frustration: Theory, design, results, and implications. *Interacting with Computers, 14*, 119–140.

Lepper, M. R., Woolverton, M., Mumme, D. L., & Gurtner, J. L. (1993). Motivational techniques of expert human tutors: Lessons for the design of computer-based tutors. *Computers as cognitive tools, S. P. Lajoie and S. J. Derry* (pp. 75–105). Hillsdale: Erlbaum.

Morency, L. P., Rahimi, A., & Darrell, T. (2003). *Adaptive view-based appearance model CVPR 2003*. Wisconsin.

Morency, L. P., Sundberg, P., & Darrell, T. (2003). Pose Estimation using 3D View-Based Eigenspaces. *ICCV Workshop on Analysis and Modeling of Face and Gesture*. Nice.

Mota, S., & Picard, R. W. (2003). Automated posture analysis for detecting learner's interest level. In: *Workshop on Computer Vision and Pattern Recognition for Human-Computer Interaction*, June 2003.

Perlin, K. (1997). Layered compositing of facial expression. *ACM SIGGRAPH 97*. New York.

Reynolds, C. (1999). *The sensing and measurement of frustration with computers*. Masters: Massachusetts Institute of Technology.

Rueda, C. (2004). Personal Conversation.

Strauss, M., Reynolds, C., Hughes, S., Park, K., McDarby, G., & Picard, R. (2005). The HandWave Bluetooth Skin Conductance Sensor. *1st International Conference on Affective Computing and Intelligent Interaction*. Beijing.

Tekscan. (1997). *Tekscan body pressure measurement system user's manual*. Tekscan Inc: South Boston.

Videre Design. (2010). http://www.videredesign.com/. MEGA-DCS Stereo Camera website SVS version 3.2 (2004).

A Motivationally Supportive Affect-Sensitive AutoTutor

Sidney K. D'Mello, Blair Lehman, and Art Graesser

Introduction

This chapter describes a fully automated affect-sensitive Intelligent Tutoring System (ITS) called the Affective AutoTutor (also called the Supportive AutoTutor). AutoTutor is an ITS that helps students learn topics in Newtonian physics, computer literacy, and critical thinking via natural language dialogues that simulate the dialogue patterns observed in human–human tutoring (Graesser, Chipman, Haynes, & Olney, 2005; Graesser et al., 2004; Storey, Kopp, Wiemer, Chipman, & Graesser, in press). The AutoTutor system uses state-of-the-art natural language understanding mechanisms to model student cognitive states and plan its dialogue moves in a manner that is sensitive to these states. The Affective AutoTutor takes the level of intelligence and interactivity even further by using emerging technologies from the field of Affective Computing (Calvo & D'Mello, 2010; McNeese, 2003; Paiva, Prada, & Picard, 2007; Picard, 1997) to model and respond to students' affective states in addition to their cognitive states.

The achievement of an affect-sensitive tutorial interaction engages the tutor and learner in an *affective loop* (Conati, Marsella, & Paiva, 2005). This includes the *identification* of the affective states relevant to learning, the real-time *detection* of those states, the *selection* of appropriate tutor actions that maximize learning while influencing learner affect, and the *synthesis* of emotional expressions by the tutor as it attempts to engage learners in a more human-like manner.

Implementing the affective loop in an integrated ITS must incorporate the perspective of both the learner and the tutor. The learner-centric view consists of analyzing the prominent affective states of the learner, assessing their potential impact

S.K. D'Mello (✉)
Department of Psychology, Institute for Intelligent Systems,
University of Memphis, Memphis, TN, USA
e-mail: sdmello@memphis.edu

R.A. Calvo and S.K. D'Mello (eds.), *New Perspectives on Affect and Learning Technologies*, 113
Explorations in the Learning Sciences, Instructional Systems and Performance Technologies 3,
DOI 10.1007/978-1-4419-9625-1_9, © Springer Science+Business Media, LLC 2011

on learning, identifying how these states are expressed by the learner, and developing automatic systems to detect these states in real time. The tutor-centric view explores how good human tutors or theoretically ideal tutors adapt their instructional agenda to encompass the emotions of the learner. This expert knowledge can then be transferred to computer tutors. Animated pedagogical agents that simulate human tutors can also be programmed to synthesize affective elements through the generation of facial expressions, inflections of speech, and the modulation of posture (Graesser, Jeon, & Dufty, 2008; Johnson, Rickel, & Lester, 2000; Moreno, Mayer, Spires, & Lester, 2001).

We have implemented aspects of both the learner-centric and tutor-centric perspectives in the Affective AutoTutor, as will be described in this chapter. We begin with a brief description of the AutoTutor system followed by an analysis on five studies that have systematically tested links between emotions and learning with AutoTutor. We then describe how the Affective AutoTutor detects, responds to, and synthesizes affect followed by the results of an experiment that evaluated the efficacy of the system in promoting learning and engagement.

AutoTutor

AutoTutor is a dialogue-based ITS for Newtonian physics, computer literacy, and critical thinking. The impact of AutoTutor on facilitating the learning of deep conceptual knowledge has been validated in over a dozen experiments on college students (Graesser et al., 2004; Storey et al., in press; VanLehn et al., 2007). Tests of AutoTutor have produced learning gains of 0.4–1.5 sigma (a mean of 0.8), depending on the learning measure, the comparison condition, the subject matter, and the version of AutoTutor. So we take it as a given that (the nonaffective) AutoTutor helps learning and now the pertinent question is whether the new Affective AutoTutor can yield further enhancements of learning.

The major components of AutoTutor include an animated conversational agent, dialogue management, speech act classification, a curriculum script, semantic evaluation of student contributions, and electronic documents (e.g., textbook and glossary). AutoTutor communicates through an animated conversational agent utilizing speech, facial expressions, and some rudimentary gestures.

AutoTutor's dialogues are organized around difficult questions or problems (called main questions) that require reasoning and explanations in the answers. When presented with these questions, students typically respond with answers that are only one word to two sentences in length, which is typically not sufficient to answer these main questions. In order to guide students in the construction of an improved answer, AutoTutor actively monitors learners' knowledge states and engages them in a turn-based dialogue.

As with most ITSs, AutoTutor fits within VanLehn's analyses of the outer loop and the inner loop when characterizing the scaffolding of solutions to problems, answers to questions, or completion of complex tasks (VanLehn, 2006).

The outer loop involves the selection of topics and problems to cover, assessments of the student's topic knowledge and general cognitive abilities, and global aspects of the tutorial interaction. The inner loop consists of covering individual steps within a problem at a micro-level.

The outer loop of AutoTutor consists of a series of didactic lessons and challenging problems or questions (such as *why, how, what-if*). An example main question is "When you turn on the computer, how is the operating system first activated and loaded into RAM?" The order of lessons, problems, and questions can be dynamically selected based on the profile of student abilities, but the order is fixed in most versions of AutoTutor we have developed.

The interactive dialogue occurs during the construction of a response to the problems and questions. The answer to a question (or solution to a problem) requires several sentences of information in an ideal answer. AutoTutor assists the learner in constructing their answer after the student enters their initial response. The inner loop of AutoTutor consists of this collaborative interaction while answering a question (or solving a problem). It is this inner loop that is the distinctive hallmark of AutoTutor. AutoTutor adaptively manages the tutorial dialogue by providing feedback on the learner's answers (e.g., "good job," "not quite"), pumps the learner for more information (e.g., "What else"), gives hints (e.g., "What about X"), prompts for specific words (e.g., "X is a type of what"), corrects misconceptions, answers questions, and summarizes topics. The inner loop dialogue between AutoTutor and the student takes approximately 100 dialogue turns to answer a single challenging question, approximately the length of a conversation with a human tutor (Graesser, Person, & Magliano, 1995).

AutoTutor can keep the dialogue on track because it is always comparing what the student says to anticipated input from a curriculum script. This constitutes AutoTutor's model of the student's knowledge and cognitive states. Pattern matching operations and pattern completion mechanisms drive the comparison. These matching and completion operations are based on symbolic interpretation algorithms (Rus & Graesser, 2007) and statistical semantic matching algorithms (Graesser, Penumatsa, Ventura, Cai, & Hu, 2007).

In summary, AutoTutor uses natural language processing techniques, recent advances in agent technologies, insights from discourse processing, the dialogue moves and tactics of human tutors, and strategies from constructivist theories of pedagogy (Chi, Roy, & Hausmann, 2008; Jonassen, Peck, & Wilson, 1999; Moshman, 1982) to allow students to chart their own course through the tutorial dialogue and to construct their own answers to difficult questions.

Identifying Affective States

What are the affective states that learners experience during interactions with AutoTutor and other learning environments? Do the "basic emotions" (anger, sadness, fear, disgust, happiness, and surprise) (Ekman, 1992), constitute learners' primary emotional reactions. Or are the "academic emotions" (e.g., anxiety, boredom) more relevant in learning contexts (see Pekrun, 2011)? We addressed this fundamental question by conducting a number of studies that aimed at identifying the affective states that learners typically experience while interacting with AutoTutor, with the expectation that these findings will generalize to other learning environments (Baker, D'Mello, Rodrigo, & Graesser, 2010).

In the *observational* study, five trained judges observed the affective states (boredom, confusion, frustration, eureka, flow/engagement, vs. neutral) of 34 students who were learning introductory computer literacy with AutoTutor (Craig, Graesser, Sullins, & Gholson, 2004b). In the *emote-aloud* study, seven college students verbalized their affective states while interacting with AutoTutor (D'Mello, Craig, Sullins, & Graesser, 2006). The *multiple-judge* study consisted of 28 learners completing a 32-min session with AutoTutor, after which their affective states were judged by the learners themselves, untrained peers, and two trained judges. Judgments were based on videos of learners' faces and computer screens which were recorded during the tutorial session (Graesser et al., 2006). The *speech recognition* study was similar to the multiple-judge study with the exception that learners spoke their responses to the AutoTutor system instead of typing them. Retrospective self-reports by the learners constituted the primary affect measure in this study (Graesser, Chipman, King, McDaniel, & D'Mello, 2007).The *physiological* study also implemented the retrospective affect judgment procedure, however, the learners were 27 engineering students from an Australian University instead of the undergraduate psychology students from the USA, who comprised the samples in the previous four studies (Pour, Hussein, AlZoubi, D'Mello, & Calvo, 2010).

When averaged across studies, flow/engagement was the most frequent state, comprising 24% of the observations. Boredom and confusion were the second most frequent states (18 and 17%, respectively) followed by frustration (13%). Neutral was reported for 19% of the observations, while delight (6%) and surprise (3%) were rare.

Although the present set of studies did not directly compare the occurrence of these learning-centered affective states with the basic emotions, other studies have demonstrated that the basic emotions are comparatively rare in learning sessions (one exception is happiness which does occur in some contexts) (Lehman, D'Mello, & Person, 2008; Lehman, Matthews, D'Mello, & Person, 2008). The basic emotions have claimed center-stage of most emotion research in the last four decades, but our results suggest that they might not be relevant to learning, at least for the short learning sessions of these studies. In contrast, confusion, frustration, and boredom, were the prevalent negative emotions, indicating that it is critically important for the Affective AutoTutor to respond to these states.

Detecting Affective States

The affect detection system monitors conversational cues, gross body language, and facial features to detect boredom, confusion, frustration, and neutral (no affect) (see Fig. 1). Automated systems that detect these emotions have been integrated into

Fig. 1 Monitoring affective states during interactions with AutoTutor

AutoTutor and have been extensively described and evaluated in previous publications (D'Mello, Craig, Witherspoon, McDaniel, & Graesser, 2008; D'Mello & Graesser, 2009). The system is capable of correctly identifying learner affect with approximately 50% accuracy (base-rate=25%) (see D'Mello & Graesser, 2009 for details).

It is beyond the scope of this chapter to describe the individual components of the system, however, it is useful to get a grasp of the multimodal affect detection system as a whole. The system uses a decision-level fusion algorithm where each channel independently provides its own diagnosis of the student's affective state. These individual diagnoses are combined with an algorithm that selects a single affective state and a confidence value of the detection. The algorithm relies on a voting rule enhanced with a few simple heuristics.

A spreading activation network (Rumelhart, McClelland, & PDP Research Group, 1986) with *projecting* and *lateral* links is used to model decision-level fusion. A sample network is presented in Fig. 2. This hypothetical network has two sensor nodes, *C1* and *C2*, and three emotion nodes, *E1, E2,* and *E3*. Each sensor is connected to each emotion by a projecting link (solid lines). The degree to which a particular sensor activates a particular emotion is based on the accuracy by which the sensor has detected the emotion in past offline evaluations (see weights in Fig. 2). So if one sensor is more accurate at detecting boredom than confusion, it will excite the boredom node more than the confusion node, even if its current estimates on the probability of both emotions are approximately equivalent.

Each emotion is also connected to every other emotion with a *lateral* link (dotted lines). These links are weighted and can be excitatory or inhibitory (see weights in Fig. 2). Related emotions excite each other while unrelated emotions inhibit each other. For example, confusion would excite frustration but boredom would inhibit engagement.

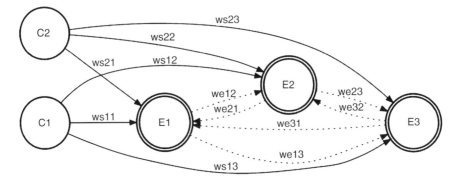

Fig. 2 Sample activation spreading network for decision-level fusion

Each emotion node receives activation from both link types and maintains an *activation value*. At any time, the emotion node with the highest activation value is considered to be the emotion that the learner is currently experiencing. The decision-level fusion algorithm operates in four phases.

1. *Detection by Sensors.* Each sensor provides an independent estimate of the likelihood that the learner is experiencing an emotion. The likelihood can be represented as a probability value for each emotion (e.g., sensor C1 expresses a .53 probability that the current emotion is E1).
2. *Activation from Sensors.* Sensors spread activation and emotion nodes aggregate this activation.
3. *Activation from Emotions.* Each emotion spreads the activation received from the sensors to the other emotions, so that some emotions are excited while others are inhibited.
4. *Decision.* The emotion with the highest activation is selected to be the emotion that the learner is currently experiencing.

Responding to Affective States and Synthesizing Affect

Despite the complexity associated with real-time affect detection, detection is only one piece of the puzzle. The next challenge is to help students regulate their affective states so that positive states such as flow/engagement and curiosity persevere, while negative states such as frustration and boredom are rapidly eradicated.

The Affective AutoTutor addresses this challenge by adapting its dialogue moves in a manner that is dynamically responsive to students' affective and cognitive states. In particular, at any given turn the Affective tutor keeps track of five informational parameters that provide the foundations for affect-sensitivity (three affective parameters and two cognitive parameters). The three affective parameters include the current affective state detected, the confidence level of that affect classification, and the previous affective state detected. The cognitive parameters include a global measure of student ability (dynamically updated throughout the session) and the conceptual quality of the student's immediate response. These cognitive measures are accessed via the use of natural language understanding techniques that monitor students knowledge trajectories by constantly comparing their responses to information in the curriculum script (Graesser, Penumatsa et al., 2007).

Taking these five parameters as input, the Affective AutoTutor is equipped with a set of production rules to map the input parameters with appropriate tutor actions. In particular, the Affective tutor responds with (a) feedback for the current answer with an affective facial expression, (b) an affective statement accompanied by a matching emotional facial and vocal expression by the tutor, and (c) the next dialogue move. Each of these components is described below.

Feedback with Affective Facial Expression: AutoTutor provides short feedback to each student response. The feedback is based on the semantic match between the response and the anticipated answer. There are five levels of feedback: positive, neutral-positive, neutral, neutral-negative, and negative. Each feedback category has a set of predefined expressions that the tutor randomly selects from. "Good job" and "Well done" are examples of positive feedback, while "That is not right" and "You are on the wrong track" are examples of negative feedback. In addition to articulating the textual content of the feedback, the affective AutoTutor also modulates its facial expressions and speech prosody. Positive feedback is delivered with an *approval* expression (big smile and big nod). Neutral-positive feedback receives a *mild approval* expression (small smile and slight nod). Negative feedback is delivered with a *disapproval* expression (slight frown and head shake), while the tutor makes a *skeptical* face when delivering neutral-negative feedback (see Fig. 3). No facial expression accompanies the delivery of neutral feedback.

Affective Response with Affective Facial Expression and Affectively Modulated Speech: After delivering the feedback, the affective AutoTutor delivers an emotional statement if it senses that the student is bored, confused, or frustrated. A non-emotional discourse marker (e.g., "Moving on," "Try this one") is selected if the

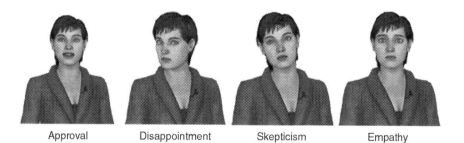

Approval   Disappointment   Skepticism   Empathy

Fig. 3 Synthesized facial expressions by the AutoTutor agent

student is neutral. AutoTutor's strategies to respond to boredom, confusion, and frustration are motivated by attribution theory (Batson, Turk, Shaw, & Klein, 1995; Heider, 1958; Weiner, 1986), cognitive disequilibrium during learning (Craig, Graesser, Sullins, & Gholson, 2004a; Festinger, 1957; Graesser & Olde, 2003; Piaget, 1952), and recommendations by pedagogical experts. In general, the Affective AutoTutor responds to the learners' affective states via empathetic and motivational responses. These responses always attribute the source of the learners' emotion to the material instead of the learners themselves. So the supportive AutoTutor might respond to mild boredom with "This stuff can be kind of dull sometimes, so I'm gonna try and help you get through it. Let's go." A response to confusion would include attributing the source of confusion to the material ("Some of this *material* can be confusing. Just keep going and I am sure you will get it") or the tutor itself ("I know I do not always convey things clearly. I am always happy to repeat myself if you need it. Try this one").

As a complete example, consider a student who has been performing well overall (high global ability), but the most recent contribution was not very good (low current contribution quality). If the current emotion was classified as boredom, with a high probability, and the previous emotion was classified as frustration, then AutoTutor might say the following: "Maybe this *topic* is getting old. I'll help you finish so we can try something new." This is a randomly chosen phrase from a list that was designed to indirectly address the student's boredom and to try to shift the topic a bit before the student becomes disengaged from the learning experience. This rule fires on several different occasions, and each time it is activated AutoTutor will select a dialogue move from a list of associated moves. In this fashion, the rules are context sensitive and are dynamically adaptive to each individual learner.

The affective response is accompanied by an emotional facial expression and emotionally modulated speech. These affective expressions include empathy, mild enthusiasm, high enthusiasm, and neutral in some cases. The facial expressions in each display were informed by Ekman's work on the facial correlates of emotion expression (Ekman & Friesen, 1978). The facial expressions of emotion displayed by AutoTutor are augmented with emotionally expressive speech synthesized by the agent. The emotional expressivity is obtained by variations in pitch, speech rate, and other prosodic features. Previous research has led us to conceptualize AutoTutor's affective speech on the indices of pitch range, pitch level, and speech rate (Johnstone & Scherer, 2000). The current quality of the emotionally modulated speech is acceptable, although there is the potential for improvement.

A screenshot of the Affective AutoTutor is shown in Fig. 4. Here the tutor is displaying a skeptical face while delivering neutral-negative feedback (e.g., "kind of," "sort of").

Next Dialogue Move: Finally, AutoTutor responds with a move to advance the dialogue. In the current version of the tutor, this dialogue move is sensitive to the learner's cognitive state but not to his or her affective state (see "AutoTutor" section). That is, affect-sensitivity is currently applied to AutoTutor's motivational (feedback and affective response) but not its pedagogical moves (i.e., hints, prompts, assertions).

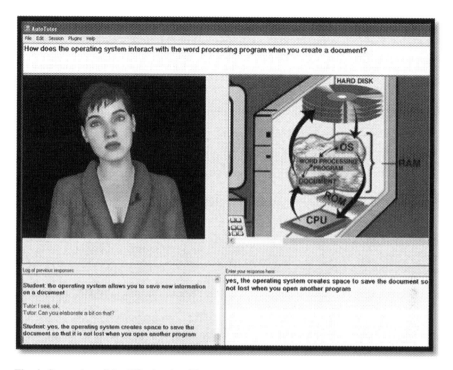

Fig. 4 Screenshot of the Affective AutoTutor

Future affect-sensitive interventions will focus on the tutor's pedagogical moves as well. This adaptation would increase the bandwidth of communication and allow the Affective AutoTutor to respond at a more sophisticated metacognitive level.

There could be many possible responses to the different affective states of the learner and the context of the interaction. If the affective state of frustration is detected, then the Affective AutoTutor could respond by changing its dialogue strategies to include more direct feedback, assertions, and corrections of detected misconceptions. If the learner is bored then the tutor could engage the learner in a task that increases interest and cognitive arousal, such as a simulation, options of choice, a challenge, or a seductive embedded game.

Confusion presents a key opportunity for the tutor to encourage deep learning. The Affective AutoTutor system could manage confusion in at least two ways. Successful learners might be allowed to work out their own confusion in a discovery learning environment (Bruner, 1961; D'Mello et al., 2010; Vavik, 1993) that requires self-regulated cognitive activities (see Azevedo & Chauncey, 2011). A second method would systematically scaffold the student out of the confused state. This method might work better for learners with lower domain knowledge and lower ability to self-regulate their learning activities.

Evaluating the Affect-Sensitive AutoTutor

We have recently conducted an experiment that evaluated the pedagogical effectiveness of the Affective AutoTutor when compared to the original tutor (D'Mello et al., 2010). Both tutors utilize identical pedagogical strategies, however, the Affective AutoTutor has enhanced motivational moves. The obvious prediction is that learning gains should be superior for the Affective AutoTutor.

The experiment utilized a between-subjects design where 84 learners (a) completed a pretest on topics in computer literacy, (b) were tutored on two computer literacy topics with either the affective or the regular AutoTutor, and (c) completed a posttest. The tests and tutorial sessions were pitched at deeper levels of comprehension with questions that required reasoning and inference instead of the recall of shallow facts and definitions. The tutorial session consisted of two 30-min sessions on different computer literacy topics but with the same version of AutoTutor (i.e., either Affective or Regular). The key dependent variable was *proportional learning gains*, computed as: (posttest scores − pretest scores)/(1 − pretest scores). Proportional learning gains represent the degree of improvement at posttest above and beyond pretest performance.

The results of this experiment indicated that the Affective AutoTutor was more effective than the regular tutor for low-domain knowledge students (identified via a median split on pretest scores) in the second session ($d = 0.713$), but not the first session (see Fig. 5). This suggests that it is inappropriate for the tutor to be supportive to low-domain knowledge students before there has been enough context to show there are problems. Simply put, do not be supportive until the students need support.

The low-domain knowledge learners also demonstrated more knowledge transfer by scoring higher on related topics that were not covered in the tutorial session. Transfer scores were higher with the Affective AutoTutor when compared to the regular tutor, thereby signaling a unique advantage for this type of motivational support.

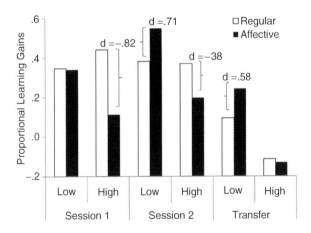

Fig. 5 Proportional learning gains separated by learning session and tutor

The students with more knowledge never benefited from the Affective AutoTutor. These students do not need the emotional support, but rather they need to go directly to the content. There are also conditions when affective support was detrimental to these high domain knowledge students. There appears to be a liability to quick support and empathy compared to no affect-sensitivity.

The central message is that there is an appropriate time for affect-sensitivity in the form of supportive dialogues. Just as there is a "time for telling"; there is a "time for emoting." We could imagine a strategy where low-knowledge students start out with a nonemotional regular tutor until they see there are problems. Then after that they need support, as manifested in the second tutorial session. Regarding high-knowledge students, they are perfectly fine working on content for an hour or more and may get irritated with an AutoTutor showing compassion, empathy, and care. But later on there may be a time when they want an Affective AutoTutor. These are all questions to explore in future research.

Conclusions

Once no more than a mere seductive vision, the idea of having a tutoring system detect, respond to, and synthesize emotions is now a reality (Picard, 1997). The fact that the Affective AutoTutor is the first affect-sensitive ITS to facilitate deep learning gains of difficult technical materials over and above nonaffective controls signals an important advancement in the field of ITSs and the more general areas of Affective Computing and Human–Computer Interaction. However, there is still much room for further research and technological development. In addition to providing affective motivational support, there is the key challenge of providing affect-sensitive pedagogical support as well. Another challenge is to provide more contextually sensitive affective responses that take into account both the causes and effects of learner emotions (see Conati, 2011). It is also important to consider the "afterglow of affect-sensitivity" which would involve monitoring the learner after an affective-sensitive intervention. One might even consider inducing certain emotions that are considered to be beneficial to learning.

Individual differences play their usual important role so more research is needed into their effects. In addition to prior knowledge, individual differences in motivation, attribution styles, academic risk taking, cognitive complexity, affective traits, and baseline mood states are likely to interact with student affect (Clifford, 1988; Clore & Huntsinger, 2007; Fletcher, Danilovics, Fernandez, Peterson, & Reeder, 1986; Hidi, 2006; Isen, 2008; McAuley, Duncan, & Russell, 1992; Meyer & Turner, 2006). Identifying how these and other individual differences moderate the experience and impact of student emotions and developing affective interventions that capitalizes on these relationships represents a significant challenge for next-generation affect-sensitive ITSs.

Acknowledgments We thank our research colleagues in the Emotive Computing Group and the Tutoring Research Group (TRG) at the University of Memphis (http://emotion.autotutor.org). We gratefully acknowledge our partners in the Affective Computing group at the MIT Media Lab.

This research was supported by the National Science Foundation (REC 0106965, ITR 0325428, HCC 0834847). Any opinions, findings and conclusions, or recommendations expressed in this paper are those of the authors and do not necessarily reflect the views of NSF.

References

Azevedo, R., & Chauncey, A. (2011). Integrating cognitive, metacognitive, and affective regulatory processes with MetaTutor. In R. Calvo & S. D'Mello (Eds.), *Affective prospecting (Explorations in the learning sciences, instructional systems and performance)*. New York: Springer.

Baker, R., D'Mello, S., Rodrigo, M., & Graesser, A. (2010). Better to be frustrated than bored: The incidence and persistence of affect during interactions with three different computer-based learning environments. *International Journal of Human-Computer Studies, 68*(4), 223–241.

Batson, C., Turk, C., Shaw, L., & Klein, T. (1995). Information function of empathic emotion – learning that we value the others welfare. *Journal of Personality and Social Psychology, 68*(2), 300–313.

Bruner, J. (1961). The act of discovery. *Harvard Educational Review, 31*(1), 21–32.

Calvo, R. A., & D'Mello, S. K. (2010). Affect detection: An interdisciplinary review of models, methods, and their applications. *IEEE Transactions on Affective Computing, 1*(1), 18–37.

Chi, M., Roy, M., & Hausmann, R. (2008). Observing tutorial dialogues collaboratively: Insights about human tutoring effectiveness from vicarious learning. *Cognitive Science, 32*(2), 301–341.

Clifford, M. (1988). Failure tolerance and academic risk-taking in ten- to twelve-year-old students. *British Journal of Educational Psychology, 58*, 15–27.

Clore, G. L., & Huntsinger, J. R. (2007). How emotions inform judgment and regulate thought. *Trends in Cognitive Sciences, 11*(9), 393–399.

Conati, C. (2011). Combining cognitive appraisal and sensors for affect detection in a framework for modeling user affect. In R. Calvo & S. D'Mello (Eds.), *Affective prospecting (Explorations in the learning sciences, instructional systems and performance)*. New York: Springer.

Conati, C., Marsella, S., & Paiva, A. (2005). Affective interactions: The computer in the affective loop. In J. Riedl & A. Jameson (Eds.), *Proceedings of the 10th International Conference on Intelligent User Interfaces* (p. 7). New York: ACM.

Craig, S., Graesser, A., Sullins, J., & Gholson, B. (2004). Affect and learning: An exploratory look into the role of affect in learning. *Journal of Educational Media, 29*, 241–250.

D'Mello, S., Craig, S., Sullins, J., & Graesser, A. (2006). Predicting affective states expressed through an emote-aloud procedure from AutoTutor's mixed-initiative dialogue. *International Journal of Artificial Intelligence in Education, 16*(1), 3–28.

D'Mello, S., Craig, S., Witherspoon, A., McDaniel, B., & Graesser, A. (2008). Automatic detection of learner's affect from conversational cues. *User Modeling and User-Adapted Interaction, 18*(1–2), 45–80.

D'Mello, S., & Graesser, A. (2009). Automatic detection of learners' affect from gross body language. *Applied Artificial Intelligence, 23*(2), 123–150.

D'Mello, S., Lehman, B., Sullins, J., Daigle, R., Combs, R., Vogt, K., et al. (2010). A time for emoting: When affect-sensitivity is and isn't effective at promoting deep learning. In J. Kay & V. Aleven (Eds.), *Proceedings of 10th International Conference on Intelligent Tutoring Systems* (pp. 245–254). Berlin: Springer.

Ekman, P. (1992). An argument for basic emotions. *Cognition & Emotion, 6*(3–4), 169–200.

Ekman, P., & Friesen, W. (1978). *The facial action coding system: A technique for the measurement of facial movement*. Palo Alto: Consulting Psychologists Press.

Festinger, L. (1957). *A theory of cognitive dissonance*. Stanford, CA: Stanford University Press.

Fletcher, G. J. O., Danilovics, P., Fernandez, G., Peterson, D., & Reeder, G. D. (1986). Attributional complexity – An individual-differences measure. *Journal of Personality and Social Psychology, 51*(4), 875–884.

Graesser, A., Chipman, P., Haynes, B., & Olney, A. (2005). AutoTutor: An intelligent tutoring system with mixed-initiative dialogue. *IEEE Transactions on Education, 48*(4), 612–618.

Graesser, A., Chipman, P., King, B., McDaniel, B., & D'Mello, S. (2007). Emotions and learning with AutoTutor. In R. Luckin, K. Koedinger, & J. Greer (Eds.), *13th International Conference on Artificial Intelligence in Education* (pp. 569–571). Amsterdam: Ios Press.

Graesser, A., Jeon, M., & Dufty, D. (2008). Agent technologies designed to facilitate interactive knowledge construction. *Discourse Processes, 45*(4–5), 298–322.

Graesser, A., Lu, S. L., Jackson, G., Mitchell, H., Ventura, M., Olney, A., et al. (2004). AutoTutor: A tutor with dialogue in natural language. *Behavioral Research Methods, Instruments, and Computers, 36*, 180–193.

Graesser, A., McDaniel, B., Chipman, P., Witherspoon, A., D'Mello, S., & Gholson, B. (2006). *Detection of emotions during learning with AutoTutor*. Paper presented at the 28th Annual Conference of the Cognitive Science Society, Vancouver, Canada.

Graesser, A., & Olde, B. (2003). How does one know whether a person understands a device? The quality of the questions the person asks when the device breaks down. *Journal of Educational Psychology, 95*(3), 524–536.

Graesser, A., Penumatsa, P., Ventura, M., Cai, Z., & Hu, X. (2007). Using LSA in AutoTutor: Learning through mixed-initiative dialogue in natural language. In T. Landauer, D. McNamara, S. Dennis, & W. Kintsch (Eds.), *Handbook of latent semantic analysis* (pp. 243–262). Mahwah, NJ: Erlbaum.

Graesser, A., Person, N., & Magliano, J. (1995). Collaborative dialogue patterns in naturalistic one-to-one tutoring. *Applied Cognitive Psychology, 9*(6), 495–522.

Heider, F. (1958). *The psychology of interpersonal relations*. New York: Wiley.

Hidi, S. (2006). Interest: A unique motivational variable. *Educational Research Review, 1*, 69–82.

Isen, A. (2008). Some ways in which positive affect influences decision making and problem solving. In M. Lewis, J. Haviland-Jones, & L. Barrett (Eds.), *Handbook of emotions* (3rd ed., pp. 548–573). New York, NY: Guilford.

Johnson, W., Rickel, J., & Lester, J. (2000). Animated Pedagogical Agents: Face-to-face interaction in interactive learning environments. *International Journal of Artificial Intelligence in Education, 11*, 47–78.

Johnstone, T., & Scherer, K. (2000). Vocal communication of emotion. In M. Lewis & J. Haviland-Jones (Eds.), *Handbook of emotions* (2nd ed., pp. 220–235). New York: Guilford Press.

Jonassen, D., Peck, K., & Wilson, B. (1999). *Learning with technology: A constructivist perspective*. Upper Saddle River, NJ: Prentice Hall.

Lehman, B., D'Mello, S., & Person, N. (2008). *All alone with your emotions: An analysis of student emotions during effortful problem solving activities*. Paper presented at the Workshop on Emotional and Cognitive issues in ITS at the Ninth International Conference on Intelligent Tutoring Systems

Lehman, B., Matthews, M., D'Mello, S., & Person, N. (2008). What are you feeling? Investigating student affective states during expert human tutoring sessions. In B. Woolf, E. Aimeur, R. Nkambou, & S. Lajoie (Eds.), *Proceedings of the 9th International Conference on Intelligent Tutoring Systems* (pp. 50–59). Berlin: Springer.

McAuley, E., Duncan, T. E., & Russell, D. W. (1992). Measuring causal attributions – the Revised Causal Dimension Scale (Cdsii). *Personality and Social Psychology Bulletin, 18*(5), 566–573.

McNeese, M. (2003). New visions of human-computer interaction: making affect compute. *International Journal of Human-Computer Studies, 59*(1–2), 33–53.

Meyer, D., & Turner, J. (2006). Re-conceptualizing emotion and motivation to learn in classroom contexts. *Educational Psychology Review, 18*(4), 377–390.

Moreno, R., Mayer, R., Spires, H., & Lester, J. (2001). The case for social agency in computer-based teaching: Do students learn more deeply when they interact with animated pedagogical agents? *Cognition and Instruction, 19*(2), 177–213.

Moshman, D. (1982). Exogenous, endogenous, and dialectical constructivism. *Developmental Review, 2*(4), 371–384.

Paiva, A., Prada, R., & Picard, R. (Eds.). (2007). *Affective computing and intelligent interaction.* Heidelberg: Springer.

Pekrun, R. (2011). Emotions as drivers of learning and cognitive development. In R. Calvo & S. D'Mello (Eds.), *Affective prospecting (Explorations in the learning sciences, instructional systems and performance).* New York: Springer.

Piaget, J. (1952). *The origins of intelligence.* New York: International University Press.

Picard, R. (1997). *Affective computing.* Cambridge: MIT Press.

Pour, P. A., Hussein, S., AlZoubi, O., D'Mello, S. K., & Calvo, R. (2010). The impact of system feedback on learners' affective and physiological states. In J. Kay & V. Aleven (Eds.), *Proceedings of 10th International Conference on Intelligent Tutoring Systems* (pp. 264–273). Berlin, Heidelberg: Springer.

Rumelhart, D., McClelland, J., & PDP Research Group. (1986). *Parallel distributed processing: explorations in the microstructure of cognition. Volume 1: Foundations.* Cambridge, MA: MIT Press.

Rus, V., & Graesser, A. (2007). Lexico-syntactic subsumption for textual entailment. In N. Nicolov, K. Bontcheva, G. Angelova, & R. Mitkov (Eds.), *Recent advances in natural language processing IV: Selected papers from RANLP 2005* (pp. 187–196). Amsterdam: John Benjamins.

Storey, J., Kopp, K., Wiemer, K., Chipman, P., & Graesser, A. (in press). Critical thinking tutor: Using AutoTutor to teach scientific critical thinking skills. *Behavioral Research Methods.*

VanLehn, K. (2006). The behavior of tutoring systems. *International Journal of Artificial Intelligence in Education., 16*(3), 227–265.

VanLehn, K., Graesser, A., Jackson, G., Jordan, P., Olney, A., & Rose, C. P. (2007). When are tutorial dialogues more effective than reading? *Cognitive Science, 31*(1), 3–62.

Vavik, L. (1993). Facilitating discovery learning in computer-based simulation learning environments. In R. Tennyson & A. Baron (Eds.), *Automating instructional design: Computer-based development and delivery tools* (pp. 403–449). Berlin: Springer.

Weiner, B. (1986). *An attributional theory of motivation and emotion.* New York: Springer.

Actionable Affective Processing for Automatic Tutor Interventions

David G. Cooper, Ivon Arroyo, and Beverly Park Woolf

Introduction: Detecting Emotion for Action

Once a tutoring system is able to detect students' emotions, it is not obvious how to change the tutor's behavior to leverage this emotion detection for the student's benefit. For instance, if students state that they are excited, then providing harder problems may be appropriate in one case, while providing actions to calm them down so that they can better focus may be the best response in other cases. Both the cognitive and emotional states are important when choosing the tutor's actions. The purpose of this chapter is to describe the elements necessary for a tutoring system that makes appropriate actions based on a detected affective state. This is broken down into three parts. First we describe several methods for emotion detection. Then we present a study using Wayang Outpost, our math tutor, using sensors to detect students' emotion and taking actions based on that emotion. Then we discuss potential actions for the detected emotions. We conclude with future steps needed to improve the actions of tutoring systems in general.

Methods for Emotion Detection

Many instructional systems can detect emotion (Ammar, Neji, & Alimi, 2005; D'Mello & Graesser, 2007; McQuiggan, Lee, & Lester, 2007; Mota & Picard, 2003; Nkambou, 2006; Qi & Picard, 2002; Ruvolo et al., 2008; Sarrafzadeh et al., 2006; Strauss et al., 2005; Xiangjie et al., 2006). They capture a person's emotion using

D.G. Cooper(✉)
Department of Computer Science, University of Massachusetts, Amherst, MA, USA
e-mail: dcooper@cs.umass.edu

R.A. Calvo and S.K. D'Mello (eds.), *New Perspectives on Affect and Learning Technologies*, 127
Explorations in the Learning Sciences, Instructional Systems and Performance Technologies 3,
DOI 10.1007/978-1-4419-9625-1_10, © Springer Science+Business Media, LLC 2011

sensors, application events, and/or dialogue information. Many emotional detection systems are used in a laboratory setting with emotion detection as the end goal of the system.

For example, researchers use videotapes of learners and ask students or experts to identify observable emotions. Seminal work by Graesser et al. (2006) studied detection of emotion on video by learners, peers (fellow students), and judges. Judgments by peers have very little correspondence to the self-reports of learners. Judges trained on Ekman's Facial Action Coding system had good inter-rater reliability, but did not match the self-reports. Afzal & Robinson (2011) discuss a similar method. It was very difficult for either students or experts to label the emotion or to segment the video into emotionally salient clips. One conclusion was that emotion judgments are generally ambiguous and subjective and have low inter-rater reliability among reviewers. The emotion reporting described above differs from the in-situ self-reports in our experiments described below. Our method more readily captures emotions as they arise.

The system described in this chapter has further constraints in that it is used in real time in classroom environments. This means that the sensors should not only be inexpensive, but also provide methods for detection that can be applied in multiple settings (e.g., in classrooms and after school activities) and should not be too cumbersome to either the school or the students using the system. This section discusses three different emotion detection methods outlined above (sensors, application events, and dialogue information).

Sensors

Sensors have been used for a very long time to detect emotion (Ekman, Levenson, & Friesen, 1983; Mandryk et al., 2006). For instance, one physiological sensor used in lie detectors tests Galvanic Skin Response based on conductivity changes in the skin on the fingertips. The basis of the lie detector test is that arousal increases relative to a baseline when people lie. Sensors can be grouped into three categories in order of decreasing level of physical invasiveness: physiological sensors, touch (haptic) sensors, and observational sensors (e.g., cameras, microphones, and eye trackers).

Physiological sensors: Physiological sensors (e.g., the wrist sensor in Fig. 1) tend to be the most physically invasive as they require contact with a particular part of the body, and usually need to be tethered to the computer that is logging the readings. A typical skin conductivity sensor connects to two fingertips and is used to detect arousal. These sensors are often used alongside a heart rate sensor (electrocardiography) that is often connected to a fingertip (Conati et al., 2003; McQuiggan et al., 2007). An electromyograph (EMG) connects to particular muscles in the face to detect muscle tension or particular muscle activity such as frowns and eyebrow raises and is tethered to the computer (Amershi, Conati, & McLaren, 2006; Conati et al., 2003). An EEG (electroencephalograph) is typically connected to points on

Fig. 1 The wrist sensor used with Wayang Outpost to detect skin conductivity during problem solving

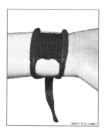

Fig. 2 *Left*. The chair sensor detects movement and posture changes. *Right*. The mouse sensor detects the amount of pressure while gripping the mouse

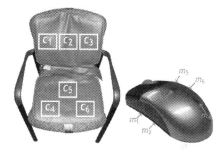

the head to detect surface brain activity (Derbali & Frasson, 2010; Heraz & Frasson, 2009; Heraz & Frasson, 2010). All of these methods, except for the heart rate sensor and some skin conductance sensors, require that a gel be placed on the electrodes for better conductivity. Attaching such electrodes can be uncomfortable and distracting. In addition, such methods are cost prohibitive in a classroom environment, since they have to be fitted to each student.

In the Wayang Tutor, described below, a skin conductance bracelet, shown in Fig. 1, is used that transmits conductivity at 1 Hz wirelessly using active RFID transmission (Cooper et al., 2009).

Haptic sensors: Sensors that detect touch or pressure, such as those in Fig. 2, can be used in a variety of ways. One way is to put pressure sensors on a computer mouse to detect the force exerted by the hand while using the mouse. Another is to put pressure sensors on the seat and back of a chair to detect movement in the chair and body posture. Studies have correlated pressure on the mouse with user frustration (Qi & Picard, 2002). In addition, different body postures have been associated with different emotions, such as sitting forward in the chair indicating user engagement or interest (Mota & Picard, 2003). These sensors are less invasive and students often do not notice them, but they require that the student physically touch the sensors and so they impede mobility.

In the Wayang Tutor, we use both a pressure-sensitive mouse and pressure-sensitive cushions placed on top of the back and seat of regular classroom chairs, shown in Fig. 2. The mouse has six pressure sensors that we aggregate, and the chair cushion has six pressure sensors, three in the seat and three in the back. The chair cushion sensor detects back motion, seat motion, and indicates a student sitting forward (Cooper et al., 2009).

Fig. 3 The camera detects facial points and translates them into mental states used by the Wayang Tutor's classifiers

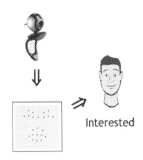

Interested

Observational sensors: Observational sensors, such as cameras (e.g., the one in Fig. 3), eye trackers, and microphones are not physically invasive; however, they can be quite distracting to students who are uncomfortable with the thought that their activities are being recorded and can be replayed and viewed by other people. Cameras have been used to classify emotional states by observing facial expressions (Cowie et al., 2001; Zeng et al., 2009). In addition, the pattern of facial expressions has been used to determine higher-level mental states in order to provide emotional intelligence to computer systems (el Kaliouby & Robinson, 2004). Microphones have also been used to determine different emotional states by analyzing pitch and amplitude information, and some experiments have sought to detect laughter (Truong & Leeuwen, 2007). In addition, an eye tracker, used to detect pupilary response, has been used in conjunction with the same chair, mouse, and skin conductance sensor described above along with text transcribed from a microphone to detect moments of Yes! (Muldner, Burleson, & VanLehn, 2010).

In the Wayang Tutor, we use a Web camera, Fig. 3, but do not keep the video information, instead we keep only the video features detected by the mind-reader software, e.g., 22 facial feature points, 12 facial expressions, and six mental states, (concentrating, thinking, etc.) (el Kaliouby & Robinson, 2004). Additionally, to protect human subjects, all identifying material about individual students is immediately replaced with anonymous labels before students even interact with the system. Thus, no information about student grades, behavior, or actions are ever associated with students personally or viewed by other people.

Application Events

When students interact with intelligent tutoring systems, they typically click buttons to progress through the tutor curriculum. This includes answering questions, asking for hints, going to the next problem, etc. These events are typically logged with time stamps so that statistics, e.g., time spent on a problem and time to the first attempt can be determined on a per problem basis. In addition, the number of hints selected, number of incorrect responses, and whether the student solved the problem on the first attempt are all application events that have been correlated with student emotion, e.g., interest, excitement, frustration, and confidence level (Arroyo et al., 2009). Since almost all tutoring systems have these events, our initial question was how well such tutor events could detect student emotion and what gains were available by adding each sensor's information.

Dialogue Information

Instructional systems that use natural language dialogue to interact with students can detect student emotions through the dialogue, as briefly discussed in this section. In a dialogue-based tutoring system, text can be evaluated for affective content (D'Mello & Graesser, 2007); keyword matching can be used to determine the student's emotion. In addition, other features of dialogue have been correlated to affective states (D'Mello, Craig, Witherspoon, McDaniel, & Graesser, 2008); the number of times the student has responded to a particular question, the number of typed characters in a response, the quality of the answer based on Latent Semantic Analysis, and the type of feedback that the tutor provides. Cohesion in dialogue is another method that is used for detecting affect (D'Mello et al., 2009); specifically a large number of negations by the student correlates with boredom, a lack of cohesion in pronoun references made by the student is correlated with confusion, a high frequency of causal words, e.g., "A caused B" compared to event and action words correlates with student flow, and a low amount of noun overlap in adjacent sentences correlates with frustration. The detected affective state based on dialogue could be used as an additional feature for emotion classifiers if a tutor has a dialogue mechanism.

The Wayang Tutor does not process the student's language; questions from the tutor are multiple-choice, so Wayang does not detect emotion through dialogue.

Case Study: Wayang Outpost with Sensors in the Classroom

Wayang Outpost (Fig. 4) is a mathematics tutoring system that tutors students by presenting them with problems of increasing or decreasing difficulty depending on the student's mastery. Problems are shown with multiple-choice answers, and students can request hints that animate the problem, point out important parts of diagrams, and speak the text that is presented in the hints. A toolbar enables students to draw and type over problems on the screen, (Figure 4, left). A learning companion, represented by an animated picture of a student who is gendered and multicultural (White, Hispanic and Black American) is provided for each student. Students interact with the learning companions that provide hints and generate behaviors based on the student's interaction. Until recently, the tutor has only adapted to students based on performance metrics (e.g., problems correct, gaming the system, etc.). The tutor's adaptations include presenting performance bars between problems, automatically

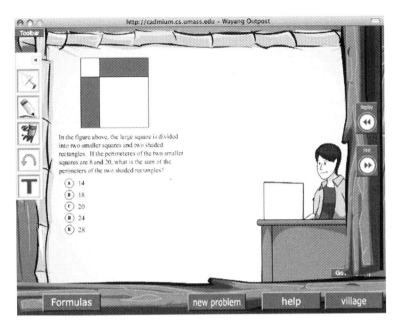

Fig. 4 An example problem of the Wayang Tutor with the White male learning companion

changing the difficulty of the next problem, and providing students with the option to change the difficulty of the next problem. With the detection of emotion, we have added actions related to the emotional state of the student (e.g., having learning companions change their expression or provide encouragement). The tutor can also offer hints or suggest that students view a video of a similar concept or problem that is solved by the tutor.

Emotion Classifiers

Wayang Outpost, described above, uses a combination of sensors and application events to detect and respond to four different affective states relevant to tutoring interactions. These states, e.g., confidence vs. anxiety, interest vs. boredom, low and high excitement, and low and high frustration, have been identified as important in human–computer interactions (Cowie et al., 1999) and education (Varlander, 2008). We intend to integrate into the tutor appropriate actions when a particular level of each affective state is detected. In order to do this we combine both sensor and application event data, correlate them with self-reported emotions, and construct classifiers based on these correlations. An example dialogue for emotional self-report is shown in Fig. 5.

Fig. 5 Students report their emotion to the tutor using a five-point scale (*top*). Four different emotions are encoded, shown with their left and right extremes (*bottom*)

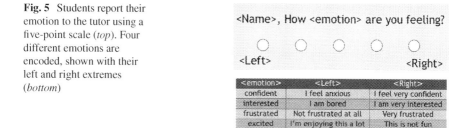

<emotion>	<Left>	<Right>
confident	I feel anxious	I feel very confident
interested	I am bored	I am very interested
frustrated	Not frustrated at all	Very frustrated
excited	I'm enjoying this a lot	This is not fun

We use a wrist sensor for skin conductance, a mouse sensor for grip pressure, chair back and seat pad sensors for detecting back motion, leg motion, and whether or not the student is sitting forward, and a camera sensor that detects the mental states of interested, agreeing, unsure, concentrating, and thinking.

We use application events on a per problem basis. The events we consider are the number of hints the student views, time to the first attempt, number of incorrect attempts, whether the student solved the problem on the first attempt, time of the session, time using the tutor, time to solve the problem, whether or not a learning companion was present, and which learning companion was present (Male, Female, or No learning companion).

Using the available sensor and application events that occur during each problem, we use step-wise linear regression to select a subset of events as features for each classifier to make the best performing classifier for each emotion. For each emotion we constructed seven classifiers. The baseline classifier chose the most common state. One classifier just used the application events. Four of the classifiers use a combination of one sensor with application events. The final classifier was constructed with all four of the sensors available plus the application events. After training our classifiers, we tested them on an entirely new population to verify the results. We do this because there is the potential that our classifiers will not generalize to a greater population. By training on data from 100 students in one semester, and testing on 400 additional students from data collection in a later semester, we were able to verify that classifiers for three emotions (low confidence, high excitement, and high interest) were better than predicting the most common emotional state (i.e., a common baseline) (Cooper et al., 2010). Frustration was the fourth emotion, and it was not classified well. Since these classifiers have been verified on a novel population, we can confidently use them to make better decisions based on affective states. The next section discusses the current actions that are available in the tutor, and other actions that could be added in the future.

Data Collection

The data collection involved two sets of data from separate populations at separate times. The first set, Sample A, involved a total of 94 students from three different schools. Each student had between one and four working sensors while using Wayang Outpost. Students worked for 1–5 sessions of 30–90 min. At intervals of 5 min, but only at the end of a problem, students were asked to self-report their emotions (either confident, interested, excited, or frustrated). Both sensor data and tutor data were logged for analysis. Data from Sample A was used to create the training set for the classifiers.

The second set of data, Sample B, involved over 500 students. These students also worked for 1–5 sessions of 30–90 min. At intervals of 3 min, students were asked to self-report about one of four emotions (either confident, interested, excited, or frustrated). Both sensor data and tutor data were logged for analysis. The Sample B data set was used only to verify that the classifiers generalize to a larger population.

Methods and Results for Detecting Emotion

We developed a five-step procedure to test the classifiers more rigorously than is commonly done for a lab-based experiment with an intelligent tutoring system.

- *First Step: Data Collection.* As described above, during data collection we use in-situ student self-reports as opposed to reporting on emotion after the fact based on a recorded video. In addition, we collect data from two separate populations, using Sample A for training and Sample B for verification.
- *Second Step: Feature Selection.* We perform feature selection on data from Sample A. Since we have nine tutor event features and 40 sensor features, it is important to use a classifier with a small combination of the features that work the best. We use step-wise linear regression to find the best features.
- *Third Step: Construct the Classifiers.* Using data from Sample A we compute a basic generalization metric based on cross-validation, using a leave-one-student-out cross-validation. This involves training the classifiers on all of the students except for one, and then testing the classifiers on the student that was left out, and repeating this for each student. We do this for accuracy, sensitivity, and specificity of our classifiers.
- *Fourth Step: Rank the results.* Once we have the results from training and cross-validation, the fourth step is to rank these results so we can definitively say that one classifier is better than another. We do this using both parametric and non-parametric methods because some of the assumputions of the parametric methods do not hold, although some parametric methods are known to be robust to violations of some assumptions.
- *Fifth Step: Test the classifiers.* Once we have the results and the rankings, constructed from our training data, the fifth and final step is to test the classifiers on the verification set from Sample B. We test each student individually, and then do the classifier rankings. We then compare these rankings to the training set, and if we have similar results that are better than our baseline classifier, then we make that classifier available for our tutoring system.

To justify this method we present here a segment of the results from feature selection, cross-validation, and ranking of the training, then the verification data to show that if only some of the steps are taken, then our tutoring system would be making decisions based on classifiers with performance that does not generalize.

If we evaluate the classifiers detecting high or low student confidence by comparing only accuracy about how often the system would correctly act? if it always believed that the student had low confidence, then the tutor would be right about 86% of the time using the best classifier, and only 66% of the time if it always thought the student had low confidence. However, when ranking these two results on a per student basis, there is no significant difference between these results. It is only when looking at the specificity $\left(\dfrac{correct\,neg.\,predictions}{neg.\,examples} \right)$ results for confidence, that the results are significantly different. The specificity results for the best classifier for confidence is 90.4% vs. 55.56% for the baseline for the training set, and for the testing set that classifier has 84.88% vs. 44.14%. This shows that the classifier is able to capture the low confidence cases very well, and should be able to act based on those, but without all of these steps, the tutor would act based on the classifier detecting high confidence as well; this would be an error.

Tutor Actions for Emotions Detected

This section describes the set of methods that we combine in Wayang Outpost along with the findings about which features are useful for the particular emotions that we study. Although some computer-based learning environments are designed (implicitly or explicitly) to take student affect into account in a nonadaptive manner, few can detect and respond dynamically (even in limited ways) to students' affective states or traits (Sarrafzadeh et al., 2006). In this section, we describe the actions we have used to respond to student affect and other possible actions/interventions to consider in the future.

Implemented Actions for Detected Emotions

We implemented affective learning companions (Fig. 6) to deliver approximately 50 different messages emphasizing the malleability of intelligence and the importance

Fig. 6 Wayang's learning companions support students affectively, acknowledging each student's automatically detected emotions (e.g., frustration)

of effort and perseverance (Arroyo et al., 2009; Woolf et al., 2010). A general goal was to train students motivationally, by emphasizing the importance of effort and perseverance and the idea that intelligence is malleable instead of a fixed trait (Dweck, 2000). This support was implemented in response to the effort exerted by students rather than to the student's emotions. Companions offered praise to students who exerted effort while solving a problem, even if their answers were wrong, highlighting that the goal is to learn through experience rather than to perform well. Characters were either unimpressed when effort was not exerted, or simply ignored the fact that the student got the right answer while not exerting effort.

In response to a detected emotion, characters empathized with students' emotion in various ways. If the student's emotion had positive valence (e.g., Interest, excitement), characters mirrored the student's emotion in a visual way with a certain probability (to ensure that companions did not look repetitive, acting the same way all the time). This happened at the beginning of a new problem, to ensure that characters did not distract students from solving the problem at hand.

If the student's emotion was negative (frustration, anxiety, boredom or low excitement) the characters first mirrored the negative emotion and then made a verbal acknowledgement of the emotion, e.g., "Sometimes I get frustrated when solving these math problems." These acknowledgements emulate a discourse that a true learning partner might pursue. The purpose of this empathic reaction is to encourage students to believe that they are not alone in their feelings toward the task, and that they are not the only ones that feel that way. Next, a verbal connector was played (e.g., "On the other hand"), followed by general affective support that provides an optimistic twist to the negative emotion. This support is meant to train students motivationally, e.g., "more important than getting the problem right is putting in the effort and keeping in mind that we can all do math if we try." While addressing emotions directly, this resolution of the conflicting emotion proved essential; as initial attempts of merely mirroring the negative emotion appeared to overemphasize the negative emotion instead of helping to resolve it.

Actions or responses to emotions detected may concentrate on affective matters ("emotion focused") or cognitive reactions ("problem-focused"). However, responding to the affective factors (e.g., by being encouraging) may impact the cognitive state of the student and vice versa. In sum, neither cognitive nor affective interactions should be considered in isolation and both may impact on learning or affective outcomes. The next section describes lines of future inquiry that follow from this approach.

Other Actions for Detected Emotions

It is important to consider both emotional and cognitive actions when thinking about responding to students' affective states. Murray and Arroyo (2002) describe thinking about the Zone of Proximal Development within a range of emotional states, the idea being that an ideal level of cognitive challenge lies between a zone of

Fig. 7 Cognitive response to affect. Extracted from Murray and Arroyo (2002)

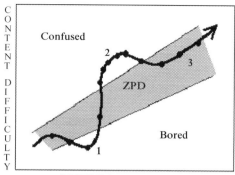

confusion and boredom (Fig. 7) that may be adjusted by varying content difficulty. Such early work considered that boredom and confusion was a simple byproduct of the interaction of students' skill level and the challenge provided in the content. In fact, students' emotions may vary for reasons beyond cognitive challenges, for example, a student might be disengaged, or be responding to pre-existing beliefs, attitudes or a daily mood, in addition to the appropriateness of content difficulty and student's skill level. Given the tools described in this chapter to detect emotional states, it is clearly possible to adjust the level of challenge provided in math problems or other activities in the software depending on automatically diagnosing boredom, disinterest or low excitement (Fig. 7 lower right quadrant) by increasing the difficulty of the content, or responding to confusion, anxiety, or frustration (Fig. 7, upper left quadrant) by decreasing the difficulty of the content.

In addition, it is possible that the reasons for students' negative feelings are based on meta-cognitive issues. For instance, students are frustrated because they do not know how to solve the current problem and take an "avoidance" attitude that makes them ignore the help provided by the software and instead quick-guess at a solution. Students might not know that one possible solution to their frustration lies in seeking help that the system provides. The system could offer such students hints, or simply show the hints, or show problems in "worked-out example mode."

Deciding to Act

The classifiers created by the process described above are a first step in integrating a variety of sensors with application event data so that the tutor can take actions based on the emotional state of students solving problems in the tutoring environment. For example, detecting low confidence or times of anxiety allows a tutor to respond in a supportive way at the appropriate time. In the future, it will be important to find better features to detect low interest, low excitement, and high frustration. This could be done in a number of ways. One way is to measure the emotion of individual students, determine a baseline behavior and construct classifiers based on changes from the baseline. Another way is to look at a sequence of problems rather than just at a per problem basis. This has been done with just tutor features, so adding sensor features may make this approach more accurate. Another way to identify useful features is to look at an individual's difference from the average behavior on a particular problem. This has also been calculated with just tutor features. A similar process could be to use sensor features and then measure the differences from the problem to determine the emotion of the student. In all future work, it is important to make sure that the classifiers created for a tutoring system either generalize to a larger population, or are able to create a baseline per student in order for the actions taken by the tutor to be useful.

In addition to detecting emotions in a general way, it is important that tutor actions based on emotions are useful for each student who expresses that emotion. In order to determine the best affective response for each student, additional user studies are required and this is part of the interplay between detecting emotion and acting based on emotion that may require some adaptation on its own. By bringing emotional detection into the classroom, we have uncovered a new set of research issues to be addressed by the educational research community.

References

Afzal, S., & Robinson, P. (2011). Natural affect data: collection and annotation. In R. Calvo & S. D'Mello (Eds.), *Affective prospecting (Explorations in the learning sciences, instructional systems and performance).* New York: Springer.

Amershi, S., Conati, C., & McLaren, H. (2006). Using feature selection and unsupervised clustering to identify affective expressions in educational games. *Workshop on Motivational and Affective Issues in ITS, 8th International Conference on Intelligent Tutoring Systems* (pp. 21–28).

Ammar, M. B., Neji, M., & Alimi, A. M. (2005). The integration of an emotional system in the intelligent system. *The 3rd ACS/IEEE International Conference on Computer Systems and Applications, 2005* (pp. 145–148). Cairo, Egypt.

Arroyo, I., Cooper, D. G., Burleson, W., Woolf, B. P., Muldner, K., & Christopherson, R. (2009). Emotion sensors go to school. *Proceeding of the 2009 conference on Artificial Intelligence in Education,* (pp. 17–24). Brighton, UK.

Arroyo, I., Woolf, B. P., Royer, J. M., & Tai, M. (2009). Affective gendered learning companions. *Proceeding of the 2009 conference on Artificial Intelligence in Education,* (pp. 41–48). Brighton, UK.

Conati, C., Chabbal, R., & Maclaren, H. (2003). A study on using biometric sensors for monitoring user emotions in educational games. *Proceedings User Modeling Workshop on "Assessing and Adapting to User Attitudes and Effect: Why, When, and How?", in conjunction with UM'03, 9th International Conference on User Modeling,* Pittsburgh, USA.

Cooper, D. G., Arroyo, I., Woolf, B. P., Muldner, K., Burleson, W., & Christopherson, R. (2009). Sensors model student self concept in the classroom. *UMAP '09: Proceedings of the 17th International Conference on User Modeling, Adaptation, and Personalization,* (pp. 30–41). Trento, Italy.

Cooper, D. G., Muldner, K., Arroyo, I., Woolf, B. P., & Burleson, W. (2010). Ranking feature sets for emotion models used in classroom based intelligent tutoring systems. *UMAP* (pp. 135–146).

Cowie, R., Douglas-Cowie, E., Apolloni, B., Taylor, J., Romano, A., & Fellenz, W. (1999). What a neural net needs to know about emotion words. *Computational Intelligence and Applications.*

Cowie, R., Douglas-Cowie, E., Tsapatsoulis, N., Votsis, G., Kollias, S., Fellenz, W. (2001). Emotion recognition in human-computer interaction. *Signal Processing Magazine, IEEE, 18,* 32–80.

D'Mello, S., Craig, S., Witherspoon, A., McDaniel, B., & Graesser, A. (2008). Automatic detection of learner's affect from conversational cues. *User Modeling and User-Adapted Interaction, 18,* 45–80.

D'Mello, S., Dowell, N., & Graesser, A. (2009) Cohesion relationships in tutorial dialogue as predictors of affective states. *Proceeding of the 2009 conference on Artificial Intelligence in Education,* (pp. 9–16). Amsterdam: IOS Press.

D'Mello, S. & Graesser, A. (2007). Mind and body: Dialogue and posture for affect detection in learning environments. *Proceeding of the 2007 conference on Artificial Intelligence in Education* (pp. 161–168). Amsterdam: IOS Press.

Derbali, L. & Frasson, C. (2010). Players' motivation and EEG waves patterns in a serious game environment. *International Conference on Intelligent Tutoring Systems* (pp. 297–299).

Dweck, C. S. (2000). *Self-theories: Their role in motivation, personality, and development.* London, UK: Psychology Press.

Ekman, P., Levenson, R., & Friesen, W. (1983). Autonomic nervous system activity distinguishes among emotions. *Science, 221,* 1208–1210.

el Kaliouby, R., & Robinson, P. (2004). Real-time inference of complex mental states from facial expressions and head gestures. *Proc. Int'l Conf. Computer Vision & Pattern Recognition, 3,* 154–173.

Graesser, A., McDaniel, B., Chipman, P., Witherspoon, A., D'Mello, S., & Gholson, B. (2006). Detection of emotions during learning with AutoTutor. *Proceedings of the 28th Annual Meetings of the Cognitive Science Society,* (pp. 285–290). Mahwah, NJ: Erlbaum.

Heraz, A. & Frasson, C. (2009). Predicting learner answers correctness through brainwaves assessment and emotional dimensions. *Proceeding of the 2009 conference on Artificial Intelligence in Education,* (pp. 49–56). Amsterdam: IOS Press.

Heraz, A. & Frasson, C. (2010). Theoretical model for interplay between some learning situations and brainwaves. *International Conference on Intelligent Tutoring Systems* (pp. 337–339).

Mandryk, R. L., Atkins, M. S., & Inkpen, K. M. (2006). A continuous and objective evaluation of emotional experience with interactive play environments. *Proceedings of the SIGCHI Conference on Human Factors in Computing Systems* (p. 1036). New York: ACM Press.

McQuiggan, S., Lee, S., & Lester, J. (2007). *Early prediction of student frustration* (pp. 698–709). Interaction: Affective Computing and Intelligent.

Mota, S., & Picard, R. W. (2003). Automated posture analysis for detecting learner's interest level. *Computer Vision and Pattern Recognition Workshop, 5,* 49.

Muldner, K., Burleson, W., & VanLehn, K. (2010). "Yes": using tutor and sensor data to predict moments of delight during instructional activities. *User Modeling, Adaptation, and Personalization, 6075,* 159–170.

Murray, T. & Arroyo, I. (2002). Toward measuring and maintaining the zone of proximal development in adaptive instructional systems. *International Conference on Intelligent Tutoring Systems* (pp. 133–145).

Nkambou, R. (2006). A framework for affective intelligent tutoring systems. *Information Technology Based Higher Education and Training, 2006. ITHET '06. 7th International Conference on* (pp. nil2–nil8).

Qi, Y. & Picard, R. W. (2002). Context-sensitive Bayesian classifiers and application to mouse pressure pattern classification. Proceedings of 16th International Conference on Pattern Recognition, 2002, vol 3 (pp. 448–451).

Ruvolo, P., Fasel, I. R., & Movellan, J. R. (2008). Auditory mood detection for social and educational robots. *ICRA* (pp. 3551–3556).

Sarrafzadeh, A., Alexander, S., Dadgostar, F., Fan, C., & Bigdeli, A. (2006). See me, teach me: facial expression and gesture recognition for intelligent tutoring systems. *Innovations in Information Technology, 2006,* 1–5.

Strauss, M., Reynolds, C., Hughes, S., Park, K., McDarby, G., & Picard, R. (2005). The handwave bluetooth skin conductance sensor. *Affective Computing and Intelligent Interaction*, (pp. 699–706).

Truong, K. P., & van Leeuwen, D. A. (2007). Automatic discrimination between laughter and speech. *Speech Communication, 49*, 144–158.

Varlander, S. (2008). The role of students emotions in formal feedback situations. *Teaching in Higher Education, 13*, 145–156.

Woolf, B., Arroyo, I., Muldner, K., Burleson, W., Cooper, D., Dolan, R., & Christopherson, R. (2010). The effect of motivational learning companions on low achieving students and students with disabilities. *International Conference on Intelligent Tutoring Systems* (pp. 327–337).

Xiangjie, Q., Zhiliang, W., Jun, Y., & Xiuyan, M. (2006). An affective intelligent tutoring system based on artificial psychology. *ICICIC '06. First International Conference on Innovative Computing, Information and Control, 2006, 3*, 402–405.

Zeng, Z., Pantic, M., Roisman, G. I., & Huang, T. S. (2009). A survey of affect recognition methods: audio, visual, and spontaneous expressions. *IEEE Transactions on Pattern Analysis and Machine Intelligence, 31*, 39–58.

Integrating Cognitive, Metacognitive, and Affective Regulatory Processes with MetaTutor

Roger Azevedo and Amber Chauncey Strain

The ubiquity of technology in schools and at home has led to an increase in the use of computer-based learning environments (CBLEs) for teaching and learning. More recently, web-based encyclopedias, educational games, and intelligent tutoring systems have become a leading source of learning where students are able to have a stronger degree of control over their learning. For example, with the advent of Wikipedia, students can expand their knowledge upon the material presented in their text books by simply typing a few keywords into the site's search engine. With just a click of the mouse students can access definitions, summaries, examples, a historical background, references, and a multitude of hyperlinks about any particular topic. One might think, with a world of knowledge at their fingertips, learners with all types of experience and competency could achieve successful learning.

Research tells us, however, that this is rarely the case (Azevedo, 2009; Azevedo, Moos, Johnson, & Chauncey, 2010; Winne & Hadwin, 1998, 2008; Zimmerman, 2000). Although CBLEs are designed to facilitate learners' understanding of complex instructional material, the sheer volume of multirepresentational material can be overwhelming and can interfere with students' ability to regulate their learning. For example, during a 2-h learning session with MetaTutor, an adaptive multi-agent hypermedia tutoring system, learners must begin by activating their prior knowledge and setting meaningful goals. They must then continuously monitor their emerging understanding of the content, assess the relevance of information sources in relation to their current goals, monitor their progress toward these goals, and select and use effective strategies to facilitate knowledge acquisition and retention.

R. Azevedo (✉)
Laboratory for the Study of Metacognition and Advanced Learning
Technologies and Department of Educational and Counselling Psychology,
McGill University, Montreal, Canada
e-mail: roger.azevedo@mcgill.ca

R.A. Calvo and S.K. D'Mello (eds.), *New Perspectives on Affect and Learning Technologies*,   141
Explorations in the Learning Sciences, Instructional Systems and Performance Technologies 3,
DOI 10.1007/978-1-4419-9625-1_11, © Springer Science+Business Media, LLC 2011

They must also engage in complex navigational behavior by returning to previously read pages, to review what they have already learned, or using the table of contents to find pages that are related to the current topic. In other words, students need to regulate their learning. In addition, they must heed advice from embedded pedagogical agents which prompt them to plan and monitor their learning, and use effective strategies.

For example, when learners are prompted to use a learning strategy like summarizing the content, there are several key steps that the student must take in order to benefit from such a prompt. First, they need to understand the prompt – i.e., what is a summary, and how should they summarize? After attempting to summarize, they need to determine if they have summarized correctly, and if not, how to rectify their mistakes. In cases where agents provide feedback on their summarization (i.e., *that summary was a little too short*), they then need to understand and integrate that feedback when they make the next attempt to summarize.

What we have just described are some of the complex cognitive and metacognitive processes that are likely to occur during learning with MetaTutor, but what about learners' affective processes? How do emotions arise, change, and decay? How do they interact with the cognitive and metacognitive processes we just described? For example, how do learners feel when they receive the feedback that they were incorrect in their use of a particular learning strategy? Do they feel frustrated because they did not understand how to use that strategy? Do they feel confused because they might have thought that they did use it correctly? Or, perhaps, do they feel angry that they are receiving negative feedback? To what or whom do they attribute their successes and failures? How do these attributions impact their subsequent use of learning strategies? These are some of the key questions that need to be investigated in our research on the cognitive, metacognitive, motivational, and affective processes during learning with CBLEs.

In this chapter, we intend to focus primarily on the affective and motivational processes which must be *continuously* and *concurrently* monitored and controlled along with cognitive and metacognitive processes, in order to achieve optimal learning. After all, at the heart of most learning experiences lies a host of potentially positive and negative academic emotions such as *confusion, frustration, boredom, excitement, surprise, anger,* and *flow* (D'Mello, Craig, & Graesser, 2009; D'Mello & Graesser, 2010; Pekrun, Goetz, Titz, & Perry, 2002). When learning with complex, multi-representational CBLEs, where there is not only pressure to learn, but perhaps more importantly, pressure to *construct* one's own learning by managing an enormous amount of information, these emotions may be even more intense and may negatively impact learning.

A recent study by D'Mello, Taylor, and Graesser (2007) examined the trajectories of learners' emotions while interacting with AutoTutor, an intelligent tutoring system. Results indicated that when learners reported being in a negative emotional state (such as boredom) at one time interval, they were likely to remain in a negative state in subsequent intervals. When learners reported being in a positive emotional state (such as delight), they tended to remain in this positive state, or transition to another positive state (such as flow). These results indicate that many affective states tend to be pervasive, meaning that once a learner enters one affective state he or she is likely to stay in that state. While these results are very informative, we still need to understand how other regulatory processes interact with affective states.

Based on these interesting results, we wonder how someone might overcome the pervasive and potentially negative effects of one's emotions during learning. Recently, cognitive and educational psychologists have attempted to answer this question by examining the steps that learners take, to *regulate their own* emotions (i.e., Schutz & Davis, 2000; Schutz & Decuire, 2002). In fact, based on results from experiments using AutoTutor, D'Mello and colleagues are beginning an innovative line of research, examining the dynamic ways in which emotions emerge during learning and if those emotions can be effectively regulated in order to achieve optimal learning performance. We feel, however, that before we can hope to understand emotional self-regulation in the context of learning, we must first understand how emotion affects other self-regulatory processes such as metacognitive monitoring, study-time allocation, and selection of learning strategies (e.g., Chauncey & Azevedo, 2010). Further, we must understand how the interaction between these processes and emotions impact learning performance.

To establish the purpose of our current program of research involving MetaTutor, we will begin by briefly discussing the strengths and weaknesses of the two traditional methods of examining the relationship between cognitive, metacognitive, and affective processes: i.e. laboratory-based research and classroom-based research. Then, we will describe our newest module of MetaTutor, which we have developed to assimilate the benefits of these two types of research while attempting to avoid some of their limitations. We will also present preliminary data that we have collected and analyzed from the ongoing MetaTutor project. Finally, we will conclude by discussing what we perceive to be the necessary future directions of this interesting, yet perplexing topic.

Two Traditions of Data Collection: Strengths and Weaknesses

Traditionally, the primary focus of learning with CBLEs has been the learner's cognitive and metacognitive processes (Astleitner & Leutner, 2000; Azevedo, 2008, 2009; Azevedo et al., 2010; Efklides & Volet, 2005; Winne & Hadwin, 1998; 2008; Zimmerman, 2008). In recent years, there has been an emerging trend toward studying the impact of emotional and motivational processes as well (Moos & Marroquin, 2010). The majority of this research falls into one of two categories: (1) laboratory research, which typically employs a pretest-intervention-posttest design, and (2) classroom research, which typically occurs over the course of a semester and data is collected with self-report measures at different time intervals. In our opinion, there are strengths and weaknesses to both of these approaches of research to aid in understanding the impact of emotion on learning. This section will describe each of these in turn.

Laboratory-Based Research

In educational research, laboratory experiments are often preferred because they allow for a degree of experimental control which cannot be obtained in classroom settings. Using CBLEs allows researchers to control *time on task* (e.g., requiring participants to spend 30 min learning), measure *study-time allocation* (e.g., setting time limits for how much time can be spent learning each subtopic), and examine *attentional deployment* (e.g., providing task-directed feedback when a participant is off-task). In cognitive and metacognitive research, laboratory-based experiments offer the additional advantage of allowing researchers to prompt for important cognitive and metacognitive processes which are known to occur infrequently during learning, such as making inferences or monitoring one's progress toward a goal or subgoal (Azevedo, 2009; Azevedo, Johnson et al., 2010). An expansive corpus of research indicates that using these processes during learning can promote deep conceptual understanding of the learning material (Azevedo, 2008; Graesser, Chipman, Haynes, & Olney, 2005; Moos & Azevedo, 2009; Veenman, 2007; Winne & Nesbit, 2009; Zimmerman, 2008). In laboratory experiments using CBLEs, researchers can prompt for these processes and examine how the use of these processes affects learning performance.

Along with the benefit of controlling and prompting various processes during learning, laboratory experiments using CBLEs have the added benefit of converging several data sources including concurrent think-alouds, video and audio time-stamp data, and log-file data, all captured during learning (see Azevedo, Moos et al., 2010). By combining several types of data, researchers are better able to understand how several complex cognitive, metacognitive, and affective processes unfold during learning. This can be particularly important for researchers who are interested in understanding not only how these processes affect learning performance, but also how these processes coalesce to influence one another.

However, despite the benefits of laboratory-based research with CBLEs, there are also several limitations. Most importantly, because learning outcomes (i.e., post-test scores) have no impact on their academic career (such as their overall GPA), some participants experience very little motivation to be engaged with the material, to overcome obstacles that arise, or to attempt to fully understand the material. Of course, there are some learners who are intrinsically motivated to learn, even when their performance has no direct effect on their academic progress. However, it seems that these learners are exceptions rather than the rule. Further, many of the proto-typical emotions that occur during learning, such as confusion, frustration, anxiety, or flow, may be unlikely to occur in the absence of intrinsic motivation. This is an especially difficult problem for researchers who are interested in examining the emotions that occur during learning. To overcome this problem, researchers can attempt to induce emotions through various methods such as using film vignettes, memory recall, or false feedback (see Chauncey & Azevedo, 2010; Gross, 2008; Koole, 2009). They can also use methods of inducing cognitive disequilibrium such as giving learners break-down scenarios of every-day devices (Graesser, Lu, Olde,

Cooper-Pye, & Whitten, 2005). These scenarios have successfully elicited emotions like confusion, frustration, and engagement in laboratory-based research (Lehman, D'Mello, Strain, Gross, Dobbins, Wallace, et al., in press). However, experimentally induced emotions may be qualitatively different from those that occur in more naturalistic contexts, which raises the issue of ecological validity. For this reason, we feel that, despite the benefits offered by laboratory-based experiments for cognitive and metacognitive research, it seems that these types of experiments may be less suitable for motivational and affective research.

Classroom-Based Research

While classroom-based research does not share some of the benefits of laboratory-based research, it can often avoid many of the limitations associated with it. The most obvious benefit of classroom-based research is that experiments can be designed as to closely resemble the typical learning context for most students. Rather than sitting in a sterile laboratory with a researcher nearby, participants in classroom-based experiments are often situated in a classroom where they learn about Biology, English, Mathematics, or History. Therefore, it is more probable that the cognitive, metacognitive, and affective processes that arise will be more natural given the situated nature of the learning context.

A second benefit is that researchers usually have access to teachers who have spent extensive time learning about their students' academic strengths and weaknesses (e.g., level and amount of help-seeking behavior, use of effective strategies, ability to make accurate judgments regarding their understanding of complex topics). With guidance from teachers, researchers can tailor their training methods to meet the needs of the students. For example, if a science teacher indicates that her students are struggling with setting achievable goals and subgoals, a researcher could potentially structure a hypermedia learning environment or intelligent tutoring system to train students to more effectively use these processes during learning.

Lastly, because students' success or failure on evaluations (such as mid-term and final exams) directly impacts their academic progress, it is (hopefully) more likely that they will be motivated to perform well. Motivation can manifest itself in many ways across many individuals, and the literature indicates that there are distinct emotions that arise with different motivation orientations. In a recent classroom study, Pekrun, Elliot, and Maier (2006) found that performance-approach (motivation to achieve competence defined by normative standards) is a predictor of emotions as pride and hope in undergraduate students. Conversely, performance-avoidance (motivation to avoid incompetence defined by normative standards) is a predictor of shame, anxiety, or hopelessness. An extensive body of research has demonstrated that these emotional states, which arise from performance-approach and performance-avoidance, can directly impact learning outcomes (Church, Elliot, & Gable, 2001; Pekrun, Maier, & Elliot, 2009; Vansteenkiste, Simons, Lens, Soenons,

Matos, 2005). Since this research indicates that a variety of emotions occur during classroom learning, and that these emotions have the potential to impact performance, it seems that classroom-based experiments are the premier testbed for examining the relationship between cognitive, metacognitive, and affective processes during learning and test-taking. This is especially true since the emotions experienced during classroom-based experiments may more closely resemble those that occur during a typical learning episode prior to a midterm or final.

In our opinion, however, there are still limitations to this method of data collection. Most importantly, classroom-based experiments tend to assess students' *trait* characteristics rather than *state* characteristics (Pekrun, Goetz, Daniels, Stupnisky, & Perry, 2010). For example, students may complete a battery of assessments at the beginning of the semester to assess the cognitive and metacognitive strategies they typically use to regulate their learning and affective strategies they use to regulate their emotions. These assessments can provide vast amounts of self-report data regarding the relationship between students' perceptions of various self-regulatory processes and learning outcomes. However, as these correlational studies do not typically track how students use these processes *during learning*, they do not provide data on how students actually monitor and control their cognitive, metacognitive, motivational and affective processes in situated contexts. For example, at the beginning of the semester a student may report typically feeling calm and at ease during test taking. She may also report that she frequently uses important learning strategies during learning such as taking notes and summarizing. However, suppose midway through the semester this learner encounters a particularly challenging topic, that despite her best efforts, she cannot seem to fully comprehend. How might her cognitive, metacognitive, and affective processes shift in this new situation? More importantly, how might researchers capture these shifts if they are not tracking these processes *during* learning (e.g., Azevedo, Moos et al., 2010)?

Recently, our research has been directed toward developing an improved module of MetaTutor, a research and learning tool which may bring the benefits of laboratory experiments mentioned above (i.e., high experimental control, prompting for important processes and tracking participants' behaviors during learning) to the classroom. Our goal is to combine the benefits of laboratory-based and classroom-based research, while finding ways to avoid the limitations of both. In the following section we will begin by briefly describing the architecture of MetaTutor and the assumptions behind its design. Then, we will discuss how we have used MetaTutor to track students' emotional states during learning.

MetaTutor: A Research and Learning Tool to Study and Foster Self-Regulated Learning (SRL)

MetaTutor is a hypermedia learning environment that is designed to detect, model, trace, and foster students' self-regulated learning about human body systems such as the circulatory, digestive, and nervous systems (Azevedo et al., 2010).

Theoretically, it is based on cognitive models of self-regulated learning (Winne & Hadwin, 1998, 2008). The underlying assumption of MetaTutor is that students should regulate the key cognitive and metacognitive processes in order to learn about the complex and challenging science topics. The design of MetaTutor is based on extensive research by Azevedo and colleagues showing that providing adaptive human scaffolding, that addresses both the content of the domain and the processes of self-regulated learning enhances students' learning about challenging science topics with hypermedia (e.g., see Azevedo, 2008; Azevedo, Moos et al., 2010; Azevedo & Witherspoon, 2009). Overall, our research has identified key self-regulatory processes that are indicative of students' learning about these complex science topics. More specifically, they include several processes related to planning, metacognitive monitoring, learning strategies, and methods of handling difficult tasks and demands.

The actual learning environment is comprised of a learning goal which is either set by the experimenter or teacher (e.g., *Your task is to learn all you can about the circulatory system. Make sure you know about its components, how they work together, and how they support the healthy functioning of the human body*), and is associated with the sub-goals box where the learner can generate several sub-goals for the learning session. A list of topics and subtopics are presented on the left-side of the interface, while the actual science content (including the text, static and dynamic representations of information) are presented in the center of the interface. The main communication dialogue box (between the learner and the environment) is found directly below the content box. The pedagogical agents are available and reside on the top right-hand corner of the interface. For example, in some cases, Mary the Monitor is available to assist the learner through the process of evaluating his/her understanding of the content. Below the agent box is a list of SRL processes that the learner can use throughout the learning session. Specifically, the learner can select the SRL process he/she is about to use by highlighting it. The goal of having learners select the processes is to enhance metacognitive awareness of the processes used during learning and to facilitate the environment's ability to trace, model, and foster learning. In addition to learner-initiated SRL, the agent can prompt learners to engage in planning, monitoring, or using strategies under appropriate conditions traced by MetaTutor.

The purpose of the MetaTutor project is to examine the effectiveness of animated pedagogical agents as external regulatory agents to detect, trace, model, and foster students' self-regulatory processes during learning about complex science topics. MetaTutor is in its infancy, thus the algorithms used to guide scaffolding and feedback to the student are currently based on system-initiated and user-initiated rules that control agents' behaviors based on several variables, including: overall learning goal, list of student-generated sub-goals, time on task and to complete session, specificity of the current sub-goal, navigation to relevant content, time on relevant content, strategies used on relevant content, several metacognitive monitoring processes used to assess various aspects of the self and context, thresholds for various behaviors (e.g., opening and closing a relevant content page too quickly), performance on embedded quizzes, judgments of performance, monitoring dynamics of the task, etc. Overall, the system behavior is quite complex as it attempts to detect, track, model and foster students' SRL and content learning. In the next section, we present preliminary data collected from a study using MetaTutor.

The current adaptive MetaTutor is an improved version of our previous nonadaptive MetaTutor (see Azevedo, Johnson et al., 2010). While our previous research using the first version of MetaTutor (MT1) was directed primarily toward recording learners' use of cognitive and metacognitive processes during learning, our new adaptive version (MT2) is designed to *detect, track, model, prompt* and *foster* these processes, along with learners' affective and motivational processes. The first goal of the MT2 project was to identify effective methods for capturing learners' emotional states during learning with MetaTutor. To take on this difficult task, we first conducted an extensive literature review to acquire knowledge about the various methods which are currently being used to detect emotions during learning. We found that a predominant amount of current studies rely heavily on human-raters to assess emotions. For example, some researchers capture video and audio recordings of their participants and use trained human raters (typically graduate and undergraduate students) to rate the frequency of several key emotions such as *frustration, confusion, boredom, flow,* or *pride* (D'Mello et al., 2007). A limitation that we find with this method is that even highly trained human raters may be incapable of accurately coding other individuals' emotions (e.g., Graesser, McDaniel, Chipman, Witherspoon, D'Mello, & Gholson, 2006). Presumably this is because individuals experience and interpret emotions differently, which makes rating *others'* emotions challenging.

To get around this limitation, some studies have used retrospective emotion-coding, in which participants watch a video of their own learning session and rate their emotions at specific intervals in the video (i.e., every 2 min) (Craig, Graesser, Sullins, & Gholson, 2004). This method may be more effective because participants are rating their *own* emotions, rather than having their emotions rated by a stranger. However, we believe it is likely that participants may not be able to accurately recall their emotions after they have occurred and diminished, even when they are able to use the videos as cues. Also, it is possible that display rules (such as not wanting to express anger or frustration) may cause participants to not report negative emotions, even if they experienced them frequently during learning.

More recently, researchers have attempted to use physiological sensors such as EMG, EKG, EEG, and GSR to assess learners' emotions during learning (see Calvo & D'Mello, 2010; Gross, 2007; Koole, 2009 for recent reviews). We feel that the use of sensors may provide the most accurate assessment of learners' emotions, because individuals' physiological responses are often closely linked to their emotional experiences. However, we find most of these sensors to be highly intrusive and may actually *induce* emotions (such as anxiety or stress) that may not have occurred in their absence. In that case, it seems necessary that we find a highly accurate method of detecting learners' emotions without inducing new emotions or significantly altering naturally occurring emotions.

To improve our own research, we have acquired FaceReader™, a software package which we believe may resolve many of the issues described above. The FaceReader is a program used for facial analysis that can detect emotional expressions in the face. It can identify the six basic emotions described by Ekman (1992): happy, sad, angry, surprised, scared, disgusted, and neutral (see Zeng, Pantic, Roisman, & Huang, 2009). The strength of the software is that it is completely non-invasive. That is, participants do not have to wear sensors during learning, and are not required to make any report of their emotional states. Rather, the software collects facial data on-line which is then processed off-line, meaning that it can use previously recorded videos from each participant's learning session. In this way, we can collect a high volume of data from each participant without being overly invasive or disruptive. We have only recently begun analyzing the extensive corpus amount of data we have collected using FaceReader™ software in the MetaTutor project. More specifically, we have started to triangulate log-file, concurrent think-alouds, eye-tracking, and facial data during 2-h experiments with MetaTutor, with pre-test and post-test data along with embedded quizzes, summaries, notes and drawings taken by college students while interacting with the MetaTutor (Azevedo, Johnson, Burkett, Chauncey, Fike, Lintean, Cai, & Rus, 2010). Converging these data streams, will allow us understand how students monitor and control their cognitive, metacognitive, and affective processes during learning with MetaTutor.

In the next section, we present some preliminary data based on a recent study with MetaTutor, where college students were randomly assigned to one of three conditions. In the *control condition* (C), students did not interact with pedagogical agents at all. Participants in the *prompt only condition* (PO) received prompts from multiple pedagogical agents on the use of specific self-regulatory processes such as activate their prior knowledge, make inferences, monitor their progress toward goals, etc. The *prompt and feedback* condition (PF) was identical to the prompting condition, except that students in the *prompt and feedback condition* also received feedback from the agent regarding their use of the prompted processes.

Affective States During Learning with MetaTutor: Preliminary Data

In this preliminary analysis, we were interested in uncovering which emotional states (neutral, happy, surprised, angry, disgusted, scared, and sad) were experienced across conditions between high and low performers. First, using a subset of participants from our MetaTutor project whose facial expressions were recorded and analyzed with FaceReader ($n = 15$), we conducted a frequency analysis to examine the frequency of each emotion across the three conditions, to determine if participants were likely to experience different types of emotions by condition. See Fig. 1 for a sample of the data on affective states experienced by condition, during a 2-h learning experiment with MetaTutor.

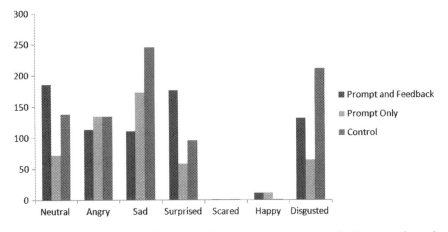

Fig. 1 Total raw frequencies of each classified emotional state across the three experimental conditions

As shown in Fig. 1, preliminary data indicates that, overall participants tended to experience the seven detected emotions differentially across conditions (although these differences failed to achieve statistical significance). Most notably, we found that participants in condition C were more likely to experience negative emotions such as sadness and disgust than those in the other two experimental conditions. Specifically, we found that 66% of all emotions detected by FaceReader for the condition C were negative (sadness, anger, and disgust). In contrast, 49% and 51% of all detected emotions were negative for the PF and PO conditions, respectively.

What are some of the possible explanations of these preliminary data? Perhaps participants who were not prompted to engage in critical cognitive and metacognitive processes which are known to improve learning, and received no feedback about their performance, were likely to feel overwhelmed by the volume and complexity of the material, and to become doubtful of their ability to successfully learn such a difficult topic. These feelings of self-doubt may have translated to the expression of negative emotions like sadness and disgust which may be directed toward oneself (i.e., the perception that one is ill-equipped to learn the material) or toward the learning environment (i.e., this is badly designed and is hindering me from learning). Perhaps those in the PF condition (who received prompts and feedback) and the PO condition (who received prompts only) were better equipped to avoid these kinds of negative emotions because they were given more guidance to help them manage their learning.

These results provide interesting insights about the relationship between computer-delivered metacognitive guidance (prompts and feedback) and emotions during learning with MetaTutor. However, we feel that it is equally important to understand how emotions are experienced differentially between high-performing and low-performing learners. To answer this question, we conducted an independent-samples t-test to determine if there were significant differences in detected emotions between participants who performed above the median, and at or below the median. This analysis revealed that high performers experienced significantly less *sadness* than low performers, $(t\,(13) = 3.67, p < 0.05, d = 1.96)$. While we found no other statistically significant differences between the two groups, we found high effect sizes for surprise $(d = 0.71)$ and disgust $(d = 0.82)$, with high performers tending to experience *more* of these emotions. One question that will need to be addressed as we investigate these preliminary data is, whether there are, indeed, significant differences between the emotions experienced by high and low performers, or if FaceReader simply detects more emotions in high performers. For example, are high performers more likely to display emotions than low performers? Are the emotions more frequently experienced by high performers, more easily detected by FaceReader, than those experienced by low performers? These are questions that will need to be addressed as we continue to analyze these data.

Further, it is important to point out that all of the basic emotions detected by FaceReader have been demonstrated in previous studies to occur infrequently during learning (see Kort, Reilly, & Picard, 2001). Instead, as stated above, empirical research has shown that learners are more likely to experience emotions like boredom, flow, frustration, and confusion. A clear limitation of the use of FaceReader is its inability to detect such emotions. As we continue examining these data in the ongoing MetaTutor experiment, we will need to search for effective ways to detect, monitor, and record these emotions throughout the learning session.

Conclusions and Future Directions

Intelligent multi-agent learning environments, like MetaTutor, represent a great leap forward in transforming how we support students' self-regulated learning. There are several multi-agent, adaptive and intelligent environments including Graesser, D'Mello and colleagues' AutoTutor (see D'Mello, Lehman, & Graesser, 2011), Biswas and colleagues' Betty's Brain (Leelawong & Biswas, 2008), Lester and colleagues' Crystal Island (Lester, McQuiggan, & Sabourin, 2011), and White and colleagues' Inquiry Island (White, Frederiksen, & Collins, 2009), that have been developed to support students' self-regulated learning. Our focus has been almost exclusively on the detection, tracking, modeling, and fostering of cognitive and metacognitive processes. In the domain of self-regulated learning, however, there are other areas that have been less extensively explored by researchers, such as motivation and affect. A comprehensive model of SRL must include cognitive, metacognitive, affective, and motivational processes. For example, one of the significant challenges recently raised by Moos and Marroquin (2010) is the neglected area of studying motivation in multimedia, hypertext and hypermedia learning environments. According to them, there is a paucity of research on the role motivational processes, mainly due to the complex construct of motivation and interest, and the difficulty in measuring and linking it to learning outcomes. Lastly, they caution researchers to take the appropriate steps in interpreting outcomes of studies using motivational constructs. As Moos and Marroquin (2010) also mention, future studies in this field require consideration of more process data, like think-aloud protocols, eye-tracking data, and data from online trace methodologies (e.g., Azevedo, Moos et al., 2010). These data will provide insights into learning processes with hypermedia and hypertext environments, and the role of motivation, interest and similar factors on degree of learning. And finally, the question needs to be investigated whether the use of all sophisticated and expensive hypermedia environment benefits the learners significantly or not, and whether it boosts their motivation, interest and learning.

The role of affect has to be taken into consideration when examining the role of self-regulated learning with advanced learning technologies. Recent work has focused on the role of affect on students' learning in Science and Mathematics and has been instrumental in detecting and classifying various emotions during learning (e.g., Calvo & D'Mello, 2010; McQuiggan, Robison, & Lester, 2010). Further work on affect, should focus on understanding how affect may influence cognitive and metacognitive processes and either (temporarily) impede learning or foster learning with advanced learning technologies. Similarly, work on affect regulation is needed to determine how learners monitor and control their emotions during learning about complex and challenging topics and domains. These are a few of the critical issues that need to be investigated so that we can advance the field of SRL and build learning technologies that are truly capable of supporting students' cognitive, metacognitive, motivational and affective self-regulatory process.

Acknowledgments The research presented in this chapter has been supported by funding from the National Science Foundation (Early Career Grant DRL 0133346, DRL 0633918, DRL 0731828, HCC 0841835) awarded to the first author. The authors would also like to thank Candice Burkett, Michael Cox, Eric Brooks, Andrew Hoff, and Rachel Anderson for the data collection, and Amy Johnson, Mihain Lintean, Z. Cai, Vasile Rus, Art Graesser, and Danielle McNamara for the design and development of MetaTutor. Current work on the MetaTutor is funded by a grant from the National Science Foundation (DRL 1008282) awarded to the first author and his colleagues, Ronald Landis and Mohammed Yeasin, at the University of Memphis.

References

Astleitner, H., & Leutner, D. (2000). Designing instructional technology from an emotional perspective. *Journal of Research on Computing in Education, 32*, 497–510.

Azevedo, R. (2008). The role of self-regulated learning about science with hypermedia. In D. Robinson & G. Schraw (Eds.), *Recent innovations in educational technology that facilitate student learning* (pp. 127–156). Charlotte, NC: Information Age Publishing.

Azevedo, R. (2009). Theoretical, methodological, and analytical challenges in the research on metacognition and self-regulation: A commentary. *Metacognition & Learning, 4*, 87–95.

Azevedo, R., Johnson, A., Burkett, C., Chauncey, A., Lintean, M., & Rus, V. (2010). The role of prompting and feedback in facilitating students' learning about science with MetaTutor. *Proceedings of the Twenty-fourth AAAI Conference on Artificial Intelligence,* Arlington, VA.

Azevedo, R., Johnson, A., Chauncey, A., & Burkett, C. (2010). Self-regulated learning with MetaTutor: Advancing the science of learning with MetaCognitive tools. In M. Khine & I. Saleh (Eds.), *New science of learning: Computers, cognition, and collaboration in education* (pp. 225–247). Amsterdam: Springer.

Azevedo, R., Moos, D., Johnson, A., & Chauncey, A. (2010). Measuring the cognitive and meta-cognitive regulatory processes during hypermedia learning: Issues and challenges. *Educational Psychologist, 45*, 210–223.

Azevedo, R., Moos, D., Witherspoon, A., & Chauncey, A. (2010). Measuring cognitive and meta-cognitive regulatory processes used during hypermedia learning: Issues and challenges. *Educational Psychologist, 45*(4), 210–223.

Azevedo, R., & Witherspoon, A. M. (2009). Self-regulated learning with hypermedia. In A. Graesser, J. Dunlosky, D. Hacker (Eds.), *Handbook of metacognition in education* (pp. 319–339). Mahwah, NJ: Erlbaum.

Calvo, R. A., & D'Mello, S. K. (2010). Affect detection: An interdisciplinary review of models, methods, and their applications. *IEEE Transactions on Affective Computing, 1*, 18–37.

Chauncey, A., & Azevedo, R. (2010). *Emotions and motivation during multimedia learning: How do I feel and why do I care?* In V. Aleven, J. Kay, & J. Mostow (Eds.), ITS 2010, Part 1, LNCS 6094, (pp.369–378).

Church, M. A., Elliot, A. J., & Gable, S. L. (2001). Perceptions of classroom environment, achievement goals, and achievement outcomes. *Journal of Educational Psychology, 93*, 43–54.

Craig, S., Graesser, A., Sullins, J., & Gholson, B. (2004). Affect and learning: An exploratory look into the role of affect in learning. *Journal of Educational Media, 29*, 241–250.

D'Mello, S. K., Craig, S., & Graesser, A. (2009). Multi-method assessment of affective experience and expression during deep learning. *International Journal of Learning Technology, 4*, 165–187.

D'Mello, S., & Graesser, A. C. (2010). Multimodal semi-automated affect detection from conversational cues, gross body language, and facial features. *User Modeling and User-adapted Interaction., 20*(2), 147–187.

D'Mello, S., Lehman, B., & Graesser, A. (2011). A motivationally supportive affect-sensitive AutoTutor. In R. Calvo & S. D'Mello (Eds.), *Affective prospecting (Explorations in the learning sciences, instructional systems and performance)*. New York: Springer.

D'Mello, S. K., Taylor, R., & Graesser, A. C. (2007). Monitoring affective trajectories during complex learning. In D. S. McNamara & J. G Trafton (Eds.), *Proceedings of the 29th Annual Meeting of the Cognitive Science Society* (pp. 203–208). Austin, TX: Cognitive Science Society.

Efklides, A. & Volet, S. (Eds.). (2005). Feelings and emotions in the learning process. *Learning and Instruction, 15* (5) [Whole issue].

Ekman, P. (1992). An argument for basic emotions. *Cognition and Emotion, 6*, 169–200.

Graesser, A. C., Chipman, P., Haynes, B. C., & Olney, A. (2005). AutoTutor: An intelligent tutoring system with mixed-initiative dialog. *Transactions on Education, 48*, 612–618.

Graesser, A. C., Lu, S., Olde, B. A., Cooper-Pye, E., & Whitten, S. (2005). Question asking and eye-tracking during cognitive disequilibrium: Comprehending illustrated texts on devices when the devices break down. *Memory and Cognition, 7*, 1235–1247.

Graesser, A. C., McDaniel, B., Chipman, P., Witherspoon, A., D'Mello, S., & Gholson, B. (2006). Detection of emotions during learning with AutoTutor. *Proceedings of the 28th Annual Conference of the Cognitive Science Society* (pp. 285–290). Washington, DC: Cognitive Science Society.

Gross, J. J. (Ed.). (2007). *Handbook of emotion regulation*. New York, NY: Guilford Press.

Gross, J. J. (2008). Emotion regulation. In M. Lewis, J. M. Haviland-Jones & L. F. Barrett (Eds.), *Handbook of emotions* (3rd ed., pp. 497–512). New York, NY: Guilford.

Koole, S. (2009). The psychology of emotion regulation: An integrative review. *Cognition & Emotion, 23*, 4–41.

Kort, B., Reilly, R., & Picard, R. (2001). An affective model of interplay between emotions and learning: Reengineering educational pedagogy–building a learning companion. In T. Okamato, R. Hartley, Kinshuk & J. P. Klus (Eds.), *Proceedings IEEE International Conference on Advanced Learning Technologies: Issues, Achievements, and Challenges* (pp. 43–38). Madison, Wisconsin: IEEE Computer Society.

Leelawong, K., & Biswas, G. (2008). Designing learning by teaching agents: The Betty's Brain system. *International Journal of Artificial Intelligence in Education, 18*, 181–208.

Lehman, B., D'Mello, S. K., Strain, A. C., Gross, M., Dobbins, A., Wallace, P., et al. (in press). Inducing and tracking confusion with contradictions during critical thinking and scientific reasoning. In S. Bull & G. Biswas (Eds.), *Proceedings of the 15th International Conference on Artificial Intelligence in Education*. New York / Heidelber: Springer.

Lester, J. C., McQuiggan, S. W., & Sabourin, J. L. (2011). Affect recognition and expression in narrative-centered learning environments. In R. Calvo & S. D'Mello (Eds.), *Affective prospecting (Explorations in the learning sciences, instructional systems and performance)*. New York: Springer.

McQuiggan, S., Robison, J., & Lester, J. (2010). Affective transitions in narrative-centered learning environments. *Educational Technology & Society, 13*, 40–53.

Moos, D. C., & Marroquin, L. (2010). Multimedia, hypermedia, and hypertext: Motivation considered and reconsidered. *Computers in Human Behavior, 26*, 265–276.

Pekrun, R., Elliot, A. J., & Maier, M. A. (2006). Achievement goals and achievement emotions: A theoretical model and prospective test. *Journal of Educational Psychology, 98*, 583–597.

Pekrun, R., Goetz, T., Daniels, L., Stupnisky, R., & Perry, R. (2010). Boredom in achievement settings: Exploring control antecedents and performance outcomes of a neglected emotion. *Journal of Educational Psychology, 102*, 531–549.

Pekrun, R., Goetz, T., Titz, W., & Perry, R. P. (2002). Academic emotions in students' self-regulated learning and achievement: A program of quantitative and qualitative research. *Educational Psychologist, 37*, 91–106.

Pekrun, R., Maier, M. A., & Elliot, A. J. (2009). Achievement goals and achievement emotions: Testing a model of their joint relations with academic performance. *Journal of Educational Psychology, 101*, 115–135.

Schutz, P. A., & Davis, H. A. (2000). Emotions during self regulation: The regulation of emotion during test taking. *Educational Psychologist, 35*, 243–256.

Schutz, P. A., & DeCuire, J. T. (2002). Inquiry on emotions in education. *Educational Psychologist, 37*, 125–134.

Vansteenkiste, M., Simons, J., Lens, W., Soenens, B., & Matos, L. (2005). Examining the motivational impact of intrinsic versus extrinsic goal framing and autonomy-supportive versus internally controlling communication style on early adolescents' academic achievement. *Child Development, 2*, 483–501.

Veenman, M. (2007). The assessment and instruction of self-regulation in computer-based environments: A discussion. *Metacognition and Learning, 2*, 177–183.

White, B., Frederiksen, J., & Collins, A. (2009). The interplay of scientific inquiry and metacognition: More than a marriage of convenience. In D. J. Hacker, J. Dunlosky, & A. C. Graesser (Eds.), *Handbook of metacognition in education* (pp. 175–205). New York: Routledge.

Winne, P. H., & Hadwin, A. F. (1998). Studying as self-regulated learning. In D. J. Hacker, J. Dunlosky, & A. Graesser (Eds.), *Metacognition and educational theory and practice* (pp. 277–304). Hillsdale, NJ: Erlbaum.

Winne, P., & Hadwin, A. (2008). The weave of motivation and self-regulated learning. In D. Schunk & B. Zimmerman (Eds.), *Motivation and self-regulated learning: Theory, research, and applications* (pp. 297–314). NY: Taylor & Francis.

Winne, P. H., & Nesbit, J. C. (2009). Supporting self-regulated learning with cognitive tools. In D. J. Hacker, J. Dunlosky, & A. C. Graesser (Eds.), *Handbook of metacognition in education* (pp. 259–277). New York: Routledge.

Zeng, Z., Pantic, M., Roisman, G. I., & Huang, T. S. (2009). A survey of affect recognition methods: Audio, visual, and spontaneous expressions. *IEEE Transaction on Pattern Analysis and Machine Intelligence, 31*, 39–58.

Zimmerman, B. (2000). Attaining self-regulation: A social cognitive perspective. In M. Boekaerts, P. Pintrich, & M. Zeidner (Eds.), *Handbook of self-regulation* (pp. 13–39). San Diego, CA: Academic.

Zimmerman, B. (2008). Investigating self-regulation and motivation: Historical background, methodological developments, and future prospects. *American Educational Research Journal, 45*(1), 166–183.

Designing Adaptive Motivational Scaffolding for a Tutoring System

Genaro Rebolledo-Mendez, Rosemary Luckin, and Benedict du Boulay

Introduction

Attribution Theory (Weiner, 1990) and Goal Orientation Theory (Ames, 1990) provide human teachers with useful guidelines to help them understand students' motivation and *personalize* their choice of educational activities. Such theories can assist teachers by informing the way they may interact with students in real class settings. However, it is less obvious how these theories can aid the development of motivationally aware educational technology. One of the strengths of educational technology, for example, intelligent tutoring systems, is the use of learner models to adapt the learning activities to the student's current abilities and needs. This adaptation has provided some degree of efficiency tailoring in educational content delivery but the resulting activities are not, necessarily, motivating for students.

The focus of this chapter is the application of the concept of personalization in tutoring systems (user modeling plus scaffolding) to implement concepts taken from theories of motivation in order to develop a motivationally aware tutoring system. The underlying reason for motivational personalization is that matching the delivery of learning material to students' motivation (or de-motivation) should improve their experience and, arguably, also their learning. Ecolab II is the intelligent tutoring system chosen to experiment with motivational scaffolding. It was selected because its underlying principles of adaptation are also applicable at a motivational level. Ecolab II is a system that is inspired by the work of Vygotsky in the sense that it models the learner's Zone of Proximal Development in order to scaffold the learning process, particularly by suggesting help and adapting task-challenge levels to individual students. The idea behind Ecolab II is to personalize the learning process

G. Rebolledo-Mendez (✉)
Faculty of Informatics, Av. Jalapa esq. Av. Avila Camacho,
Col. Centro, 91020, Jalapa, Veracruz, Mexico
e-mail: grebolledo@uv.mx

R.A. Calvo and S.K. D'Mello (eds.), *New Perspectives on Affect and Learning Technologies*,   155
Explorations in the Learning Sciences, Instructional Systems and Performance Technologies 3,
DOI 10.1007/978-1-4419-9625-1_12, © Springer Science+Business Media, LLC 2011

by suggesting increasingly complex activities or different levels of help. The result can be seen as a virtual more able partner who provides activities that are part of the students' education but slightly beyond his or her independent ability (Luckin & du Boulay, 1999).

There are two difficulties in working with learner's motivation in computer-based settings, the first is how to detect varying states of motivation and the second is how to remediate negative states. The problem of detection has been considered for other tutoring systems, see for example (de Vicente & Pain, 1998) and in the Ecolab II (Rebolledo-Mendez, 2003). This chapter deals with the second problem (remediation) and presents the design process for the motivational scaffolding of the same tutoring system.[1] This chapter does not address issues such as affect (Burleson & Picard, 2004) or emotions but focuses on how to motivate learners considering the theories of motivation presented in the Background Section. Designers of motivational scaffolding, it is hoped, may benefit from the design process presented in this chapter as it describes how motivation was conceptualized and then made explicit in the tutoring system. The chapter also presents the result of an initial evaluation suggesting a positive influence of the motivating techniques.

Background

Motivation is a term that has been understood differently by different researchers. If one considers motivation to be concerned with what induces a student to learn then the differences in definition relate to the perceived cause of that inducement. Some researchers believe that the cause is external and based on stimulus–response connections; others believe that it is internal and originating in beliefs, thoughts or objectives. Educational technology has borrowed concepts from some theories of motivation to design tutoring systems that consider motivation. One of the first examples of a tutoring system addressing the issue of motivational detection was MORE (del Soldato & du Boulay, 1996). Other works which consider motivation include the Genetics System (Song & Keller, 2001) where Keller's (1983) model of motivation called Attention Relevance Confidence and Satisfaction (ARCS for short) was implemented, the Virtual Factory Teaching System (Qu & Johnson, 2005) which utilizes biometrics based on the learners' gaze to model motivation, and the My Pet Our Pet system (Chen, Deng, Chou, & Chan, 2005) which motivates learners to collaborate in computer-mediated instruction. Corresponding to the richness and diversity of motivational strategies, their implementation in tutoring systems reflects the designers' understanding of motivation. For the purposes of this chapter, motivation is understood as the student's desire to expend effort in the pursuit of learning activities while seeking less help and greater task challenges

---

[1] There is evidence suggesting the problem of remediation of de-motivation is also true among teachers (Balaam, 2007).

(Rebolledo-Mendez, 2003). For an historical perspective on the study of motivation in education please refer to (Weiner, 1990).

This chapter starts with the notion that motivation is linked to the desire for performing learning activities based on acting as a response to expectancies and values (Rotter, 1954). Expectancy is referred to as the state of mind that triggers different types of behaviors in individuals in order to achieve goals. These behaviors are regulated by the expectancy of the reward and by the value of the reward. Expectancy shifts were typical when people's performance was attributed to skill. As such, performance is controllable and expectancy increments may be expected after success; when performance is not controllable, expectancy decrements may be expected after failure (Rotter, 1954). Based on the idea of expectancy, other concepts entered motivational research. For example, an extension to the idea of expectations, specific behaviors associated with expectancies can be defined (Cantor, 1990): high achievers display an optimistic behavior to reinforce their success whereas defensive pessimists expect to do poorly or anticipate a variety of negative scenarios. Helplessness is another behavior that is used to explain lack of motivation in students who often do not exert enough effort: learned helplessness is due to the student's belief that success is out of their control (Dweck, 1975).

Achievement theory (Atkinson, 1964) considers the notion of triumph in undertaking a goal: individuals with higher needs for recognition prefer tasks of intermediate difficulty. Achievement theory evolved into Goal Theory (Ames, 1990) which studies the types of goals and their impact on learning. Goal theory combines the concepts of involvement, rewards and social comparisons as indicators of success and ability. Intrinsic and extrinsic motivation are other concepts that might explain the influence of motivation on learning (Deci, 1975; Sansone & Harackiewicz, 2000). Extrinsic motivation prompts behaviors that arise as the direct influence of externally administered rewards (pay, possessions, prestige, positive feedback, for example). In contrast, intrinsic motivation is believed to exist when the behavior displayed is inspired by learning for its own sake rather than to obtain material or social reinforcement. The term intrinsic implies internal, psychological needs that reinforce students' behaviors (Sansone & Harackiewicz, 2000). Key intrinsic motivators include responsibility, challenge, achievement, variety and advancement opportunity.

An interesting angle on motivation incorporates the idea of positive feedback as a kind of retribution or praise (Deci, 1975). A series of studies showed that humans perceive positive feedback after an easy task as denoting low ability on their part (Deci, 1975). However, positive feedback after a difficult task was considered as very rewarding. Other studies show the effects of feedback interventions as altering the person's motivational state depending on their source: results suggested that people feel less intimidated by computer feedback than they are by human feedback (Kluger & de Nisi, 1996).

There are also practical approaches to defining motivation, such as the ARCS model (Keller, 1983) mentioned before. In ARCS, motivation is regarded as being influenced by four major factors: Attention, Relevance, Confidence and Satisfaction. Attention is the first requirement to achieve motivation; it has to be obtained and appropriately directed by cues that engage the student in the learning activity. Acquiring attention is often not difficult but the challenge is in sustaining it during the learning process. Attention can be subdivided into the visual and the cognitive, having curiosity as its main component. Relevance is the second requirement to achieve motivation. Tutors must demonstrate the relevance of the material so that the students perceive a degree of meaningfulness in what is being taught. Even if the tutor improves the learners' attention and sense of relevance, motivation may not be achieved due to too little or too much confidence, which could be related to the learner's expectancy of success. Tutors should be able to detect and correct any excess or lack of confidence through the use of tailored strategies. By doing so students will become more realistic about what they can learn given the context of the lesson. Finally, satisfaction must be created in the learner to give the learning a sense of fulfillment. The provision of rewards should also be included in instructional design to achieve greater degrees of satisfaction. As a consequence, to achieve a more effective learning experience, instruction needs to place a special emphasis on optimizing the four factors of the model. Motivational diagnosis demands that the teacher constantly assesses any change in these variables, which could be the basis to trigger or withdraw motivational support. A practical applications of the ARCS model in a tutoring system is provided by Song and Keller (2001).

This chapter addresses the design process pertaining to the inclusion of motivational elements in the Ecolab II, an intelligent tutoring system for Ecology. This process involved the application of learner-centered design techniques to define motivational scaffolding for Ecolab II. We adopted the "prototypes for rapid visualization" approach (Curtis & Vertelney, 1990), in which different prototypes were designed, tested and rebuilt, eventually leading to the final version. The methodology of rapid visualization does not define a predetermined number of cycles before a final user interface is created although the starting point is always an analysis of user needs. Because of the evolutionary nature of this model, the process is very flexible and allows the participation of learners during some or all of the stages of designing and testing. The methodology emphasizes that the system's designer should use the results of the tests to build an improved version of the previous prototype. The following section describes the design process including the conception and testing of motivating elements for the tutoring system.

Developing Scaffolding for a Tutoring System

The tutoring system chosen to incorporate motivational scaffolding is called Ecolab II. This tutoring system is based on the Ecolab system (Luckin & du Boulay, 1999), an implementation of a Vygotskyan-inspired design framework. This includes a learner model that records the actions successfully completed by each learner and the amount of system assistance that the learner required in order to achieve that success. The design of this learner model is based upon an interpretation of

Vygotsky's Zone of Proximal Development (ZPD). The design framework also includes an embodiment of a virtual more able partner that provides help and challenges the learner to complete slightly more difficult learning options during the learning process (Luckin & du Boulay, 1999). Ecolab II teaches the concepts of food webs and food chains to children aged 10 and 11. It provides a flexible environment offering the student different perspectives on ecological concepts as well as increasingly complex activities organized in a learning curriculum. The activities are adjustable to the students' ability and challenge-taking preferences. To support this level of personalization, Ecolab II maintains a learner model which quantifies the student's Zone of Proximal Development (ZPD), indicating which areas of the curriculum are beyond what the student can do alone but are achievable when the system, acting as the more able partner, provides appropriate support. The learner model provides Ecolab II with elements to take decisions about how much support he or she needs to ensure that the learner is successful when interacting with activities within the curriculum. The decisions taken by Ecolab II are based on the learner model and can be thought of as those of a virtual more able partner offering the learner activities slightly beyond her current understanding but within her capacity. It was considered important that the inclusion of motivational scaffolding should be consistent with the Vygotskyan nature of Ecolab II and should provide motivational help consisting of varying motivational support based on a motivational model of the learner. The rationale for personalizing motivational help is outlined in a previous paper (Rebolledo-Mendez, 2003).

The design process that led to the development of M-Ecolab (motivational Ecolab) involved the application of learner-centered design techniques and the development of "prototypes for rapid visualization" to design motivating elements to build the motivational scaffolding for Ecolab II. Five prototypes were designed, tested and rebuilt in five phases, eventually leading to the final version of the tutoring system.

Phase 1: The Effects of Feedback Interventions in Ecolab II

An exploratory learner-centered study was carried out to assess the influence of feedback interventions (Deci, 1975; Kluger & de Nisi, 1996) in the target tutoring system. The purpose was to see the effects of the wording of feedback on different learners. There were two male participants aged 9, both Year 4 (fourth grade) students. The two participants each experienced a different version of Ecolab II's help messages: one with flattering feedback and the other with factual feedback. The help messages were developed considering the following criteria: (a) the flattering feedback included messages containing praise and favorable words referring to the student in the first person; (b) the factual-feedback included help messages containing words describing facts using impersonal words and no praise was given. To measure motivation a self-assessment questionnaire pretest was constructed based on Keller's (1983) theory of motivation. The learners were then asked to interact with Ecolab II for as long as they wanted. After the interaction, a posttest was administered to give an indication of the degree of satisfaction with the system.

Considering the answers in the pretest, one of the participants showed a clear interest in the topic of food chains and webs and expressed his desire to become a zoo keeper or a safari rider; he was particularly interested in animals' eating habits. This participant happened to be assigned to the factual feedback condition. The other participant did not show any interest towards science; he happened to be in the flattering feedback condition. An analysis of the interactions showed that both children spent the same amount of time interacting with Ecolab II. However, the child in the factual feedback condition, being motivated towards food chains, completed a considerably larger number of learning activities than the other participant. An analysis of the posttests showed that the student interacting with the factual version of M-Ecolab was more interested, considering the number of questions related to Ecolab II that were answered. Although it is not possible to draw firm conclusions from such a small study, it explored the nature of motivating feedback and its implications for less-motivated learners.

Phase 2: Developing a Quiz and a Crossword Puzzle

It was decided to try out other elements that could arouse students' curiosity and interest in the learning material presented in Ecolab II. A quiz and a crossword puzzle were thought of as elements that might arouse curiosity and interest, in line with Keller's (1983) suggestions on how to increase learner's attention, the first major variable in the ARCS model (Keller, 1983). Low-tech materials were used for the development of the prototypes; the questions for the quiz and the words for the crossword were obtained from the domain of Ecolab II's curriculum. The evaluation was intended to uncover usability problems using established human factors principles. The participants in this evaluation were six usability experts and the materials used consisted of the prototypes presented via slides. The procedure involved asking the evaluators to express their opinions with written comments about the prototypes. The results revealed problems with several aspects of the designs including the lack of rules to operate both the quiz and the crossword puzzle, which were familiar to the evaluators but not necessarily to the children. There was also a recommendation to personalize the quiz by referring to learners by name and also to adjust the difficulty of the questions to the degree of challenge that learners were willing to take, making use of one of the existing features of Ecolab II. The interface envisaged for the quiz needed to be more explanatory and it was suggested that the system could provide explanations for different elements when the mouse pointer was on them. The crossword did not need to have an elaborated description as it was thought that children would be familiar with it. The interface for the crossword was intuitive but the definition of its components (vertical and horizontal words) used complicated words that, it was thought, children would find difficult to grasp.

The final recommendation was that both prototypes needed an exit button that would allow the learners to leave the facilities whenever they wished.

Phase 3: An Improved Quiz and Crossword

Phase 2 provided useful results but it was still not clear whether the quiz and crossword would motivate Ecolab II learners. To find out, it was necessary to have input from learners themselves to produce a more robust prototype. A participatory design setting was devised in which learners and designers collaborated to create a newer prototype. The study used a combination of high- and low-tech materials including two card-based games. The low-tech card-based games consisted of color printouts of the quiz and crosswords prototypes as described earlier that worked in conjunction with a computer with Ecolab II running. The new quiz included the same questions as in the previous version with three possible answers to choose from. An example question is "In the Ecolab, can you find out what eats caterpillars?" with a set of possible answers such as voles, toads, or thrushes. For the crossword puzzle a new set of words was developed, the new words were expected to be understandable for the target population.

The aim of evaluating the new quiz and crossword was to find out whether these were suitable to work in conjunction with Ecolab II and whether learners thought these materials were suitable for Ecolab II. The participants were two boys and one girl aged between 9 and 11. They were asked to interact with both Ecolab II and the low-tech prototypes. The participants were taught how to interact with Ecolab II and told what the software was intended for. Five minutes free-play time was allowed after instruction. Once the learners were comfortable with the software, they were informed of the objectives of this experiment and were asked to play with the card-based quiz and crossword games described earlier. Participants were encouraged to suggest improvements or new games to make Ecolab II more fun. The interaction with the low-tech prototypes and Ecolab II continued for 30 min while the participants were talking aloud. The results of this experiment suggested the wording of both the quiz and the crossword was appropriate. It was also evident that the participants did not spend much time reading the feedback provided by the software and preferred to continue exploring the software by themselves. According to the learners' later comments, the prototypes were experienced as somewhat detached from Ecolab II both physically and conceptually and consequently did not reflect what was being taught. The participants suggested that a story would be preferred to isolated games such as the crossword and quiz. When asked about the nature of the narrative, the participants recommended that a plot could be integrated and emphasized that the use of characters would make it "more fun." The idea of the character was interesting as it was thought it could be employed to create expectations in learners (Rotter, 1954) via spoken feedback. Another possibility was to use the character as a mechanism to deliver varying motivational feedback that could be matched to the perceived state of motivation. Even though the number of participants was very limited, the suggestions were taken into account.

Phase 4: Designing a Narrative

Narrative Centered Informant Design (Waraich, 2002) was considered in order to design the story for Ecolab II. A strong requirement for the new narrative was to preserve Ecolab II's interface, user model and metaphor and to include either the quiz or the crossword puzzle. The existing features of Ecolab II could be used to model motivation (Rebolledo-Mendez, 2003) and provide a platform through which to display the story. To inform the design of the narrative, two 9–11-year-old learners, one boy and one girl, were interviewed. They were asked to suggest characters and a story for a virtual ecology laboratory. Their answers were video taped. Conversations with the learners revealed that they were enthusiastic about a treasure-hunting story for Ecolab II. They also suggested help could be provided by the character when a difficult task was given. To keep consistent with the Vygotskyan approach of Ecolab II, a virtual partially embodied more able partner was considered. This character could convey motivating spoken and domain-specific feedback, adapting its tone by considering the learner model (Rebolledo-Mendez, 2003) maintained by the tutoring system. The learners showed a preference for cartoon-like characters to maintain consistency with the look of Ecolab II. For the learners, one important trait of the character would be its ability to change its gestures and tone of voice to match events in Ecolab II. One feature that could not be defined at this stage was the character's spoken feedback. This was not a simple task as the feedback could cause an important change in the student's motivation.

Considering Kluger and de Nisi's (1996) idea that computer-based feedback could be less intimidating, it was decided that the rationale for the characters' changes of intonation would be determined by changes in the learner's motivation. By doing this, the characters' believability could be increased, which might lead to improving motivational states in the students. For example, by making the character say the phrase "try to put more effort" (in a "worried" tone), the learner would react differently than if the character said the same phrase in a "happy" tone. Considering the young learners' suggestions, the character (nicknamed Paul) would use "kid's language" and two tones (worried and normal, see Fig. 1).

Fig. 1 Facial expression variations

Table 1 Variations of Paul's feedback

Motivation	Preactivity feedback		Postactivity feedback	
	Tone of voice	Facial expression	Tone of voice	Facial expression
Low	Normal	Normal	Worried	Worried
High	Normal	Normal	n/a	n/a

If the learner's motivation were high, the intonation would be happy, else it would be worried. The presented feedback would consider the assumed cause of de-motivation and the context of the learning activities. To keep consistency with Ecolab II activities, the character would produce feedback at two points: before and after an activity. Preactivity feedback provided variations of tone of voice and facial expressions considering (1) the student's motivation and (2) the correctness of her responses in the previous activity. Postactivity feedback was only given when the student had low motivation during the activity, see Table 1.

To evaluate this prototype, low-tech materials and Ecolab II were used in a Wizard of Oz style study. The participants were five 9–11-year-olds, one girl and four boys. They all agreed to take part in the study and worked individually. The setting for this new study involved individual learners interacting concurrently with two computers: one with Ecolab II and the other with the narrative and the character presented using Microsoft's Power Point. In this setting, one researcher (the wizard) could see the students' actions in Ecolab II in an adjacent room and the assessment of his/her motivation using a model of motivation (Rebolledo-Mendez, 2003). The information provided by the model allowed the wizard to control the spoken feedback provided by the character. Examples of spoken feedback included: "Be bold and take more challenge" or "Try to use less help." At the end of the interaction individual learners were interviewed.

An analysis of the learner's reactions, in conjunction with the perceptions of the motivational states recorded on the wizard's computer provided indications about the nature of the motivational reactions for Ecolab II: (1) it was easy for learners to ignore written feedback; instead they tended to focus on spoken feedback; (2) the content of the spoken feedback in the prototype was out of sync with the actions and inconsistent with the learning activities; (3) the participants unanimously liked the cartoon-like character; (4) the participants agreed that Paul's voice was unclear and difficult to understand. The results suggested that less motivated students were particularly enthusiastic about the narrative and perceived the characters as being very useful in providing guidance during the interaction as well as being helpful and empathetic.

Phase 5: M-Ecolab Takes Shape

The findings in the previous phase signaled specific changes. Given that participants tended to focus on the spoken feedback, they could be directed by the character's instructions. Paul's voice needed to be clearer. The motivation model as presented in Rebolledo-Mendez (2003) would automatically detect motivation and underpin the behavior of Paul in the context of M-Ecolab. Automatic detection of the degree of motivation was made by measuring problem-solving effort, number and type of help requests and the degree of task-challenge chosen. Learners were prompted by Ecolab II to select among three levels of challenge and four levels of help (Luckin & du Boulay, 1999). The idea to integrate the motivation model and the motivation reactions by Paul was in order to offer personalized motivational techniques to the learners. If the learner's motivation was low at the end of an activity, postactivity feedback would be provided using a worried tone (see Table 1). The content of the spoken feedback provided by Paul was related to the perceived symptom of the de-motivation, namely lack of effort, over-dependence on the tutor's help or unwillingness to take on challenging activities. For example, if the symptom was lack of independence, Paul would say *"for the next activity try to use less help"*; another example for lack of confidence is: *"be bold and take a greater challenge."*

To test the integration of the motivation modeler and the character a new evaluation was designed to analyze its effects. This study adopted a between-subjects design comparing the original Ecolab II with M-Ecolab that had gone through the enhancement process described above. The students' domain knowledge about food webs and food chains was measured pre and post using the same test as in previous studies of Ecolab II (Luckin & du Boulay, 1999). The test consists of 11 questions and an accompanying sheet depicting a small food chain. The questions consist of a mixture of open-ended, multiple choice and drawing instructions which are marked 1 for tentative knowledge demonstrated, 2 for some knowledge demonstrated and 3 for firm knowledge demonstrated. Because of this marking scheme the maximum possible score was 33 and the minimum score was 0 (Luckin & du Boulay, 1999). The students' ability was measured using the National Curriculum Assessment (referred to colloquially as SAT) results in Science for the previous year. The SAT's were used to assess students' knowledge in England and were divided into Key Stages. For Key Stage 2 (11-year-old) students were assessed in English, Mathematics, and Science. Motivation was measured via an adaptation of the self-report scale of intrinsic vs. extrinsic orientations in the classroom (Harter, 1981). All these measurements were conducted before the interaction, immediately after the interaction and again 2 weeks after the interaction. The participants ($n=29$) were students from two Year-Five classes in a semirural primary (elementary) school in Horsham, England with an average age of 9.3 years. None of them had been involved in the previous design studies. The students used tablet PCs with either Ecolab II or M-Ecolab and were allowed to interact with the software for 40 min.

To assess the effects on learning (see Table 2) with the motivation-aware M-Ecolab, a set of statistical tests was used. In what follows we note that the cell

Table 2 Descriptive statistics for the Ecology test scores at three points of the interaction

	Control ($n=10$)	Experimental ($n=19$)
Ecology pretest	16.70 (5.208)	20.16 (5.65)
Ecology posttest	17.60 (3.718)	24.95 (4.129)
Delayed ecology posttest	20.60 (5.641)	26.39 (3.987)

sizes are small so the results need to be treated with care. We report only those that were of interest for the investigation of the effects of M-Ecolab. Two between-groups t-tests considering ability and pretest domain knowledge showed no significant differences suggesting homogeneity. At posttest, however, results showed the students using M-Ecolab had significantly higher scores in the domain knowledge test than students in the Ecolab II condition ($p<0.001$). Similarly, a comparison for delayed posttest showed that M-Ecolab students had significantly higher scores than Ecolab II students ($p<0.01$).

By using the learners' motivational state prior to the interaction, between-subjects analyses revealed that the control and experimental groups were not statistically different in their initial motivation towards Science (see Table 3), suggesting homogeneity. The scores of the Ecology posttest indicated that less-motivated learners (i.e., those whose scores on Harter's test were below average) in the experimental condition had significantly higher scores than their counterparts in the control group ($n=7$) (t(13)$=-2.280$, $p<0.05$). Likewise, more-motivated students under the experimental condition had significantly higher scores in the posttest than those in the control condition ($n=3$) (t(12)$=-5.050$, $p<0.001$).

Analyses of the changes of motivation during the interaction were performed using the student's motivational state during the interaction as recorded by M-Ecolab's model of motivation. The results of between-subject analyses revealed that there was no significant difference for effort or confidence between Ecolab II and M-Ecolab II users but there was a significant difference (t(25)$=2.069$, $p<0.05$) in the independence component. This result indicated that Ecolab II students requested less help from the system than M-Ecolab learners did (Rebolledo-Mendez, du Boulay, & Luckin, 2005). This result suggests that M-Ecolab students might have been prompted to request more help by Paul. From a motivational point of view, this result might indicate a greater degree of engagement, which was the intended purpose of the motivational scaffolding. However, this result might also indicate a greater level of dependence on the system help and, from a nonmotivational point of view, it suggests students might have fallen into a kind of gaming the system behavior (Baker, Roll, Corbett and Koedinger, 2008). Because there were significant differences in the scores of the Ecology test there is an indication that the help-seeking behavior could have been beneficial for the students. However,

Table 3 Descriptive statistics for learning test scores considering learner motivation before the interaction

	Ecology pretest	Ecology posttest	Delayed ecology posttest
Control, less-motivated ($n=7$)	16.86 (3.485)	18.43 (3.910)	21.71 (6.047)
Experimental, less-motivated ($n=8$)	18.50 (6.928)	23.75 (5.203)	26.13 (4.086)
Control, motivated, Ecolab II ($n=3$)	16.33 (9.238)	15.67 (2.887)	18.00 (4.359)
Experimental, motivated ($n=11$)	21.36 (4.478)	25.82 (3.125)	26.60 (4.115)

future studies might shed light onto this particular behavior. These results can only show interesting trends since the sample was very small. Future evaluation might throw more light onto these trends and the nature of motivational scaffolding in M-Ecolab.

Summary

This chapter has presented an example of the way in which the influence of theoretical concepts can shape the nature of motivational scaffolding. The development of the final prototype progressed via a series of mock-ups that gradually led to the definition of a narrative-supported environment within which different motivational elements were framed. The design methodology adopted in this research paved the way for the creation of a new motivationally aware tutoring system called M-Ecolab. An initial evaluation of the final version of the prototype (Phase 5 of the design) produced useful information particularly related to the type of behavior students displayed in the presence of motivational scaffolding: it seems students benefitted by making numerous help requests.

There are two main conclusions derived from the design process itself. The first is that the methodology used for the design proved particularly suitable since constant small evaluations of the prototypes helped identify potential errors at early stages, in this case, details of the use of a puzzle and a crossword. The technique also allowed the inclusion of many elements taken directly from theoretical concepts. In particular, the theoretical concepts that have informed the design of the motivational scaffolding include the following: (1) Rotter's (1954) idea of expectancy, expressed through the messages delivered to the students by Paul; (2) Deci's (1975) and Kluger and de Nisi's (1996) concepts related to spoken feedback and its delivery; (3) Keller's (1983) strategies to increase attention (including attractive elements on the environment encompassing the look and sounds of the character) and relevance (providing a meaningful and guided interaction with the tutoring system). There were other elements that have not been included but could be incorporated in future versions of M-Ecolab such as extrinsic motivators (rewards in the form of points or stars) or an exploration of intrinsic motivators.

The second conclusion of these studies is that motivation is an important factor and could improve students' learning in a motivationally aware tutoring system. The results presented here are preliminary and a larger sample should be tested in subsequent evaluations. One interesting finding is that the motivation strategies as implemented in M-Ecolab prompted students to display the sort of help-seeking behavior that brought about better learning results. In particular, M-Ecolab students displayed a behavior which was conducive of better learning gains but underpinned by significantly more dependence on the tutor. This behavior may correspond to a gaming the system variant associated with better learning gains as defined by Baker et al. (2008). Future studies will allow the collection of more volumes of data and the application of educational data mining techniques to examine whether this behavior is in fact positive gaming the system behavior and whether the type of motivational scaffolding in M-Ecolab prompts learners to behave this way. Data mining techniques might also be used to study whether other behaviors of interest, such as Cantor's (1990) *high achievers* or *defensive pessimistic* are present. It would also be interesting to further study Ames' (1990) goal orientation profiles and whether they can be detected in M-Ecolab, in a similar fashion to the goal-orientated work of Harris, Bonnett, Luckin, Yuill, and Avramides (2009) and Martinez-Miron, Harris, du Boulay, Luckin and Yuill (2005).

References

Ames, C. A. (1990). Motivation: What teachers need to know. *Teachers College Record, 91*(3), 409–421.

Atkinson, J. (1964). *An introduction to motivation*. Princeton: Van Nostrand.

Baker, R S Jd, Roll, I., Corbett, A. T., & Koedinger, K. R. (2008). Developing a generalizable detector of when students game the system. *User Modeling and User-Adapted Interaction, 18*(3), 287–314.

Balaam, M. (2007) *Exploring the emotional experiences of high school students with a subtle stone technology*. University of Sussex, School of Science and Technology Department of Informatics. Sussex University Theses, S 6754.

Burleson, W., & Picard, R. (2004). *Affective agents: sustaining motivation to learn through failure and a state of 'stuck*. Paper presented at the Social and Emotional Intelligence in Learning Environments Workshop In Conjunction with the 7th International Conference on Intelligent Tutoring Systems, Maceio, Brasil.

Cantor, N. (1990). From thought to behaviour: "Having" and "doing" in the study of personality and cognition. *American Psychologist, 45*, 735–750.

Chen, Z. H., Deng, Y. C., Chou, C. Y., & Chan, T. W. (2005). *Motivating learners by nurturing animal companions: My-pet and Our-pet*. Paper presented at the 12th Artificial Intelligence in Education: Supporting Learning through Intelligent and Socially Informed Technology.

Curtis, G., & Vertelney, L. (1990, April 2). *Storyboards and Sketch Prototypes for Rapid Interface Visualization (Tutorial 33)*. Paper presented at the CHI '90, Seattle, Washington.

de Vicente, A., & Pain, H. (1998). *Motivation diagnosis in ITS Systems*. Paper presented at the 4th International Conference on Intelligent Tutoring Systems, San Antonio, TX.

Deci, E. L. (1975). *Intrinsic motivation*. New York: Plenum Press.

del Soldato, T., & du Boulay, B. (1996). Implementation of motivational tactics in tutoring systems. *Journal of Artificial Intelligence in Education, 6*(4), 337–378.

Dweck, C. S. (1975). The role of expectations and attributions in the alleviation of learned helplessness. *Journal of personality and social psychology, 31*(4), 674–685.

Harris, A., Bonnett, V., Luckin, R., Yuill, N. & Avramides, K. (2009). Scaffolding effective help-seeking behaviour in mastery and performance oriented learners. In: Dimitrova, V. Mizogucji, R., du Boulay. & Graesser, A. (Eds.). Artificial Intelligence in Education (pp. 425–432). Amsterdam, Netherlands: IOS Press.

Harter, S. (1981). A new self report scale of intrinsic versus extrinsic orientation in the classroom: motivational and informational components. *Developmental Psychology, 17*(3), 300–312.

Keller, J. M. (1983). Motivational Design of Instruction. In C. M. Reigeluth (Ed.), *Instructional-Design theories and models: An overview of their current status* (pp. 383–434). Hillsdale: Erlbaum.

Kluger, A. N., & de Nisi, A. (1996). The effects of feedback on Performance: A Historical review, a meta analysis, and a preliminary feedback intervention Theory. *Psychological Bulletin, 119*(2), 255–284.

Luckin, R., & du Boulay, B. (1999). Ecolab: The development and evaluation of a Vygostskian design framework. *International Journal of Artificial Intelligence, 10*, 198–220.

Martinez-Miron, E., Harris, A., du Boulay, B., Luckin, R., & Yuill, N. (2005). *The role of learning goals in the design of ILE's: Some issues to consider.* Paper presented at the 12th Conference on Artificial Intelligence in Education, Amsterdam, The Netherlands.

Qu, L., & Johnson, W. L. (2005). *Detecting the learner's motivational states in an interactive learning environment.* Paper presented at the 12th Conference on Artificial Intelligence in Education, Amsterdam, The Netherlands.

Rebolledo-Mendez, G. (2003). *Motivational Modelling in a Vygotskyan ITS.* Paper presented at the 11th International Conference on Artificial Intelligence in Education, Sydney, Australia.

Rebolledo-Mendez, G., du Boulay, B., & Luckin, R. (2005). "Be bold and take a challenge": Could motivational strategies improve help-seeking? Paper presented at the 12th Conference on Artificial Intelligence in Education, Amsterdam, The Netherlands.

Rotter, J. B. (1954). *Social Learning and clinical psychology.* New York: Prentice-Hall.

Sansone, C., & Harackiewicz, J. M. (Eds.). (2000). *Intrinsic and extrinsic motivation: the search for optimal motivation and performance.* San Diego, CA: Academic.

Song, S. H., & Keller, J. M. (2001). Effectiveness of motivationlly adaptive computer-assisted instruction on the dynamic aspect of motivation. *Educational technology research and development, 49*(2), 5–22.

Waraich, A. (2002). *Designing motivating narratives for interactive learning environments.* Leeds: University of Leeds.

Weiner, B. (1990). History of motivational research in education. *Journal of Educational Psychology, 82*(4), 616–622.

Annotating Disengagement for Spoken Dialogue Computer Tutoring

Kate Forbes-Riley, Diane Litman, and Heather Friedberg

Introduction

Within tutoring systems research, there has been a lot of recent interest in developing systems that adapt their responses to the student's changing affect and attitude as conveyed during the human–computer interaction (e.g., (Forbes-Riley & Litman, 2011b; Conati & Maclaren, 2009; D'Mello, Craig, Witherspoon, McDaniel, & Graesser, 2008; McQuiggan, Robison, & Lester, 2008; Porayska-Pomsta, Mavrikis, & Pain, 2008; Wang et al., 2008; Arroyo et al., 2007; Pon-Barry, Schultz, Bratt, Clark & Peters, 2006; Gratch & Marsella, 2003; de Vicente & Pain, 2002; Kort, Reilly, & Picard, 2001)). The hypothesis underlying this research is that responding to student affect and attitude will improve system performance, particularly as measured by student learning. However, this is a challenging task, which usually involves three main steps.

The first step involves identifying the target affect/attitude state and labeling it in a dataset of student–system interactions. Typically, these target states are not among the "six basic emotions" (i.e., anger, disgust, fear, happiness, sadness, surprise) (Ekman & Friesen, 1978) that have received significant attention in the wider psychological literature on emotion. Tutoring researchers have shown via annotation studies of interactions between students and tutoring systems that a different range of affect and attitude is displayed by tutoring system users (e.g., (Lehman, Matthews, D'Mello, & Person, 2008)). States that have been reported as relevant to tutoring systems are numerous and overlapping and include uncertainty, confusion, self-efficacy, irritation, frustration, boredom, disengagement, curiosity, flow, and interest, among others. Tutoring researchers have further shown that some states,

K. Forbes-Riley (✉)
Learning Research and Development Center, University of Pittsburgh,
Pittsburgh, PA, USA
e-mail: forbesk@cs.pitt.edu

R.A. Calvo and S.K. D'Mello (eds.), *New Perspectives on Affect and Learning Technologies*, 169
Explorations in the Learning Sciences, Instructional Systems and Performance Technologies 3,
DOI 10.1007/978-1-4419-9625-1_13, © Springer Science+Business Media, LLC 2011

such as uncertainty, confusion, and boredom, correlate with learning and thus are of particular interest from a performance point of view (Craig, Graesser, Sullins, & Gholson, 2004; Forbes-Riley, Rotaru, & Litman, 2008).[1] However, the best way to label students' internal affective state(s) is still an open question. Many learning systems researchers rely on trained judges (e.g., (Pon-Barry et al., 2006; Porayska-Pomsta et al., 2008)) while others use student self-reports (e.g., (Conati & Maclaren, 2009; McQuiggan, Mott, & Lester, 2008; Yannakakis, Hallam, & Lund, 2008; Arroyo et al., 2007)). Both methods are problematic; for example, both are rendered inaccurate when students mask their true feelings. D'Mello et al. (2008) compare self-reports, peer labelers, trained judges, and combinations of labelers. Similarly, Afzal and Robinson (2011) compare self-reports, trained judges and online labelers. Both studies illustrate the common finding that human annotators display relatively low interannotator reliability for affect annotation, and both studies show that expert judges yield the highest reliability on this task.

The second step involves developing and evaluating an automatic detection model for the target affective state. Development can be done using statistical learning methods, which use the labeled dataset from step one for training and testing, or using appraisal theory methods, which only need step one for empirical testing of the theory-based model (Gratch, Marsella, Wang, & Stankovic, 2009). Numerous affect detection models have been evaluated in the computer tutor literature. These models use a wide range of learner-based cues, including linguistic, visual, and physiological information, and/or features of the learning environment, to predict student affective states (D'Mello et al., 2008; Forbes-Riley & Litman, 2011a; Conati & Maclaren, 2009; McQuiggan, Robison, et al., 2008; Porayska-Pomsta et al., 2008; Pon-Barry et al., 2006; de Vicente & Pain, 2002). However, despite these demonstrated advances, affect detection techniques do not yet consistently perform on par with humans.

The third step involves developing and evaluating an automatic adaptation model for the target state. Again development can be data-driven, using analysis of the labeled dataset from step one, and/or theory driven. To date there have been few reported evaluations of affect-adaptive computer tutors; this is likely due to the difficulty of the annotation and detection tasks, and the fact that it is not clear what constitutes a maximally effective response in this complex domain. Most evaluations have used a "Wizard of Oz" scenario, where a human performs tasks such as natural language recognition or understanding, or affect detection or adaptation. These studies have shown that in these ideal (wizarded) conditions, affect-adaptive computer tutors can improve performance, measured as user satisfaction, student persistence, or learning (e.g., (Tsukahara & Ward, 2001; Aist, Kort, Reilly, Mostow, & Picard, 2002; Wang et al., 2008)). In most of these systems, the affect adaptation consisted only of simple emotional feedback (Aist et al., 2002; Tsukahara & Ward, 2001). There have been very few reported evaluations of fully automated affect-adaptive computer dialogue tutors that respond to affective states with substantive

---

[1] To simplify our discussion hereafter, we use the term "affect" to cover the variety of different emotions, moods, and attitudes displayed by students in interactions with tutoring systems.

content (Pon-Barry et al., 2006; D'Mello et al., 2010). Neither system yielded a significant overall learning improvement; however, the D'Mello et al. (2010) affect-adaptive tutor yielded significant learning gain for a subset of students when compared to a non affect-adaptive tutor. More generally, tutoring researchers are beginning to address the need for fully automated computer tutors that provide contentful adaptations to multiple affective states (e.g., (Conati & Maclaren, 2009; Porayska-Pomsta et al., 2008)).

Our prior work has addressed each of these three steps. First, we performed a pilot annotation study of student affect in a spoken dialogue tutoring system corpus collected with ITSPOKE (*I*ntelligent *T*utoring *SPOKE*n dialogue system), a speech-enhanced and modified version of the Why2-Atlas physics tutor (VanLehn et al., 2002). This study showed that student uncertainty occurs more frequently than any other state in our system dialogues (Forbes-Riley, Rotaru, & Litman, 2008).[2] We developed an automatic system affect adaptation that provides additional substantive content after uncertain student turns. We evaluated the adaptation both in a wizarded version of ITSPOKE where a human performed uncertainty detection and natural language understanding, and in a fully automated version of ITSPOKE where all tasks were performed by the system. The wizarded uncertainty-adaptive ITSPOKE significantly improved overall student learning (Forbes-Riley & Litman, 2011b). While the fully automated uncertainty-adaptive ITSPOKE also improved learning, this result was only significant for a subset of students. System error analysis suggests that this result would improve by improving the recall of our automatic uncertainty detector (Forbes-Riley & Litman, 2011a).

Our current work focuses on enhancing uncertainty-adaptive ITSPOKE (wizarded and fully automated versions) to provide substantive adaptations to multiple student affective states. In this paper, we focus on the first step of this goal: annotating a second affective state in our ITSPOKE corpora. Our prior pilot annotation study showed that *disengagement* is the second-most frequently occurring student affective state in our corpora. We have also found a negative interaction between low motivation (a related construct) and learning in ITSPOKE (Ward, 2010). Here we present a scheme for annotating student disengagement, along with its source (or cause) in our corpora (Section "Annotating Disengagement"). Our scheme draws on prior work from various human–computer interaction domains (Section "Related Work on Defining and Labeling Disengagement"). Though based on observations of student behavior in our data, our scheme should generalize to other domains. We then present an interannotator agreement study showing that our Disengagement (0.55 Kappa) and Source (0.43 Kappa) labels can be annotated with moderate reliability on par with prior work (Section "Interannotator Agreement"). We conclude by discussing how our Source labels can be used to automatically detect and adapt to disengagement (Section "Conclusions and Future Directions").

---

[2] Other computer tutoring researchers have found similar results for the closely related state of confusion (D'Mello et al., 2008; Afzal & Robinson, 2011).

Related Work on Defining and Labeling Disengagement

Affective systems research across domains has shown that users display a range of affective states and attitudes while interacting with computer systems. User displays of (dis)engagement (or the closely related states of boredom or indifference, and interest, curiosity, flow or motivation) are of particular interest to the computer tutoring community (along with uncertainty and frustration), due to their relation to student learning (e.g., (Lehman et al., 2008; Porayska-Pomsta et al., 2008; Hershkovitz & Nachmias, 2008; Arroyo et al., 2007; Beck, 2005; de Vicente & Pain, 2002)). User displays of (dis)engagement are also of interest in the wider affective systems community due to their relation to system usability (e.g., (Bohus & Horvitz, 2009; Martalo, Novielli, & de Rosis, 2008; Yannakakis et al., 2008; Sidner & Lee, 2003)).

Generally, affective systems researchers agree that disengagement is a complex internal state evidenced by simpler affective displays, such as boredom, disinterest, gaming, or irritation during the human–computer interaction. Disengagement is also associated with interactive, facial and/or gestural signals, such as a lack of attention or participation, gaze avoidance or looking at something besides the computer, finger tapping, etc.[3] Specific definitions of disengagement vary depending on the researcher, with the intention of being coherent within the application domain and being relevant to the specific adaptation goal (Martalo et al., 2008).[4]

Pekrun (2010) summarizes the wider psychological literature on disengagement (specifically, boredom) and provides a detailed theoretical analysis that distinguishes overlapping terms (e.g., lack of interest) and describes boredom and its effects on academic performance in terms of control and value appraisal. This analysis is validated across five empirical studies using boredom self-reporting. The studies all found that perceived levels of control and task value negatively predicted boredom. Moreover, boredom was related to increased attention problems and decreased motivation, effort, use of elaboration strategies, self-regulation, and performance.

The work described in Lehman et al. (2008) and de Vicente and Pain (2002) is most closely related to our approach, not only in terms of application domain, which is also computer tutoring, but also in terms of the methods used for labeling disengagement (or motivation). These methods are briefly summarized below, along with related methods by other researchers. Our approach (Section "Annotating Disengagement") combines aspects of these methods with systematic observations of our data. The remaining disengagement research cited above either used

---

[3] Note that such signals can also signal fleeting disengagement, or distraction, due to an unexpected event (e.g., a knock on the door), followed by reengagement.

[4] Martalo et al. (2008) and Hershkovitz and Nachmias (2008) both provide useful summaries of relevant literature in the tutoring and affective systems community on engagement and the related notions of user motivation.

self-reports or used observed user features to approximate disengagement; while we did not use these methods to label disengagement, we do intend to use them in the future to help automatically diagnose disengagement in our disengagement-adaptive system (see Section "Conclusions and Future Directions").

In Lehman et al. (2008), two independent coders labeled videotaped spoken dialogue human tutoring sessions for multiple affective states; when a nonneutral affective state was labeled, the student's engagement level was also labeled with one of four labels: *Disengaged* refers to students who are bored or uninterested in the topic. *Socially Attending* refers to students who attend to conversational conventions but whose responses are nonsubstantive. *Actively Attending* refers to students who attend to content and give content-driven responses. *Full Engagement* refers to students whose mental resources are fully invested in the topic. Interannotator agreement is not provided for disengagement, but the study finds that full disengagement and full engagement, along with the accompanying states of boredom and flow, respectively, were extremely rare, while low engagement (socially attending) occurred in 23% of labeled affective turns and high engagement (actively attending) occurred in the remaining 77%. Kapoor and Picard (2005) also find that complete boredom is extremely rare in a corpus of videotaped interactions between students and an educational computer game that is labeled by experienced teachers. Their dataset contains roughly equal occurrences of high and low interest (Kappa = 0.79). Martalo et al. (2008) combine low and no engagement into a single label which, as labeled by two independent labelers, occurs in 44% of dialogues between users and an embodied conversational agent in the healthcare domain (Kappa 0.90).

In de Vicente and Pain (2002), ten experienced tutors were each shown a personality trait self-report for a different student. They then labeled student motivation during a recorded screen interaction between the student and a computer tutor for learning Japanese numbers. The labelers were encouraged to explain their reasoning for each label. Note that the labelers could only see the screen actions, not the participants themselves. Motivation was labeled in terms of five categories: confidence, satisfaction, effort, cognitive (task) interest, and sensory (interface) interest. In total, 85 labels were obtained. The authors derived 61 "rules" from analysis of the labelers' reasoning and labels. The rule outputs were one of the five motivation categories. The rule inputs included performance aspects such as speed and correctness, mouse movements, tutoring aspects such as difficulty and presentation, personality traits, and the other motivational categories. An example rule is provided which predicts high satisfaction if a subject performs the task quickly and in a directed manner while displaying high task interest, confidence and performance. However, the study does not present the set of derived rules or a distribution of the rule output categories. Porayska-Pomsta et al. (2008) used a similar but more far-reaching protocol, in which human math tutors interacting with students via a chat interface labeled 8 "situational" factors including student interest, confidence, aptitude and correctness, and difficulty and importance of the material, while also verbalizing aloud all aspects of their reasoning during the tutoring.

Annotating Disengagement

Our annotation scheme for binary student disengagement was developed over several annotation rounds in the corpus resulting from our evaluation of our fully automated uncertainty-adaptive ITSPOKE system (UNC-ITSPOKE corpus). The UNC-ITSPOKE corpus contains 360 spoken dialogues (five per student) from 72 students (7,216 student turns). Annotations were performed while listening to the turns of each student sequentially (as many times as needed) and reading along with the transcript.

The first round of preliminary annotation was performed by a single annotator. Two more rounds were then performed by the first annotator and a second annotator who was trained on annotations from the first annotator. Each round was followed by discussion of the (dis)agreements between the two annotators and subsequent modification of the annotation scheme based on these discussions. The final annotation scheme contains two components, presented below.

Basic Definition of the Disengagement Label (DISE): Annotators were instructed to use the DISE label as follows:

> Use the DISE label if you feel the student clearly seems to have little or no engagement in the tutoring process. That is, you feel that s/he is giving the answer without trying to work it out and without caring whether it is correct. S/he may also show overt signs of inattentiveness, boredom, or irritation (pertaining to the tutor/tutoring environment). Clear examples of DISE turns include very fast answers spoken in monotone or with a sarcastic or flippant or very playful tone, or answers spoken with signs of distraction, such as continuous rhythmic tapping, singing, or a clicking sound indicating they are playing with electronics, etc. Often DISE turns are not so clear-cut. Do not use the DISE label if you are not sure that a turn is DISE, or it seems only a little DISE. Recalibrate your use of the DISE label relative to each student, because students vary in how they express DISE.

This definition draws on the prior work in Section "Related Work on Defining and Labeling Disengagement" as well as on specific observations of student behavior in our data. Based on the finding by Lehman et al. (2008) and others (and ourselves) that total disengagement is rare in human–computer interactions, our DISE label is used for turns that display either no or low engagement; all other turns are labeled nonDISE by default.

Basic Definitions of Sources of Disengagement: We found during the intermediary annotation rounds that there could be multiple sources of disengagement, each of which might require a different adaptation. Our method for developing our six Source categories was similar to that used in the de Vicente and Pain (2002) study (Section "Related Work on Defining and Labeling Disengagement") to develop their "motivation rule inputs."[5] In particular, during each annotation round, annotators discussed the reasoning behind their DISE labels with the intention of elucidating all underlying sources (i.e., causes) of disengagement. Our Source categories were

---

[5] Conati and Maclaren (2009) also delineate data- and theory-driven causes of emotions, but their research currently does not include (dis)engagement or related states such as boredom or interest.

thus based on specific observations in our data, but overlap with disengagement causes previously proposed (e.g., difficulty of material) and should also generalize to other domains. The six Source definitions below describe the underlying cause of the disengagement *as well as* the behavior that evidences it. In particular, the Sources distinguish different student reactions to the system's limited natural language understanding abilities (Language/Gaming), different student perceptions of the tutoring material (Easy/Hard/Presentation), and a final "catch-all" category describing student reactions as the tutoring session progresses (Done).

- *Language*: Student is distracted and hyperarticulates his/her answer[6] (with or without irritation) because the system has misunderstood an immediately prior student answer due to its limited natural language understanding capabilities.
- *Gaming*: Student does not try to work out the answer but instead deliberately gives an incorrect answer that attempts to fool the system into marking it correct due to its limited natural language understanding capabilities. Examples include deliberately gives two opposite answers (e.g., "up and down"), leaves off a requested element of the answer (e.g., units in a numerical answer) or gives an obviously wrong or vague answer.
- *Presentation*: Student does not pay attention to the tutor turn because the material is not presented in a way that is helpful for this student. The most common example is very long tutor turns. Students can both hear the tutor turns and see the text of the tutor turns in the student interface. Some students may lose focus during long tutor turns because they perceive it as too long and boring.
- *Easy*: Student finds the material too easy so s/he loses interest. Note that this student will usually give the correct answer, but s/he may also give an incorrect answer if s/he does not hear the question properly. Common examples include simple questions that are repeated across problems, such as "What is the direction of gravity?" (answer: down). Some students gain confidence by answering these repeated questions correctly. Other students become bored because the question was already asked and answered.
- *Hard*: Student finds the material too hard so s/he loses interest. Note that this student will usually give an incorrect answer, but s/he may also give the correct answer by guessing. Common examples include questions asking for physics law definitions. Some students attempt to work out the answer based on the discussion, while others disengage and do not try to work out the answer.
- *Done*: Student just wants the experiment to be over – s/he appears bored, tired, and/or disinterested in answering questions anymore. Note that this source typically occurs later in the dialogues, and should only be used when the other sources do not fit.

Finally, note that discussion during the preliminary annotation rounds led to the use of the DISE label by default for all turns where the student does not provide any speech at all, based on the reasoning that the student is not attending to conversational

---

[6] That is, gives the answer with unnatural pitch, cadence, stress, loudness in an attempt to make the computer better understand him/her.

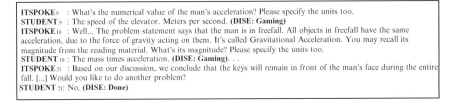

ITSPOKE₉   : What's the numerical value of the man's acceleration? Please specify the units too.
STUDENT₉ : The speed of the elevator. Meters per second. **(DISE: Gaming)**
ITSPOKE₁₀ : Well... The problem statement says that the man is in freefall. All objects in freefall have the same acceleration, due to the force of gravity acting on them. It's called Gravitational Acceleration. You may recall its magnitude from the reading material. What's its magnitude? Please specify the units too.
STUDENT₁₀ : The mass times acceleration. **(DISE: Gaming)**. . .
ITSPOKE₂₁ : Based on our discussion, we conclude that the keys will remain in front of the man's face during the entire fall. [...] Would you like to do another problem?
STUDENT₂₁: No. **(DISE: Done)**

Fig. 1 ITSPOKE corpus example illustrating DISE annotation scheme

conventions by at least acknowledging their turn to speak. Figure 1 provides an example from our ITSPOKE dialogues to illustrate the use of the DISE and Source labels. The first two turns were labeled as DISE with Gaming source by both annotators, because the student avoided giving a specific numerical value, offering instead a vague (and incorrect) answer. The third turn was labeled by both annotators as DISE with Done source, because the student answered "No" semi-jokingly in regard to continuing the experiment.

Interannotator Agreement

Reliability of the final disengagement annotation scheme discussed in Section "Annotating Disengagement" was computed between the two annotators on the tutoring sessions for four students in the UNC-ITSPOKE corpus. The four students were randomly selected and all the turns for those students were annotated sequentially as discussed above, yielding 393 total student turns. Each turn was either labeled as DISE with a single Source, or was otherwise labeled nonDISE by default. The confusion matrix in Table 1 summarizes the interannotation for the DISE/nonDISE labels, which yielded agreement of 86% (0.55 Kappa).[7]

As the table shows, the percent of DISE labeled by the two annotators differed slightly; one annotator labeled DISE in 80 turns, the other in only 66, and each annotator yielded at least 20 DISE turns which the other annotator labeled nonDISE. The diagonal shows that the agreed percentage of DISE is 12%, which is similar to the percentage of uncertainty found in this and prior ITSPOKE corpora (Forbes-Riley & Litman, 2011a). Note that Rodrigo (2011) similarly finds a boredom incidence score of 10% on average across seven computer learning environments.

Discussion of the disagreements revealed two main ongoing DISE-labeling difficulties that are not resolved in the current scheme. First, there were a number of turns where the annotators could not agree whether the answer was DISE or was a

---

[7] Although interpreting Kappa values is somewhat controversial and depends on the application, we find the Landis and Koch (1977) standard to be a useful guideline: 0.21–0.40 = "Fair"; 0.41–0.60 = "Moderate"; 0.61–0.80 = "Substantial"; 0.81–1.00 = "Almost Perfect."

Table 1 Confusion matrix for reliability analysis of disengagement (DISE) labels

	DISE	nonDISE	Total
DISE	46	20	66
nonDISE	34	293	327
Total	80	313	393

Table 2 Confusion matrix for reliability analysis of disengagement source labels

	Done	Easy	Gaming	Hard	Language	Presentation	Total
Done	24	4	0	2	2	3	35
Easy	1	1	0	0	0	0	2
Gaming	1	0	3	0	0	0	4
Hard	0	0	0	3	0	0	3
Language	1	0	0	0	0	0	1
Presentation	0	0	0	0	0	1	1
Total	27	5	3	5	2	4	46

certain but monotone response to the (largely) monotone tutor. For example, a monotone answer given quickly and without hesitation may indicate that the student is confident, or it may indicate that s/he is not trying to work out the answer and does not care whether it is correct or not. For some students, context was useful for distinguishing these cases, by comparing the current turn to other turns by the same student that were more clearly disengaged or certain. However, for other students, this process would merely yield a larger set of turns scattered throughout the session which all sounded similar and were not clearly ambivalent or certain to both annotators. Prior work suggests that making ITSPOKE more affective could help relieve this labeling difficulty; more socially aware computer tutors can yield greater social responses from the student (Wang et al., 2008).

Second, there were a number of turns which both annotators felt displayed clear acoustic and/or prosodic changes, but the annotators could not agree on which affective state(s) was being expressed. Usually, one annotator interpreted the acoustic/prosodic changes as signaling vacillating engagement levels, while the other annotator interpreted the acoustic/prosodic changes as signaling constant engagement with vacillating uncertainty levels.

The confusion matrix in Table 2 summarizes the interannotation for the Source labels on the 46 turns that both annotators agreed were DISE. Agreement for the Source labels on these 46 turns was 70% (0.43 Kappa).

As the table shows, Done was the most frequent source labeled by both annotators. The remaining sources were all selected much less frequently by both annotators; moreover, their distribution differs across annotators. One annotator used each of the remaining five labels at least twice across almost half of the turns (19/46), while the other annotator used these five labels only for a quarter of the turns (11/46) and their distribution was much more skewed.

Discussion of the agreements and disagreements revealed some ongoing DISE Source labeling difficulties that are not resolved in the current scheme. Most importantly, the Done category is too vague and needs to be subdivided. Some instances of "Done" may be due to some internal source related to personality type (e.g., introverted vs. extroverted); similarly to the use of personality and motivational traits as "motivation rule inputs" in de Vicente and Pain (2002) and as potential emotion causes in Conati and Maclaren (2009), we plan to investigate whether labeling student personality traits can help distinguish internal and external sources of disengagement (rather than using the "catch-all" Done source for these turns). Other instances of "Done" may be attributed to some aspect of the tutoring. For example, repeatedly encountering questions that are too hard – or too easy – may eventually cause some students to just want the experiment to be over, even if the first few encounters do not trigger a disengagement display. Similarly, repeatedly encountering system misunderstandings that cause answers to be treated as incorrect when they are correct (or vice versa) may also eventually cause some students to just want the experiment to be over. Since in the current annotation scheme all sources are defined locally in terms of the current answer, they do not capture the idea of disengagement that has a more complex repetitive source, or a source that is not immediately displayed.

Conclusions and Future Directions

We presented a scheme for annotating the presence of student disengagement and the source of that disengagement in a spoken dialogue computer tutoring corpus. Our scheme is based on specific observations in our data but draws on prior work from, and should generalize to, other human–computer interaction domains. Our interannotator agreement study shows that our Disengagement and Source labels can both be annotated with moderate reliability on par with that of prior work on emotion annotation (e.g., (Lehman et al., 2008; D'Mello et al., 2008)). However, the agreement study also showed that the Done source category should be subdivided.

Our Source labels will be used in the next two steps of this research: developing automatic methods for detecting and adapting to multiple affective states in our spoken dialogue tutoring system – specifically, student disengagement and uncertainty.

First, numerous computer learning researchers have used (potentially) causal information about emotions (e.g., tutor or user goals) to automatically predict emotional states (Conati &Maclaren, 2009; Forbes-Riley & Litman, 2011a; McQuiggan, Mott, et al., 2008; D'Mello et al., 2008; Gratch & Marsella, 2003). Our existing Source labels can be approximated using automatically available features in our system, and then used in combination with other features such as timing features, which have previously been shown to be related to disengagement (Arroyo et al., 2007; Baker, Corbett, Roll, & Koedinger, 2008; Beck, 2005), as well as other acoustic, prosodic and lexical features, to predict the presence of disengagement. For example, the speech recognizer's confidence score for this turn, along with running averages of confidence scores over all turns by this student and over all students for this question can be used to represent the Language source, because the speech recognizer's confidence score provides a good indication of how well the student speech is being understood by the system. The semantic recognizer's correctness label for this turn, along with running averages for correctness over all turns for this student and over all students for this question can be used to represent the Easy and Hard Sources. Features related to the tutor turn, such as number of words, temporal length, and dialogue acts can be used to represent the Presentation Source. A number of automatically available features in computer tutoring have previously been shown to be useful for predicting gaming, such as how quickly a student moves through tutor questions after previously answering one incorrectly (e.g., (Baker et al., 2008)).

Second, computer learning researchers, particularly those using appraisal theory methods, have hypothesized that identifying the causes of student affect can help the agent determine how to best respond (e.g., (Conati & Maclaren, 2009; Gratch & Marsella, 2003)). Analysis of our existing Source labels suggests different adaptation approaches depending on the source of disengagement, which can be triggered by our approximated Source features. For example, Hard Sources of disengagement can be handled by providing the student with a simplified (e.g., multiple choice) version of the prior tutor question along with motivational feedback, while Easy Sources can be handled by providing a more challenging related question and/or motivating feedback such as "That was an easy one to make sure you are paying attention" (depending on the question). Presentation Sources can be handled by providing a shorter version of the same question again along with a reminder about why the question is important. Language Sources can be handled by providing a system apology along with a reminder to try to ignore system understanding errors and focus on the tutoring content. Gaming Sources can be handled by providing an explicit request to supply the missing information, along with additional content focused on helping them supply it; prior research suggests that gaming is often due to frustration at not having the knowledge needed to answer the question, and responding to the gamed question with supplementary material has been shown to help reduce gaming and improve learning (Baker et al., 2006). A more generic disengagement adaptation (e.g., for use after Done sources) can consist of motivating feedback and/or productive learning tips, along with progress reports summarizing correctness so far; (Arroyo et al., 2007) show that combining progress reports and learning tips can be effective at increasing learning, engagement, and user satisfaction. These disengagement adaptations will be combined with our existing uncertainty adaptation when a turn is labeled as both uncertain and disengaged.

Finally, we also plan to include student personality and motivation self-reports in our future system evaluations; these self-reports can be used in real-time during the experiment to help diagnose disengagement and its source as the tutoring proceeds.

Acknowledgments This material is based upon work supported by the National Science Foundation (Grant #0914615, #0631930).

References

Afzal, S., & Robinson, P. (2011). Natural affect data: collection and annotation. In R. Calvo & S. D'Mello (Eds.), *Affective prospecting (explorations in the learning sciences, instructional systems and performance)*. New York: Springer.

Aist, G., Kort, B., Reilly, R., Mostow, J., & Picard, R. (2002). Experimentally augmenting an intelligent tutoring system with human-supplied capabilities: Adding human-provided emotional scaffolding to an automated reading tutor that listens. *Proceedings of the 4th IEEE International Conference on Multimodal Interfaces (ICMI)* (pp. 483–490). Pittsburgh, PA.

Arroyo, I., Ferguson, K., Johns, J., Dragon, T., Merheranian, H., Fisher, D., Barto, A., Mahadevan, S., & Woolf, B. (2007). Repairing disengagement with noninvasive interventions. *Proceedings of Artificial Intelligence in Education (AIED)* (pp. 195–202). Amsterdam: IOS Press.

Baker, R. S., Corbett, A., Koedinger, K., Evenson, S., Roll, I., Wagner, A., Naim, M., Raspat, J., Baker, D., & Beck, J. (2006). Adapting to when students game an intelligent tutoring system. In *Proceedings of the 8th International Conference on Intelligent Tutoring Systems* (pp. 392–401). Amsterdam: IOS Press.

Baker, R. S., Corbett, A., Roll, I., & Koedinger, K. (2008). Developing a generalizable detector of when students game the system. *User Modeling and User-Adapted Interaction (UMUAI), 18*(3), 287–314.

Beck, J. (2005). Engagement tracing: using response times to model student disengagement. *Proceedings of the 12th International Conference on Artificial Intelligence in Education (AIED)* (pp. 57–64). Amsterdam: IOS Press.

Bohus, D., & Horvitz, E. (2009). Models for multiparty engagement in open-world dialog. Proceedings of SIGdial. London, UK

Conati, C., & Maclaren, H. (2009). Empirically building and evaluating a probabilistic model of user affect. *User Modeling and User-Adapted Interaction (UMUAI), 19*(3), 267–303.

Craig, S., Graesser, A., Sullins, J., & Gholson, B. (2004). Affect and learning: an exploratory look into the role of affect in learning with AutoTutor. *Journal of Educational Media, 29*(3), 214–250.

D'Mello, S. K., Craig, S. D., Witherspoon, A., McDaniel, B., & Graesser, A. (2008). Automatic detection of learner's affect from conversational cues. *User Modeling and User-Adapted Interaction: The Journal of Personalization Research, 18*, 45–80.

D'Mello, S., Lehman, B., Sullins, J., Daigle, R., Combs, R., Vogt, K., Perkins, L., & Graesser, A. (2010). A time for emoting: When affect-sensitivity is and isn't effective at promoting deep learning. In *Intelligent Tutoring Systems Conference* (pp. 245–254). Pittsburgh, PA, USA.

de Vicente, A., & Pain, H. (2002). Informing the detection of the students' motivational state: An empirical study. *Proceedings of the Intelligent Tutoring Systems Conference (ITS)* (pp. 933–943). Berlin: Springer.

Ekman, P., & Friesen, W. V. (1978). *The facial action coding system: A technique for the measurement of facial movement*. Palo Alto: Consulting Psychologists Press.

Forbes-Riley, K., & Litman, D. (2011a). Benefits and challenges of real-time uncertainty detection and adaptation in a spoken dialogue computer tutor. *Speech Communication* (in press).

Forbes-Riley, K., & Litman, D. (2011b). Designing and evaluating a wizarded uncertainty-adaptive spoken dialogue tutoring system. *Computer Speech and Language (CSL), 25*(1), 105–126.

Forbes-Riley, K., Rotaru, M., & Litman, D. (2008). The relative impact of student affect on performance models in a spoken dialogue tutoring system. *User Modeling and User-Adapted Interaction, 18*(1–2), 11–43.

Gratch, J., & Marsella, S. (2003). Fight the way you train: The role and limits of emotions in training for combat. *The Brown Journal of World Affairs, 10*(1), 63–76.

Gratch, J., Marsella, S., Wang, N., & Stankovic, B. (2009). Assessing the validity of appraisal-based models of emotion. *Proceedings of ACII*. Amsterdam, Netherlands.

Hershkovitz, A., & Nachmias, R. (2008). Developing a log-based motivation measuring tool. *The First International Conference on Educational Data Mining (EDM'08)*. Montreal, Canada.

Kapoor, A., & Picard, R. W. (2005). Multimodal affect recognition in learning environments. *13th Annual ACM International Conference on Multimedia* (pp. 677–682). Singapore.

Kort, B., Reilly, R., & Picard, R. (2001). An affective model of interplay between emotions and learning: Reengineering educational pedagogy-building a learning companion. In T. Okamoto, R. Hartley, J. Kinshuk, & P. Klus (Eds.), *Proceedings IEEE International Conference on Advanced Learning Technology: Issues, Achievements and Challenges* (pp. 43–48). Madison, WI.

Landis, J. R., & Koch, G. G. (1977). The measurement of observer agreement for categorical data. *Biometrics, 33*, 159–174.

Lehman, B., Matthews, M., D'Mello, S., & Person, N. (2008). What are you feeling? Investigating student affective states during expert human tutoring sessions. *Intelligent Tutoring Systems Conference (ITS)* (pp. 50–59). Montreal, Canada.

Martalo, A., Novielli, N., & de Rosis, F. (2008). Attitude display in dialogue patterns. *Proceedings of AISB 2008 AISB 2008 Symposium on Affective Language in Human and Machine* (pp. 1–8). Aberdeen, Scotland.

McQuiggan, S., Mott, B., & Lester, J. (2008). Modeling self-efficacy in intelligent tutoring systems: An inductive approach. *User Modeling and User-Adapted Interaction (UMUAI), 18*(1–2), 81–123.

McQuiggan, S. W., Robison, J. L., & Lester, J. C. (2008). Affective transitions in narrative-centered learning environments. *Proceedings of the 9th International Intelligent Tutoring Systems Conference.* Montreal, Canada.

Pekrun, R., Goetz, T., Daniels, L., Stupinsky, R., & Perry, R. (2010). Boredom in achievement settings: Exploring control-value antecedents and performance outcomes of a neglected emotion. *Journal of Educational Psychology, 102*(3), 521–549.

Pon-Barry, H., Schultz, K., Bratt, E. O., Clark, B., & Peters, S. (2006). Responding to student uncertainty in spoken tutorial dialogue systems. *International Journal of Artificial Intelligence in Education, 16*, 171–194.

Porayska-Pomsta, K., Mavrikis, M., & Pain, H. (2008). Diagnosing and acting on student affect: the tutor's perspective. *User Modeling and User-Adapted Interaction: The Journal of Personalization Research, 18*, 125–173.

Rodrigo, T. (2011). Comparing the Incidence and Persistence of Learners' Affect During Interactions with Different Educational Software Packages. In R. Calvo & S. D'Mello (Eds.), *Affective prospecting (explorations in the learning sciences, instructional systems and performance).* New York: Springer.

Sidner, C., & Lee, C. (2003). An architecture for engagement in collaborative conversations between a robot and a human. Tech. Rep. TR2003-12, MERL.

Tsukahara, W., & Ward, N. (2001). Responding to subtle, fleeting changes in the user's internal state. *Proceedings of SIG-CHI on Human factors in computing systems* (pp. 77–84). Seattle, WA.

VanLehn, K., Jordan, P. W., Rosé, C., Bhembe, D., Böttner, M., Gaydos, A., Makatchev, M., Pappuswamy, U., Ringenberg, M., Roque, A., Siler, S., Srivastava, R., & Wilson, R. (2002). The architecture of Why2-Atlas: A coach for qualitative physics essay writing. *Proceedings of the International Conference on Intelligent Tutoring Systems.* London: Springer.

Wang, N., Johnson, W., Mayer, R. E., Rizzo, P., Shaw, E., & Collins, H. (2008). The politeness effect: Pedagogical agents and learning outcomes. *International Journal of Human-Computer Studies, 66*(2), 98–112.

Ward, A. (2010). *Reflection and learning robustness in a natural language conceptual physics tutoring system.* Ph.D. thesis, University of Pittsburgh.

Yannakakis, G. N., Hallam, J., & Lund, H. H. (2008). Entertainment capture through heart rate activity in physical interactive playgrounds. *User Modeling and User-Adapted Interaction: The Journal of Personalization Research, 18*, 207–243.

Comparing the Incidence and Persistence of Learners' Affect During Interactions with Different Educational Software Packages

Ma. Mercedes T. Rodrigo and Ryan S.J.d. Baker

In recent years, and throughout this book (e.g., Cooper, Arroyo, & Woolf, 2011; D'Mello, Lehman, & Graesser, 2011; Forbes-Riley, Litman, & Friedberg, 2011; Lester, McQuiggan, & Sabourin, 2011), there have been an increasing number of studies investigating patterns of learner affective states, including both the incidence of specific affective states and their persistence, within specific educational technologies. Technologies for learning influence affect (Calvo & D'Mello, 2011). However, it is not yet clear to what degree student affective states vary among learning systems, and whether specific learning systems are associated with characteristic patterns of learner affect. In this chapter, we review a set of studies conducted by our research group that, as a group, have the potential to shed light on this question. Across the studies, we collected data on affect within three intelligent tutoring systems and two educational games, each addressing a different domain. The three intelligent tutors were Aplusix, an intelligent tutor for prealgebra and algebra; Ecolab and M-Ecolab, intelligent tutors for ecology (differing principally in that M-Ecolab added a motivational agent); and two versions of the Scatterplot Tutor, with and without a pedagogical agent focused on student misuse of the tutor. The two educational games were The Incredible Machine, a problem solving/logic puzzle game, and Math Blaster 9–12, a game for prealgebra. These studies were conducted with the same methodology (except for some differences in study time), by the same research group, using similar populations. Given the high degree of difference among these systems and their domains, and the highly similar nature of the studies, we are able to study which patterns of student affective states generalize across these environments – representing to some degree affective constants among learners,

Ma. M.T. Rodrigo (✉)
Department of Information Systems and Computer Science,
Ateneo de Manila University, Metro Manila 1108, Philippines
e-mail: mrodrigo@ateneo.edu

R.A. Calvo and S.K. D'Mello (eds.), *New Perspectives on Affect and Learning Technologies*, 183
Explorations in the Learning Sciences, Instructional Systems and Performance Technologies 3,
DOI 10.1007/978-1-4419-9625-1_14, © Springer Science+Business Media, LLC 2011

corresponding to the affect corner of the affect–technology–learning triangle in (Calvo & D'Mello, 2011). The seven studies presented in this paper represent seven different combinations of technologies and learning outcomes, and as such the findings which generalize across these seven studies can be seen as general properties of student affect during learning.

At the same time, we are able to study which patterns are more influenced by the learning environment and the domain of the learning activity, corresponding to the other two corners of the affect–technology–learning triangle. Within this paper, we present a set of studies that cross several domains, but for which most of the domains involve two systems, allowing some consideration of the different impacts of domain and learning environment on affective patterns.

This chapter compares affective patterns in two fashions. First, we investigate the proportion of a set of affective across environments. In this chapter, we consider these issues across a broad set of learning environments and domains, enabling us to make broad comparisons of affective incidence across learning environments, toward making initial inferences about what types of learning system promote different types of affect.

Second, we investigate the persistence of different affective states across learning environments, studying which affective states fall into virtuous cycles and vicious cycles (cf. D'Mello, Taylor, & Graesser, 2007). Virtuous cycles and vicious cycles can involve either repeated transitions between two affective states with the same valence (e.g., a vicious cycle could involve transitions from frustration, to boredom, back to frustration), or the persistence of a specific affective state over time (which can be conceptualized as repeated self-transitions in a state diagram – an example of this type of vicious cycle is when a student is "bored, bored, bored, bored, bored, bored…"). Understanding the overall persistence of affective states will enable us to understand, as a field, when a result is noteworthy. For instance, if a negative affective state such as boredom is persistent across studies, and a new learning environment does not have persistent boredom, we can hypothesize that this environment may be disrupting boredom, even prior to a two-condition comparison. Previously, Baker, D'Mello, Rodrigo, and Graesser (2010) compared affect between three learning environments, in an investigation which varied research methods considerably (for instance, measuring affect by quantitative field observations in some studies and by retrospective self-reports in other studies), as well as populations (high school students in classrooms in the Philippines, college undergraduates in a lab setting in the USA). This prior investigation allowed us to see what affective states were persistent across different learning systems, research methods, and populations. In particular, boredom was found to be persistent. In this chapter, we look at a considerably greater number and diversity of learning systems, but with a single research method and in populations within a single age group and country, allowing us to study in detail what affective states are persistent across learning environments – and correspondingly, what affective states are more or less persistent in different types of learning environments.

Descriptions of the Learning Environments

Data was gathered from different sets of students using seven learning environments that ranged from intelligent tutors to serious games: Aplusix, Ecolab, M-Ecolab, the Scatterplot Tutor with and without a pedagogical agent, the Incredible Machine, and Math Blaster 9–11.

Aplusix

An intelligent tutor for prealgebra and algebra, Aplusix: Algebra Assistant (Nicaud, Bouhineau, & Chaachoua, 2004; Nicaud, Bouhineau, Mezerette, & Andre, 2007) (http://aplusix.imag.fr/) provides students with practice opportunities in six content areas: numerical calculation, expansion and simplification, factorization, solving equations, solving inequations, and solving systems. Each area has four to nine levels of difficulty. Aplusix presents the student with a mathematics problem from the student's chosen problem set and allows the student to solve the problem one step at a time, more or less as he or she would be using a paper and pen. At each step, Aplusix displays equivalence feedback: two black parallel bars mean that the current step is equivalent to the previous step, two red parallel bars with an X mean that the current step is not equivalent to the previous step (see Fig. 1). This informs the student about the state of the problem in order to guide him or her toward the final solution. Students can end the exercise when they believe they are done. Aplusix then tells the student whether errors still exist along the solution path or whether the solution is not in its simplest form yet. The student has the option of looking at the solution, a "bottom out" hint (cf. Aleven & Koedinger, 2000) with the final answer.

Ecolab/M-Ecolab

The ecology intelligent tutoring systems Ecolab and M-Ecolab (Fig. 2) assist primary school children in the process of learning feeding relationships between different species. They are based on the metaphor of an ecology laboratory and enable learners to add plants and animals to a virtual environment. Learning activities in both Ecolab and M-Ecolab consist of a network of ten learning nodes where cognitive help specific to every learning node is provided with four levels of help messages.

The difference between the two systems is that M-Ecolab provides learners with help at the motivational level as well, via an affective learning companion, Paul. Paul's demeanor changes with respect to the learner's degree of motivation as assessed by a motivational model (Rebolledo-Mendez, 2003). Paul helps students solve the learning activities for which the learner's motivation is low. For example, if a low state of motivation is detected, the affective companion uses a worried

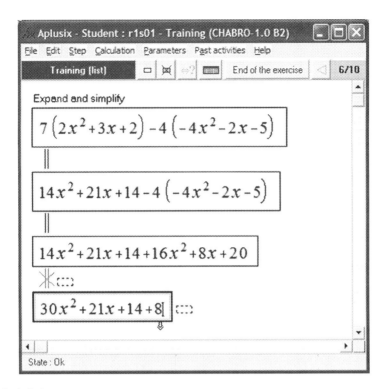

Fig. 1 Aplusix

Fig. 2 Ecolab basic user interface (*top*). Below, happy (*left*) and less positive (*right*) facial expressions in the context of M-Ecolab

facial expression (motivation enhancing strategy on right, Fig. 2) and gives the spoken feedback: "You're doing well but now try to do even more actions within the activity and if you make an error try again to do the correct action!" A more detailed description of M-Ecolab's motivational support is provided in (Rebolledo-Mendez, du Boulay, & Luckin, 2006; Rebolledo-Mendez, Luckin, & du Boulay, 2011).

The Scatterplot Tutor

As the name suggests, the Scatterplot Tutor (Fig. 3) teaches students how to create and interpret scatterplots of data. To this end, the tutor gives students scatterplot problem sets of progressive levels of difficulty. The student must successfully answer

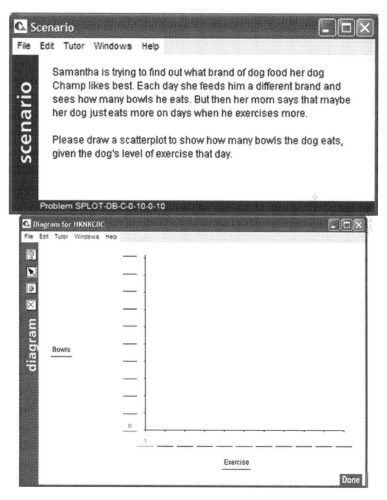

Fig. 3 Scatterplot tutor (not all screens shown) at top

questions regarding the nature of the data available to him or her and determine whether it is appropriate or inappropriate for a scatter plot. The student then plots the data on a given graphical area, shown in the figure. By answering the questions on the scaling tool, students determine the correct starting value of each axes and the appropriate increments. Each action a student takes when using the software is associated with one or more component skill that, when attained, lead to the mastery of the topic. To help students solve the problems, the tutor provides step-by-step guidance such as contextual hints about what to do next, feedback on correctness, and just-in-time messages for common errors (Koedinger & Corbett, 2006).

Baker et al. developed a second version of the Scatterplot Tutor with a pedagogical agent, "Scooter the Tutor." Scooter was designed to both reduce the incentive to game the system (misusing system features to progress through the curriculum without learning – Baker, Corbett, Koedinger, & Wagner, 2004), and to help students learn the material that they were avoiding by gaming, while affecting nongaming students as minimally as possible. When a student is not gaming, Scooter looks happy (Fig. 4, left) and occasionally gives the student positive messages. If the detector assesses that the student has been gaming, Scooter displays increasing levels of displeasure, terminating in expressions of anger, shown in Fig. 4 (right), as well as offering supplementary exercises that give students additional alternatives to learn content bypassed via gaming. Both this version of the Scatterplot tutor, as well as the original version (with no pedagogical agent), were studied.

The Incredible Machine

As shown in Fig. 5, the Incredible Machine: Even More Contraptions (Sierra Online Inc., 2001) is a simulation environment where students complete a series of logical puzzles. In each puzzle, the student is given (a) objects with limited interactivity, including mechanical tools like gears, pulleys, and scissors; (b) more active objects such as electrical generators and vacuums; and (c) animals. The student must combine

Fig. 4 Happy (*left*) and angry (*right*) expressions of scooter

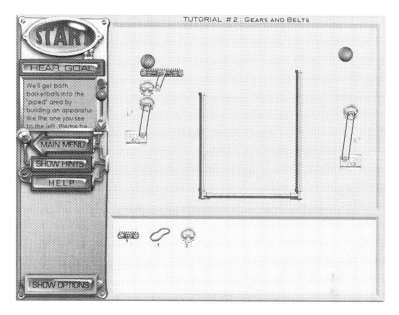

Fig. 5 The incredible machine

these objects in a creative fashion to accomplish each puzzle's goal. Goals range from relatively straightforward goals, such as lighting a candle, to more complex goals, such as making a mouse run. If a student is stuck, he or she can ask for a hint; hint messages display where items should be located in a correct solution to the current problem (without displaying which items should be placed in each location). The Incredible Machine does not explicitly adapt to student learning, knowledge, or motivational state, although challenges increase in difficulty as students complete easier problems.

Math Blaster 9–12

A popular mathematics game from the 1990s, Math Blaster 9–12 (Fig. 5) is published by Davidson (1997). Current versions of the "Blaster" series are published by Knowledge Adventure. Math Blaster is a collection of prealgebra drills embedded in an adventure game. The premise of the game is that a galactic commander is stranded on a planet of monkeys. To help the commander escape, the player has to collect medallions that the commander can then offer to the monkey king. In order to win the medallions, the player has to engage in prealgebra games that require him or her to add, subtract, multiply or divide positive and negative whole numbers, decimals, or fractions. The participants were asked to focus on three activities within the game: Crater Crossing (Fig. 6), Banana Splat and Bridge Builder. These activities were selected because they required the direct and immediate application of basic arithmetic operation. The students were not asked to play the two other games

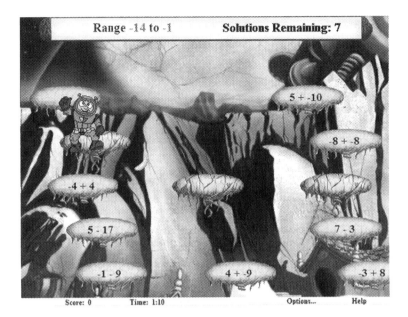

Fig. 6 Crater crossing in math blaster

within Math Blaster because these games involved logic puzzles rather than mathematics. MathBlaster does not explicitly adapt to student learning, knowledge, or motivational state, although challenges increase in difficulty as students complete easier problems.

Methods

The students who participated in these studies were drawn from four private schools and one public school within an urban area of the Philippines and one private school in Cavite, a rural area south of Manila. All student–software interactions took place within a school computer laboratory. In all cases, the students used the software under study for the first time. The details of the user characteristics, environment characteristics, system characteristics, and methodological characteristics of each study are found in Table 1. It is worth noting that, within the Philippines, students in private schools tend to have greater access to computers and related technologies than students in public schools (Rodrigo, 2005). Students in public schools are only rarely required to use computers as part of their regular school work. However, aside from this factor, the populations were quite similar between studies.

A uniform observation protocol was used to record the affective states of students using these different learning environments. Pairs of observers carried out the affect observations. The observers were Masters students in Education or

Table 1 Summary of different studies

Dimension	Factor	Aplusix	Ecolab	M-Ecolab
User characteristics	Number of participants	140	90	90
	Age	12–15	9–13	9–13
	Gender	83F+57M	29F+61M	47F+43M
Environment characteristics	School location	4 urban; 1 rural	1 urban; 1 rural	1 urban; 1 rural
	School ownership	Private	Private	Private
Learning interaction characteristics	Domain	Algebra	Ecology	Ecology
	System type	Computer tutor	Computer tutor	Computer tutor
Methodological characteristics	Interaction time (min)	45	40	40
	Sampling rate (s)	200	200	200
	Interrater reliability (kappa)	0.63	0.73	0.71

Dimension	Factor	Scatterplot tutor (control group)	Scatterplot tutor (with agent)	The incredible machine	Math blaster 9–12
User characteristics	Number of Participants	59	68	36	30
	Age	12–14	12–14	14–19	12–13
	Gender	35F+24M	42F+26M	17F+19M	30M
Environment characteristics	School location	1 urban	1 urban	1 urban	1 urban
	School ownership	Public	Public	Private	Private
System characteristics	Domain	Graphing	Graphing	Logic puzzles	Prealgebra
	System type	Cognitive tutor	Cognitive tutor	Serious game	Serious game
Methodological characteristics	Interaction time (min)	80	80	10	40
	Sampling rate (s)	200	200	60	200
	Interrater reliability (kappa)	0.54		0.63	0.77

Computer Science. Most had teaching experience. The observers trained for the task through a series of preobservation discussions on the meaning of the categories they were coding and through a pilot observation exercise conducted at a different school. Observations were conducted according to a guide that gave examples of actions, utterances, facial expressions, or body language that would imply an affective state, and observers practiced the coding categories during a pilot observation period prior to the studies.

The observers coded a set of affective categories drawn from D'Mello, Craig, Witherspoon, McDaniel, and Graesser (2005): boredom, confusion, delight, engaged concentration, frustration, surprise and neutral. It is worth noting that two of the affective states studied, engaged concentration, a subset of flow (Csikszentmihalyi, 1990), and confusion, have significant cognitive components. For this reason, some researchers have termed these two states *cognitive-affective* states (cf. Baker et al., 2010). However, in this paper, for simplicity of discussion, we refer to the full set of states as affective states. Considering them in this fashion does not signify that these states do not have a cognitive component; it simply allows us to focus on the affective aspect of these states.

The observers attempted to conduct observations in a fashion that did not make students aware that they were being observed at a given moment. To this end, students were observed through quick glances, through using peripheral vision, or by pretending they were looking at another student, so as to minimize the effects of the observations. Each observation lasted 20 s. If two distinct affective states were seen during an observation, only the first affective state observed was coded. Each pair of observers was assigned to a group of students. Observers rotated among students in a predetermined order, and conducted all observations in synchrony. Each observation lasted 20 s.

The set of studies varied somewhat in observation length, due to the different original research goals of each study. The majority of the studies were 40–45 min long. The two Scatterplot Tutor studies were 80 min long, in order to conform with the exact design of a previous study of the same tutor (e.g., Baker, Corbett, Roll, & Koedinger, 2008). The study of The Incredible Machine was 10 min long, and was initially designed as a preliminary test of the study methodology before the Aplusix study (although the two studies involved different populations). There is some risk of bias due to these differences – the expected bias is that boredom should increase over time, and confusion should decrease over time. However, these biases were not seen in the results (see below). Hence, the differences between the Scatterplot Tutor and the other environments, and The Incredible Machine and the other environments, should be considered with this possible confound in mind. However, similarities in affective patterns seen between environments can be considered robust to this difference in study desing.

Incidence of Affective States

We examined the extent to which students exhibited each affective state (Table 2). Across most of the studies, engaged concentration was the most prevalent state, observed over 60% of the time in students using Aplusix, Ecolab, M-Ecolab, the Incredible Machine and Math Blaster. Confusion was typically the second most commonly exhibited affective state, observed between 10 and 15% of the time among students using Aplusix, Ecolab, M-Ecolab and The Incredible Machine.

Table 2 Incidence of affective states (data are in percentages)

Affective state	Aplusix	Ecolab	M-Ecolab	Scatterplot tutor (control group)	Scatterplot tutor (with agent)	The incredible machine	Math blaster
Boredom	3	15	12	6	7	7	22
Confusion	14	13	13	47	52	11	2
Delight	6	3	4	1	1	6	12
Engaged concentration	73	62	67	43	38	61	63
Frustration	3	6	3	0.5	0.2	7	0
Surprise	0.3	1	1	0.1	0.1	3	0
Neutral	1	0.3	0.01	1	2	5	1

However, the opposite pattern was observed among students using the two versions of the Scatterplot Tutor. These students most commonly exhibited confusion (47% in the control group; 52% in the group using the agent) followed by engaged concentration (43% in the control group; 38% in group using the agent). We hypothesize that confusion was more prevalent than engaged concentration because of the relative difficulty of the subject matter and the novelty of using computers for mathematics. This suggests that domain likely plays a large role in the prevalence of different affective states. However, it is worth noting that there are a pair of confounds between these studies – the Scatterplot Tutor studies involved public school students and had a longer observation period. The difference in population suggests an alternate hypothesis, that public school students in the Philippines may find intelligent tutors or mathematics more difficult than private school students. In terms of the difference in study time, it seems unlikely that studying the same material for more time would lead to greater confusion.

Boredom varied fairly significantly in frequency between environments, from a low of 3% in Aplusix to a maximum of 22% in Math Blaster. Interestingly, students using Math Blaster experienced high degrees of boredom (22%) and delight (12%). The high incidence of delight implies that specific game experiences such as hopping from one pod to another and throwing bananas at monkeys, may have created superficial moments of entertainment, but that the overall experience did not sustain high levels of engagement, somewhat contrary to some theory on how games impact student engagement (cf. Gee, 2003).

Comparing the educational games with the intelligent tutors, we find that game formats, while associated with relatively high amounts of delight, were not associated with more engaged concentration. Indeed, students can find game formats more frustrating, as in the case of The Incredible Machine, or more boring, as in the case of Math Blaster. The substantial differences in affective prevalence between Aplusix and MathBlaster in particular suggests that the type of learning environment may substantially impact affect, as these two very different learning environments involved similar mathematical content.

However, it appears that large-scale differences in learning environments (such as game vs. intelligent tutor) impact affect more than small-scale differences such as the incorporation of a pedagogical agent. Neither Paul, the motivational agent of M-Ecolab, nor Scooter, the agent in the Scatterplot Tutor, influenced student affect in a statistically detectible way.

Persistence of Affective States

We analyze the persistence of affective states using the transition likelihood metric L, from D'Mello et al. (2007). L provides an indication of the probability of any transition taking place, above and beyond the base rate of each affective category. For instance, engaged concentration was the most common affective category in Aplusix, Ecolab, M-Ecolab, the Incredible Machine and Math Blaster, whereas confusion was the most common affective category in the two conditions of the Scatterplot Tutor; therefore, these affective states are likely to be the most common affective state that follows *any* other affective state in these environments. L can be computed for any pair of states {prev, next}. In this chapter, we use L to compute persistence by looking at the probability that a state follows itself – e.g., that prev state and next state are the same state.

L explicitly accounts for the base rate of each affective category when assessing how likely a transition is, given the probability that a transition between two affective states occurs, and given the base frequency of the destination state. L is computed as shown in (1):

$$L = \frac{\Pr(NEXT \,|\, PREV) - \Pr(NEXT)}{(1 - \Pr(Next))}. \tag{1}$$

A value of 1 means that the transition will always occur; a value of 0 means that the transition's likelihood is exactly what it would be given only the base frequency of the destination state. Values above 0 signify that the transition is more likely than it could be expected (i.e., greater than the base frequency of the destination state), and values under 0 signify that the transition is less likely (i.e., less than the base frequency of the destination state). Table 3 summarizes the L-values for boredom, confusion, delight, engaged concentration and frustration for the seven studies. L-values are not given for surprise, because it was very rare across all seven studies.

Across all seven learning systems, we examined the L-values to determine which states tended to be persistent (Table 3). We found that the affective state of boredom proved to be the most persistent. When students are bored, they tend to stay bored, regardless of what type of educational application they are using. This result was statistically significant in five of the seven studies, and marginally significant in the other two studies (The Incredible Machine and MathBlaster). This result was consistent across intelligent tutors, educational games (marginally in both cases), systems with and without pedagogical agents, and both public and private schools. This result also replicated the finding in Baker et al. (2010). Across the seven environments, the average L for boredom was 0.238.

Engaged concentration persisted in four out of seven educational environments: Ecolab, both conditions of the Scatterplot Tutor, and The Incredible Machine (marginal). Though the result did not appear in all systems, it did appear across types of learning environment and school settings. However – interestingly – this result did not appear in either of the two very different learning environments in the domain of prealgebra, MathBlaster and Aplusix, suggesting a role for the domain in predicting the persistence of engaged concentration. Across the seven environments, the average L was 0.140.

Confusion was persistent in two out of the seven environments – the two Scatterplot Tutors. Given the higher overall confusion in these two environments, there is evidence either that this domain is particularly difficult for students, or that the public school population is less well-prepared to learn from intelligent tutors than the private school population which used Aplusix, Ecolab, and M-Ecolab.

Table 3 L-values for boredom, confusion, delight, engaged concentration and frustration across the seven learning environments

Affect	Aplusix	Ecolab	M-Ecolab	Scatterplot tutor (control group)	Scatterplot tutor (with agent)	The incredible machine	Math blaster 9–12
Boredom	**0.212**	**0.283**	**0.267**	**0.20**	**0.28**	*0.261*	*0.16*
Confusion	0.0076	−0.018	0.013	**0.21**	**0.22**	0.097	**−0.02**
Delight	0.047	0.041	**0.120**	0.05	0.03	0.096	0.15
Engaged concentration	0.062	**0.188**	0.109	**0.18**	**0.14**	0.202	0.10
Frustration	*0.071*	**0.206**	**0.148**	0.08	0.06	0.12	Never detected

Values in **bold** are statistically significant ($p \le 0.05$) while values in *italics* are marginally significant ($0.05 < p \le 0.10$)

Confusion was actually significantly less likely than chance to persist in MathBlaster. Across the seven environments, the average L for confusion was 0.073.

Frustration, by contrast, persisted in three environments – Ecolab, M-Ecolab, and Aplusix. Frustration was not extremely common in any of these environments, but when it occurred, it persisted. It is worth noting that all three of these environments were intelligent tutoring systems. Frustration was not different from chance in The Incredible Machine, and was never observed in MathBlaster. This difference is particularly salient in the case of Aplusix and MathBlaster, which were in the same domain, and suggests that educational games are more effective at disrupting frustration than intelligent tutors. Across the seven environments, the average L for frustration was 0.114.

One interesting note is that there are relatively few differences in affective persistence between environments. For instance, the pedagogical agents had relatively few impacts. The motivational agent in M-Ecolab appeared to lead to delight being more persistent, $(t(30) = 2.13, p = 0.04)$, a relationship not seen in Ecolab; the apparent trend toward more persistent engaged concentration was not significant, $t(178) = 0.85, p = 0.39$. (The difference in degrees of freedom is because not all students displayed all affective states) but there was at the same time a nonsignificant trend toward less persistent engaged concentration in M-Ecolab. There was no such pattern with the pedagogical agent in the Scatterplot Tutor, but this may be because of the different focus of the agents. Games also did not have any more engaged concentration than intelligent tutors did, although the games did yield more delight on the whole than the other environments (with the exception of the motivational agent in M-Ecolab). The persistence of affect did not appear to be radically different when students from public schools were compared to students in private schools.

Conclusions

In this chapter, we discussed the incidence and persistence of affective states across seven learning environments, studied with an identical observation protocol in high schools in the Philippines. The seven studies presented in this paper represent seven different combinations of technologies and learning outcomes, and as such the findings which generalize across these seven studies can be seen as general properties of the affect corner of the affect–technology–learning triangle in (Calvo & D'Mello, 2011). The studies, when taken together, reveal several patterns that transcend learning environment, domain, and population.

At the same time, these seven studies are selected to cut across a small number of themes in the technology and learning corners of the affect–technology–learning triangle. The seven studies involve four domains, two types of learning system (game and intelligent tutor), and the presence or absence of pedagogical agents. The studies also involve both public and private schools in the Philippines. Both of the two technology variables cut across domains. This semi-systematic variation enables us to study which patterns are more influenced by the learning environment and the domain of the learning activity.

Clear patterns emerged in the overall frequency of affective states. Engaged concentration was the most common affective state, by a large margin, in all studies run in private schools in the Philippines; confusion was slightly more common than engaged concentration in the two public school (Scatterplot Tutor) studies. However, this result may also have been due to the difficulty of the material in the tutors used in that study. Other affective states, particularly boredom, varied considerably between environments – surprisingly, the intelligent tutor for prealgebra was the least boring environment, whereas the educational game for prealgebra was the most boring. Delight was more common in the games than the other environments, but engaged concentration was not more prevalent, somewhat contrary to prior theory. Neither pedagogical agent influenced the incidence of affect in a substantial fashion.

Across all seven learning environments, boredom was persistent; this replicated earlier findings reported by Baker et al. (2010). As boredom precedes behaviors that lead to poorer learning (Baker et al. 2010), this finding suggests that future educational technology must find a way to disrupt boredom and reengage bored students, in order to promote optimal engagement and learning. Other negative affect states, such as frustration, were considerably less persistent – in particular, educational games appeared to disrupt frustration more than intelligent tutors. Engaged concentration was persistent in many studies, but appeared to be less persistent within prealgebra than in the other domains, for reasons that are not yet completely understood.

Hence, as a whole, it appears that there are some affective patterns that transcend learning environment and domain – in particular, the persistence of boredom and low persistence of frustration. Interestingly, though boredom's persistence is constant, its prevalence is highly variable, suggesting that learning environments are generally more able to prevent boredom than to disrupt it once it emerges. At the same time, it appears that both domain and the learning environment have substantial impacts on affective patterns, as engaged concentration was less persistent in the two very different prealgebra environments than in the other environments, even as the overall pattern of affect in those two environments were very different. However, our results suggested that high-level differences between environments (e.g., games vs. tutors) have a bigger impact than relatively smaller differences, such as the introduction of pedagogical agents.

One valuable step for validating the generalizability of this work will be for replication of this overall program of research in other nations. However, the results presented in this chapter already present a major challenge for the field – to reduce the persistence of boredom. Boredom is highly persistent, across learning environments, but differs considerably in overall prevalence between learning environments. This suggests that boredom is easier to prevent through generally engaging educational design, than to disrupt (for instance with delight-causing game features). Understanding how to design learning environments that prevent boredom is therefore an important area of future work. Interestingly, despite the common hypothesis that games should improve engagement (e.g., Gee, 2003), one game (Math Blaster) was associated with fairly high boredom (despite high delight), and an intelligent tutor (Aplusix) had the lowest boredom. This suggests that there is still a considerable amount to learn about how to most effectively reduce and disrupt learner boredom within educational technology.

Acknowledgments We thank the Philippines Department of Science and Technology (DOST) Engineering Research and Development for Technology Consortium for the grant entitled "Multidimensional Analysis of User-Machine Interactions Towards the Development of Models of Affect," the DOST Philippine Council for Advanced Science and Technology Research and Development for the grant entitled "Development of Affect-Sensitive Interfaces," the Ateneo de Manila University and the Pittsburgh Science of Learning Center (National Science Foundation) via grant "Toward a Decade of PSLC Research," award number SBE-0836012. We thank all the graduate students and colleagues who volunteered as coders. We thank the Ateneo Center for Educational Development, the Department of Information Systems and Computer Science of the Ateneo de Manila University and the faculty, staff, and students of Ateneo de Manila High School, Kostka School of Quezon City, School of the Holy Spirit Quezon City, St. Alphonsus Liguori Integrated School, St. Paul's College Pasig, and Ramon Magsaysay Cubao High School for their support in this project. We also thank Jean-Francois Nicaud and Genaro Rebolledo-Mendez for making their learning software available for use in our research.

References

Aleven, V., & Koedinger, K. R. (2000). Limitations of student control: Do students know when they need help? *Proceedings of the 5th International Conference on Intelligent Tutoring Systems* (pp. 292–303). London: Springer.

Baker, R. S. J. d., Corbett, A. T., Roll, I., & Koedinger, K. R. (2008). Developing a generalizable detector of when students game the system. *User Modeling and User-Adapted Interaction: the Journal of Personalization Research, 18*(3), 287–314.

Baker, R. S. J. d., D'Mello, S. K., Rodrigo, M. M. T., & Graesser, A. C. (2010). Better to be frustrated than bored: the incidence, persistence, and impact of learners' cognitive-affective states during interactions with three different computer-based learning environments. *International Journal of Human-Computer Studies, 68*(4), 223–241.

Baker, R. S. J. d., Corbett, A. T., Koedinger, K. R., & Wagner, A. Z. (2004). Off-task behavior in the cognitive tutor classroom: When students "Game the system". *Proceedings of ACM CHI 2004: Computer-Human Interaction* (pp. 383–390). Washington, DC: Association for Computing Machinery.

Calvo, R. A., & D'Mello, S. (2011). Introduction. In R. Calvo & S. D'Mello (Eds.), *Explorations in the learning sciences, instructional systems and performance technologies*. New York: Springer.

Cooper, D. G., Arroyo, I., & Woolf, B. P. (2011). Actionable affective processing for automatic tutor interventions. In R. Calvo & S. D'Mello (Eds.), *Explorations in the learning sciences, instructional systems and performance technologies*. New York: Springer.

Csikszentmihalyi, M. (1990). *Flow: The psychology of optimal experience*. New York: Harper and Row.

D'Mello, S., Lehman, B., & Graesser, A. (2011). A motivationally supportive affect-sensitive auto-tutor. In R. Calvo & S. D'Mello (Eds.), *Explorations in the learning sciences, instructional systems and performance technologies*. New York: Springer.

D'Mello, S. K., Taylor, R. S., & Graesser, A. (2007). Monitoring affective trajectories during complex learning. In D. S. McNamara & J. G. Trafton (Eds.), *Proceedings of the 29th Annual Cognitive Science Society* (pp. 203–208). Austin: Cognitive Science Society.

Davidson and Associates. (1997). Math Blaster 9–12 [Computer Software].

D'Mello, S. K., Craig, S. D., Witherspoon, A., McDaniel, B., & Graesser, A. (2005). Integrating affect sensors in an intelligent tutoring system. *Proceedings of Affective Interactions: The Computer in the Affective Loop Workshop* (pp. 7–13). Washington, DC: Association for Computing Machinery.

Forbes-Riley, K., Litman, D., & Friedberg, H. (2011). Annotating disengagement for spoken dialogue computer tutoring. In R. Calvo & S. D'Mello (Eds.), *Explorations in the learning sciences, instructional systems and performance technologies*. New York: Springer.

Gee, J. P. (2003). *What video games have to teach us about learning and literacy*. Hampshire: Palgrave MacMillan.

Koedinger, K. R., & Corbett, A. T. (2006). Cognitive tutors: Technology bringing learning sciences to the classroom. In R. K. Sawyer (Ed.), *The Cambridge handbook of the learning sciences* (pp. 61–77). New York: Cambridge University Press.

Lester, J. C., McQuiggan, S. W., & Sabourin, J. L. (2011). Affect recognition and expression in narrative-centered learning environments. In R. Calvo & S. D'Mello (Eds.), *Explorations in the learning sciences, instructional systems and performance technologies*. New York: Springer.

Nicaud, J.-F., Bouhineau, D., & Chaachoua, H. (2004). Mixing microworld and CAS features in building computer systems that help students learn algebra. *International Journal of Computers for Mathematical Learning, 9*, 169–211.

Nicaud, J. F., Bouhineau, D., Mezerette, S., & Andre, N. (2007). Aplusix II [Computer software].

Rebolledo-Mendez, G. (2003). Motivational modelling in a Vygotskyan ITS. *Proceedings of the 11th International Conference on Artificial Intelligence in Education* (pp. 537–538). Amsterdam: IOS Press.

Rebolledo-Mendez, G., du Boulay, B., & Luckin, R. (2006) Motivating the learner: an empirical evaluation. *Proceedings of the 8th International Conference on Intelligent Tutoring Systems* (pp. 545–554). Heidelberg, Springer: Germany.

Rebolledo-Mendez, G., Luckin, R., & du Boulay, B. (2011). Designing adaptive motivational scaffolding for a tutoring system. In R. Calvo & S. D'Mello (Eds.), *Explorations in the learning sciences, instructional systems and performance technologies*. New York: Springer.

Rodrigo, M. M. T. (2005). Quantifying the divide: A comparison of ICT usage of schools in metro manila and IEA-surveyed countries. *International Journal of Educational Development, 25*, 53–68.

Sierra Online. (2001). The Incredible Machine: Even More Contraptions [Computer Software].

Part III
Interdisciplinary Views

Cognitive Load in Adaptive Multimedia Learning

Slava Kalyuga

Introduction

The design of innovative learning environments that are adaptive to the affective states of the learner (affective learning technologies) should be based on clearly understood links between emotions, cognition, and motivation. There is evidence indicating that affective states of learners may significantly influence learning (e.g., Craig, Graesser, Sullins, & Gholson, 2004; Linnenbrink & Pintrich, 2002). Affective states may also be influenced by the cognitive load experienced by learners. Therefore, considering cognitive load aspects of affective learning could broaden the focus of research and enhance understanding of the emotional processes that underlie learning. Potentially, cognitive load framework can also offer some novel methodologies for investigating affect and learning. The aim of this chapter is to advance research in cognitive load aspects of affective learning technologies by reviewing recent applications of cognitive load theory to the design of adaptive multimedia learning, their potential relations with affect-sensitive learning, and setting the stage for future research in this area.

Research in adaptive multimedia and hypermedia learning environments has been focused mostly on technical issues related to adapting instructional content to student preferences, interests, or previous online behavior patterns (e.g., Brusilovsky, 2001; Ghazarian & Noorhosseini, 2010). Even though these are important parameters to consider, fundamental cognitive characteristics of learners have not been given sufficient attention by both researchers and designers of multimedia learning environments. Research in expert–novice differences in cognitive science has demonstrated that the most important cognitive characteristic that influences learning is

S. Kalyuga (✉)
School of Education, University of New South Wales, Sydney, New South Wales, Australia
e-mail: s.kalyuga@unsw.edu.au

R.A. Calvo and S.K. D'Mello (eds.), *New Perspectives on Affect and Learning Technologies*,   203
Explorations in the Learning Sciences, Instructional Systems and Performance Technologies 3,
DOI 10.1007/978-1-4419-9625-1_15, © Springer Science+Business Media, LLC 2011

the learner prior knowledge base (for an overview, see Bransford, Brown, & Cocking, 1999).

Studies within the cognitive load framework have indicated that instructional design formats and procedures that are effective with low-knowledge individuals can lose their effectiveness and even have negative consequences for more knowledgeable learners, and vice versa (expertise reversal effect; see Kalyuga, 2007 for a recent overview). The major instructional design implication of this reversal in the relative effectiveness of instructional methods is the need to dynamically adapt instructional techniques and procedures as learners acquire more expertise in a specific domain. The following sections of this chapter will focus primarily on characteristics of human cognitive architecture that are directly related to the expertise reversal effect, main empirical findings associated with this effect in multimedia and hypermedia learning environments, their interpretation within cognitive load theory, and implications for research in affective learner-tailored multimedia environments.

Role of Prior Knowledge in Cognition and Learning

Our cognitive architecture includes two essential components that define how we process information and learn. One of these components is long-term memory representing our knowledge base with effectively unlimited capacity and duration. Most of organized knowledge is stored in the form of schemas – generic knowledge structures that are used to mentally categorize and represent concepts and procedures, and govern our behavior. Another essential component of our cognitive system represents a mechanism that limits the scope of immediate simultaneous changes to the knowledge base. This mechanism is associated with the concept of working memory as a conscious processor of information within the focus of attention. Working memory is severely limited in capacity and duration when dealing with novel information (Cowan, 2001; Miller, 1956). Most of contemporary models of working memory include separate limited processing channels for visual and auditory information modalities (e.g., Baddeley, 1986). Processing limitations of working memory are responsible for learner cognitive overload and profoundly influence the effectiveness of instruction.

The interaction between the above two components is critical for efficient cognitive functioning. Knowledge base in long-term memory may effectively reduce limitations of working memory by encapsulating many elements of information into higher-level units that are treated as elements in working memory (Ericsson & Kintsch, 1995). For example, knowledge of written English words allows readers of this text to encapsulate many separate letters into meaningful words and treat them as single elements in working memory. With sufficient reading experience, whole phrases and combinations of words are also treated as single processing units. Another way of reducing cognitive load is practicing skills until they can operate under automatic rather than controlled processing (Shiffrin & Schneider, 1977). For example, when basic routine operations in mathematics are processed automatically, learners can devote working memory resources to handing more complex problems without cognitive overload.

Thus, more knowledgeable learners use their available knowledge structures for managing cognitive load. However, if task-relevant knowledge structures are not available in long-term memory, learners may need to simultaneously process many new elements of information in working memory resulting in a cognitive overload. Appropriate external guidance may be required to assist these learners in acquiring new knowledge structures in a cognitively efficient and nonstressful manner. In the absence of a relevant knowledge base or external instructional guidance, the learners may need to rely on weak problem-solving methods based on random search processes such as means–ends analysis or trial-and-error attempts. These methods usually result in excessive levels of cognitive load and consequently, minimal (if any) learning.

If, on the other hand, detailed instructional guidance is provided to more experienced learners who have an adequate knowledge base in long-term memory for dealing with the learning task, these learners would need to relate and reconcile the corresponding components of their knowledge and external information. Such coreferencing processes may cause additional cognitive load that would inevitably reduce working memory resources available for learning (e.g., making appropriate generalizations or further strengthening and automating schemas). These are the mechanisms that are believed to be behind the expertise reversal effect from a purely cognitive perspective (Kalyuga, 2007). As levels of learner expertise increase, relative effectiveness of learning tasks with different levels of instructional guidance may reverse. Presenting more knowledgeable learners with detailed external instructional guidance may inhibit their learning relative to the outcomes that could be achieved with minimal guidance. The provided instructional guidance causes an extraneous cognitive load, one of the two major types of cognitive load considered in cognitive load theory.

Recently, there have been suggestions that affective and motivational factors may also influence the effect (e.g., Paas, Tuovinen, van Merrienboer, & Darabi, 2005). It may be plausible that, for example, feelings of boredom or angst for the "waste" of time spent on studying a redundant extra feedback may prevent efficient learning for more knowledgeable individuals. The inclusion of such factors in research on expertise reversal effect needs further research.

Types of Cognitive Load

In most cases, when dealing with novel information, no learning occurs without a cognitive load associated with effortful conscious processing of essential interacting elements of information in working memory. Some notable exceptions include further strengthening of knowledge structures that have already been mostly automated due to extended practice or learning knowledge that we are genetically and evolutionary predisposed to acquire implicitly, effortlessly, and mostly without conscious processing (biologically primary knowledge according to Geary, 2007). For example, we do not seem to experience a cognitive load when learning to speak our first language or engage in common social interactions. However, the acquisition of knowledge that has been generated at later stages of the development of human culture (biologically secondary knowledge, including subjects thought at schools) requires cognitive load. This essential, necessary, productive, and useful load required for achieving specific learning goals is called intrinsic cognitive load.

Intrinsic cognitive load is caused by specific cognitive activities resulting in new or modified knowledge structures in long-term memory. Such activities involve concurrent processing of interacting elements of information in working memory and integrating them with available knowledge structures in accordance with specific learning goals. Intrinsic load is associated with internal complexity of the learning task and, therefore, is always relative to the level of learner expertise since what is complex for novices may be simple for experts. In order to achieve meaningful learning outcomes, it is necessary to accommodate this load without exceeding available working memory resources. If these resources are not available and there are no other means of providing them (such as reducing extraneous load, see below), intrinsic cognitive load could be reduced by dividing the learning goal into a series of subgoals and accordingly, segmenting learning tasks into smaller units that require less working memory resources (segmenting principle, Mayer, 2009). Some of the essential interactions between elements of information could also be excluded from learning at initial stages followed by fully interactive materials later (Pollock, Chandler, & Sweller, 2002).

In contrast to intrinsic load, extraneous cognitive load is a nonessential, unnecessary, and wasteful type of load caused by cognitive activities and processes that are irrelevant to learning goals. This type of load is usually caused by poor instructional designs, for example, unsuitable presentation formats (e.g., separating related sources of information in space and/or time or duplicating the same information simultaneously in different modalities) or inappropriate selection and sequencing of learning activities with inadequate levels of instructional support (e.g., using unguided exploratory activities with beginner learners). It should be noted that the difference between extraneous and intrinsic cognitive load could be relative to levels of learner expertise: some parts of cognitive load that are essential (intrinsic) for novice learners could become extraneous (irrelevant) for relatively more experienced learners, and vice versa.

Working memory resources that are actually devoted to dealing with intrinsic cognitive load and lead to learning are germane resources in contrast to extraneous working memory resources that are devoted to dealing with extraneous cognitive load (Sweller, 2010). This separate dimension of actually allocated working memory resources stresses the role of germane resources in learner engagement in processing relevant aspects of a task and importance of instructional methods that motivate and engage students in learning-effective cognitive activities. More engaged and motivated learners invest more of their working memory resources into dealing with intrinsic load thus leading to better learning (Schnotz, 2010). The actual amount of working memory resources invested in learning activities would depend on levels of motivation, attitudes, and affective characteristics of the learner in relation to the activity itself. This relationships between the individual, the activity and the technology (or media) through which they interact is a common theme of this book.

Together, the added intrinsic and extraneous cognitive load determines the total cognitive load imposed on the learner by the learning task. This load determines working memory resources required for processing all the involved elements of information and achieving learning goals by a fully engaged learner. However, it does not necessarily determine actually allocated working memory resources in a specific learning situation. The amount of actually devoted working memory resources depends on how well and fully the learner is engaged in the learning environment. It is therefore important to develop effective learning environments that motivate learners into devoting their working memory resources to achieving learning goals, even though this task stretches beyond specific methods of cognitive load theory.

Instructional situations that cause extraneous cognitive load resulting in an expertise reversal effect could be divided in two types depending on which side of the novice–expert continuum they apply to. In one type of situations applying to novice learners, insufficient external instructional guidance may not compensate for limited knowledge of these learners thus forcing them into applying search-based processes resulting in extraneous cognitive load. In another type of situations applying to more experienced learners, the knowledge base of these learners overlaps with provided instructional guidance. In this case, relating and cross-referencing the overlapping internal and external representations of the same information may impose an additional extraneous load. Consequently, less capacity could be available for new knowledge acquisition and performance improvement, resulting in the expertise reversal effect (Kalyuga, 2007).

Thus, cognitive load consequences of using different learning formats and procedures depend on levels of learner expertise and may result in different affective states. If challenges of the task significantly exceed the available learner knowledge base, the task could cause cognitive overload and emotional unease. On the other hand, when these challenges are too low relative to the available knowledge and skills, the task could be easy and boring, with corresponding emotional consequences for the learner. A well fitted learning task that provides challenges just above the level of learner available knowledge base could provide the best motivating power and emotional state. Both unguided effortful search for solutions by novice learners and allocating unnecessary attention to information that could otherwise be processed automatically and effortlessly by more experienced learners would reduce cognitive resources available for effortful cognitive activities related to learning meaningful domain patterns. Such unnecessary diversion of attention may emotionally upset and de-motivate the learners.

Expertise Reversal Effect in Multimedia Learning

According to the expertise reversal effect, multimedia formats that are optimal for novices may hinder performance of relatively more experienced learners. For example, when different related sources of information (e.g., text and pictures) that require mental integration for understanding are separated in space or time, the process of their integration (e.g., visual search-and-match) may substantially increase extraneous cognitive load and inhibit learning. Physically integrated or embedded verbal and pictorial representations may reduce or eliminate this load. Such integrated formats could be effective alternatives to "split-source" instructions (split-attention effect; e.g., Mayer & Gallini, 1990; Sweller, Chandler, Tierney, & Cooper, 1990).

However, for more knowledgeable learners, eliminating nonessential redundant textual explanations could be more effective than processing the redundant material, especially if this information is embedded into the pictures without the possibility of ignoring it. Kalyuga, Chandler, and Sweller (1998) demonstrated that with novice electrical apprentices the split-attention rather than the redundancy effect was obtained when learning from wiring diagrams with accompanying textual explanations. Students learned poorly from a diagram alone and best from a physically integrated diagrams and text. After extensive training in the domain, when the same learners became more experienced, a reversed pattern was obtained: the effectiveness of the integrated diagram and text condition decreased while the effectiveness of the diagram alone condition increased. Textual explanations that were essential for novices became redundant for more knowledgeable learners.

Split-attention situations may also be avoided by using different modalities, since working memory includes separate subsystems for storing and processing visual and auditory information (Baddeley, 1986). Integrating verbal auditory and pictorial visual information may not overload working memory if its capacity is effectively expanded by using a dual-mode presentation (modality effect; Mayer, 1997; Mousavi, Low, & Sweller, 1995; Tindall-Ford, Chandler, & Sweller, 1997). Kalyuga, Chandler, and Sweller (2000) demonstrated that replacing on-screen textual explanations of procedural steps in using charts for setting up industrial machinery with corresponding narrated explanations was beneficial for novice learners. However, when these learners became more experienced in this task domain after a series of intensive training sessions, an interactive diagram-only presentation became more beneficial than the diagram with narrated explanations. Accordingly, subjective ratings of learning difficulty indicated that the learners in the diagram-only condition experienced a lower level of cognitive load.

The pattern of results in the above experiments is typical for many other studies that demonstrated the expertise reversal effect. For example, Lee, Plass, and Homer (2006) investigated two different modes of visual representations in a gas law simulation for middle-school chemistry students. Essential gas characteristics were presented either in symbolic form only (words "temperature," "pressure," and "volume" with corresponding numerical values) or by adding iconic information to the symbolic representations (e.g., burners for temperature, weighs for pressure). While low prior knowledge learners benefited more from added iconic representations than from symbolic formats only, high prior knowledge learners benefited more from symbolic only representations. Iconic representations were redundant for these learners and inhibited their learning.

Animated visualizations that represent movements and processes are commonly believed to be appropriate for presenting dynamic information. However, no convincing evidence has been obtained indicating higher learning effects of animations as compared to static diagrams (Hegarty, Kriz, & Cate, 2003; Park & Hopkins, 1993; Tversky, Morrison, & Betrancourt, 2002). According to cognitive load theory, continuous animations could be too cognitively demanding for novice learners because of high levels of transitivity. These learners could benefit more from studying a set of static diagrams. On the other hand, knowledge structures of more experienced learners may help them in handling the transitivity of animations, as they may have sufficient working memory resources for constructing and running dynamic mental representations. Static graphics could be less beneficial for these learners because their knowledge structures would need to be integrated and reconciled with redundant (for them) details displayed in graphics, thus unnecessarily consuming additional cognitive resources.

A number of studies demonstrated interactions between levels of learner expertise and effectiveness of animated and static visualizations. For example, Kalyuga (2008a) demonstrated that less knowledgeable learners performed significantly better after studying static procedural examples in mathematics. Learners with higher levels of prior knowledge showed better results after studying animated instructions. Schnotz and Rasch (2005) demonstrated that less knowledgeable and able learners performed better after learning with static than with animated pictures, while more knowledgeable and able students performed equally in both conditions.

The levels of learner prior knowledge also influence the effectiveness of hypermedia learning environments. Novice learners may experience excessive levels of cognitive load when they need to maintain goals in working memory while searching for relevant information in hyperspace. The search processes may leave no resources available for constructing relevant knowledge structures. Extraneous cognitive load could be further increased by the need to choose among a variety of possible navigational paths. Therefore, learners with lower levels of prior knowledge may need more instructional support when using such environments. On the other hand, the available knowledge base could guide more experienced learners in their exploration of unsupported hypermedia environments (Gerjets & Scheiter, 2007).

Accordingly, Simons and Klein (2007) demonstrated the effectiveness of providing compulsory embedded scaffolds in a problem-based hypermedia learning environment for seventh grade students. Studies of the role of prior knowledge in learning from hypertext have indicated that low prior knowledge learners benefit more from well structured texts (Calisir & Gurel, 2003; Potelle & Rouet, 2003; Shin, Schallert, & Savenye, 1994). Only relatively more knowledgeable learners are able to handle split-attention situations caused by relating unordered segments of text without cognitive overload (DeStefano & LeFevre, 2007) or benefit from other nonlinear environments and network structures (Jacobson, 1994; Spiro, Feltovich, Jacobson, & Coulson, 1991).

Tailoring Multimedia Learning Based on the Expertise Reversal Effect

A major instructional implication of the expertise reversal effect is the need to adapt dynamically instructional formats and levels of instructional guidance to current levels of learner expertise. Changes in learner knowledge levels need to be dynamically monitored as they gradually change during learning and specific instructional procedures adjusted accordingly. For example, relatively less-guided exploratory or problem-based environments could gradually replace direct instruction methods as levels of learner expertise increase.

An important part of such adaptive multimedia learning environments is the set of assessment tools that are able to diagnose levels of learner expertise rapidly and in real time. A possible method for rapid assessment of expertise could be based on observing how learners approach briefly presented tasks. For example, in the first-step diagnostic method, learners are asked to rapidly indicate their first step toward the solution of a task presented to them for a limited time. More experienced learners are able to use their well-learned solution schemas to skip some intermediate steps and rapidly indicate more advanced steps of the solution as their first steps. On the other hand, less experienced learners may only generate a very first immediate move according to the detailed procedure they have learned. Complete novices could at best be able to indicate only their first attempt in using trial-and-error or means–ends analysis approaches.

The first-step diagnostic technique was applied in several domains (algebra, geometry, and arithmetic word problems) and indicated sufficiently high levels of concurrent validity (Kalyuga, 2006c; Kalyuga & Sweller, 2004). In an alternative method, students could be briefly presented with potential solution steps at various stages of advancement and asked to rapidly verify their correctness (a rapid verification method). This method was validated using mathematics as well as kinematics and sentence comprehension tasks that represented relatively less-structured domains (Kalyuga, 2006b, 2008b).

The rapid diagnostic methods were used in adaptive computer-based tutorials in the domains of linear algebra equations (Kalyuga & Sweller, 2004, 2005) and vector addition motion problems in kinematics (Kalyuga, 2006a). According to the dynamic tailoring approach, the tutorials provided levels of instructional guidance that were optimal for learners with different levels of expertise as measured by rapid methods. At the beginning of training sessions, each learner was provided with an appropriate level of instructional guidance according to the outcome of the initial rapid pretest. Depending on the outcomes of the ongoing rapid probes during the session, the learner proceeded to the next learning stage or was required to repeat the same stage and then take the rapid test again. At each subsequent stage, a lower level of guidance was provided to learners. Worked-out components of solution procedures were gradually omitted and progressively replaced with problem-solving steps. In Kalyuga and Sweller (2005) and Kalyuga (2006a), the rapid measures of expertise were combined with measures of cognitive load based on subjective ratings of task difficulty. Research studies in evaluating levels of mental workload have indicated that subjective measures of mental load are sufficiently reliable and correlate highly between themselves and with objective measures (Braarud, 2001; Eggemeier, 1988; Moray, 1982; O'Donnell & Eggemeier, 1986). Subjective ratings of learning difficulty or mental effort associated with learning instructional materials have been used in many studies within a cognitive load framework as they are easy to implement and do not intrude on primary task performance (Paas, Tuovinen, Tabbers, & van Gerven, 2003). Since the expertise is associated not only with relatively higher-level but also lower-effort performance, combining both measures could produce a better indicator of learner expertise in a domain. Results indicated that both adaptive conditions outperformed the non-adapted condition; however, there were no significant differences between the adaptation procedures.

The above approaches to dynamic tailoring of instruction to levels of learner expertise used system-controlled formats: a computer program dynamically selected an instructional method that was most appropriate for the current level of learner expertise. An alternative approach is a learner-controlled individualization of instruction. However, students control over the content and instructional sequences may possibly be effective only when they have sufficient prior knowledge of the task domain. Novice learners could not be able to effectively use the allowed levels of control. As a results, they could be engaged in poor instructional sequences and require appropriate assistance. Not surprisingly, the empirical evidence related to the effectiveness of learner control has been inconclusive and more often negative rather than positive despite the expectations of enhanced motivational aspects such as positive learner attitudes and a sense of control (Chung & Reigeluth, 1992; Niemec, Sikorski, & Walberg, 1996).

Within a cognitive load framework, shared control approaches as alternatives to system-controlled task selection models were suggested (Van Merriënboer et al., 2006). For example, Corbalan, Kester, and van Merriënboer (2006) investigated a shared control model that first selected a subset of tasks based on learner performance scores and cognitive load ratings (a system-controlled component). As the learner proceeded through the training session, the system continuously assessed performance and invested mental effort and selected an optimal subset of tasks for the following learning step. This subset was presented to the learner who made the final selection (a learner-controlled component).

This model was compared to a fully system-controlled procedure in an experiment using a simulation-based learning environment in the domain of dietetics. The results demonstrated that the shared control was more effective and more efficient than fully system-controlled condition. Shared control condition resulted in higher learner posttest performance scores and lower invested mental effort. Measures of motivation using interest/enjoyment subjective rating scale indicated marginally significant differences favoring the shared instructional control condition, thus supporting the suggestion that learner control may have enhanced learner motivation (Corbalan et al., 2006). Adaptive guidance and adaptive formative feedback approaches (Bell & Kozlowski, 2002; Shute, 2008) could also be used in adaptive multimedia learning to continuously monitor learners progress and provide them with diagnostic information, feedback, and individual tailored recommendations on the following learning tasks and activities.

Conclusion

Cognitive load associated with imbalances between provided instructional guidance and available knowledge base may emotionally upset and de-motivate learners and thus further strengthen the expertise reversal effect. Affective aspects of the effect could also be considered in relation to learning goals. When motivated by consciously chosen goals, learners experience a sense of control and meaningfulness of their experience. Learning goals represent an important part of a learner prior knowledge that performs an important guiding role in cognitive processing. Balancing external guidance with learner internal goal structures is important for creating positive affective states and higher levels of motivation.

There is a close relationship between affective states and the operation of working memory that are linked through attention mechanisms (Eysenck, 1982; Simon, 1967). Cognitive load caused by instructional guidance that is not tailored to learner prior knowledge and learning goals could lower the level of motivation, thus providing an additional complementing explanation of the expertise reversal effect. However, in cognitive load theory, affective and motivational factors have not been considered until very recently (Paas et al., 2005). The inclusion of affective and motivational factors in research on expertise reversal effect remains an essential direction for future research in this area (Paas et al., 2005; Tobias, 1989, 2010). Establishing connections between affective variables and cognitive load factors, and using methods of affective computing could enhance capabilities of multimedia environments in tailoring learning to cognitive characteristics of individual learners.

Even though most studies within a cognitive load framework used very rough self-report measures of cognitive load, there have been some other techniques proposed (for overviews, see Brünken, Plass & Leutner, 2003; Paas et al., 2003). Research in new approaches to measuring cognitive load may provide more reliable objective and real-time dynamic indicators. More research is needed to investigate behavioral patterns associated with increased cognitive load in tasks incorporating multimodal features. In this respect, studies in multimodal affect detecting tools that combine conversational cues, gross body language, and facial features (D'Mello & Graesser, 2010) could be of great interest to the cognitive load research field.

In summary, when instructional support provided to learners is not tailored to levels of their prior knowledge, the resulting extraneous cognitive load may emotionally upset and de-motivate learners and thus influence the learning outcomes. This chapter described features of our cognitive architecture that are directly related to the effect of learner prior knowledge, empirical findings associated with this effect in multimedia learning environments, and some implications of these findings for research in affective learner-tailored multimedia environments

References

Baddeley, A. D. (1986). *Working memory*. New York: Oxford University Press.

Bell, B. S., & Kozlowski, S. W. J. (2002). Adaptive guidance: Enhancing self-regulation, knowledge, and performance in technology-based training. *Personnel Psychology., 55*, 267–306.

Braarud, P. O. (2001). Subjective task complexity and subjective workload: Criterion validity for complex team tasks. *International Journal of Cognitive Ergonomics, 5*, 261–273.

Bransford, J. D., Brown, A. L., & Cocking, R. R. (Eds.). (1999). *How people learn: Mind, brain, experience, and school*. Washington: National Academy Press.

Brünken, R., Plass, J., & Leutner, D. (2003). Direct measurement of cognitive load in multimedia learning. *Educational Psychologist, 38*, 53–61.

Brusilovsky, P. (2001). Adaptive hypermedia. *User Modeling and User-Adapted Interactions, 11*, 87–110.

Calisir, F., & Gurel, Z. (2003). Influence of text structure and prior knowledge of the learner on reading comprehension, browsing and perceived control. *Computers in Human Behavior., 19*, 135–145.

Chung, J., & Reigeluth, C. M. (1992). Instructional prescriptions for learner control. *Educational Technology., 32*, 14–20.

Corbalan, G., Kester, L., & van Merriënboer, J. J. G. (2006). Towards a personalized task selection model with shared instructional control. *Instructional Science, 34*, 399–422.

Cowan, N. (2001). The magical number 4 in short-term memory: A reconsideration of mental storage capacity. *Behavioral and Brain Sciences., 24*, 87–114.

Craig, S. D., Graesser, A. C., Sullins, J., & Gholson, B. (2004). Affect and learning: an exploratory look into the role of affect in learning with auto tutor. *Journal of Educational Media, 29*, 241–250.

D'Mello, S., & Graesser, A. C. (2010). Multimodal semi-automated affect detection from conversational cues, gross body language, and facial features. *User Modeling and User-adapted Interaction., 20*(2), 147–187.

DeStefano, D., & LeFevre, J.-A. (2007). Cognitive load in hypertext reading: A review. *Computers in Human Behavior., 23*, 1616–1641.

Eggemeier, F. T. (1988). Properties of workload assessment techniques. In P. A. Hancock & N. Meshkati (Eds.), *Human mental workload* (pp. 41–62). Amsterdam: Elsevier.

Ericsson, K. A., & Kintsch, W. (1995). Long-term working memory. *Psychological Review, 102*, 211–245.

Eysenck, M. W. (1982). *Attention and arousal: Cognition and performance*. Berlin: Springer.

Geary, D. (2007). Educating the evolved mind: Conceptual foundations for an evolutionary educational psychology. In J. S. Carlson & J. R. Levin (Eds.), *Psychological perspectives on contemporary educational issues* (pp. 1–99). Greenwich: Information Age Publishing.

Gerjets, P., & Scheiter, K. (2007). Learner control in hypermedia environments. *Educational Psychology Review., 19*, 285–307.

Ghazarian, A., & Noorhosseini, S. M. (2010). Automatic detection of users' skill levels using high-frequency user interface events. *User Modeling and User-Adapted Interactions., 20*(2), 109–146. doi: 10.1007/s11257-010-9073-5.

Hegarty, M., Kriz, S., & Cate, C. (2003). The roles of mental animations and external animations in understanding mechanical systems. *Cognition and Instruction., 21*, 325–360.

Jacobson, M. J. (1994). Issues in hypertext and hypermedia research: Toward a framework for linking theory-to-design. *Journal of Educational Multimedia and Hypermedia., 3*(2), 141–154.

Kalyuga, S. (2006a). Assessment of learners' organized knowledge structures in adaptive learning environments. *Applied Cognitive Psychology., 20*, 333–342.

Kalyuga, S. (2006b). Rapid assessment of learners' proficiency: A cognitive load approach. *Educational Psychology., 26*, 613–627.

Kalyuga, S. (2006c). Rapid cognitive assessment of learners' knowledge structures. *Learning and Instruction., 16*, 1–11.

Kalyuga, S. (2007). Expertise reversal effect and its implications for learner-tailored instruction. *Educational Psychology Review., 19*, 509–539.

Kalyuga, S. (2008a). Relative effectiveness of animated and static diagrams: An effect of learner prior knowledge. *Computers in Human Behavior., 24*, 852–861.

Kalyuga, S. (2008b). When less is more in cognitive diagnosis: A rapid assessment method for adaptive learning environments. *Journal of Educational Psychology, 100*, 603–612.

Kalyuga, S., Chandler, P., & Sweller, J. (1998). Levels of expertise and instructional design. *Human Factors., 40*, 1–17.

Kalyuga, S., Chandler, P., & Sweller, J. (2000). Incorporating learner experience into the design of multimedia instruction. *Journal of Educational Psychology., 92*, 126–136.

Kalyuga, S., & Sweller, J. (2004). Measuring knowledge to optimize cognitive load factors during instruction. *Journal of Educational Psychology., 96*, 558–568.

Kalyuga, S., & Sweller, J. (2005). Rapid dynamic assessment of expertise to improve the efficiency of adaptive e-learning. *Educational Technology Research and Development., 53*, 83–93.

Lee, H., Plass, J. L., & Homer, B. D. (2006). Optimizing cognitive load for learning from computer-based science simulations. *Journal of Educational Psychology., 98*, 902–913.

Linnenbrink, E. A., & Pintrich, P. R. (2002). The role of motivational beliefs in conceptual change. In M. Limon & L. Mason (Eds.), *Reconsidering conceptual change: Issues in theory and practice* (pp. 115–135). Dordrecht: Kluwer Academic Publishers.

Mayer, R. E. (1997). Multimedia learning: Are we asking the right questions? *Educational Psychologist., 32*, 1–19.

Mayer, R. E. (2009). *Multimedia learning*. New York: Cambridge University Press.

Mayer, R., & Gallini, J. (1990). When is an illustration worth ten thousand words? *Journal of Educational Psychology., 82*, 715–726.

Miller, G. A. (1956). The magical number seven, plus or minus two: Some limits on our capacity for processing information. *Psychological Review, 63*, 81–97.

Moray, N. (1982). Subjective mental workload. *Human Factors, 24*, 25–40.

Mousavi, S. Y., Low, R., & Sweller, J. (1995). Reducing cognitive load by mixing auditory and visual presentation modes. *Journal of Educational Psychology., 87*, 319–334.

Niemec, P., Sikorski, C., & Walberg, H. (1996). Learner-control effects: A review of reviews and a meta-analysis. *Journal of Educational Computing Research., 15*, 157–174.

O'Donnell, R. D., & Eggemeier, F. T. (1986). Workload assessment methodology. In K. R. Boff, L. Kaufman, & J. P. Thomas (Eds.), *Handbook of perception and human performance (Chapter 42)* (Vol. 2, pp. 1–49). New York: Wiley.

Paas, F., Tuovinen, J., Tabbers, H., & van Gerven, P. (2003). Cognitive load measurement as a means to advance cognitive load theory. *Educational Psychologist, 38*, 63–71.

Paas, F., Tuovinen, J. E., van Merrienboer, J. J. G., & Darabi, A. A. (2005). A motivational perspective on the relation between mental effort and performance. *Educational Technology Research and Development, 53*, 25–34.

Park, O.-C., & Hopkins, R. (1993). Instructional conditions for using dynamic visual displays. *Instructional Science., 21*, 427–449.

Pollock, E., Chandler, P., & Sweller, J. (2002). Assimilating complex information. *Learning and Instruction., 12*, 61–86.

Potelle, H., & Rouet, J. F. (2003). Effects of content representation and readers' prior knowledge on the comprehension of hypertext. *International Journal of Human-Computer Studies., 58*, 327–345.

Schnotz, W. (2010). Reanalyzing the expertise reversal effect. *Instructional Science, 38*, 315–323.

Schnotz, W., & Rasch, T. (2005). Enabling, facilitating, and inhibiting effects of animations in multimedia learning: Why reduction of cognitive load can have negative results on learning. *Educational Technology Research and Development., 53*, 47–58.

Shiffrin, R., & Schneider, W. (1977). Controlled and automatic human information processing: II. Perceptual learning, automatic attending, and a general theory. *Psychological Review., 84*, 127–190.

Shin, E. C., Schallert, D. L., & Savenye, W. C. (1994). Effects of learner control, advisement, and prior knowledge on young students' learning in a hypertext environment. *Educational Technology Research and Development., 42,* 33–46.

Shute, V. J. (2008). Focus on formative feedback. *Review of Educational Research, 78,* 153–189.

Simon, H. A. (1967). Motivational and emotional controls of cognition. *Psychological Review, 74,* 29–39.

Simons, K. D., & Klein, J. D. (2007). The impact of scaffolding and student achievement levels in a problem-based learning environment. *Instructional Science., 35,* 41–72.

Spiro, R. J., Feltovich, P. J., Jacobson, M. J., & Coulson, R. L. (1991). Knowledge representation, content specification, and the development of skill in situation-specific knowledge assembly: Some constructivist issues as they relate to cognitive flexibility theory and hypertext. *Educational Technology., 31*(9), 22–25.

Sweller, J. (2010). Element interactivity and intrinsic, extraneous, and germane cognitive load. *Educational Psychology Review, 22,* 123–138.

Sweller, J., Chandler, P., Tierney, P., & Cooper, M. (1990). Cognitive load and selective attention as factors in the structuring of technical material. *Journal of Experimental Psychology: General., 119,* 176–192.

Tindall-Ford, S., Chandler, P., & Sweller, J. (1997). When two sensory modes are better than one. *Journal of Experimental Psychology: Applied., 3*(4), 257–287.

Tobias, S. (1989). Another look at research on the adaptation of instruction to student characteristics. *Educational Psychologist, 24,* 213–227.

Tobias, S. (2010). The expertise reversal effect and aptitude treatment interaction research. *Instructional Science, 38,* 309–314.

Tversky, B., Morrison, J. B., & Betrancourt, M. (2002). Animation: Does it facilitate learning? *International Journal of Human-Computer Studies., 57,* 247–262.

Van Merriënboer, J. J. G., Sluijsmans, D., Corbalan, G., Kalyuga, S., Paas, F., & Tattersall, C. (2006). Performance assessment and learning task selection in environments for complex learning. In D. Clark & J. Elen (Eds.), *Advances in learning and instruction* (pp. 201–220). Amsterdam: Elsevier Science.

The Role of Affect in Creative Minds

Andy Dong

Introduction

From the joy experienced by children in making a castle out of used appliance cardboard boxes to the pleasure of the "flow" reported by inventors when fully immersed in a state of discovery (Csikszentmihalyi, 1996), positive feelings are associated with creative activities. We have all experienced the effects of positive affect on creative thinking and the feedback effect of creativity in generating heightened feelings of positive affect.

Feelings of positive affect do more than make our creative minds feel "happy." Several authors have established that inherently creative tasks may be facilitated by positive affect (Forgas, 2000). Solovoya identified that emotions serve as a reservoir for conceptual inspiration and "influences the formation of the belief and value system of a designer" (Solovoya, 2003). The positive emotions that we feel as a response to an affective appraisal, appetitive (positive) or aversive (negative), of a creative experience account for the enhanced creative and exploratory behavior congruent with positive affect (Blascovich & Mendes, 2000). In contrast to positive affective states (emotions) influencing generative and creative thinking, negative affect has an opposite effect. Fiedler's computational model known as BIAS, which represents concepts as affective states, simulates the effect of evaluative judgments on affective states (Fiedler, 2000). The model supports the assertion that negative affective states promote detail and procedurally oriented thinking.

When it comes to the effects of emotions on creative thinking, there is little doubt that positive emotions enrich motivational tendencies (Pekrun, 2011), leading to enhanced creativity. Creativity, though, is not only about making novel and useful

A. Dong (✉)
Faculty of Architecture, Design and Planning,
University of Sydney, Sydney, New South Wales, Australia
e-mail: andy.dong@sydney.edu.au

R.A. Calvo and S.K. D'Mello (eds.), *New Perspectives on Affect and Learning Technologies*, 217
Explorations in the Learning Sciences, Instructional Systems and Performance Technologies 3,
DOI 10.1007/978-1-4419-9625-1_16, © Springer Science+Business Media, LLC 2011

objects. It is also associated with creative problem solving and learning, both of which recruit the cognitive processes underlying creativity. Creative problem solving entails finding a novel solution to a problem, often by framing the problem in a new way rather than strict analysis. Our creative minds recruit affect as an ineluctable part of creativity because affect provides a framing for propositions. These affective frames provide our creative minds with critical information upon which to base actions and tasks. This emphasis on being imaginative in thinking about problems is also a means to enhance learning, such as increasing the retention of a subject matter by imagining creative uses of the knowledge rather than memorizing the knowledge (Bromage & Mayer, 1981). In terms of teaching, the benefits of taking a creative problem solving approach have been amply documented, particularly in contrasting the motivational effects of taking a creative problem solving approach compared to a procedural approach.

While creativity is a central aspect of many human activities, it is an essential aspect in professions related to the practice of design including architecture, engineering, and fashion. The field of design research was developed to study the tools, methods, practices, and cognitive processes of designers in practice with an eye toward progressive refinement of design processes and designed objects. Within this area of research, creativity is seen as essential, but the real challenge is conducting the research in naturalistic settings, which is becoming the norm (McDonnell & Lloyd, 2009).

I will present a linguistically derived approach to describe the representation of emotions in language. Human language is vital to the expression of feelings and is comparatively easier to access than physiological or bio-physiological indicators of emotions. Language enables us to express our conscious awareness of affective states. In order to study how affect affects thinking in design, examining the linguistic structure by which designers express affect can expose the way that affect is drawn into their perception and interpretation of situations during creative activities. Once this is isolated, we are in the position to evaluate the role of affect in creative minds. I will study this designerly language within the industrial context of creative practitioners in the areas of architecture, engineering design (Dong, Kleinsmann, & Valkenburg, 2009), and interaction design (Dong, 2006). Studying creative practitioners engaged in practice provides a suitable test bed within which to study the interplay of affect and creative thinking. Based on some evidence uncovered in prior studies, I hypothesize that affect serves three meta-functions[1] in creative minds:

1. To help break stimulus–response bonds
2. To control the pacing and sequencing of actions
3. To evaluate according to beliefs and values

I will start by describing the linguistic analysis approach. I will then present a discussion of the three meta-functions in relation to the roles that affect plays in creative minds.

---

[1] Taking a functionalist view of affect, I use the term meta-function because each of these has a different concern and may recruit a number of behavior-regulatory and internal-regulatory functions to achieve their effects.

What You Say About What You Feel

The linguistic underpinnings and full implementation of the semantic and grammatical analyses to derive representations of emotions from language use in creative activities are dealt with in other publications (Dong, 2009; Dong et al., 2009). Here, I present a general overview of the method so that subsequent reports on evidence of emotions expressed during creative activities can be understood.

To understand how language represents emotions, we need to first agree upon what it is we mean by "affect" and "emotions." Affect is the neurobiological state incorporating emotion, feelings and other affective phenomena such as mood and temperament. According to the *appraisal theory of emotions*, emotions arise from the appraisal of circumstances (Ellsworth & Scherer, 2003). Appraisal is believed to be related to the evolutionarily conserved instinct for survival. The affective networks in the brain allow an organism to reference stimuli and behaviors in relation to their survival value; further, it is believed that affective states help organisms to unconditionally and conditionally valuate situations (Burgdorf & Panksepp, 2006). Whether or not a valuation is unconditional or conditional depends upon the extent to which executive functions are exercised in responses to stimuli.

Affective appraisals, as an antecedent and participant in emotion, are hypothesized to be indicated by a linguistic appraisal to circumstances encountered during creative activities. A linguistic appraisal is an overt, verbal realization of the appraisal of circumstances, that is, a comment or a judgment. In linguistics, this process is called appraisal. Appraisal theory in linguistics deals with the ways speakers express evaluation, attitude and emotions through language. The hypothesis that language is a reliable way to get at emotions is supported by research in cognitive science and psychology on the relation between language use and affective state. Ortony, Clore, and Foss (1987) established an "affective lexicon" to categorize words about affect into affective, behavioral and cognitive "foci" based upon the extent to which the word refers to how one is feeling (affect), acting (behavior), or thinking (cognitive). Pennebaker and King (1999) point to systematic approaches to derive reliable linguistic resources that deal with both the representation and the representability of feelings through language.

At present, computational methods for the analysis of appraisals in language, called sentiment analysis, are unable to reliably deal with the full range of linguistic resources that deal with both the representation and the representability of feelings through language (Turney & Littman, 2003; Whitelaw, Garg, & Argamon, 2005). As such, it is essential to apply manual analysis of language in order to gain a robust understanding.

The methodological question that is raised in the development of a linguistic framework to describe the way that designers represent affective states is to determine the "situations" that provide stimuli and hence may produce an emotion. Three categories of circumstances can provide sources of appraisal during creative activities: the Product (the creative work), the Process (tasks and activities associated with creativity) and the People (the agent(s) involved in creative activities). Appraisals of products are one way in which we offer subjective, personal assessments or apply normative judgments based on best practices and external authoritative critique. Whereas the appraisal of products is associated with a tangible object, an appraisal of a process is associated with activities and tasks. The appraisal of a process is identified by taking stances toward tangible tasks and actions. The evaluation associates a position toward the state of being of an action and can normally be identified by asking, "What is being/was done?" and then "What is/was the stance toward the action?" Finally, appraisal of people includes internal, mental states of affect, cognitive states, cognitive–behavioral states, and physical functioning or capability to undertake a tangible action. Using Ortony, Clore and Foss's affective lexicon (Ortony et al., 1987), sample words are: (affect) at-ease, bitter, happy, irritated; (cognitive) amazed, inspired, interested; (cognitive–behavioral) cautious, lazy, sensitive. Words describing physical functioning or capability include novice, expert, visionary, and integrative.

There are several linguistic analysis techniques that offer methods to analyze the relation between language and what is being thought or felt while expressing a verbalization. However, the linguistic realization of appraisals has been theorized most prominently within the linguistic theory of Systemic-Functional Linguistics (SFL) (Halliday, 2004; Halliday & Matthiessen, 1999). SFL examines how the semantic resources of a language (i.e., its semantics and grammar) create a system of options for speakers to enact the three main meta-functions of language: (1) ideational: to represent ideas; (2) interpersonal: to function as a medium of exchange between people; and (3) textual: to organize, structure, and hold itself together (Halliday, 2004). SFL is concerned with the system of grammar within a genre of text (i.e., magazine, academic journal, personal letters) and how the grammar produces meaning and relates experiences in the text. The text itself is considered to be strongly associated with a social situational context within which the text is produced. How I express my disregard toward a matter with my immediate friends at home would strongly differ with a similar statement in a work environment, and these may differ again if I make the statement in Australia or in the USA. Within each specific genre, SFL theory holds that the system of grammar of a language constrains the choices available to a speaker to generate meaning using language. SFL specifies a lexicogrammatical framework which constrains the features available to speakers. For example, in academic writing, evaluative statements about research are generally implicit rather than explicit (Hood, 2004). To make the evaluation that current research is more correct than prior research, rather than explicitly saying so, I might write, "In the past, cognitive science research tended to separate cognition and affect into two distinct systems. However, contemporary theorists treat them as inseparable aspects of the texture of cognition." The constraints imposed by the structure of a grammar yield the potential to analyze how the structural consequences of that choice relate to how the speaker utilized language as a tool for representing knowledge or for making meaning (Halliday & Matthiessen, 1999).

The interpersonal meta-function is realized through the system of APPRAISAL. (Consistent with the theory, systems are identified by CAPITALIZATION). SFL linguists (Martin, 2000; Martin & White, 2005) define five high-level resources for conveying appraisals: attitude, engagement, graduation, orientation, and polarity.

Each resource has a set of attributes (Fig. 1). Any noun, verb, adjective, or adverb which functions to express meaning related to these resources for appraisal is considered a term of appraisal. The clause within which the term appears is an appraisal.

Attitude has to do with ways of taking evaluative stances (or what linguists call attitudinal positioning), which can be done through descriptions of mental states (affect), personal tastes and dispositions (appreciation), or norms and mores with reference to behavioral norms and conventions (judgment). Engagement is the commitment to an appraisal and is often considered an appraisal of the appraisal. It deals with subtle grading of the speaker's commitment to what is said. Graduation deals with the strength or "size" of the evaluation. Orientation relates to whether the appraisal is positive or negative. Polarity is labeled as marked or unmarked depending upon whether the appraisal is scoped. Table 1 presents some sample semantic resources of appraisal.

Table 2 shows examples of appraisals employing each of these semantic resources with various attributes, which will be evident from the content of the appraisal.

I apply the analysis technique of functional grammar to the analysis of language (Eggins, 2004, pp. 206–253). I will use the example "I certainly love the delightful

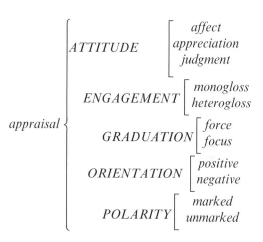

Fig. 1 Semantic resources for appraisal and their attributes

Table 1 Sample resources and attributes in appraisals

Semantic resource	Attribute	Sample words
Attitude	Affect	Like, dislike, enjoy
		Ill-at-ease, dissatisfied, apprehensive
Graduation	Force	Very, really, extremely, at the moment, recent, right now
	Focus	In particular, effectively
Engagement	Monogloss	In my opinion, in my view, I believe
	Heterogloss	It is said, so to speak, it seems, probably, perhaps, maybe, sort of

Table 2 Sample appraisals

Appraisal	Semantic resource and attribute
This is a [good] design	[good] (attitude: appreciation; orientation: positive)
She is a [great] designer	[great] (attitude: judgment; orientation: positive; graduation: force)
I [really] [think] she is a [great] designer	[really] (graduation: force); [think] (attitude: affect) [great] (attitude: judgment; orientation: positive; graduation: force)
This is a [good] design, [maybe]	[good] (attitude: appreciation; orientation: positive); [maybe] (engagement: monogloss)
This is [not] a [good] design process	[not] (polarity: marked); [good] (attitude: appreciation; orientation: negative)

tactile feel of multitouch interfaces" to illustrate the functional grammar approach to the identification of the semantic resources of appraisal:

1. Identify the verb clause. This is known as the PROCESS.
2. Identify the Participants with the verb clause.

I	certainly	love	the delightful tactile feel of multitouch interfaces
Participant		Process	Participant

3. Using the rules of the TRANSITIVITY system in SFL, decide the appropriate PROCESS type: mental (thinking), material (doing), relational (having, being), existential (existing) or behavioral (behaving) and the corresponding participant types. Code the Participant(s) according to their respective categories based on the PROCESS type.

I	certainly	love	the delightful tactile feel of multitouch interfaces
Sensor	Intensifier	Process: mental	Phenomenon:act

4. Identify the semantic resources for APPRAISAL. If there is no semantic resource evident, the clause is not an appraisal. Interpret whether the orientation of the appraisal is positive or negative. The semantic resources for APPRAISAL are indicated by [].

I	[certainly]	[love]	the [delightful] feel of multitouch interfaces
Sensor	Graduation: force	Process: mental Attitude: affect	Attitude: appreciation; orientation: positive

5. Classify the clause as being about Product, Process, or People to describe the design situations (states) and events which may be the stimuli of affective judgment and therefore the object of the linguistic appraisal.

Category:	Product		
I	[certainly]	[love]	the [delightful] feel of multitouch interfaces
Sensor	Graduation: force	Process: mental Attitude: affect	Attitude: appreciation; orientation: positive

In summary, the analysis of linguistic appraisals in creative activities includes the identification of an appraisal and the object of the appraisal. This appraisal analysis is meaningful and relevant toward identifying emotions according to the appraisal theory of emotions because it considers the representation of the emotion in light of the external (stimuli) of the appraisal, that is, Product, Process, or People. While the analysis of appraisals in actual language use in creative activities is more complicated than these examples would imply, and required modifications from Martin and White's original formulation (Martin & White, 2005), this model of linguistic analysis has shown to be well suited for bridging the representational gap between emotions and creative activities (Dong, 2006; Dong et al., 2009; Kleinsmann & Dong, 2007).

In the next sections, I will present some findings on the role of affect in creative minds and compare them to other research on the interplay between affect and cognition.

What You Feel Will Set You Free

What design, invention and innovation – all canonical creative activities – share, as Thomas Edison once said, is that "To invent, you need imagination and a pile of junk." What he meant is that you need to be able to see new ideas from old ones; the more ideas you have lying around, the more likely you are to be able to come up with a new one. Therein lays the problem. To what extent is the ability to invent in the mind of the inventor or in the intrinsic properties of the idea? While the answer is not an either-or proposition, affect plays a role in a person's ability to "see" something new from something old, that is, to "see" in the set of ideas a new idea that no one else has considered before.

This ability to "see" something new from what is already there in ambient reality or in our memory is partially enabled by the network architecture of the brain. Our brain's neural architecture allows the activation of mental representations that are not part of ambient reality because sensory information undergoes extensive associative transformations with similar sets of sensory inputs and with our memory (Mesulam, 1998). More important, it is also known that modulation of the sensory input is driven in part by emotion. That is, even though the brain can produce multiple conceptions, there must be an impulse to do so. There is a broad consensus that novelty seeking is a primary driver in this emotional modulation. Creative minds can give rise to new interpretations of old ideas because the brain is innately motivated "to seek and create novelty and change" (Mesulam, 1998, p. 1044). I define this motivation as design curiosity, which is likely to play a role in evoking the construction of alternative representations from the same sensation.

Design curiosity is not the same as the sort of curiosity associated with the goal of seeking out new information as models of curiosity advocated by Berlyne (Berlyne, 1954) and Littman (Litman, 2008) would suggest. The goal of creative activities is not necessarily satisfied simply by the discovery of new (to the information seeker) ideas or information-seeking behavior. We can derive satisfaction from designing our dream home in our heads without ever building it. There is an intrinsic curiosity that is satisfied by "doing" creative activities even when these activities have no manifest practical outcome, and new knowledge is secondary to the creative act itself. Creative thinking is motivated by curiosity, for example, to modify the current circumstances to produce a new creative outcome through an expansion or projection of possibilities (Dong, McInnes, & Davies, 2005). Design curiosity can help to explain how our creative minds loosen stimulus – response bonds to allow us to inhibit a preexisting representation (the world as it is) to try a new one (the world as it could be), and thereby see new ideas from old ones.

In the following excerpt, a team of professionals from different design-related industries are playing an urban design game named "Kantjil" (Kleinsmann & van der Lugt, 2007). The game simulates the urban design of a fictitious planet. Each player has one of four roles, and the team's major goal was to create an island that can accommodate as many inhabitants as possible, in such a way that the island's inhabitants feel happy. One of the challenges of the game is that the players' objectives apparently conflict if the players interpret the game rules and instructions literally. To succeed, the players must reduce the complexity of the game by "seeing" alternative "rules" for configuring the game pieces on the board.

One team of professional architects and industrial designers was able to do so by creating a module (a set of game pieces in a specific configuration) with "connections" that was replicated several times. In the following excerpt, the team designs the type of connections that would result in a module that balances all of their competing objectives. The architect starts by proposing a layout. Whereas most of the team participants present rather pessimistic appraisals of the layout currently on the game board, with the culture expert being particularly negative, the architect generally remains positive, and then proposes a "smart connection." (Appraisals are in **bold face** in the excerpts.)

Excerpt 1 (Dong et al., 2009)

Architect	maybe we can think, **this is very structured**, if we multiply this we have **the right combination, the right balance**
Energy	**that's true** but for the energy, to get energy from that **it's really**
Health	**not good**
Health	**not good** because **I have one big connected place**
Culture	**it's better** to have big blue and green
Architect	but maybe **we need a smart connection** then
Energy	**that's possible**
Health	you are looking for the optimum right?
Architect	yeah
Health	something yes
Energy	then you can
Culture	you don't like the cities to be big so **we can't build a really big city with a big for my point of view that would be best to have a big city, one big piece of water** and **one big piece of green for my opinion that would be the most perfect**

After a short discussion analyzing the configuration, the architect eventually designs a "smart connection."

Architect   can't we make a smart connection and if we link this to this they're linked
              so maybe it's behaving like a metropolis if we multiply this but **it's still
              a very open and friendly living environment** so we

In this excerpt, we can identify several linguistic characteristics signaling a design curiosity driven expansion of possibilities. Verbal auxiliaries such as *maybe*, *can*, etc., signal when the architect is opening up a space of speculation and suggestion. The architect is attempting to find an alternative interpretation ("*maybe* we can think") for the configuration. The "if" in "*if* we multiply this" operates in a similar fashion as an interrogative or questioning form of language, signaling a possible configuration of the game pieces without the expectation of a direct answer. The health expert seems to understand that the architect is engaged in this design curiosity driven exploration for an alternative configuration and interpretation in saying "you are looking for the optimum right?" The architect maintains the curiosity by proposing "*maybe* we need a *smart* connection." The alternative configuration is finally proposed when the architect says, "can't we make a smart connection and if we link this to this" and builds it on the game board. The architect makes a new interpretation of the connected modules as "behaving like a metropolis."

We can observe from this example that linguistic appraisals of stimuli (the game board pieces in the above excerpt) signal a problem that requires the attention of the designers, because the layout cannot satisfy the design requirements. Whereas some of the designers address the problem in a detail-oriented, bottom-up processing style by examining if the configuration can satisfy the game requirements, the architect seems motivated by a different affective state, that of design curiosity. The architect's curiosity seems to elicit the architect's focus on the possibilities rather than material that is directly content relevant. Thus, at the same time that affect is providing the impulse (for the architect) to find alternative ideas, it is also influencing information processing activities of the other team members. We pursue this second meta-function in the next section.

I Don't Feel I Know Enough Yet

The bulk of the evidence on the interplay between feeling and thinking is that cognitive processes are tuned to meet the situational requirements signaled by feelings (Schwarz & Clore, 2007). Internal and external cues that signal a benign or problematic situation have different cognitive and motivational consequences, as shown in the prior example. The amount of attention and resources devoted to "thinking" about a situation is tuned such that problem signals foster vigilance and the adoption of detail-oriented processing of information, whereas the converse is not associated with any particular information processing style. If we feel that something is a problem, even without objective evidence to support that feeling, it turns out that we cannot readily and "consciously" override this feeling to ignore the problem signal; systematic information processing fostered by negative moods is difficult to override (Bless & Schwarz, 1999). Feelings can also change the priority of goals. If we feel confident about a situation, then we may explore new, unusual and creative associations. This does not mean that this exploration is not without its downsides; we could feel overconfident and overestimate our knowledge. This problem of "deceptive clarity" occurs in children's learning of scientific phenomena from scientific visualizations which appear "too good" (Linn, Chang, Chiu, Zhang, & McElhaney, 2010).

In Excerpt 2 taken from a design student's blog, the appraisals offer us a glimpse into how mood and negative feelings influence the actions of the designer. The designer is developing a data visualization system to identify illegal stock trading, such as bidding up the price of a stock. The designer ruminates about the next design "move." While it is not clear what the designer will actually do, we are told a bit about the designer's mood.

Excerpt 2 (Dong, 2006)

> I have spent all afternoon cleaning up my viz- **the animation for April and May was really retarded** in my last prototype… I also finished adding the remaining May data. AND I have just used graphics to label April and May- last time **I was lazy** and just dragged in the buttons I made for another prototype.. hehe. And I made an intro!!! Yay! **Nothing too flash**, but **I was reeeally fussy with it**. But **I am satisfied**… **Actually** no, **I am not. I want it to look cuter**. I may change it at the last minute if I have the time. Hopefully I can get a working timeline and mouse overs up and running tonight! For now, it's a shower and then dinner! =)

The negative appraisals of the designer's cognitive–behavioral state ("I was lazy") and negative opinion of the current implementation of the prototype ("the animation … was really retarded") informs the reader that the designer was probably in a negative mood, possibly caused by the poor outcome of the design work. Faced with a problematic situation, the designer is motivated to rectify the design work. During this negative mood, the designer is systematic ("I was really fussy with it") in producing the new prototype, wherein being "fussy" connotes having a narrow focus of attention on each feature of the visualization. Nonetheless, the designer is not satisfied with the outcome. The consideration of feelings was at least as important as aesthetic principles about visual communication in assessing the potential for fulfilling experiential goals (Would the visualization be aesthetically pleasing to view?) rather than instrumental goals (Would the visualization be informative?), and is consistent with the finding that feelings are more informative when the judgment itself is about a feeling, that is, affective in nature (Pham, 2004). To repair the designer's mood ("I *want* it"), the designer resolves to make the visualization "look cuter." In short, how the designer feels about the creative work controlled the pacing of design actions, by being "reeaally fussy" and the sequencing of actions, in undertaking further revisions of the work to make it "look cuter." This example shows that affect frames propositions and provides information content that serves as the basis for actions. In our other research, we found that design actions are framed by episodes of low to high to low affective content (number of linguistic appraisals), and peaks of positive affect reliably signal the end of a design episode

(Kleinsmann & Dong, 2007). This framing effect is more pronounced in situations in which we must deal with our values and beliefs.

It Just Doesn't Feel Right

We turn our attention from issues associated with creative activities in a general sense toward an issue more relevant to the professional practice of design. Value-sensitive design is a framework for the principled and systematic handling of the ways in which principles, standards, and qualities guide designers' actions (Friedman & Kahn, 2003). Design is steeped in ethical considerations wherein designers make judgments that resolve ethical issues and a deceptively simple aesthetic decision can easily have moral consequences (Lloyd, 2009). Designers may be called upon to deal with moral issues such as privacy, trust, child protection, freedom of information, and democracy in their work. In such situations, there is no objective knowledge to serve as the basis of "right" and "wrong" because decisions of "right" and "wrong" are by nature ethical. Regardless of what the values are, they motivate the decisions and guide the actions of designer, and ultimately serve as the basis for how the designer assesses the design work.

If designers are making decisions based on values, then their decisions may be particularly sensitive to affect, especially when objective knowledge is not available as a basis for the decision. If we take the definition of affect as the appetitive or aversive response to stimuli, then designers could use their affective response as the basis of their decisions (Schwarz, 2000). In other words, designers may be asking themselves, "How do I feel about this?" rather than "What do I know about this?" in justifying their decisions. Further, they will draw upon their past affective experiences, such that their positive or negative affective responses to a few existing products may dominate their response to the current one (Fredrickson, 2000).

The influence of affective appraisals when the subject of the appraisal is closely tied to the person's beliefs rather than objective knowledge is demonstrated in our analyses of design meetings (McDonnell & Lloyd, 2009). In the following excerpt, an architect and a client are discussing the number of cremators in a new crematorium (Dong et al., 2009).

Excerpt 3 (Dong et al., 2009)

Architect	well this is **fairly fundamental**-
Client	yes
Architect	deciding the number of cremators
Client	yes
Architect	because originally there were going to be no cremators
Client	no that's right
Architect	and then we said there were two
Client	yep
Architect	erm if you want us to look at three **this might have a fundamental change on the whole width of this bay** and so **I think we need a clear direction** from yourselves of how many cremators we are to t- look at

There is a discrepancy between what the architect thinks should be the best number of cremators based on a belief in symmetry and what the clients objectively know as the correct number given the functional requirements based on historical evidence.

Excerpt 4 (Dong et al., 2009)

Client	yep so you know but its not so much a third cremator but **just enough space** to + put all the add on bits that probably might come with it such as a stairwell that sort of type o- its just the th- just the two doors on either side just making me think whether they might want to be-
Architect	yeah I mean I think this was put in for architectural reasons
Client	right
Architect	because **it's such a symme/trical**
Client	/metrical\
Architect	building
Client	yeah OK
Architect	you know I mean **if you wanted us to look at seriously at putting in a third cremator** I think **we'd have to review this whole area the chances are we couldn't + retain the symmetry** erm in that way if you would like us to look at a third cremator we can do that I think we

The architect's belief in symmetry is affect sensitive; as the final statement indicates, the architect clearly feels strongly about the symmetry, appears to be in a negative mood about any changes, and is not entirely amenable to changing the design despite the needs stated by the client (Luck, 2009).

In contrast, in another discussion, the same architect and client discuss a footpath over a stream. While they will later recognize the perils of the footpath (Later, the client comments about a possible sign indicating, "yeah do not fall over watch where you're going."), they proceed with the footpath and stepping stones nonetheless.

Excerpt 5 (Dong et al., 2009)

Client	I think something that looks like a bridge would be well or something that's solid would be the unfortunately although I can see the benefit of having I mean **I quite like the idea of stepping stones**
Client	yes I do **I like the idea**
Architect	well if you like it **why don't we run with it** until somebody says you don't want to do that

In both instances, decisions are being made based on how the architect and/or the client feel about the situation. In the first episode, the architect appears to want to ignore the objective requirements and while the architect tries to mount a logical argument, the client is more obviously keying into the architect's desire for symmetry. In summary, decision-making based on feelings toward values and beliefs may be a simplifying heuristic short-cut for complex decisions. It is commonly seen in design situations, because design problems can be complex and it is simply not possible for the designer to evaluate all the possible information that could feed into a decision. Instead, designers rely on affective responses, and the affective responses are value-driven.

Affect in Learning

What then can be said about the role of affect in learning about creativity, that is, learning to be a creative designer? As both du Boulay and Pekrun have already articulated in this book, motivational states generally influence both the psychology of learning (du Boulay) and cognitive processes associated with learning (Pekrun). The data presented here likewise suggest a multifaceted role for affect and, consequently, challenges for learning technologies when it comes to developing systems supporting learning to do creativity. Despite no firm study on emotions in learning about design, the data presented suggest that design education could benefit from an increased focus on using emotions as a "sixth sense" alongside the analytical, theoretical and critical forms of judgment taught in design curricula.

A core skill in design practice is the ability to manage the uncertainty and ill-defined nature of design problems. Managing and dealing with the peaks (positive) and troughs (negative) of emotions as a consequence of these characteristics of designing is a part of design learning. In particular, students should learn to appreciate appetitive appraisals during periods of impasse and incubation as what they are – part of the process. The design student working on the data visualization (Excerpt 2) is an apt example of harnessing appetitive appraisals as a guide for focusing efforts. At other times, positive affect can be used to break existing ways of seeing the world, which partially explains why brainstorming sessions are often conducted in a "fun" way while suspending any form of judgment that may potentially inhibit feelings of positive affect. When learning how to produce a creative solution to ill-defined problems, students often experience problems in overcoming past examples. Fixation has been used to describe this block, and various methods have been proposed to overcome fixation. Affective framing of design concepts may help to reduce cognitive workload in assessing them so that more cognitive resources could be applied toward detecting and eliminating the inappropriate carryover of features from prior examples.

Finally, affective experience is a basis for the evaluation of a design work when values and beliefs enter the desiderata. Students can learn to apply their affective experiences as part of their repertoire of tools for critical analysis and inquiry, particularly when objective evidence fails to deliver a clear answer. Consider, for a moment, helping a student to assess whether the visual design of the student's poster, which advocates a political matter you disagree with vehemently, is *acceptably* vulgar since the vulgarity is part of the strategy for persuasion to elicit an emotion from viewers. The acceptable level of vulgarity is both a matter of community standards, for which we can make assessments based on evidence, and a matter of emotional awareness. The discussion between instructor and student on such an issue must occur on both a critical level and a level of emotional awareness, but priority in this case is likely to be given to the emotional factors. The student is more likely to draw on past affective experience to judge the level of emotional response elicited by the poster than on analytical design principles.

The multifaceted role for affect, as briefly outlined above, is a challenge for affective learning technologies. A key challenge for learning technologies in discerning emotions lays in the fine-grained understanding of the object of the appraisal that led to the emotion in addition to the emotion itself. This problem could partially be overcome by eliciting both the emotion and the object of the appraisal underlying the emotion from the student. Sentiment analysis tools currently identify only the orientation of the emotion. However, if we were to build a more robust sentiment analysis tool to understand linguistic appraisals, the sentiment analysis tool must *simultaneously* understand the content of the appraisal, that is, whether the appraisal is about Product, Process or People, and the orientation (positive or negative) of the appraisal. It turns out that this is possible, but it is not as accurate as identifying the topic of a text or the orientation of a text separately (Wang & Dong, 2008). Furthermore, the tight interweaving of linguistic features that characterize subject matter and sentiment means that supervised machine learning methods would be limited in their ability to operate between one corpus and another. The training and target corpus must be semantically similar. Further work in this area is needed to make emotion detection in learning technologies up to the task. Nonetheless, the data and analyses presented show that understanding the representation of emotions in language is a robust pathway to understanding the role of affect in creativity.

Conclusions

From analyses of linguistic appraisals during creative situations, we find that affect exercises regulatory effects on creative thinking. The extent of the effect is not quantifiable from the data sets, but some of its influences have been described. The research method to extract affective content from language use in creative situations is intended to link affective content to creative thinking. The research method responds to the need to theoretically explain in naturalistic creative situations affect's congruity effects or the absence of any effects with theories of cognition.

The challenging view made in this research is that the affective content of our creative mind is accessible through the language of linguistic appraisals. It is possible that affective appraisals are occurring in the brain with no manifestation linguistically or otherwise. When appraisals are consciously and linguistically manifested, though, they provide a means to parse creative activities and to align affective processing with logical thinking.

References

Berlyne, D. E. (1954). A theory of human curiosity. *British Journal of Psychology, 45*, 180–191.
Blascovich, J., & Mendes, W. B. (2000). Challenge and threat appraisals: The role of affective cues. In J. P. Forgas (Ed.), *Feeling and thinking: The role of affect in social cognition.* Cambridge: Maison des Science de l'Homme and Cambridge University Press.

Bless, H., & Schwarz, N. (1999). Sufficient and necessary conditions in dual process models: The case of mood and information processing. In S. Chaiken & Y. Trope (Eds.), *Dual-process theories in social psychology*. New York: Guilford.

Bromage, B. K., & Mayer, R. E. (1981). Relationship between what is remembered and creative problem-solving performance in science learning. *Journal of Educational Psychology, 73*, 451–461. doi: 10.1037/0022-0663.73.4.451.

Burgdorf, J., & Panksepp, J. (2006). The neurobiology of positive affect. *Neuroscience & Biobehavioral Reviews, 30*, 173–187. doi: 10.1016/j.neubiorev.2005.06.001.

Csikszentmihalyi, M. (1996). *Creativity: Flow and the psychology of discovery and invention*. New York: Harper Collins Publishers.

Dong, A. (2006). How am I doing? The language of appraisal in design. In J. S. Gero (Ed.), *Design computing and cognition '06 (DCC06)* (pp. 385–404). Dordrecht: Kluwer.

Dong, A. (2009). *The language of design: Theory and computation*. London: Springer.

Dong, A., Kleinsmann, M., & Valkenburg, R. (2009). affect-in-cognition through the language of appraisals. *Design Studies, 30*, 138–153. doi: 10.1016/j.destud.2008.12.003.

Dong, A., McInnes, D., & Davies, K. P. (2005). Exploring the relationship between lexical behavior and concept formation in design conversations. *17th International Conference on Design Theory and Methodology*. New York: ASME Press, DETC2005-84407.

Eggins, S. (2004). *An introduction to systemic functional linguistics*. London: Continuum International Publishing Group.

Ellsworth, P. C., & Scherer, K. R. (2003). Appraisal processes in emotion. In R. J. Davidson, K. R. Scherer, & H. H. Goldsmith (Eds.), *Handbook of affective sciences [electronic resource]*. New York: Oxford University Press.

Fiedler, K. (2000). Toward and integrative account of affect and cognition phenomena using the BIAS computer algorithm. In J. P. Forgas (Ed.), *Feeling and thinking: The role of affect in social cognition*. Cambridge: Maison des Sciences de l'Homme and Cambridge University Press.

Forgas, J. P. (2000). Feeling and thinking: Summary and integration. In J. P. Forgas (Ed.), *Feeling and thinking: The role of affect in social cognition*. Cambridge: Maison des Sciences de l'Homme and Cambridge University Press.

Fredrickson, B. L. (2000). Extracting meaning from past affective experiences: The importance of peaks, ends, and specific emotions. *Cognition Emotion, 14*, 577–606. doi: 10.1080/026999300402808.

Friedman, B., & Kahn, P. H., Jr. (2003). *Human values, ethics, and design. The human-computer interaction handbook: Fundamentals, evolving technologies and emerging applications*. London: L. Erlbaum Associates.

Halliday, M. A. K. (2004). *An introduction to functional grammar*. London: Arnold.

Halliday, M. A. K., & Matthiessen, C. M. I. M. (1999). *Construing experience through meaning: A language-based approach to cognition*. London: Cassell.

Hood, S. (2004). Managing academic writing in undergraduate academic writing: A focus on the introductions to research reports. In L. Ravelli & R. A. Ellis (Eds.), *Analysing academic writing: Contextualized frameworks*. London: Continuum.

Kleinsmann, M., & Dong, A. (2007). Investigating the affective force on creating shared understanding. *19th International Conference on Design Theory and Methodology*. New York: ASME Press, DETC2007-34240.

Kleinsmann, M., & van der Lugt, R. (2007). Design games for simulating design communication. *Proceedings of the 16th International Conference on Engineering Design (ICED07)*. Paris: The Design Society.

Linn, M. C., Chang, H.-Y., Chiu, J., Zhang, H., & McElhaney, K. (2010). Can desirable difficulties overcome deceptive clarity in scientific visualizations. In A. S. Benjamin (Ed.), *Successful remembering and successful forgetting: a Festschrift in honor of Robert A Bjork*. London: Psychology Press.

Litman, J. A. (2008). Interest and deprivation factors of epistemic curiosity. *Personality and Individual Differences, 44*, 1585–1595. doi: 10.1016/j.paid.2008.01.014.

Lloyd, P. (2009). Ethical imagination and design. *Design Studies, 30*, 154–168. doi: 10.1016/j. destud.2008.12.004.

Luck, R. (2009). 'Does this compromise your design?' Interactionally producing a design concept in talk. *CoDesign: International Journal of CoCreation in Design and the Arts, 5*, 21–34. doi: 10.1080/15710880802492896.

Martin, J. R. (2000). Beyond exchange: APPRAISAL systems in English. In S. Hunston & G. Thompson (Eds.), *Evaluation in text: Authorial stance and the construction of discourse.* Oxford: Oxford University Press.

Martin, J. R., & White, P. R. R. (2005). *The language of evaluation: Appraisal in English.* New York: Palgrave Macmillan.

McDonnell, J., & Lloyd, P. (Eds.). (2009). *About: Designing – analysing design meetings.* London: Taylor and Francis.

Mesulam, M. M. (1998). From sensation to cognition. *Brain, 121*, 1013–1052. doi: 10.1093/ brain/121.6.1013.

Ortony, A., Clore, G. L., & Foss, M. A. (1987). The referential structure of the affective lexicon. *Cognitive Science, 11*, 341–364.

Pekrun, R. (2011). Emotions as drivers of learning and cognitive development. In R. Calvo & S. D'Mello (Eds.), *Explorations in the learning sciences, instructional systems and performance technologies.* New York: Springer.

Pennebaker, J. W., & King, L. A. (1999). Linguistic styles: Language use as an individual difference. *Journal of Personality and Social Psychology, 77*, 1296–1312. doi: 10.1037/0022-3514.77.6.1296.

Pham, M. T. (2004). The logic of feeling. *Journal of Consumer Psychology, 14*, 360–369. doi: 10.1207/s15327663jcp1404_5.

Schwarz, N. (2000). Emotion, cognition, and decision making. *Cognition Emotion, 14*, 433–440. doi: 10.1080/026999300402745.

Schwarz, N., & Clore, G. L. (2007). Feelings and phenomenal experiences. In A. W. Kruglanski & E. T. Higgins (Eds.), *Social psychology: Handbook of basic principles.* New York: Guilford.

Solovyova, I. (2003). Conjecture and emotion: An investigation of the relationship between design thinking and emotional content. In N. Cross & E. Edmonds (Eds.), *Expertise in design: Design thinking research symposium 6.* Sydney: Creativity and Cognition Studios Press.

Turney, P. D., & Littman, M. L. (2003). Measuring praise and criticism: Inference of semantic orientation from association. *ACM Transactions on Information Systems, 21*, 315–346. doi: 10.1145/944012.944013.

Wang, X., & Dong, A. (2008). A case study of computing appraisals in design text. In J. S. Gero & A. Goel (Eds.), *Design computing and cognition DCC'08* (pp. 573–592). Dordrecht: Springer.

Whitelaw, C., Garg, N., & Argamon, S. (2005). Using appraisal groups for sentiment analysis. *CIKM '05: Proceedings of the 14th ACM international conference on Information and knowledge management* (pp. 625–631). New York: ACM. doi: 10.1145/1099554.1099714.

Perspectives from Social and Affective Neuroscience on the Design of Digital Learning Technologies

Mary Helen Immordino-Yang and Vanessa Singh

The past decade has seen major advances in cognitive, affective, and social neuroscience that have the potential to revolutionize educational theories about learning, especially in technology-rich environments. In this chapter, we lay out two general, complementary findings that have emerged from neuroscience research on emotion and social processing, with the goal of beginning a dialog about the meaning of these findings for the design of emotionally responsive learning technologies. First, emotion and cognition are intertwined, and involve interplay between the body and mind. Second, social processing and learning happen in part by internalizing our subjective interpretations of other people's beliefs, goals, feelings and actions, and vicariously experiencing these in some ways as if they were our own. Together, these two results from neuroscience could have important implications for the design of technologies for learning and teaching, because they suggest that (1) social emotions and learning are intimately subjective processes, heavily influenced by social and cultural experience and individual predispositions and preferences; (2) affective responses involve a dynamic interplay between bottom-up and top-down processing. We conclude with a prospective discussion of the implications for affective computational systems design.

M.H. Immordino-Yang (✉)
Brain and Creativity Institute, University of Southern California, Los Angeles, CA, USA
and
Rossier School of Education, University of Southern California, Los Angeles, CA, USA
e-mail: immordin@usc.edu

R.A. Calvo and S.K. D'Mello (eds.), *New Perspectives on Affect and Learning Technologies*, 233
Explorations in the Learning Sciences, Instructional Systems and Performance Technologies 3,
DOI 10.1007/978-1-4419-9625-1_17, © Springer Science+Business Media, LLC 2011

Humans and Computers Interacting: Reframing the Digital Learning Experience as a Social Encounter

We begin with a familiar scenario: a group of high school students are sitting in a computer classroom. Some are slumped over their desks or staring aimlessly out of the window. Others, though, appear to be highly engaged in the task, working in pairs or alone and obviously absorbed in the digital environment. What accounts for the differences between these groups? How is it that some students may find a digital learning environment engaging and useful, while others may wonder, "why am I doing this?"

Both social-affective neuroscientists and learning technology designers are interested in scenarios such as this one, and in explaining the motivation and learning differences between the two groups of students. However, while the neuroscientists would focus on the question of how neural systems enable some students to experience the digital classroom as a motivating environment and how both perception and learning are altered as a result, learning technology designers would focus on the tools and setup that characterize the digital environment as their starting point, asking "what technology designs promote more efficient and effective learning?"

In this chapter, we argue for a different, complementary approach – one that advocates that social-affective neuroscientists and digital learning designers meet in the middle. In this productive middle ground, we suggest, a new question emerges: "How could digital learning environments be designed more effectively if we were to consider digital learning as happening through a dynamic interaction between the person and the computer?" In this view, the use of a computer learning technology by a person would be akin to a social encounter between a mind and a machine. While there is a long tradition of studying mind–machine interfaces, our hope is that framing the problem in terms of the neurobiology of human social emotion may give technology designers a new perspective into their craft, by paving the way for a dialog with affective and social neuroscientists about what we can expect from social humans when they interact with each other or, by extension, when they interact with silicon.

Embodied Brains, Social Minds: The Neurobiology of Being Human

Think back to the atrocities committed on 9/11/2001. How do we know these actions were wrong? And why do most Americans have such a difficult time understanding how the terrorists were able to carry out these plans? To decide these things, we automatically, albeit many times nonconsciously, imagine how the passengers on those planes must have felt, empathically experiencing both what they were thinking about and their emotions around these thoughts by imagining ourselves in the fateful plane. For many, just thinking of the images of planes hitting buildings induces a fearful mindset with all its physiological manifestations, like a racing heart and anxious thoughts. By contrast, we have difficulty empathizing with the terrorists who brought down the planes, because the values, morals, and emotions that motivated these men are so different from our own.

Recent advances in methodologies such as brain imaging have led to unprecedented explorations into the neuroscientific bases of such social processing, affective responding, and their relation to learning, and have shed new light on their workings. These new discoveries link body and mind, self and other, in ways that call into question the traditional dissection of the mind and the brain into modality and domain-specific modules, underlain by unique and nonoverlapping physiological and brain responses. In demonstrating the functional overlap between low-level systems for physiological regulation and somatosensation with systems involved in the most complex of mental states (Immordino-Yang, McColl, Damasio, & Damasio, 2009), these discoveries dissolve traditional boundaries between nature and nurture in development (Immordino-Yang & Fischer, 2009). They suggest instead that complex social and emotional processing co-opt and specialize regions originally evolved for more primitive functions, such as homeostatic regulation, consciousness regulation, and the feeling of the body (Immordino-Yang, Chiao, & Fiske, 2010). Further, these findings underscore the importance of emotion in "rational" learning and decision-making in both social and nonsocial contexts (Damasio, 2005; Haidt, 2001; Immordino-Yang & Damasio, 2007), demonstrating the primacy of evaluative, reward-based and pain-based processing to learning, and our human propensity toward subjective, social thinking.

These new discoveries stand in contrast to traditional Western views of the mind and body, such as that of Descartes, that divorced high-level, rational thought from what were thought of as the basal, emotional, instinctual processes of the body (Damasio, 1994/2005). Far from divorcing emotions from thinking, the new research collectively suggests that emotions, such as anger, fear, happiness and sadness, are cognitive and physiological processes that involve both the body and mind (Barrett, 2009; Damasio, 1994/2005; Damasio et al., 2000). As such, emotions utilize brain systems for body regulation (e.g., for blood pressure, heart rate, respiration, digestion) and sensation (e.g., for physical pain or pleasure, for stomach ache). They also influence brain systems for cognition, changing thought in characteristic ways – from the desire to seek revenge in anger, to the search for escape in fear, to the receptive openness to others in happiness, to the ruminating on lost people, opportunities or belongings in sadness. In each case, the emotion can be played out on the face and body, a process that is felt via neural systems for sensing and regulating the body. And in each case, these feelings interact with other thoughts to change the mind in characteristic ways, and to help people learn from their experiences.

Further, educators have long known that thinking and learning, as simultaneously cognitive and emotional processes, are not carried out in a vacuum, but in social and cultural contexts (Fischer & Bidell, 2006). A major part of how people make decisions has to do with their past social experiences, reputation, and cultural history. Now, social neuroscience is revealing some of the basic biological mechanisms by which social learning takes place (Frith & Frith, 2007; Mitchell, 2008).

According to current evidence, social processing and learning generally involve internalizing one's own subjective interpretations of other people's feelings and actions (Uddin, Iacoboni, Lange, & Keenan, 2007). We perceive and understand other people's feelings and actions in relation to our own beliefs and goals, and vicariously experience these feelings and actions using some of the same brain systems that would be invoked if the feelings and actions were our own (Immordino-Yang, 2008). Just as affective neuroscientific evidence links our bodies and minds in processes of emotion, social neuroscientific evidence links our own selves to the understanding of other people.

For example, it is now known that the key brain systems involved in the direct sensation of physical pain, especially systems for the sensation of the gut and viscera (e.g., during stomach ache or cigarette craving), are also involved in the feeling of one's own social or psychological pain (Decety & Chaminade, 2003; Eisenberger & Lieberman, 2004; Panksepp, 2005), as well as in the feeling of social emotions about another person's psychologically or physically painful, or admirable, circumstances (Immordino-Yang et al., 2009). Put simply, the poets had it right all along: feeling emotions about other people, including in moral contexts for judgments of fairness, virtue, and reciprocity, involve the brain systems responsible for "gut feelings" like stomach ache (Greene, Sommerville, Nystrom, Darley, & Cohen, 2001; Lieberman & Eisenberger, 2009), and systems that are responsible for the construction and awareness of one's own consciousness (i.e., the experience of "self"; Damasio, 2005; Moll, de Oliveira-Souza, & Zahn, 2008). Overall, affective neuroscience, together with psychology, are documenting the myriad ways in which the body and mind are interdependent during emotion, and therefore the myriad ways in which emotions organize (and bias) reasoning, judgments of self and others, and retrieval of memories during learning (Immordino-Yang & Damasio, 2007).

Related to this, the physiology of the social emotions that govern our interpersonal relationships and moral sense appears to involve dynamic interactions between neural systems for bodily sensation and awareness – the same systems that are known to be involved in the feeling of basic emotions like anger, fear, and disgust – and systems that support other aspects of cognition and emotion regulation, including regions involved in episodic memory retrieval and perspective-taking in relation to the self (Harrison, Gray, Gianaros, & Critchley, 2010; Zaki, Ochsner, Hanellin, Wager, & Mackey, 2007). During complex social emotions like admiration and compassion, for example, neural regions associated with memory and social cognitive functions appear to be functionally interconnected, or "talking," with neural systems involved in somatosensation for the internal, visceral body, and systems involved in consciousness regulation (i.e., brainstem systems responsible for sleep–wake cycles, arousal, etc.), in patterns that reflect not only involvement in the induction or onset of the emotion, but in its maintenance and experiential aspects as well. The cross talk between these neural systems suggests that social emotions endure, guiding our decisions, ongoing engagement, and learning. Moreover, the data suggest that these emotions may get their motivational power through coordinating neural mechanisms responsible for complex computations and knowledge with mechanisms that facilitate retrieval of our own personal history, all the while colored by reactions played out on homeostatic regulatory systems that, in the most basic sense, keep our bodies alive and our minds attentive.

Information Processing in Humans and Computers: Top-Down, Bottom-Up, and the Fundamental Importance of Human Subjectivity

Let us begin this section with a simple question: why are you, the reader, interested in neuroscientific perspectives on the design of digital learning environments? Of all the possible range of intelligent behaviors available to you, from planting a garden to playing a piano sonata to drinking a coffee with friends, you chose to spend energy on thinking about ideas and evidence pertinent to this topic at this moment. Why?

We suspect that, although this obvious question may initially puzzle you, it would then compel you to respond to the effect that you feel this topic is useful, engaging and warrants attention, that designing better digital learning technologies will help learners and may gain you recognition and notoriety in the process, that you take pleasure in working on this problem, or a myriad of other possible answers in the same vein. And your answers would reveal a central and common misconception in understanding learning: that rational, logical intelligence is somehow separable or independent from emotion, and from subjective, self-relevant goals.

Human cognition, or the faculties for processing information, applying knowledge, and making decisions, differs greatly from the way information is represented and processed by computers. Most importantly, human information processing is driven by subjective and culturally founded values. Building from what we saw in the previous section, these values are instantiated – they come to organize our behavior – through dynamic interplays between complex thought and knowledge, and generally nonconscious, low level physiological reactions that shape our feelings and behavior and motivate us toward particular forms of engagement. Put another way, we humans are capable of both top-down and bottom-up strategies of attending and information processing; our cognition involves decomposing or breaking information into its composite parts, as well piecing together and integrating information into more complex representations (Immordino-Yang & Fischer, 2009). What is more, because these processes happen in accordance with prior learning and expectations, both top-down and bottom-up processing are organized by our desires, needs, and goals, sometimes conscious and sometimes not. As biological beings, a central part of explaining *how* we do things lies in explaining *why* we do them.

To see what we mean, let us return to the neurobiological evidence presented above, concerning the relationship between the body and the mind. If the feeling of the body (or simulated body) during emotion can shape the way we think, which ample evidence suggests that it can, this shaping would happen via the sensing of the body, or via perception. However, such sensations are not merely recorded in a value-neutral or objective way. All sensations are not of equal importance. Rather, sensations are assigned valence, starting with pleasure and pain and growing from there in complexity. Even the simple visual perception of objects or situations in the environment is understood in terms of its propensity to cause harm or good in relation to the current situation and context. In turn, we respond accordingly to maximize good and avoid harm, as we subjectively perceive and understand the consequences. Depending on the context, these responses can relate to our wellbeing in a basic survival sense, or in a more evolutionarily evolved, sociocultural sense.

Taken together, these appraisals, values and sensations lead to emotion, which supports and drives what we traditionally call cognition. Quite literally, and as the term "emotion" suggests, we are "moved by" the valences we assign to perceptions (or simulated perceptions); and in this way our perceptions and simulated perceptions "motivate" us to behave in meaningful ways (Immordino-Yang & Sylvan, 2010). Although a purely cognitive account of information processing describes perfectly the computations that govern artificial intelligence and embodiment (in the form of mobile robots' behavior), from our perspective this represents a fundamental rift between artificial and biological intelligence that must be dealt with in the design of interfaces that facilitate useful interactions between the two.

From Me to It and It to Me: Applying Principles from Affective and Social Neuroscience to Design Better Learning Technologies

Humans are born with the propensity to impose order, to classify and organize our environment in accordance with our individual ways of theorizing about and acting in the world. The content and order of these theories and actions is the result of interaction between biological, social and cultural life experiences. As children develop, they encounter new experiences that shape and reshape existing neural networks and schemas, and impact their cognitive, social, and emotional development. Because of this, the hard-wired patterns of neural connectivity that underlie innate functional modules, such as those that facilitate social evaluation, are dynamically sculpted by social and cultural experiences as they are subjectively perceived and emotionally "felt." In short, our personal experiences through development provide a platform on which to understand and relate to the thoughts and actions of other people.

But what if our social companion is not an acculturated, sentient, subjectively evaluating biological being, but instead a computer? How, then, can our past experiences and cultural knowledge help us to predict our computer companion's actions, to understand its purpose, to collaborate on problem solving? Normally, the design of digital environments focuses on how computers can most effectively accommodate humans, and adapt to their needs and situations. But what about considering the complementary process – how humans adapt to computers – in designing the digital environment? New advances in social and affective neuroscience are making increasingly clear that humans use subjective, emotional processing to think and to learn, and that they use emotional and social processing to adapt to the current context and accommodate their social partners. Given the various forms of evidence that humans naturally anthropomorphize computers, a better understanding of the socio-emotional nature of computer users' struggles to adapt to the digital context might afford a new vantage point from which to predict, and eventually influence, human users' adaptations and learning.

In a learning environment such as a traditional classroom, each student brings her unique goals, knowledge and decisions that have been shaped by her social and cognitive experiences and that she must learn to use empathically to understand the teacher's actions, whether the teacher is a person or a computer. For example, to learn how to build a model using a computer, the student must first understand the goal of the exercise, be able to relate this goal to her own skills and memories, and be able to translate her skills into commands that describe the procedures of the computer. Using computers and other technologies to learn and perform tasks presents the student with the challenge of mentally discerning and reconstructing actions with often times invisible goals and procedures. Not only do these processes depend upon knowledge of how computers work, they vary with the student's subjective, emotional and personal history, and with her present interests and goals.

Here we suggest that perhaps one of the main difficulties that humans (and especially computer novices) have with computer interfaces is that the humans have trouble anticipating and understanding what the computer will do and why – in effect, because we have never lived as a computer, we have trouble "empathizing" with them and sharing their processing state, the way we would naturally strive to do with another person. If this is the case, perhaps rather than striving to build computer interfaces that seem as human-like and emotionally competent as possible, we should aim instead to make the programs and interfaces as transparent as possible. This does not mean that the technical information that makes the computer run would necessarily be available, but that the *goals* and the *motivations* of the digital environment would be readily apparent. A learner using the digital environment would understand what the program is good for, what the learning goal is, and therefore how best to engage with the computer without frustration or boredom.

Related to this, because computers do not have emotion, why not find ways that the human user can supply the emotion-relevant features to the human–computer interaction by giving the person some control over the critical aspects of how the interface and environment look, feel, and behave? A vast body of literature in education implicates "locus of control" as an important consideration when helping students in higher education environments to perform better (Dweck, 1999; Pekrun, 2011). That is, when students perceive that they have intrinsic control over the content, context, and pace of their learning, they begin to believe that they can be successful, and they invest more personal effort toward the academic task. Drawing from this, it seems crucial for learning technologies to be designed such that they do not give the students using them a sense of reliance or dependence on the machine, but instead foster a sense of agency that empowers the student to master skills that he could not have managed without computerized assistance. Engaging the student in an interaction rather than in a unidirectional manipulation by one conversational partner or the other (where either the person or the machine drive), students may be more likely to productively interact with the digital learning environment and to use it to facilitate performance (see also D'Mello, Lehman, & Graesser, 2011).

From Social Interactions to Digital Media for Learning

We began our chapter with a scenario involving students interacting with digital media, and asked why some students may be engaged with the activity, while others may be bored and listless. How can this question be informed by the above discussions on the embodiment of emotion, the interdependence of the body and mind, and the involvement of self-related processing in social emotions and motivation?

Affective and social neuroscience findings are suggesting that emotion and cognition, body and mind, work together in students of all ages. People behave in accordance with subjective goals and interests, built up over a lifetime of living and acting in a social and emotional world. By contrast, the values, judgments and calculations made by computers follow from the data, algorithms, and system constraints that their programmers choose to give them. Because the parameters governing these calculations are decided beforehand and are mainly invisible to the novice human user, many people may have trouble understanding and predicting the computer's actions. In effect, they may have trouble "empathizing" – and therefore become frustrated and disengaged. For the actions and responses of the digital interface to be perceived as useful and productive, and for novice learners to effectively engage the digital learning environment as a collaborative partner, digital media designers might consider ways to make human–computer exchanges more akin to good social encounters: the goals should be transparent, the computer partner's actions should be predictable and related to the subjective needs of the human learner, and each partner in the exchange should have an appropriate share of the control.

References

Barrett, L. F. (2009). Variety is the spice of life: A psychological construction approach to understanding variability in emotion. *Cognition & Emotion, 23*(7), 1284–1306.

D'Mello, S., Lehman, B., & Graesser, A. (2011). A motivationally supportive affect-sensitive autotutor. In R. Calvo & S. D'Mello (Eds.), *Explorations in the learning sciences, instructional systems and performance technologies*. New York: Springer.

Damasio, A. R. (1994/2005). *Descartes' error: Emotion, reason and the human brain*. London: Penguin Books.

Damasio, A. R. (2005). The neurobiological grounding of human values. In J. P. Changeux, A. R. Damasio, W. Singer, & Y. Christen (Eds.), *Neurobiology of human values*. London: Springer.

Damasio, A. R., Grabowski, T. J., Bechara, A., Damasio, H., Ponto, L. L. B., Parvizi, J., et al. (2000). Subcortical and cortical brain activity during the feeling of self-generated emotions. *Nature Neuroscience, 3*(10), 1049–1056.

Decety, J., & Chaminade, T. (2003). Neural correlates of feeling sympathy. *Neuropsychologia, 41*(2), 127–138.

Dweck, C. S. (1999). *Notes to guided reading self-theories*. Philadelphia: The Psychology Press.

Eisenberger, N. I., & Lieberman, M. D. (2004). Why rejection hurts: A common neural alarm system for physical and social pain. *Trends in Cognitive Sciences, 8*(7), 294–300.

Fischer, K. W., & Bidell, T. (2006). Dynamic development of action and thought. In W. Damon & R. Lerner (Eds.), *Handbook of child psychology, Vol. 1: Theoretical models of human development* (6th ed., pp. 313–399). Hoboken: Wiley.

Frith, C. D., & Frith, U. (2007). Social cognition in humans. *Current Biology, 17*(16), R724–R732.

Greene, J. D., Sommerville, R. B., Nystrom, L. E., Darley, J. M., & Cohen, J. D. (2001). An fMRI investigation of emotional engagement in moral judgment. *Science, 293*(5537), 2105–2108.

Haidt, J. (2001). The emotional dog and its rational tail: A social intuitionist approach to moral judgment. *Psychological Review, 108*(4), 814–834.

Harrison, N. A., Gray, M. A., Gianaros, P. J., & Critchley, H. D. (2010). The embodiment of emotional feelings in the brain. *Journal of Neuroscience, 30*(38), 12878–12884.

Immordino-Yang, M. H. (2008). The smoke around mirror neurons: Goals as sociocultural and emotional organizers of perception and action in learning. *Mind, Brain, and Education, 2*(2), 67–73.

Immordino-Yang, M. H., Chiao, J. Y., & Fiske, A. P. (2010). Neural reuse in the social and emotional brain. [Commentary]. *Behavioural and Brain Sciences, 33*(4), 275–276.

Immordino-Yang, M. H., & Damasio, A. R. (2007). We feel, therefore we learn: The relevance of affective and social neuroscience to education. *Mind, Brain and Education, 1*(1), 3–10.

Immordino-Yang, M. H., & Fischer, K. W. (2009). Neuroscience bases of learning. In V. G. Aukrust (Ed.), *International encyclopedia of education, 3rd edition, section on learning and cognition* (pp. 310–316). Oxford: Elsevier.

Immordino-Yang, M., McColl, A., Damasio, H., & Damasio, A. (2009). Neural correlates of admiration and compassion. *Proceedings of the National Academy of Sciences, 106*(19), 8021–8026.

Immordino-Yang, M. H., & Sylvan, L. (2010). Admiration for virtue: Neuroscientific perspectives on a motivating emotion. *Contemporary Educational Psychology, 35*(2), 110–115.

Lieberman, M. D., & Eisenberger, N. I. (2009). Pains and pleasures of social life. *Science, 323*(5916), 890–891.

Mitchell, J. P. (2008). Contributions of functional neuroimaging to the study of social cognition. *Current Directions in Psychological Science, 17*(2), 142–146.

Moll, J., de Oliveira-Souza, R., & Zahn, R. (2008). The neural basis of moral cognition: Sentiments, concepts, and values. *Annals of the New York Academy of Sciences, 1124*, 161–180.

Panksepp, J. (2005). Why does separation distress hurt? Comment on MacDonald and Leary (2005). *Psychological Bulletin, 131*(2), 224–230.

Pekrun, R. (2011). Emotions as drivers of learning and cognitive development. In R. Calvo & S. D'Mello (Eds.), *Explorations in the learning sciences, instructional systems and performance technologies*. New York: Springer.

Uddin, L. Q., Iacoboni, M., Lange, C., & Keenan, J. P. (2007). The self and social cognition: The role of cortical midline structures and mirror neurons. *Trends in Cognitive Sciences, 11*(4), 153–157.

Zaki, J., Ochsner, K. N., Hanellin, J., Wager, T. D., & Mackey, S. C. (2007). Different circuits for different pain: Patterns of functional connectivity reveal distinct networks for processing pain in self and others. *Social Neuroscience, 2*(3–4), 276–291.

Affect, Technology and Convivial Learning Environments

Peter Goodyear

To formulate a theory about a future society both very modern and not dominated by industry, it will be necessary to recognize natural scales and limits. We must come to admit that only within limits can machines take the place of slaves; beyond these limits they lead to a new kind of serfdom. Only within limits can education fit people into a man-made environment: beyond these limits lies the universal schoolhouse, hospital ward, or prison … Once these limits are recognized, it becomes possible to articulate the triadic relationship between persons, tools, and a new collectivity. Such a society, in which modern technologies serve politically interrelated individuals rather than managers, I will call "convivial." (Illich, 1980)

Introduction

This chapter is an attempt to weave together some strands in my thinking about learning, technology and design. It takes the form of an argument, with illustrations, rather than a report of new empirical research or a description of a specific technological innovation. It will mainly be of interest to those who are concerned about the broad intellectual framing of the fields of practice and inquiry in which technology, learning and affect meet.

The short version of my argument is as follows.

- We cannot understand affect in isolation from activity – feelings are entwined with personal projects, including the work we do to make sense of ourselves and our world, and to help others make sense of us.
- Activity is both socially and physically situated. A person's activity is shaped, in ways that can be subtle and powerful, by the situation in which it unfolds.

P. Goodyear (✉)
CoCo Research Centre, University of Sydney, Sydney, New South Wales, Australia
e-mail: Peter.Goodyear@sydney.edu.au

R.A. Calvo and S.K. D'Mello (eds.), *New Perspectives on Affect and Learning Technologies*, 243
Explorations in the Learning Sciences, Instructional Systems and Performance Technologies 3,
DOI 10.1007/978-1-4419-9625-1_18, © Springer Science+Business Media, LLC 2011

- There is a valuable class of activities and human relationships, which – following Illich – I will label "convivial". It is important to be able to understand the qualities of situations that afford conviviality and to understand what, if anything can be done to construct and preserve such situations, and strengthen such affordances.
- In scoping the field of learning, technology and affect, it would be a great mistake to focus on taken-for-granted but obsolescent educational goals and processes. Optimising instruction for nineteenth-century outcomes is not the direction in which we should be heading.

Since most activity results in some learning, we can think of all situations as affording learning. While such a general case might be made, I will focus here on situations in which people are consciously and collaboratively trying to make sense of the world, to co-construct interpretations, to improve and apply ideas for some valued purpose. The challenge then is to understand the qualities of environments that afford convivial learning – at a minimum to satisfy our curiosity as learning scientists, but ideally to a level where we can design and help construct (parts of) such environments.

As with the older body of research and development (R&D) on intelligent tutoring systems, much of the work reported in this book focuses on modelling the changing state of an individual learner: the earlier emphasis being on cognitive states, represented in student models; the present work introducing an affective dimension. This focus on interactions between a computer system and an *individual* learner is a sensible R&D strategy, insofar as dealing with multiple learners might be thought of as a harder problem, but also one where solutions for individual learners might simply be aggregated to deal with multiple learners. Part of the point of the argument I am trying to develop in this chapter is that we should (also?) be considering other research strategies. The field can make some useful advances by producing clearer accounts of how tools for learning evolve, and how human practices and capacities evolve with them. Such an account cannot be constructed through methodological individualism (reducing all social phenomena to the actions of individuals); we need richer ways of understanding technology, social practice, collective enterprises and their relations with individual thought, feeling and action.

Moreover – thinking about a robust and properly ambitious research strategy for the field – we ought also to be careful to avoid narrow, conventional delimitations of what counts as learning. While my title, and some of the ideas developed in this chapter, draw inspiration from the writings of Ivan Illich – author of *"Deschooling Society"* – I do not want to underestimate the importance of helping young people achieve the goals set for them within prevailing educational systems. Action *in the short term* that persuades young people that such goals are delusions, conjured up to suit the needs of organised capitalism, typically injures the already marginalised more than the privileged. Thus the chapters in this book which show how a better understanding of affect can improve educational outcomes in established curriculum areas are – at least in the short term – of practical value. But if we are thinking longer term and more broadly about the constitution of this research field, it seems to me that we ought to be open to taking into account the full range of circumstances in which people learn. Otherwise, our enacted definition of the "science and technologies of learning" is too narrowly and partially circumscribed. A broader view also makes sense in terms of practical benefit, since much of what people learn (and value) occurs in the years after formal schooling has ended, and outside the schoolroom. An appropriate meta-level question we should be asking ourselves, from time to time, is whether the technologies we are helping build are primarily aimed at improving the efficiency with which learners achieve outmoded educational goals and, as Illich puts it, introducing "new kinds of serfdom" in the process.

To understand the relations between learning, affect and technology, so that we can make some more informed decisions about promising research directions for the field, it helps to have a sense of how technology is evolving, and to have some ethical principles about how we might best help it evolve. This is tricky work, and likely to involve some embarrassing failures. But the alternative implicit strategy of taking technology for granted simply will not do.

The next section of this chapter defines some of the key terms needed to frame the argument. After that, I explore some of the main issues involved in considering the evolution of convivial learning technologies, illustrating with some fragments of real-world practice.

Key Terms

Learning Environment

In much of the literature on technology-enhanced learning, a learning environment is something created by software and which sits within a computer. For example, one may read of interactive, intelligent and/or adaptive learning environments (Clancey & Soloway, 1990; de Corte, Linn, Mandl, & Verschaffel, 1992; Jones & Winne, 1992; Lajoie, 2000), virtual and online learning environments (Weller, 2007) or immersive learning environments (Peachey et al., 2010). In the broader literature of educational research, "learning environment" takes on a more diffuse set of meanings, and is often complicated by a conflation of objective/physical elements and subjective/mental elements. In such literature, important distinctions are some-times missed between (say) the assessment demands inscribed in course documen-tation and students' interpretations of the best strategies for meeting those demands (Entwistle, 1996; Goodyear, 1997).

I prefer to use the term "learning environment" to mean: a complex set of nested structures which provide the physical setting for the work of a community of learners. This physical setting can include all sorts of learning tools, spaces and resources – what we conventionally think of as hardware and software but also other knowledge objects produced through interactions between members of the learning commu-nity. I also take "physical" to include both the "material" and the "virtual," while recognising that each interpenetrates the other.

On this view, a learning environment may be constituted from things as small as a mouse and as large as a campus; as small as a button, as large as the Web. For any one specific situated activity, not everything in the world can usefully be deemed part of the situating environment. Those things which readily "come to hand" are more significant; as may be those things which intrude on perception. But the notion of "nesting" is also important, not least because proximal and distal affordances (and constraints) can interfere with each other (Luckin, 2010; Resnick, 2010). Affect plays into this conception of learning environment in two main ways: first, any device/machine which is affect sensitive is a component of the learning environment; second, the feelings of people engaged in learning activity will be shaped, in part, by characteristics of the learning environment.

Architecture

I take architecture to be a set of practices which focus on understanding and arranging relationships between form and function. The etymological roots refer to a chief (ρχι) builder (Τεκτονικ). Conventionally, architecture is the art and science of designing buildings and other structures. By extension, it is now also used to refer to the masterminding of structures in complex computer systems (e.g. hardware and software architecture; systems architecture) including information systems (information architecture). Some inherent attractiveness of the term means that it is also being applied much more broadly (e.g. organisational architecture; policy architecture) and loosely (e.g. "experience architecture"). In my view, the last of these takes the term too far since it muddles experience (a relation between a person and a phenomenon) with the phenomenon itself. An architect might legitimately be said to design and/or create a set of things which are available to experience, but they cannot create the experiences themselves. In the same way, it is a mistake to think of a "learning architect." One may design and/or create an environment conducive to learning, but one cannot create *learning* for others. Architecture, as a practice, is both analytic and creative. It seeks to understand relations between form and function but also to create new forms aligned with desired functions. Through analysis, it seeks to understand how a building (for example) may be decomposed into constituent parts and how the relations between these parts (the structure) relates to function – the way people *use* that building. ("Use" here needs to be interpreted broadly, so that it includes how people understand the building, how they feel about it, what they are readily able to do in it, etc.)

Affordance

The cluster of ideas around the term "affordance" provides some useful ways of understanding relations between form and function, between built space and its use, between a learning environment and learning activity. As is now well-documented, the term originates with the ecological psychologist James Gibson (e.g. Gibson, 1977) and was introduced into the human–computer interaction and product design communities – with a twist – by Don Norman (e.g. Norman, 1990; see also Norman, 1999; Turner, 2005). It penetrated into writing about the psychology of learning (e.g. Greeno, 1994) and is used both rigorously and loosely in the literature of educational technology (Conole & Dyke, 2004; Oliver, 2005). Recent writing critical of the concept has tended to dwell on slippage in usages, which have muddied thinking about whether affordances are objective features of the physical world, or ways in which the environment's opportunities are perceived. Design theorists have introduced the idea of "conventional affordances," to capture such things as the suggestions of use embodied in the appearance of items on a computer desktop. ("Desktop" being an example.) I do not want to dwell on these important arguments and reservations, but observe that it is useful to have a term whose connotations include the provision of thoughtful guidance, balancing structure with user autonomy, principled scaffolding for activity, etc. (Maier, Fadel, & Battisto, 2009). This allows us to tread a more credible and productive middle course, from both analytic and designerly perspectives, between the extremes of determinism and *laissez faire*.

Conviviality

I have appropriated this term from the writings of Ivan Illich (notably, Illich, 1980). Like Illich, I *don't* use it to mean "tipsy jolliness" (though that affective state is pleasant enough from time to time). Rather, it is a way of denoting human, social and working relationships in which the interests of autonomously creative but politically interrelated individuals are served, rather than the interests of managers or capital. For Illich, conviviality is in stark contrast to highly industrialised modes of production, and their associated values and relationships.

> A convivial society should be designed to allow all its members the most autonomous action by means of tools least controlled by others. People feel joy, as opposed to mere pleasure, to the extent that their activities are creative; while the growth of tools beyond a certain point increases regimentation, dependence, exploitation, and impotence.

Illich is careful to explain that he uses the term "tool" very broadly, to include

> …simple hardware such as drills, pots, syringes, brooms, building elements, or motors, and not just large machines like cars or power stations [but also] productive institutions such as factories that produce tangible commodities like corn flakes or electric current, and productive systems for intangible commodities such as those which produce "education," "health," "knowledge," or "decisions." I use this term because it allows me to subsume into one category all rationally designed devices, be they artifacts or rules, codes or operators… School curricula or marriage laws are no less purposely shaped social devices than road networks.

Moreover, tools are not just means for accomplishing practical goals, they are intrinsic to social relationships:

> An individual relates himself in action to his society through the use of tools that he actively masters, or by which he is passively acted upon. To the degree that he masters his tools, he can invest the world with his meaning; to the degree that he is mastered by his tools,

the shape of the tool determines his own self-image. Convivial tools are those which give each person who uses them the greatest opportunity to enrich the environment with the fruits of his or her vision. Industrial tools deny this possibility to those who use them and they allow their designers to determine the meaning and expectations of others. Most tools today cannot be used in a convivial fashion. (Illich, 1980)

Combining these ideas, we may sketch a conceptual frame in which a learning environment provides tools that afford certain kinds of valued human activity. Understanding the nature and evolution of the architecture of such learning environments is scientifically valuable – there is scope for interesting and worthwhile investigative work. It also has practical value in helping us see how to engage with others in designing new, or helping improve existing, learning environments. Notions of improvement inevitably invoke questions of value – what do we mean by "better"? Acknowledging the importance of human feelings in the design space means that our notions of "better" have to move on from mere instructional efficiency.

Illustrating the Argument

It is time to use some analysis of concrete examples to illuminate these abstract ideas about relationships between tools, learning, conviviality and feelings. There is only space in this chapter to choose two such examples, and to provide a first-pass analysis, but I trust this will be sufficient to clarify the basic point.

Diabetes Daily

Diabetes daily (DD) is a large and complex Web site dedicated to the needs of those affected by diabetes, including people who have diabetes as well as their friends, family, carers, etc. Among many other tools and resources, it hosts a set of online discussion fora. The individual fora are clustered under a number of themes, such as "peer groups" and "daily living" (the former allows peer groups, such as teens with diabetes, or parents with diabetic children, to talk together). One can read the posts without being a registered member of the site. As of 12 August 2010, the DD community had over 34,000 members and over 400,000 posts.

The following posts come from the "complications: eyes" forum. The selected thread begins on 22 June 2010. It is headed: *blurry vision and freaking out.* (In the text below, T2 refers to Type 2 diabetes, BG(L) is blood glucose level, Endo is endocrinologist.)

> *Plinstedt*: Hello- I am T2 and thinking I could keep my BG under control w/ diet, exercise and oral meds, I quit taking my insulin for 3 months. Had my a1c on 6/1 and it went from 6.1 to10! Needless to say, I am back on humalog and levemir. A few days after starting the insulin again, my vision became very blurry. Saw my ophthalmologist this morning and he said he saw no diabetic eye problems. He said my vision might return to normal or might not.

Endo says wait at least a month before purchasing glasses. I used to use 1.25 reading glasses but now need 2.5 glasses. Please give me some encouragement that I will have my vision will return to normal.

This post elicited seven replies in the next 24 h, of which the following are a sample:

Nan-OH: We can't tell you that it will happen the way you want. Many people will have improvement in their vision when their bgl comes back under control. It takes a bit of time. Listen to your Endo, and keep as much control of your bgl as you can. Diabetes and its control is an individual thing. Eating less carbs works for all of us, but what foods work for one person does not work for another. Don't get too upset, yet. Relax and see what happens in the next few months.

NewdestinyX: Our bodies LOVE consistency. When we choose to make a major change like coming off the insulin -- or coming off another med.. and that change affects our Bg level balances enough to go from 6 to 10 in a short period of time -- the body reacts. Now -- you're back on the wagon and things SHOULD readjust. My doc also finds now diabetic eye complications but yet I have this 'shifting sand' with my eyes too. Remember too that for many of us we're in mid-life or older and eye changes, even quick ones are commonplace even amongst NON-diabetics.. So hang in there and look at the long haul. I take EVERY weirdness in my 48 year old body as if it were a potential complication of my Diabetes and keep tightening my control. I'm not a Dr Bernstein - all numbers under 100 - guru/zealot - but I still like to keep tighter control than the ADA standards -- hedging against risk.

CalgaryDiabetic: I think it will although 3 months of super high BG is a long time. Remember many so called type 2 are insulin deficient and no amount of exercise, low carb or metformin will do any good.

Premonitions of blindness are understandably emotion-charged and I think two points are worth making here. First, the other contributors to this thread are framing their responses in ways that intertwine emotional support with expertise. The emotional support has a tough strand to it ("we can't tell you it will happen the way you want…"; "don't get too upset, yet"; "hang in there and look at the long haul"). Moreover, many of the contributions mobilise specialist knowledge, expressed in specialist language. This is clearly a place in which "expert patients" gather and converse. Fox, Ward, and O'Rourke (2005) use this term to denote "those who can manage their own illnesses and conditions by developing knowledge relevant to maintaining health and countering illness".

Then consider the environment(s) in which this building of shared understanding is taking place. Whether one wants to conceive of it as a single environment, or a set of intersecting environments – one per participant – the discourse within the forum only makes sense through shared reference to a multiplicity of tools, test results, drugs, symptoms and people outside the forum. The forum alone would not be sufficient to constitute an effective learning environment. It has to be understood as part of something more extensive: part of a Web or network of tools that collectively enable that which we are glimpsing. Emotions are influenced by this distributed environment, but also emotions influence how the environment is perceived – among other things, they influence the focus of attention (Most, Scholl, Clifford, & Simons, 2005), and thereby shape the functioning of affordances.

Lastly (for want of space), it is worth noting that the basic form of the forum has been around for some while now – threaded discussion has been in use for several decades. Although connection speeds and interface design have improved, with some consequent benefits for ease and efficiency of use, the DD fora could function perfectly well with the technology of the 1980s. How would new affect-sensitive technology make a difference? What would be the most appropriate level at which to model affect? Is it most sensible to try to detect the changing affective states of each participant in the forum, or even of each reader? Does it make sense to model the affective charge between individuals (Nan-OH and Plinstedt, or NewdestinX and Plinstedt)? Is there likely to be value in modelling the affective state of a system or community? (We speak loosely of the "mood of the meeting" or the "morale of the workforce". If such constructs *help* with coming to understand complex situations, and deciding how to act, then presumably they should be "in scope" for R&D in affective computing).

Inception

I now want to shift to what may appear to be a trivial illustration – insofar as the focus of the sense-making activity I am about to describe may seem far-removed from the gritty realities of managing chronic disease. But this example also has some impressive characteristics, and I would like any accounts that we create of the relationships between learning, technology and affect to be able to deal with such examples.

In July 2010, Warner Brothers released the science fiction movie *Inception*. The film received critical acclaim and grossed over half a billion dollars (US) in its first month. A premise of the movie is that dreams and reality are interwoven, which makes it hard to summarise the plot. Suffice to say that it involves dreams within dreams within dreams (nested to four or perhaps five levels), characters interacting within and across levels, including characters who (separately) have the dream and "architect" the landscape within which a dream plays out. Understanding which "level" contains the current action, and whether the "top level" is reality or actually another, encompassing, dream, are key intellectual and perceptual challenges for the audience.

Within hours of its release, movie commentators had written pieces on the Web – including on movie blog sites that allow readers to provide feedback by adding comments. One example is the site *RopesofSilicon*, hosted by Brad Brevet.

Brad Brevet (2010) provided his own interpretation of the movie in a 1700 word blog posting, illustrated with stills from the movie, on sixteenth July (the first day on general release). He invited readers to comment on his analysis, especially of the key question of whether the final scenes are reality or another (level of) dream.

By 10 August 2010, there were 425 postings in response. The comment tool in this particular blog allows people to post a response to the original piece by Brevet or to add responses to other people's responses. Thus the comments take the form of a shallow threaded discussion.

Almost all of the comments are contributions to a shared project of sense-making. (A few comments talk about how much the respondent enjoyed the film, but do not add to the interpretive work). Many comments refer to very brief and apparently inconsequential passages in the movie – such as whether the lead character was or was not wearing a wedding ring at a such and such a point in the action. Observations of this kind are deployed in arguments that seek to establish whether – at that time – we were witnessing a dream or reality and, if a dream, at what level the dream was nested.

An important element of the architecture here is that most respondents were making contributions based on (recent) memories of the film. (Some may have already acquired bootleg copies of the movie, but in many cases, respondents are referring to a complex event in which they participated some hours previously.) Crucially, there is very limited access to the key source (the movie) and so the responses have to use text to establish the context for any given piece of observation/evidence, relying on the accuracy of the readers' memories of the film in so doing.

That said, what's striking about the unfolding discourse is the extent of careful reasoning that draws on both (a) observation of details in the movie and (b) an emerging shared theory about how things might be, in the world of *Inception*. Take the following sequence as an example:

Mason (July 17th, 2010-11:47 am) I'm not going to go too far into the movie right now, because I'd like to see it at least once more before I come up with my official interpretation. However, I just have a little thought that I'd like to propose and I don't know if it's been brought up yet because I didn't exactly want to read through all 97 comments.

It seems to me that throughout the whole movie, Christopher Nolan is not only trying to make us question what is reality and what is just a dream in context of the film, but also, it is to raise questions about our actual lives. Could it be possible that our real lives take place within our dreams, and this "reality" is actually just an escape? This seems to be the thought that Mal contemplates, resulting in her suicide. Nolan may be trying to get us to see the same thing as Mal. Therefore, the final frame becomes a bit more understandable. Whether or not the ending is a dream or reality is practically irrelevant to me. I do think it is a dream, yes. But the fact that the top wobbles in the last frame shows to me the parallel between the real world and the dream world. It shows that perhaps our perception of reality is actually quite shaky.

Idk (July 17th, 2010-1:50 pm) How come when Fischer woke up, he didn't recognize that the people around him were all a dream? I think he was in on it. Or that Miles did really plan a double-inception.

After all, Dom did say that Miles was the one who taught him to manipulate minds. Miles also taught architecture. Maybe HE was the true master of inception? I do agree with the idea that Ellen Page's character was specially chosen, somehow. And that Mol was right in killing herself to go BACK to reality. I also believe there is some connection between Fischer's relationship with his father, and Miles and Dom's relationship. Ultimately, I believe that Mol and Miles were trying to get him back home, and to release everything and wake up from his dream. THAT is what Mol's totem was able to fall at the end. But again, I am not sure with my conclusion. There are MANY scenes left in the film that are needed to be pieced together. DOES ANYBODY CARE TO HELP ME OUT?

Joe (July 17th, 2010-4:47 pm) To idk: I am glad you have brought this up. After my post last night I began thinking about the moment when Fischer must have woken up and seen all of the people sitting on the plane around him. Surely he would have immediately recognized them and known they had performed an inception on him. Thus it could not have been real. Saito, Ariadne, and the others are not real. Ariadne's name is what convinces me that she is not real (in Greek mythology Ariadne helps Theseus escape the labyrinth).

I agree that Mal was right and she does return to reality, while Dom remains behind. I think the "fourth-level" (actually fifth-level) confrontation with Mal is the moment when he finally comes to terms with his guilt. This is the real inception, planted by Ariadne, who has been constructed by Miles. Dom then returns to the first-level dream world which we see at the end of the movie.

The point is that Dom no longer has his guilt to interfere with him. He will ultimately realize that he is still in a dream, and finally be able to return to reality. Anyway, I have not had a chance to see it for a second time yet, I am interested to see how all of these theories will hold up after a second viewing.

Setting aside, for a moment, the fictive referent of this discussion, one cannot fail to be impressed by the careful writing, intricate reasoning and use of evidence. (Many teachers would be delighted to get this quality of work in their students' online discussions.) The text is also imbued with *motivation* – the contributors are *driven* by a passion to make sense of the film's puzzles, and they expertly invoke motivational explanations for the characters' actions, and the intentions of the director. A sceptic may argue that this passion for collaborative sense-making is misdirected – why waste intellectual energy on a fictional puzzle? But I think we should learn from this example that the right combination of deep mystery, discussion tools and urgency can prove very fruitful.

The question of time plays differently in our two examples. In a few short weeks, the *Inception* discussions will be of historical interest. Somebody happening across the fora next year may be intrigued by the discussion, but it will be too late to contribute. The writers and readers will have moved on. Conversely, the DD fora gain value over time – every day sees an addition of new experience, insights and explanations that can be searched by subsequent visitors. Computing affect would be tricky here. It would, at least, need a theory of currency and decay, allowing reasonable inferences to be drawn about changes over time in relevance and affective charge. For example, what is the relationship, if any, between the emotions frozen into the fora and the feelings of the contributors today? If we imagine an emotionally intelligent agent sitting over the DD fora, what personal theories of affect would it need in order to compute whether to link newcomers with new issues (like Plinstedt) to people who had felt deeply about these issues 2 years ago?

Another contrast between the two fora stems from their respective relationships to face-to-face (F2F) discussions. It is easy to see the *Inception* forum as a close analogue of the kinds of discussion that a group of friends might have as they come out of the movie – and for several hours afterwards. Of course, it has different affordances. The forum has the virtue of crystallising ideas, evidence and inferences – they are frozen in time and can be read and re-read. It is much harder to remember and revisit ideas (etc.) that are articulated in a rapid F2F group conversation, where words disappear into the ether. In contrast, there really is no satisfactory F2F equivalent of the DD fora. Of course, there are self-help groups which meet F2F, but they cannot have the numbers, breadth of experience or record of past discussions that are core to DD.

Discussion

There are thousands of fora like DD. There are even several fora that have run in parallel with the Brevet-stimulated interpretations of *Inception*. This kind of collaborative technology-mediated sense-making and knowledge sharing – often involving the joint creation of complex explanations – is not rare. Within these activities and spaces we can see expressions of what Illich would label "conviviality" – people are appropriating simple online tools and using them in joint creative enterprises which, one way or another, *matter* in their lives. (It is worth mentioning that Illich wrote speculatively about the value of such "learning webs" in *Deschooling Society* – 20 years in advance of the technology that now supports them).

How then should we be scoping the field of learning, technology and affect? I suggest that we need to consider at least the following:

(a) We are unlikely to make a success of modelling feelings that matter to people if we ignore, or assume away, large parts of the environment in which they are thinking, learning, deciding, conversing, etc. A classic user: computer dyad may feel manageable, for the purposes of advancing the technology of affective computing. Improvements in the effectiveness of educational tools and tutors, brought about by better handling of affect, are also of practical value – when judged within the frames of current educational goals and practices. However, from time to time we should also pause and reflect on a properly ambitious scope for the field, and also ask ourselves *whose* framing of what is educationally valuable are we reinforcing? In my view, a systemic, holistic, ecological or architectural conception of learning environments is likely to be necessary to scientific progress.

(b) R&D in affective technology is set in a dialectic between predicting technological trends and creating new technology. (We help shape the world, but not in conditions of our own making. Making best guesses about the pace and direction of technological change is necessary if we are to time our own research such that it intercepts with people's needs and practices.) There is value in taking a moral position – it is partly in our hands to decide whether our tools are tools for conviviality or machines that perpetuate serfdom.

References

Brevet, B. (2010). RopesofSilicon, http://www.ropeofsilicon.com/article/wake-up-lets-talk-about-inception-heres-my-interpretation, accessed August 10, 2010.

Clancey, W., & Soloway, E. (Eds.). (1990). *Artificial intelligence and learning environments.* Cambridge: MIT Press.

Conole, G., & Dyke, M. (2004). What are the affordances of information and communication technologies? *ALT-J: Research in Learning Technology, 12*, 113–124.

de Corte, E., Linn, M., Mandl, H., & Verschaffel, L. (Eds.). (1992). *Computer-based learning environments and problem solving.* Berlin: Springer.

Diabetes Daily. (2010). Accessed August 10, 2010, http://www.diabetesdaily.com/

Entwistle, N. (1996). Recent research on student learning and the learning environment. In J. Tait & P. Knight (Eds.), *The management of independent learning.* London: Kogan Page.

Fox, N., Ward, K., & O'Rourke, A. (2005). The 'expert patient': Empowerment or medical dominance? The case of weight loss, pharmaceutical drugs and the Internet. *Social Science & Medicine, 60*, 1299–1309.

Gibson, J. (1977). The theory of affordances. In R. Shaw & J. Bransford (Eds.), *Perceiving, acting, and knowing: Toward an ecological psychology* (pp. 67–82). Hillsdale, New Jersey: Lawrence Erlbaum Associates.

Goodyear, P. (1997). The ergonomics of learning environments: Learner-managed learning and new technology. *Creacion de materiales para la innovacion educativa con nuevas tecnologias.* Malaga: Instituto de Ciencias de la Educacion, Universidad de Malaga.

Greeno, J. (1994). Gibson's affordances. *Psychological Review, 101,* 336–342.

Illich, I. (1973). *Deschooling society.* Harmondsworth: Penguin.

Illich, I. (1980). *Tools for conviviality.* New York: Harper.

Jones, M., & Winne, P. (Eds.). (1992). *Adaptive learning environments: Foundations and frontiers.* Berlin: Springer.

Lajoie, S. (Ed.). (2000). *Computers as cognitive tools: No more walls theory change, paradigm shifts, and their influence on the use of computers for instructional purposes.* Mahwah: Lawrence Erlbaum Associates.

Luckin, R. (2010). *Re-designing learning contexts: Technology-rich, learner-centred ecologies.* New York: Routledge.

Maier, J., Fadel, G., & Battisto, D. (2009). An affordance-based approach to architectural theory, design and practice. *Design Studies, 30,* 393–414.

Most, S., Scholl, B., Clifford, E., & Simons, D. (2005). What you see is what you set: Sustained inattentional blindness and the capture of awareness. *Psychological Review, 112,* 217–242.

Norman, D. (1990). *The design of everyday things.* Garden City: Doubleday.

Norman, D. (1999). Affordance, conventions and design. *Interactions, 6,* 38–43.

Oliver, M. (2005). The problem with affordance. *The E-Learning Journal, 2*(4), 402–423.

Peachey, A., Gillen, J., Livingstone, D., & Smith-Robbins, S. (Eds.). (2010). *Researching learning in virtual worlds.* New York: Springer.

Resnick, L. (2010). Nested learning systems for the thinking curriculum. *Educational Researcher, 39,* 183–197.

Turner, P. (2005). Affordance as context. *Interacting with Computers, 17*(6), 787–800.

Weller, M. (2007). *Virtual learning environments.* New York: Routledge.

Significant Accomplishments, New Challenges, and New Perspectives

Sidney K. D'Mello and Rafael A. Calvo

Introduction

Times have changed indeed. Although emotion research has actively progressed since Darwin's (1872) seminal work, *The Expression of Emotions in Man and Animals*, it is much more recently that emotion has claimed its rightful place in mainstream psychology, which has traditionally focused on cognitive processes such as perception, memory, attention, and action. At the time of this writing, in 2010, the journal *Emotion* is less than a decade old, while the journal *Cognition* is rapidly approaching its fortieth anniversary. *Emotion Review*, a new journal which publishes surveys and review articles in the affect sciences, is merely a year old, while *Psychological Review*, which features the occasional emotion article, is over a century old. This discrepancy in research between the affect and cognitive sciences is puzzling because the link between emotion and cognition is so compelling that some even consider the distinction between affective and cognitive processes to be arbitrary, artificial, and of little relevance (Lazarus, 1991, 2000).

A paucity of research on emotion has also plagued the field of education. Although test anxiety has received substantial attention in educational research (Zeidner, 2007), other critical emotions such as boredom and frustration have been relinquished to the sidelines. For example, there is an order of magnitude difference between the precious few studies on boredom in academic settings when compared to the approximately 1,000 studies on anxiety (Pekrun, Goetz, Daniels, Stupnisky, & Raymond, 2010). Similar to the increased emphasis on emotions in psychology, the last decade has witnessed a refreshing infusion of research that systematically

S.K. D'Mello (✉)
Department of Psychology Institute for Intelligent Systems,
University of Memphis, Memphis, TN, USA
e-mail: sdmello@memphis.edu

R.A. Calvo and S.K. D'Mello (eds.), *New Perspectives on Affect and Learning Technologies*,   255
Explorations in the Learning Sciences, Instructional Systems and Performance Technologies 3,
DOI 10.1007/978-1-4419-9625-1_19, © Springer Science+Business Media, LLC 2011

studies emotions during learning, culminating in Pekrun and Schutz's 2007 edited volume entitled *Emotions in Education*.

But perhaps the most compelling change in the last decade is the infusion of emotion into computer science and engineering. There was a time when a murky, fuzzy, diffuse psychological construct such as emotion had no place in these so-called technical sciences which focus on formal specifications of algorithms and concrete systems (Picard, 2010). However, pioneered by Picard and other visionaries, affective computing has emerged as a novel, exciting, and foundational area of research that has been embraced by computer scientists and engineers alike. In 2010, the Institute for Electrical and Electronic Engineers (IEEE), the largest professional organization in the world, published the first issue of a new journal entitled *Transactions in Affective Computing*. The fact that emotion is now placed alongside publications on circuits, antennas, transducers, dielectrics, and control systems is perhaps the ultimate testament of these changing times.

This infusion of research on emotion in psychology, education, and technology brings us to this very unique book which features an interdisciplinary fusion of research in these three areas. A little more than a decade ago, the idea of a computer tutor automatically detecting and responding to a learner's emotions was nothing more than a seductive vision (Picard, 1997). This vision is now becoming a reality as affect-sensitive learning environments are coming online (see chapters by Burleson, 2011; Conati, 2011; Cooper, Arroyo, & Woolf, 2011; D'Mello, Lehman, & Graesser, 2011; Lester, McQuiggan, & Sabourin, 2011). As highlighted in the introduction and evidenced by the chapters in this volume, the importance of broad integrative research that encompasses psychology, education, and technology is essential toward unraveling the mysteries of academic emotions. Only then can we make genuine progress toward the goal of developing next-generation learning environments that help students acquire knowledge at new levels of mastery in a manner that optimally coordinates emotion and cognition.

This concluding chapter discusses some of the important milestones achieved toward tackling this goal before highlighting some of the open problems and suggestions of promising areas for future work.

Significant Accomplishments

The significant accomplishments discussed in this book span basic research on links between affect and cognition during learning to technological solutions that advance the goal of developing emotionally intelligent learning environments. These are discussed below.

Infusion of Theories on Emotions and Learning: As Graesser and D'Mello discuss in their chapter, there was a time when there were over two dozen emotion theories, which were underspecified. These theories conveyed general links between affect and cognition, instead of making explicit predictions on the emotions that would accompany learning activities. Fortunately, the last few decades have witnessed an influx of emotion theories that are very relevant to learning. Some of these theories, particularly those emerging from psychology, pertain to a more general set of emotions. Although most of the empirical research that systematically tests these theories focuses on the basic emotions such as anger, sadness, fear, disgust, happiness, and surprise (Ekman, 1992), the theories themselves are highly relevant toward the study of learning-centered emotions (or academic emotions) because they specify the antecedents and consequents of emotions. This information can be leveraged to develop affect-sensitive ITSs, as is elaborated below.

Table 1 lists some of the contemporary emotion theories from psychology that are of potential relevance to affective processes during learning and problem solving. For example, the theory of basic emotions and perspectives that emphasize coordinated bodily and physiological changes during the experience of emotions underlies current affect detection systems (Calvo & D'Mello, 2010). Appraisal theories, on the contrary, focus on how emotions arise from situational appraisals of affect-inducing events. These theories can be used to develop predictive models of student affect, as demonstrated by Conati's (2011). Mandler's theory on the importance of interruptions as a gateway to consciousness (Mandler, 1976, 1999), coupled with the goal appraisal theory of Stein (Stein & Albro, 2001; Stein & Levine, 1991; Stein et al., 2008), emphasizes the importance of events that facilitate or hinder goals as being particularly diagnostic of emotions.

Some of the theories can also be used to develop interventions to help learners regulate harmful negative emotions such as boredom and frustration. For example, the emotion regulation literature has highlighted critical meta-affective processes that can be viable methods to prevent the onset of negative emotional states and

Table 1 General theories on emotion

Theory	Reference
Basic emotions, expressions, and embodiments	Darwin (1872); Ekman (1984; 1992); Izard (2007); Tomkins (1962); Wassmann (2010)
Network theories and the affect infusion model	Bower (1992); Forgas (1995); Isen (2008)
Feelings as information theory	Schwarz (1990, in press)
Appraisal theories	Arnold (1960); Lazarus (1991); Ortony, Clore, and Collins (1988); Scherer, Schorr, and Johnstone (2001); Smith and Ellsworth (1985)
Expectancies, interruptions, and goal appraisal	Mandler (1976, 1984, 1999); Stein, Hernandez, and Trabasso (2008); Stein and Levine (1991)
Core affect and psychological construction	Barrett (2006); Barrett, Mesquita, Ochsner, and Gross (2007); Russell (2003)
Component-process model	Scherer and Ellgring (2007); Scherer (2009a)
Self-organization and dynamical system models	Camras and Witherington (2005); Lewis (2005)
Attribution theories	Gotlib and Abramson (1999); Heider (1958); Weiner (1986)
Social constructivist approaches	Averill (1980); Parkinson (1995); Peterson (2006); Salovey (2003); Stets and Turner (2008)
Emotion regulation	Gross (1998, 2008); Joormann (2010)

Table 2 Theories on emotions during learning

Theory	Reference
Impasses, cognitive disequilibrium, and confusion	Graesser, Lu, Olde, Cooper-Pye, and Whitten (2005); Graesser and Olde (2003); Piaget (1952); Vygotsky (1978)
Control–value theory	Pekrun (2006, 2010); Pekrun et al. (2010)
Academic risk theory	Clifford (1988); Meyer and Turner (2006)
Flow theory	Csikszentmihalyi (1975, 1990)
Interest	Ainley (2008); Alexander and Jetton (1996); Dewey (1913); Guthrie et al. (2006); Hidi (2006); Hidi and Renninger (2006); Tobias (1994)
Motivation and mindset	Dweck (1986, 2002, 2006); Harter (1992); Stipek (1988)
Circumplex model (adapted by Linnenbrink)	Linnenbrink (2007)

manage them when they occur (Gross, 1998, 2008). Some of these affect-regulatory processes include *cognitive reappraisal* (changing the perceived meaning of a situation to alter its emotional content), *suppression* (suppressing thoughts and behaviors associated with an emotional experience), *distraction* (focusing attention on nonemotional aspects of a situation), and *rumination* (perseverating on the feelings and consequences associated with an emotional event). Some of these emotion regulation strategies can be applied to help learner's regulate negative emotions as they occur, while others need to be avoided because they have detrimental effects on learning (Strain & D'Mello, in press).

In addition to the general emotion theories that do not explicitly address academic emotions (per se), a number of theories that directly specify links between emotions and learning have emerged. A sample of these theories is listed in Table 2. As with the more general emotion theories, these theories on affect-learning connections can and must play an important role in the development of affect-sensitive learning environments. For example, the "zone of flow" has been hypothesized to be the optimal experience for learning (Csikszentmihalyi, 1990). The zone of flow occurs when the learners face just the right sort of materials, challenges, and problems to the point of being totally absorbed in the learning activity – in fact, the learners are so engaged that they stop perceiving (to some degree) the passage of time and fatigue. Csikszentmihalyi recommends three important strategies to sustain the zone of flow; these can be implemented in next-generation learning environments. Similarly, Dweck's strategies on keeping students motivated by rewarding effort instead of failure and nurturing a "growth" instead of a "fixed" mindset can be applied when a computer senses that a student is frustrated due to persistent failure and risks giving up and disengaging from the session (Dweck, 1986, 2002, 2006).

Identification of Affective States that are Relevant to Learning: Approximately a decade ago, there was no clear consensus on the specific emotions that accompany learning activities. Since then, considerable empirical research has converged upon a set of emotions that are more relevant to learning (although there still is no consensus). One important conclusion is that the six "basic" emotions proposed by

Ekman (anger, disgust, fear, joy, sadness, and surprise) and other emotion taxonomies commonly used in the psychological literature might not be very relevant in learning contexts. This has been empirically verified in a number of studies, which indicate that the basic emotions are not routinely observed in learning sessions that span 30 min to 1.5 h (Craig, D'Mello, Witherspoon, & Graesser, 2008; D'Mello, Lehman, & Person, in press; Lehman, Matthews, D'Mello, & Person, 2008). However, these emotions might be more relevant over longer time spans that last several weeks to a year, such as completing a college course or writing a dissertation.

In contrast to the basic emotions, states such as confusion, frustration, boredom, flow, curiosity, anxiety, and delight are more relevant during learning and problem solving (e.g., chapters by Rodrigo, Baker, and Pekrun). Some of these emotions can be grouped into Pekrun's taxonomy of academic emotions, which include achievement emotions, epistemic emotions, topic emotions, and social emotions (see Pekrun, 2011).

Importantly, the discovery that a somewhat different set of emotions is relevant during learning activities represents an important point of divergence between general emotion research, which primarily focuses on the basic emotions, and the specialized niche of learning environments, where the academic emotions are more prominent. It is these academic emotions that should be on the radar of affect-sensitive ITSs.

Automatic Detection of Learner Affect: An affect-sensitive learning environment can never respond to users' affective states if it cannot sense their affective states. Affect detection need not be perfect but must be approximately on target. Affect detection is, however, a very challenging problem because emotions are psychological constructs (i.e., conceptual quantities that cannot be directly measured) with fuzzy boundaries and with substantial individual difference variations in expression and experience.

The recent explosion of research activities that focuses on fully automated systems to detect learner affect represents an important accomplishment toward the development of affect-sensitive learning environments. As demonstrated by numerous chapters in this volume (e.g., Burleson, 2011; Conati, 2011; Cooper et al., 2011), these systems are capable of automatically sensing, for example, when a learner is interested, bored, confused, and frustrated by monitoring facial cues, paralinguistic features of speech, posture, peripheral physiology, and contextual cues. Systems that couple diagnostic assessments of emotions (from sensors) with predictive assessments (from context and appraisal models) represent significant progress in this area. Even more impressive are recent efforts to deploy these systems in real classrooms (see chapter by Cooper et al., 2011); this is a crucial goal for widespread use and acceptance.

Fully Automated Affect-Sensitive Learning Environments: Perhaps the singular accomplishment that best captures the integration of emotion theory, learning models, and technology is the development of some of the first fully automated affect-sensitive learning environments (see chapters by Burleson, D'Mello, Lester, Cooper, etc.). Emerging evidence suggests that these systems can be effective in increasing positive affective experience and learning gains when compared to nonaffective counterparts. For example, Woolf and colleagues provide evidence that affective learning companions helped low-achieving students engage in productive behaviors, while simultaneously increasing their confidence and reducing frustration (Woolf et al., 2010). D'Mello et al. (2011) show that the affect-sensitive AutoTutor was quite effective at promoting learning gains for low-domain knowledge students, when compared to a version of the tutor that only responds to their cognitive states.

It is important to note that many of these systems are still early prototypes, and substantial testing is required before their impact can be fully understood. Nevertheless, the fact that researchers have been able to endow computer tutors with a modicum of emotional intelligence in a relatively short period of time is an important accomplishment and a cue to stay tuned for more progress ahead.

New Challenges and New Perspectives

After highlighting some of the significant accomplishments in the area of affect-sensitive learning technologies, we turn the spotlight to some of the challenges and opportunities for future innovation. Broadly, these challenges can be grouped into opportunities for basic research on emotions and learning, and suggestions for possible fruitful areas of research for affect-sensitive learning environments.

Obtaining Coherence Among Multiple Levels of Analysis: As described in the chapter by Azevedo and Strain (2011), there are two traditions of research on emotions during learning. Some of the research has focused on student emotions in classrooms, where a broad array of affective responses are elicited in a number of contexts (Daniels et al., 2009; Meyer & Turner, 2006; Pekrun, 2010; Schutz & Pekrun, 2007; Zeidner, 2007). These contexts include classroom activities such as lectures and discussions that can evoke curiosity or boredom, examinations and quizzes that may induce confidence or anxiety, and peer interactions where social emotions such as pride or shame play a major role (Meyer & Turner, 2006; Schultz & Pekrun, 2007). While much of this research uses self-reports as the primary methodology and focuses on correlational links between affect and learning, other research has focused on a more in-depth analysis of a smaller set of emotions that arise during deep learning and over shorter time spans (see chapters by Azevedo, Afzal, Lester, and D'Mello). These learning contexts include a multitude of computer environments, high-stakes test taking, human tutoring, reading comprehension, and essay writing.

Both of these research traditions have unique advantages and disadvantages. Presumably, the most defensible position is to adopt research protocols that capitalize on the merits of each tradition, while simultaneously avoiding the inherent pitfalls of each. For example, according to the control–value theory, the academic emotions arise from cognitive appraisals of control and value, and there are reciprocal connections among the emotions, their antecedents, and consequents (Pekrun, 2006; Pekrun, Elliot, & Maier, 2006). This theory has obtained considerable support with correlational classroom studies that primarily rely on self-reports (for obvious reasons). The challenge is to test some of its critical predictions in controlled experiments, which are best facilitated in environments that afford high experimenter control, such as the laboratory. Alternatively, a theory can first be tested by performing controlled experiments in the laboratory and later retested via quasi-experimental designs (if strict experimentation is not feasible) in more ecological contexts such as classrooms (see chapter by Cooper).

Modeling Complex Interactions between Traits, Moods, and Events: Affective states arise out of complex multilevel interactions between disparate systems operating across multiple time scales (Barrett et al., 2007; Russell, 2003; Scherer, 2009a). These levels can be considered to be stable individual differences (long time scale), baseline moods (intermediate time scale), and immediate events (short time scale) (Rosenberg, 1998). Individual differences in affective traits, cognitive abilities, motivation orientations, and learning styles play an important role in predicting emotions and their consequents. Affective traits are particularly relevant and can be considered to be relatively stable, mostly unconscious predispositions toward particular emotional experiences. They operate by lowering the threshold for experiencing certain emotional states (i.e., hostile people have a lower threshold for experiencing anger but not necessarily other negative emotions). Moods also perform a threshold reduction function on emotional elicitation, but are considered to be more transitory and have a background influence on consciousness. In stark contrast to affective traits and moods, emotions are brief, intense, states that occupy the forefront of consciousness; have significant physiological and behavioral manifestations; and rapidly prepare the bodily systems for action. According to this framework, affective traits occupy the highest position, emotions the lowest, and moods an intermediate position along the dimensions of duration, pervasiveness in consciousness, and distributive breadth (i.e., the extent of the influence each has on other psychological and physiological processes). The challenge is to develop models that encompass critical interactions between these entities.

Incorporating Temporal Dependencies and Dynamics: One important aspect of the affect–cognition relationship that has not been adequately addressed is the temporal dynamics of affective experience, called *affective chronometry* (Davidson, 1998; Rosenberg, 1998). At this point in science, there is insufficient empirical research to support a categorization of the academic emotions on a temporal dimension. We know that emotions are quite brief (approximately 0.5–4s) when they are measured from facial expressions (Ekman, 1984). However, reports of subjective experience of emotion provide much longer estimates ranging from minutes to hours (Frijda, Mesquita, Sonnemans, & Van Goozen, 1991); some of these estimates might be more indicative of moods than emotions per se (Rosenberg, 1998; Watson & Clark, 1994). Recent evidence from affective neuroscience also indicates that there are graded differences in the recovery time from positive and negative affective experiences (Davidson, 1998; Garrett & Maddock, 2001; Hemenover, 2003).

An understanding of the temporal dynamics of particular classes of affective states is necessary for a satisfactory model that integrates affect with complex learning. For example, impasse-driven theories of learning (VanLehn, Siler, Murray, Yamauchi, & Baggett, 2003) would predict that there are learning benefits from episodes of confusion. In these episodes, the learner experiences cognitive disequilibrium and is forced to reflect, problem solve, and deliberate in an effortful manner in order to restore cognitive equilibrium (Graesser et al., 2005; VanLehn et al., 2003). Understanding the temporal dynamics of emotional experiences as they unfold is necessary in order to distinguish (a) occurrences of productive confusion that lead to learning and eventually some positive emotions from (b) occurrences of hopeless confusion that presumably have no pedagogical value. Integrating the temporal dimension into existing models of emotion is an important area of future work and a ripe area for insightful discoveries.

Reconceptualizing Affect Detection Systems: In a recent survey on affect detection systems, we argued that affective computing cannot be divorced from the century long psychological research on emotion (Calvo & D'Mello, 2010). This is because affective computing, which focuses on developing practical applications (including affect-sensitive learning environments) that are responsive to user affect, is inextricably bound to the affective sciences that attempt to understand human emotions.

While most would not disagree with this assertion, there are still some fundamental points of divergence between the theoretical underpinnings of most affect detection systems (including the ones described in this volume) and recent conceptualizations of the experience and the expression of emotion (Barrett, 2006; Barrett et al., 2007). Most of the problematic assumptions of current affect detection systems stem from widespread adoption of traditional models that view emotions as being produced by "affect programs" that, when triggered by the appropriate events, produce widespread reactions in behavior, physiology, action, and subjective experience (Ekman, 1992; Rosenberg & Ekman, 1994; Tomkins, 1962). This view has been recently challenged by new models that view emotions as entities that emerge from the intrinsic dynamics of loosely coupled, diffuse, self-organizing systems (Barrett, 2009; Camras & Witherington, 2005; Coan, 2010; Lewis, 2005; Scherer, 2009b).

Although it is beyond the scope of this chapter to address the major limitations of current affect detection systems highlighted by Calvo and D'Mello (2010), these can be succinctly summarized as (a) expectation of one-to-one mapping between experience and expression of emotions, (b) assumption of coherence among multiple components of an emotion, (c) focus on prototypical emotions in a generally nonemotional world, (d) context-free affect detection, (e) affect detection in socially divorced contexts, (f) failure to reconcile between categorical and dimensional models of affect, and (g) problems with evaluation of affect detection systems. Although these issues have been addressed at length by emotion theorists, no widely accepted solutions have emerged, thereby indicating that these are significant opportunities for basic research in this area.

Another limitation of current affect detection systems is that these systems primarily rely on physiological sensors and combinations of audio-visual signals (Caridakis et al., 2006; Chen, Huang, Miyasato, & Nakatsu, 1998; Dasarathy, 1997; Picard, Vyzas, & Healey, 2001; Yoshitomi, Sung-Ill, Kawano, & Kilazoe, 2000; Zeng et al., 2009). Although these sensor-based systems represent viable approaches for detecting affect in laboratory settings, they require expensive hardware and software and considerable expertise to operate. Furthermore, while it is possible to conduct brief studies with affect sensors in schools (Arroyo et al., 2009; Dragon et al., 2008), it is unlikely that the average classroom of the next 5 or 10 years will be equipped with physiological and behavioral affect-sensing devices. This raises some challenges for those who want to extend this program of research for long-term use in classrooms.

Finally, there is the issue of whether fully automated affect detection systems will ever be sufficiently accurate at diagnosing learner emotions. Considerable evidence indicates that humans are not very reliable at detecting emotions in naturalistic contexts (Russell, Bachorowski, & Fernandez-Dols, 2003) including learning (Afzal & Robinson, 2009; D'Mello, Taylor, Davidson, & Graesser, 2008; Graesser et al., 2006). Although more research is needed before the limits of automated affect detection systems can be fully understood, it might be beneficial to pursue alternate research paths in conjunction with refining existing affect detectors. For example, in addition to the predictive and diagnostic models discussed above, a computer tutor can engage the student in some form of dialog in order to get a better handle on their affective states.

Revisiting Reactive Emotion Regulation Strategies: Much of the effort so far has been devoted to developing systems to detect affect. Of equal importance, and an area that is quite impoverished, is the challenge of responding to affect in order to promote learning (see chapters by du Boulay, 2011; Rebolledo-Mendez, Luckin, & du Boulay, 2011). It should be noted that learning environments that aspire to coordinate emotions with learning should attempt to do more than merely promote a positive learning experience. This is because some of the negative states can actually have a positive impact on learning (see the confusion example above). Affect-sensitive ITSs must, therefore, be more than mere cheerleaders who constantly encourage students and try to promote positive moods, because failure naturally accompanies deep learning activities.

Importantly, learners can benefit from failure, especially when they resolve troublesome impasses and discard misconceptions (VanLehn et al., 2003). For example, VanLehn et al. (2003) reported that comprehension of physics concepts was rare when students did not reach an impasse, irrespective of quality of the explanations provided by tutors. Similarly, learning is presumably not directly caused by the state of confusion, but rather by the cognitive activities that accompany its experience.

It is also clear that there is no one-size-fits-all approach to learning. Hence, it is important for ITSs to regulate negative emotions in a manner that is dynamically sensitive to each learner's needs and styles. For example, in the case of confusion, the learning environment might want to keep the learner confused (i.e., in a state of cognitive disequilibrium) and leave it to the learner to deliberate and reflect actively on how to restore equilibrium. This strategy is expected to be more effective for motivated knowledgeable learners and is consistent with a Piagetian theory (1952) that stipulates that students need to experience cognitive disequilibrium for a sufficient amount of time before they adequately deliberate and reflect via self-regulation. Alternatively, a Vygotskian theory (Vygotsky, 1978) suggests that it is not productive to have low ability students spend a long time experiencing negative affect in the face of failure. If so, the tutor should give more direct hints and explanations.

This strategy might be more effective for cautious learners who might be hesitant to step up and confront their confusion because of self-doubt and the threat of failure (Clifford, 1988).

Toward Proactive Emotionally Intelligent Strategies: Despite the impressive progress in affect-sensitive ITSs, it should be noted that affect detectors and reactors, which detect and respond to learners' emotions, do not represent the entire gamut of emotionally intelligent pedagogical strategies. Emerging research suggests that these systems need to be affect *anticipators, forestallers*, and *inducers* as well. Affect anticipators and forestallers would be required to predict and prevent the occurrence of persistent negative affective states such as boredom and presumably frustration. Prediction and prevention are necessary to address boredom because boredom begets frustration and even more boredom (D'Mello & Graesser, 2010; D'Mello, Taylor, & Graesser, 2007). More importantly, tutorial interventions are not very effective in alleviating boredom when learners tend to experience harmful oscillations between boredom and frustration.

Proactively responding to boredom would involve engaging the learner in a task that increases interest and cognitive arousal, such as a challenge, an interactive simulation, or a seductive embedded serious game. These difficult tasks have a high likelihood of getting students to reengage with the material. Another strategy is to provide learners with a choice of tasks and topics so they might pick one that is more relevant to their interests. Curiosity and engagement are enhanced by the learner's freedom of choices (Lepper & Woolverton, 2002).

On the contrary, the positive link between confusion and learning suggests that learning environments need to challenge students substantially in order to illicit critical thought and deep inquiry. Therefore, a promising strategy to promote opportunities for deep learning is to develop affect induction interventions that jolt students out of their perennial state of blasé comprehension by presenting challenges with contradictions, incongruities, anomalies, system breakdowns, and difficult decisions (Bjork & Linn, 2006; Festinger, 1957; Graesser & Olde, 2003; Schwartz & Bransford, 1998). Learners experience impasses, cognitive disequilibrium, and confusion in these conditions. Cognitive equilibrium is restored after thought, reflection, problem solving, self-explanations, and other effortful cognitive activities that force learners to engage in effortful cognitive activities in order to resolve impasses.

Broadening the Scope of Affect and Learning Research: Interdisciplinary endeavors require scholarly venues for experts in each discipline to come together and build a new understanding, and possibly a new discourse that is more encompassing and reflective of the knowledge of the research community as a whole. From its inception, this book aimed to promote an interdisciplinary discourse by featuring chapters from researchers with different backgrounds, but with a common interest in affect, learning, and technology (see chapters by Kalyuga, Dong, and Immordino-Yang and Singh). There are, however, additional opportunities to foster interdisciplinary collaborations. Two specific examples, encompassing neuroscience and social constructivist approaches to emotion, are described below.

Neuroscientific approaches to studying mental phenomena provide important insights into how we learn, how we feel, and how we use technology (see the chapter by Immordino-Yang and Singh). The inception and impact of journals such as *Brain, Mind and Education* demonstrate that a large community of researchers recognizes the potential of neuroscience techniques to reveal new insights that can inform our instructional designs and technologies. Neuroscience research reminds us of the multiple ways in which cognition and emotion are embodied, and how they play out during interactions between learners and other humans or computer-based learning systems. A key contribution in the last two decades has been an abundance of evidence challenging the notion that emotions are subcortical and limbic, whereas cognition is cortical. This notion was reinforcing the flawed Cartesian dichotomy between thoughts and feelings (Damasio, 2003). There is now ample evidence that the neural substrates of cognition and emotion overlap substantially (Dalgleish, Dunn, & Mobbs, 2009). Cognitive processes such as memory encoding and retrieval, causal reasoning, deliberation, goal appraisal, and planning operate continually throughout the experience of emotion. This evidence points to the importance of considering the affective components of learners during interactions with computer environments, thereby validating one of the underlying assumptions adopted by much of the research described in this book. Furthermore, it suggests that theoretical perspectives on emotion that inform the design of affect-sensitive learning environments must be continually revised in order to be consistent with emerging neuroscience evidence.

There is also much to learn from social constructivist conceptualizations of emotions (Averill, 1980; Parkinson, 1995; Peterson, 2006; Salovey, 2003; Stets & Turner, 2008). Most affect detection research has been influenced by perspectives that view emotions as expressions, embodiments, and products of cognitive appraisal (Calvo & D'Mello, 2010). Other schools of psychology, particularly social perspectives on emotion, have been on the sidelines of this research. This is an unfortunate consequence, as highlighted by Parkinson in his criticism of the three major thrusts of emotion research including individual, interpersonal, and the representational components of emotion (Parkinson, 1995). More specifically, since several emotions serve social functions, there is the question of how they are expressed in the absence of social contexts, as is the case when a student interacts with an ITS. One complication with applying sociologically inspired emotion theories to computer-based learning environments is that these theories are aimed at interactions among people, but users of affect-sensitive learning environments are more often dealing with objects (i.e., the computer tutor or animated pedagogical agent), rather than people. Hence, it is important to understand the emotional impact that artifacts (such as computer applications) have on their users emotions (Boehner, DePaula, Dourish, & Sengers, 2007; Norman, 2005).

Concluding Remarks

As learning scientists and technologists, we often have the tendency to try to build technologies that "fix" the problems that we observe in current learning activities, which are designed for current learning objectives. But what if these learning objectives (and therefore the activities) are not what we should really be aiming for in the first place? What if the technological solutions we are developing are really "improving the efficiency with which learners achieve outmoded educational goals?" (Goodyear, 2011). Goodyear critically examines some of the general assumptions that explicitly or implicitly underlie the affect-aware systems we are building. His proposal is not to focus on building systems that aim at increasing learning efficiency in outdated learning processes (e.g., learning by rote in order to pass an examination). Instead, it might be more fruitful to develop systems that are consistent with the learning styles of the twenty-first century and beyond (e.g., just in time learning to solve problems of immediate interest to the learner). Supporting affective interactions in socially situated ecological learning contexts of the future will require novel research paradigms that transcend the affordances of the laboratory, bold technological innovations, and interdisciplinary cross-fertilizations. Together, these will sustain a rewarding and productive research program for several decades.

Acknowledgments Sidney D'Mello was supported by the National Science Foundation (ITR 0325428, HCC 0834847) and the Institute of Education Sciences (R305A080594). Any opinions, findings, and conclusions, or recommendations expressed in this chapter are those of the authors and do not necessarily reflect the views of NSF and IES.

References

Afzal, S., & Robinson, P. (2009). *Natural affect data – collection & annotation in a learning context.* Paper presented at the Proceedings of 2009 International Conference on Affective Computing & Intelligent Interaction, Amsterdam.

Ainley, M. (2008). Interest: A significant thread binding cognition and affect in the regulation of learning. *International Journal of Psychology, 43*(3–4), 17–18.

Alexander, P. A., & Jetton, T. L. (1996). The role of importance and interest in the processing of text. *Educational Psychology Review, 8*(1), 89–121.

Arnold, M. B. (1960). *Emotion and personality.* New York: Columbia University Press.

Arroyo, I., Woolf, B., Cooper, D., Burleson, W., Muldner, K., & Christopherson, R. (2009). Emotion sensors go to school. In V. Dimitrova, R. Mizoguchi, B. Du Boulay, & A. Graesser (Eds.), *Proceedings of 14th International Conference on Artificial Intelligence In Education* (pp. 17–24). Amsterdam: IOS Press.

Averill, J. R. (1980). A constructivist view of emotion. In R. Plutchik & H. Kellerman (Eds.), *Emotion: Theory, research and experience: Vol. I. Theories of emotion* (pp. 305–339). New York: Academic.

Azevedo, R., & Strain, A. C. (2011). Integrating cognitive, metacognitive, and affective regulatory processes with MetaTutor. In R. Calvo & S. D'Mello (Eds.), *Explorations in the learning sciences, instructional systems and performance technologies.* New York: Springer.

Barrett, L. (2006). Are emotions natural kinds? *Perspectives on Psychological Science, 1*, 28–58.

Barrett, L. F. (2009). Variety is the spice of life: A psychological construction approach to understanding variability in emotion. *Cognition & Emotion, 23*(7), 1284–1306.

Barrett, L., Mesquita, B., Ochsner, K., & Gross, J. (2007). The experience of emotion. *Annual Review of Psychology, 58*, 373–403.

Bjork, R. A., & Linn, M. C. (2006). The science of learning and the learning of science: Introducing desirable difficulties. *American Psychological Society Observer, 19*, 3.

Boehner, K., DePaula, R., Dourish, P., & Sengers, P. (2007). How emotion is made and measured. *International Journal of Human-Computer Studies, 65*(4), 275–291.

Bower, G. (1992). How might emotions affect learning. In S. A. Christianson (Ed.), *The handbook of emotion and memory: Research and theory* (pp. 3–31). Hillsdale: Erlbaum.

Burleson, W. (2011). Advancing a multi-modal real-time affective sensing research platform. In R. Calvo & S. D'Mello (Eds.), *Explorations in the learning sciences, instructional systems and performance technologies.* New York: Springer.

Calvo, R. A., & D'Mello, S. K. (2010). Affect detection: An interdisciplinary review of models, methods, and their applications. *IEEE Transactions on Affective Computing, 1*(1), 18–37.

Camras, L. A., & Witherington, D. C. (2005). Dynamical systems approaches to emotional development. *Developmental Review, 25*(3–4), 328–350.

Caridakis, G., Malatesta, L., Kessous, L., Amir, N., Paouzaiou, A., & Karpouzis, K. (2006). *Modeling naturalistic affective states via facial and vocal expression recognition.* Paper presented at the International Conference on Multimidal Interfaces. Banff, Canada.

Chen, L., Huang, T., Miyasato, T., & Nakatsu, R. (1998). Multimodal human emotion/expression recognition. *Proceedings of the Third IEEE International Conference on Automatic Face and Gesture Recognition* (pp. 366–371). Washington, DC: IEEE Computer Society.

Clifford, M. (1988). Failure tolerance and academic risk-taking in ten- to twelve-year-old students. *British Journal of Educational Psychology, 58,* 15–27.

Coan, J. A. (2010). Emergent ghosts of the emotion machine. *Emotion Review, 2*(3), 274–285.

Conati, C. (2011). Combining cognitive appraisal and sensors for affect detection in a framework for modeling user affect. In R. Calvo & S. D'Mello (Eds.), *Explorations in the learning sciences, instructional systems and performance technologies.* New York: Springer.

Cooper, D. G., Arroyo, I., & Woolf, B. P. (2011). Actionable affective processing for automatic tutor interventions. In R. Calvo & S. D'Mello (Eds.), *Explorations in the learning sciences, instructional systems and performance technologies.* New York: Springer.

Craig, S., D'Mello, S., Witherspoon, A., & Graesser, A. (2008). Emote aloud during learning with AutoTutor: Applying the facial action coding system to cognitive-affective states during learning. *Cognition & Emotion, 22*(5), 777–788.

Csikszentmihalyi, M. (1975). *Beyond boredom and anxiety.* San Francisco: Jossey-Bass.

Csikszentmihalyi, M. (1990). *Flow: The psychology of optimal experience.* New York: Harper and Row.

D'Mello, S., & Graesser, A. (2010). Modeling cognitive-affective dynamics with Hidden Markov Models. In R. Catrambone & S. Ohlsson (Eds.), *Proceedings of the 32nd Annual Cognitive Science Society* (pp. 2721–2726). Austin: Cognitive Science Society.

D'Mello, S., Lehman, B., & Graesser, A. (2011). A motivationally supportive affect-sensitive auto-tutor. In R. Calvo & S. D'Mello (Eds.), *Explorations in the learning sciences, instructional systems and performance technologies.* New York: Springer.

D'Mello, S., Taylor, R., Davidson, K., & Graesser, A. (2008). Self versus teacher judgments of learner emotions during a tutoring session with AutoTutor. In B. Woolf, E. Aimeur, R. Nkambou, & S. Lajoie (Eds.), *Proceedings of the 9th international conference on Intelligent Tutoring Systems.* Berlin: Springer.

D'Mello, S., Taylor, R., & Graesser, A. (2007). Monitoring affective trajectories during complex learning. In D. McNamara & G. Trafton (Eds.), *Proceedings of the 29th Annual Cognitive Science Society* (pp. 203–208). Austin: Cognitive Science Society.

Dalgleish, T., Dunn, B., & Mobbs, D. (2009). Affective neuroscience: Past, present, and future. *Emotion Review, 1*(4), 355–368.

Damasio, A. (2003). *Looking for Spinoza: Joy, sorrow, and the feeling brain.* Orlando: Harcourt.

Daniels, L. M., Pekrun, R., Stupnisky, R. H., Haynes, T. L., Perry, R. P., & Newall, N. E. (2009). A longitudinal analysis of achievement goals: From affective antecedents to emotional effects and achievement outcomes. *Journal of Educational Psychology, 101*(4), 948–963.

Darwin, C. (1872). *The expression of the emotions in man and animals.* London: John Murray.

Dasarathy, B. (1997). Sensor fusion potential exploitation: Innovative architectures and illustrative approaches. *Proceedings IEEE, 85,* 24–38.

Davidson, R. J. (1998). Affective style and affective disorders: Perspectives from affective neuroscience. *Cognition & Emotion, 12*, 307–330.

Dewey, J. (1913). *Interest and effort in education*. Boston: Riverside.

Dragon, T., Arroyo, I., Woolf, B. P., Burleson, W., el Kaliouby, R., & Eydgahi, H. (2008, Jun 23–Jul 27). *Viewing student affect and learning through classroom observation and physical sensors*. Paper presented at the 9th International Conference on Intelligent Tutoring Systems, Montreal.

du Boulay, B. (2011). Towards a motivationally-intelligent pedagogy: How should an intelligent tutor respond to the unmotivated or the demotivated? In R. Calvo & S. D'Mello (Eds.), *Explorations in the learning sciences, instructional systems and performance technologies*. New York: Springer.

Dweck, C. (1986). Motivational processes affecting learning. *American Psychologist, 41*(10), 1040–1048.

Dweck, C. (2002). Messages that motivate: How praise molds students' beliefs, motivation, and performance (in surprising ways). In J. Aronson (Ed.), *Improving academic achievement: Impact of psychological factors on education* (pp. 61–87). Orlando: Academic.

Dweck, C. (2006). *Mindset*. New York: Random House.

Ekman, P. (1984). Expression and the nature of emotion. In K. Scherer & P. Ekman (Eds.), *Approaches to emotion* (pp. 319–344). Hillsdale: Erlbaum.

Ekman, P. (1992). An argument for basic emotions. *Cognition & Emotion, 6*(3–4), 169–200.

Festinger, L. (1957). *A theory of cognitive dissonance*. Stanford: Stanford University Press.

Forgas, J. P. (1995). Mood and judgment – the affect infusion model (AIM). *Psychological Bulletin, 117*(1), 39–66.

Frijda, N. H., Mesquita, B., Sonnemans, J., & Van Goozen, S. (1991). The duration of affective phenomena, or emotions, sentiments, and passions. In K. Strongman (Ed.), *International review of emotion and motivation* (pp. 187–225). New York: Wiley.

Garrett, A. S., & Maddock, R. J. (2001). Time course of the subjective emotional response to aversive pictures: Relevance to fMRI studies. *Psychiatry Research, 108*(1), 39–48.

Goodyear, P. (2011). Affect, technology and convivial learning environments. In R. Calvo & S. D'Mello (Eds.), *Explorations in the learning sciences, instructional systems and performance technologies*. New York: Springer.

Gotlib, I., & Abramson, L. (1999). Attributional theories of emotion. In T. Dalgleish & M. Power (Eds.), *Handbook of cognition and emotion*. Wiley: Sussex.

Graesser, A., Lu, S., Olde, B., Cooper-Pye, E., & Whitten, S. (2005). Question asking and eye tracking during cognitive disequilibrium: Comprehending illustrated texts on devices when the devices break down. *Memory and Cognition, 33*, 1235–1247.

Graesser, A., McDaniel, B., Chipman, P., Witherspoon, A., D'Mello, S., & Gholson, B. (2006). Detection of emotions during learning with AutoTutor. In R. Sun & N. Miyake (Eds.), *Proceedings of the 28th Annual Conference of the Cognitive Science Society* (pp. 285–290). Austin: Cognitive Science Society.

Graesser, A., & Olde, B. (2003). How does one know whether a person understands a device? The quality of the questions the person asks when the device breaks down. *Journal of Educational Psychology, 95*(3), 524–536.

Gross, J. (1998). The emerging field of emotion regulation: An integrative review. *Review of General Psychology, 2*, 271–299.

Gross, J. (2008). Emotion regulation. In M. Lewis, J. Haviland-Jones, & L. Barrett (Eds.), *Handbook of emotions* (3rd ed., pp. 497–512). New York: Guilford.

Guthrie, J. T., Wigfield, A., Humenick, N. M., Perencevich, K. C., Taboada, A., & Barbosa, P. (2006). Influences of stimulating tasks on reading motivation and comprehension. *Journal of Educational Research, 99*(4), 232–245.

Harter, S. (1992). The relationship between perceived competence, affect, and motivational orientation within the classroom: Process and patterns of change. In A. Boggiano & T. Pittman (Eds.), *Achievement and motivation: A social-developmental perspective* (pp. 77–114). New York: Cambridge University Press.

Heider, F. (1958). *The psychology of interpersonal relations*. New York: Wiley.

Hemenover, S. H. (2003). Individual differences in rate of affect change: Studies in affective chronometry. *Journal of Personality and Social Psychology, 85*, 121–131.

Hidi, S. (2006). Interest: A unique motivational variable. *Educational Research Review, 1*, 69–82.

Hidi, S., & Renninger, K. A. (2006). The four-phase model of interest development. *Educational Psychologist, 41*(2), 111–127.

Isen, A. (2008). Some ways in which positive affect influences decision making and problem solving. In M. Lewis, J. Haviland-Jones, & L. Barrett (Eds.), *Handbook of emotions* (3rd ed., pp. 548–573). New York: Guilford.

Izard, C. E. (2007). Basic emotions, natural kinds, emotion schemas, and a new paradigm. *Perspectives on Psychological Science, 2*(3), 260–280.

Joormann, J. (2010). Cognitive inhibition and emotion regulation in depression. *Current Directions in Psychological Science, 19*(3), 161–166.

Lazarus, R. (1991). *Emotion and adaptation*. New York: Oxford University Press.

Lazarus, R. (2000). The cognition-emotion debate: A bit of history. In M. Lewis & J. Haviland-Jones (Eds.), *Handbook of emotions* (2nd ed., pp. 1–20). New York: Guilford Press.

Lehman, B., Matthews, M., D'Mello, S., & Person, N. (2008). What are you feeling? Investigating student affective states during expert human tutoring sessions. In B. Woolf, E. Aimeur, R. Nkambou, & S. Lajoie (Eds.), *Proceedings of the 9th International Conference on Intelligent Tutoring Systems* (pp. 50–59). Berlin: Springer.

Lepper, M., & Woolverton, M. (2002). The wisdom of practice: Lessons learned from the study of highly effective tutors. In J. Aronson (Ed.), *Improving academic achievement: Impact of psychological factors on education* (pp. 135–158). Orlando: Academic.

Lester, J. C., McQuiggan, S. W., & Sabourin, J. L. (2011). Affect recognition and expression in narrative-centered learning environments. In R. Calvo & S. D'Mello (Eds.), *Explorations in the learning sciences, instructional systems and performance technologies*. New York: Springer.

Lewis, M. D. (2005). Bridging emotion theory and neurobiology through dynamic systems modeling. *Behavioral and Brain Sciences, 28*(2), 169–245.

Linnenbrink, E. (2007). The role of affect in student learning: A mulit-dimensional approach to considering the interaction of affect, motivation and engagement. In P. Schutz & R. Pekrun (Eds.), *Emotions in education* (pp. 107–124). San Diego: Academic.

Mandler, G. (1976). *Mind and emotion*. New York: Wiley.

Mandler, G. (1984). *Mind and body: Psychology of emotion and stress*. New York: W.W. Norton & Company.

Mandler, G. (1999). Emotion. In B. M. Bly & D. E. Rumelhart (Eds.), *Cognitive science. Handbook of perception and cognition* (2nd ed., pp. 367–382). San Diego: Academic.

Meyer, D., & Turner, J. (2006). Re-conceptualizing emotion and motivation to learn in classroom contexts. *Educational Psychology Review, 18*(4), 377–390.

Norman, D. A. (2005). *Emotional design: Why we love (or hate) everyday things*. New York: Basic Books.

Ortony, A., Clore, G., & Collins, A. (1988). *The cognitive structure of emotions*. New York: Cambridge University Press.

Parkinson, B. (1995). *Ideas and realities of emotion*. London: Routledge.

Pekrun, R. (2006). The control-value theory of achievement emotions: Assumptions, corollaries, and implications for educational research and practice. *Educational Psychology Review, 18*(4), 315–341.

Pekrun, R. (2010). Academic emotions. In T. Urdan (Ed.), *APA educational psychology handbook* (Vol. 2). Washington: American Psychological Association.

Pekrun, R. (2011). Emotions as drivers of learning and cognitive development. In R. Calvo & S. D'Mello (Eds.), *Explorations in the learning sciences, instructional systems and performance technologies*. New York: Springer.

Pekrun, R., Elliot, A., & Maier, M. (2006). Achievement goals and discrete achievement emotions: A theoretical model and prospective test. *Journal of Educational Psychology, 98*(3), 583–597.

Pekrun, R., Goetz, T., Daniels, L., Stupnisky, R. H., & Raymond, P. (2010). Boredom in achievement settings: Exploring control–value antecedents and performance outcomes of a neglected emotion. *Journal of Educational Psychology, 102*(3), 531–549.

Peterson, G. (2006). Cultural theory and emotions. In J. Stets & J. Turner (Eds.), *Handbook of the sociology of emotions* (pp. 114–134). New York: Springer.

Piaget, J. (1952). *The origins of intelligence.* New York: International University Press.

Picard, R. (1997). *Affective computing.* Cambridge: MIT Press.

Picard, R. (2010). Affective computing: From laughter to IEEE. *IEEE Transactions on Affective Computing, 1*(1), 11–17.

Picard, R., Vyzas, E., & Healey, J. (2001). Toward machine emotional intelligence: Analysis of affective physiological state. *Ieee Transactions on Pattern Analysis and Machine Intelligence, 23*(10), 1175–1191.

Rebolledo-Mendez, G., Luckin, R., & du Boulay, B. (2011). Designing adaptive motivational scaffolding for a tutoring system. In R. Calvo & S. D'Mello (Eds.), *Explorations in the learning sciences, instructional systems and performance technologies.* New York: Springer.

Rosenberg, E. (1998). Levels of analysis and the organization of affect. *Review of General Psychology, 2*(3), 247–270.

Rosenberg, E., & Ekman, P. (1994). Coherence between expressive and experiential systems in emotion. *Cognition & Emotion, 8*(3), 201–229.

Russell, J. (2003). Core affect and the psychological construction of emotion. *Psychological Review, 110*, 145–172.

Russell, J. A., Bachorowski, J. A., & Fernandez-Dols, J. M. (2003). Facial and vocal expressions of emotion. *Annual Review of Psychology, 54*, 329–349.

Salovey, P. (2003). Introduction: Emotion and social processes. In R. Davidson, K. Scherer, & H. Goldsmith (Eds.), *Handbook of affective sciences.* New York: Oxford University Press.

Scherer, K. R. (2009a). The dynamic architecture of emotion: Evidence for the component process model. *Cognition & Emotion, 23*(7), 1307–1351.

Scherer, K. R. (2009b). Emotions are emergent processes: They require a dynamic computational architecture. *Philosophical Transactions of the Royal Society B-Biological Sciences, 364*(1535), 3459–3474.

Scherer, K., & Ellgring, H. (2007). Multimodal expression of emotion: Affect programs or componential appraisal patterns? *Emotion, 7*(1), 158–171.

Scherer, K., Schorr, A., & Johnstone, T. (Eds.). (2001). *Appraisal processes in emotion: Theory, methods, research.* London: London University Press.

Schultz, P., & Pekrun, R. (Eds.). (2007). *Emotion in education.* San Diego: Academic.

Schutz, P., & Pekrun, R. (Eds.). (2007). *Emotion in education.* San Diego: Academic.

Schwartz, D., & Bransford, D. (1998). A time for telling. *Cognition and Instruction, 16*(4), 475–522.

Schwarz, N. (1990). Feelings as information: Informational and motivational functions of affective states. In E. Higgins & R. Sorrentino (Eds.), *Handbook of motivation and cognition* (pp. 527–561). New York: Guilford Press.

Schwarz, N. (in press). Feelings-as-information theory. In P. Van Lange, A. Kruglanski & T. Higgins (Eds.), *Handbook of theories of social psychology.* Sage.

Smith, C., & Ellsworth, P. (1985). Patterns of cognitive appraisal in emotion. *Journal of Personality and Social Psychology, 48*(4), 813–838.

Stein, N. L., & Albro, E. R. (2001). The origins and nature of arguments: Studies in conflict understanding, emotion, and negotiation. *Discourse Processes, 32*(2), 113–133.

Stein, N., Hernandez, M., & Trabasso, T. (2008). Advances in modeling emotions and thought: The importance of developmental, online, and multilevel analysis. In M. Lewis, J. M. Haviland-Jones, & L. F. Barrett (Eds.), *Handbook of emotions* (3rd ed., pp. 574–586). New York: Guilford Press.

Stein, N., & Levine, L. (1991). Making sense out of emotion. In A. O. W. Kessen & F. Kraik (Eds.), *Memories thoughts and emotions: Essays in honor of George Mandler* (pp. 295–322). Hillsdale: Erlbaum.

Stets, J., & Turner, J. (2008). The sociology of emotions. In M. Lewis, J. Haviland-Jones, & L. Barrett (Eds.), *Handbook of emotions* (3rd ed., pp. 32–46). New York: Guilford.

Stipek, D. (1988). *Motivation to learn: From theory to practice*. Boston: Allyn and Bacon.

Strain, A. C., & D'Mello, S.K. (in press). Emotion regulation during learning. In S. Bull & G. Biswas (Eds.), *Proceedings of the 15th International Conference on Artificial Intelligence in Education* (pp. 566–538). New York / Heidelberg: Springer.

Tobias, S. (1994). Interest, prior knowledge, and learning. *Review of Educational Research, 64,* 37–54.

Tomkins, S. S. (1962). *Affect imagery consciousness: Volume I, the positive affects*. London: Tavistock.

VanLehn, K., Siler, S., Murray, C., Yamauchi, T., & Baggett, W. (2003). Why do only some events cause learning during human tutoring? *Cognition and Instruction, 21*(3), 209–249.

Vygotsky, L. (1978). *Mind in society: The development of higher psychological processes*. Cambridge: Harvard University Press.

Wassmann, C. (2010). Reflections on the body loop: Carl Georg Lange's theory of emotion. *Cognition & Emotion, 24*(6), 974–990.

Watson, D., & Clark, L. A. (1994). Emotions, moods, traits, and temperaments: Conceptual distinctions and empirical findings. In P. Ekman & J. Davidson (Eds.), *The nature of emotion: Fundamental questions* (pp. 89–93). New York: Oxford University Press.

Weiner, B. (1986). *An attributional theory of motivation and emotion*. New York: Springer.

Woolf, B., Arroyo, I., Muldner, K., Burleson, W., Cooper, D., Dolan, R., et al. (2010). The effect of motivational learning companions on low achieving students and students with disabilities. In J. Kay & V. Aleven (Eds.), *Proceedings of 10th International Conference on Intelligent Tutoring Systems* (pp. 327–337). Berlin: Springer.

Yoshitomi, Y., Sung-Ill, K., Kawano, T., & Kilazoe, T. (2000). Effect of sensor fusion for recognition of emotional states using voice, face image and thermal image of face. In P. o. t. I. I. W. o. R. a. H. I. Communication (Ed.), (pp. 178–183). Osaka: IEEE.

Zeidner, M. (2007). Test anxiety in educational contexts: Concepts, findings, and future directions. In P. Schutz & R. Pekrun (Eds.), *Emotions in education* (pp. 165–184). San Diego: Academic.

Zeng, Z., Pantic, M., Roisman, G., & Huang, T. (2009). A survey of affect recognition methods: Audio, visual, and spontaneous expressions. *IEEE Transactions on Pattern Analysis and Machine Intelligence, 31*(1), 39–58.

Index

R.A. Calvo and S.K. D'Mello (eds.), *New Perspectives on Affect and Learning Technologies*,   273
Explorations in the Learning Sciences, Instructional Systems and Performance Technologies 3,
DOI 10.1007/978-1-4419-9625-1, © Springer Science+Business Media, LLC 2011